THE TICKLISH SUBJECT

WO ES WAR

A series from Verso edited by Slavoj Žižek

Wo es war, soll ich werden – Where it was, I shall come into being – is Freud's version of the Enlightenment goal of knowledge that is in itself an act of liberation. Is it still possible to pursue this goal today, in the conditions of late capitalism? If 'it' today is the twin rule of pragmatic-relativist New Sophists and New Age obscurantists, what 'shall come into being' in its place? The premiss of the series is that the explosive combination of Lacanian psychoanalysis and Marxist tradition detonates a dynamic freedom that enables us to question the very presuppositions of the circuit of Capital.

The Ticklish Subject

The Absent Centre of Political Ontology

SLAVOJ ŽIŽEK

VERSO

London • New York

First published by Verso 1999
© Slavoj Žižek 1999
Paperback edition first published Verso 2000
© Slavoj Žižek 2000
All rights reserved

5 7 9 10 8 6 4

Verso
UK: 6 Meard Street, London W1F 0EG
US: 180 Varick Street, New York, NY 10014–4606

Verso is the imprint of New Left Books

ISBN 1–85984–291–7

British Library Cataloguing in Publication Data
A catalogue record for this book is available from the British Library

Library of Congress Cataloging-in-Publication Data
A catalog record for this book is available from the Library of Congress

Typeset by SetSystems Ltd, Saffron Walden, Essex
Printed and bound in Great Britain by Bookmarque Ltd, Croydon

Contents

Introduction: A Spectre Is Haunting Western Academia . . .

. . . the spectre of the Cartesian subject. All academic powers have entered into a holy alliance to exorcize this spectre: the New Age obscurantist (who wants to supersede the 'Cartesian paradigm' towards a new holistic approach) and the postmodern deconstructionist (for whom the Cartesian subject is a discursive fiction, an effect of decentred textual mechanisms); the Habermasian theorist of communication (who insists on a shift from Cartesian monological subjectivity to discursive intersubjectivity) and the Heideggerian proponent of the thought of Being (who stresses the need to 'traverse' the horizon of modern subjectivity culminating in current ravaging nihilism); the cognitive scientist (who endeavours to prove empirically that there is no unique scene of the Self, just a pandemonium of competing forces) and the Deep Ecologist (who blames Cartesian mechanicist materialism for providing the philosophical foundation for the ruthless exploitation of nature); the critical (post-)Marxist (who insists that the illusory freedom of the bourgeois thinking subject is rooted in class division) and the feminist (who emphasizes that the allegedly sexless *cogito* is in fact a male patriarchal formation). Where is the academic orientation which has not been accused by its opponents of not yet properly disowning the Cartesian heritage? And which has not hurled back the branding reproach of Cartesian subjectivity against its more 'radical' critics, as well as its 'reactionary' adversaries?

Two things result from this:

1. Cartesian subjectivity continues to be acknowledged by all academic powers as a powerful and still active intellectual tradition.

2. It is high time that the partisans of Cartesian subjectivity should, in the
   face of the whole world, publish their views, their aims, their tendencies, and meet this nursery tale of the Spectre of Cartesian subjectivity
   with the philosophical manifesto of Cartesian subjectivity itself.

This book thus endeavours to reassert the Cartesian subject, whose
rejection forms the silent pact of all the struggling parties of today's
academia: although all these orientations are officially involved in a deadly
battle (Habermasians versus deconstructionists; cognitive scientists versus
New Age obscurantists . . .), they are all united in their rejection of the
Cartesian subject. The point, of course, is not to return to the *cogito* in the
guise in which this notion has dominated modern thought (the self-
transparent thinking subject), but to bring to light its forgotten obverse,
the excessive, unacknowledged kernel of the *cogito*, which is far from the
pacifying image of the transparent Self. The three parts of the book focus
on today's three main fields in which subjectivity is at stake: the tradition
of German Idealism; post-Althusserian political philosophy; the 'deconstructionist' shift from Subject to the problematic of multiple subject-
positions and subjectivizations.[1] Each part starts with a chapter on a
crucial author whose work represents an exemplary critique of Cartesian
subjectivity; a second chapter then deals with the vicissitudes of the
fundamental notion that underlies the preceding chapter (subjectivity in
German Idealism; political subjectivization; the 'Oedipus complex' as the
psychoanalytic account of the emergence of the subject).[2]

Part I begins with a detailed *confrontation with Heidegger's endeavour to
traverse the horizon of modern Cartesian subjectivity*. Again and again, the
inherent logic of their philosophical project compelled the authentic
philosophers of subjectivity to articulate a certain excessive moment of
'madness' inherent to *cogito*, which they then immediately endeavoured to
'renormalize' (the diabolical Evil in Kant, the 'night of the world' in
Hegel, etc.). And the problem with Heidegger is that his notion of
modern subjectivity does not account for this inherent excess – it simply
does not 'cover' that aspect of *cogito* on account of which Lacan claims
that *cogito* is the subject of the Unconscious. Heidegger's fatal flaw is
clearly discernible in the failure of his reading of Kant: in his focus on
transcendental imagination, Heidegger misses the key dimension of
imagination: its disruptive, anti-synthetic aspect, which is another name
for the abyss of freedom; this failure also casts new light on the old
question of Heidegger's Nazi engagement. So, after this confrontation,
the second chapter endeavours to elaborate the status of subjectivity in

Hegel, focusing on the link between the philosophical notion of reflexivity and the reflexive turn that characterizes the (hysterical) subject of the Unconscious.

Part II contains a systematic confrontation with the four philosophers who, in one way or another, took Althusser as their starting point, but later, via a criticism of Althusser, developed their own theory of political subjectivity: Laclau's theory of hegemony, Balibar's theory of *égaliberté*, Rancière's theory of *mésentente*, Badiou's theory of subjectivity as fidelity to the Truth-Event. The first chapter focuses on Badiou's attempt to formulate a 'politics of truth' that could undermine today's deconstructionist and/or postmodernist stance, with a special emphasis on his pathbreaking reading of St Paul. Although I am in solidarity with Badiou's attempt to reassert the dimension of universality as the true opposite of capitalist globalism, I reject his criticism of Lacan – that is, his thesis that psychoanalysis is not able to provide the foundation of a new political practice. The next chapter analyses the ways in which the four authors tackle the predominant 'post-political' liberal-democratic stance which is the political mode of today's global capitalism, each of them deploying his own version of political subjectivization.

Part III deals with those tendencies of today's 'postmodern' political thought which, against the spectre of the (transcendental) Subject, endeavour to assert the liberating proliferation of the multiple forms of subjectivity – feminine, gay, ethnic. . . . According to this orientation, one should abandon the impossible goal of global social transformation and, instead, focus attention on the diverse forms of asserting one's particular subjectivity in our complex and dispersed postmodern universe, in which cultural recognition matters more than socioeconomic struggle – that is to say, in which cultural studies have replaced the critique of political economy. The most representative and persuasive version of these theories, whose practical expression is multiculturalist 'identity politics', is Judith Butler's performative theory of gender formation. So the first chapter of this part engages in a detailed confrontation with Butler's work, focusing on those of its aspects which make possible a productive dialogue with Lacanian psychoanalysis (her notions of 'passionate attachments' and the reflexive turn constitutive of subjectivity). The last chapter then directly confronts the key issue of 'Oedipus today': is the so-called Oedipal mode of subjectivization (the emergence of the subject through the integration of the symbolic prohibition embodied in the paternal Law) today really in decline? And if so, what is replacing it? In a confrontation with the proponents of the 'second modernization' (Giddens,

Beck), it argues for the continuous actuality of the 'dialectic of Enlightenment': far from simply liberating us from the constraints of patriarchal tradition, the unprecedented shift in the mode of functioning of the symbolic order that we are witnessing today engenders its own new risks and dangers.

While this book is philosophical in its basic tenor, it is first and foremost an engaged political intervention, addressing the burning question of how we are to reformulate a leftist, anti-capitalist political project in our era of global capitalism and its ideological supplement, liberal-democratic multiculturalism. One of *the* photos of 1997 was undoubtedly that of members of some indigenous tribe from Borneo carrying water in plastic bags to put out gigantic fires which were destroying their habitat, the ridiculous inadequacy of their modest effort matched by the horror of seeing their entire life-world disappear. According to newspaper reports, the gigantic cloud of smoke covering the entire area of northern Indonesia, Malaysia and the southern Philippines derailed nature itself, its normal cycle (because of the continuous darkness, bees were unable to accomplish their part in the biological reproduction of plants). Here we have an example of the unconditional Real of global Capital perturbing the very reality of nature – the reference to global Capital is necessary here, since the fires were not simply the result of the 'greed' of local wood merchants and farmers (and of corrupt Indonesian state officials allowing it), but also of the fact that because of the El Niño effect, the extraordinary drought did not end in the rains which regularily quench such fires, and the El Niño effect is *global*.

This catastrophe thus gives body to the Real of our time: the thrust of Capital which ruthlessly disregards and destroys particular life-worlds, threatening the very survival of humanity. What, however, are the implications of this catastrophe? Are we dealing merely with the logic of Capital, or is this logic just the predominant thrust of the modern productivist attitude of technological domination over and exploitation of nature? Or furthermore, is this very technological exploitation the ultimate expression, the realization of the deepest potential of modern Cartesian subjectivity itself? The author's answer to this dilemma is the emphatic plea of 'Not guilty!' for the Cartesian subject.

In her careful editing of my manuscripts for Verso, Gillian Beaumont regularly catches me with my (intellectual) pants down: her gaze unerringly discerns repetitions in the line of thought, moronic inconsistencies of the argumentation, false attributions and references that display my lack of general education, not to mention the awkwardness of style ... how can I not feel ashamed, and thus *hate* her? On the other hand, she has every reason to hate *me*. I constantly bombard her with late insertions and changes of the manuscript, so that I can easily imagine her possessing a voodoo doll of me and piercing it in the evenings with a gigantic needle. This mutual hatred, as they would have put it in the good old days of classic Hollywood, signals the beginning of a beautiful friendship, so I dedicate this book to her.

Notes

1. For a detailed confrontation with the critical rejection of the Cartesian subjectivity in cognitive sciences, see Slavoj Žižek, 'The Cartesian Subject versus the Cartesian Theatre', in *Cogito and the Unconscious*, ed. Slavoj Žižek, Durham, NC: Duke University Press 1998.

2. Interestingly enough, the three parts also correspond to the geographic triad of German/French/Anglo-American tradition: German Idealism, French political philosophy, Anglo-American cultural studies.

PART I

The 'Night of the World'

1

The Deadlock of Transcendental Imagination, or, Martin Heidegger as a Reader of Kant

One of the enigmatic features of 'progressive' postmodernist thought, from Derrida to Fredric Jameson, lies in its ambiguous relationship to Heidegger's philosophy: Heidegger is treated with due respect, often referred to in a noncommittal way, the way one refers to an undisputed authority; yet, simultaneously, an unease, never fully explicated, prevents full endorsement of his position, as if a kind of invisible prohibition tells us that something must be fundamentally wrong with Heidegger, although we are not (yet) in a position to determine what this is. Even when authors do risk a full confrontation with Heidegger (as Derrida does in *On the Spirit*[1]), the result is, as a rule, ambiguous; one endeavours to gain a distance from Heidegger while somehow staying on his path (Heidegger still remains a philosopher of Origins and authentic Presence, although he did the most to 'deconstruct' the metaphysical logic of Origins . . .). On the other hand, those who adopt one of the two extreme positions, and either engage in a desperate attempt at a politically 'progressive' appropriation of Heidegger (like Reiner Schürmann's 'anarchic' reading[2]) or propose a thorough rejection of his thought (like Adorno[3] or Lyotard[4]), can be convincingly dismissed as dealing with a simplified image of Heidegger that does not live up to his own philosophical stringency. The ethico-political roots of this deadlock of the deconstructionist reference to Heidegger were perhaps best formulated by Derrida in his interview with Jean-Luc Nancy:

> I believe in the force and the necessity (and therefore in a certain irreversibility) of the act by which Heidegger *substitutes* a certain concept of *Dasein* for a concept of subject still too marked by the traits of the being as *vorhanden*, and

hence by an interpretation of time, and insufficiently questioned in its ontological structure ... The time and space of this displacement opened up a gap,
marked a gap, they left fragile, or recalled the essential ontological fragility of,
the ethical, juridical, and political foundations of democracy and of every
discourse that one can oppose to National Socialism in all its forms (the 'worst'
ones, or those that Heidegger and others might have thought of opposing).
These foundations were and remain essentially sealed within a philosophy of
the subject. One can quickly perceive the question, which might also be the
task: can one take into account the necessity of the existential analytic and what
it shatters in the subject and [can one] turn towards an ethics, a politics (are
these words still appropriate?), indeed an 'other' democracy (would it still be a
democracy?), in any case towards another type of responsibility that safeguards
against what a moment ago I very quickly called the 'worst'? ... I think that
there are a certain number of us who are working for just this, and it can only
take place by way of a long and slow trajectory.[5]

That is the terrible deadlock: if one endorses Heidegger's 'deconstruction' of the metaphysics of subjectivity, does one not thus undermine the
very possibility of a philosophically grounded democratic resistance to the
totalitarian horrors of the twentieth century? Habermas's answer to this
question is a definitive and pathetic 'Yes!', and, for that reason, he also
opposed Adorno's and Horkheimer's *Dialectic of Enlightenment*, a book
which – in a way not totally dissimilar to Heidegger – locates the roots of
the 'totalitarian' horrors in the basic project of Western Enlightenment.
Heideggerians, of course, would retort that one cannot simply oppose
democratic subjectivity to its 'totalitarian' excess, since the latter is the
'truth' of the former – that is to say, since phenomena like 'totalitarianism'
are effectively grounded in modern subjectivity. (This is how – to put it in
a somewhat simplified way – Heidegger himself explains his brief Nazi
engagement: by the fact that the project of *Being and Time* was not yet
wholly freed of the transcendental approach.)

The same ambiguity also seems to determine Lacan's own (often
inconsistent) reference to Heidegger, oscillating between appropriation
of some key Heidegger terms as providing the sought-after foundation for
psychoanalysis, and a series of dismissive passing remarks in his last years
(like the one qualifying his earlier references to Heidegger as purely
external and didactic). Against the background of this imbroglio, our
thesis will be that Lacan succeeds where Habermas and other 'defenders
of the subject', including Dieter Henrich, fail: the Lacanian (re)reading
of the problematic of subjectivity in German Idealism enables us not only
to delineate contours of a notion of subjectivity that does not fit the frame

of Heidegger's notion of the nihilism inherent to modern subjectivity, but also to locate the point of the inherent failure of Heidegger's philosophical edifice, up to the often-discussed question of the eventual philosophical roots of his Nazi engagement.

Heideggerian Political (Dis)Engagement

Let us take as our starting point Nietzsche's critique of Wagner: this critique was appropriated by Heidegger as the paradigmatic rejection of all critiques of subjectivism that remain within the horizon of Cartesian subjectivity (say, of the liberal-democratic criticisms of the 'totalitarian' excess of subjectivity). Nietzsche possessed an unerring instinct that enabled him to discern, behind the sage who preaches the denial of the Will to Life, the *ressentiment* of the thwarted will: Schopenhauer and his like are comical figures who converted and elevated their impotent envy, their lack of life-asserting creativity, into the pose of resigned wisdom. (Does not Nietzsche's diagnosis also hold for today's attempts to 'overcome' the Cartesian paradigm of domination by means of a new holistic attitude of renouncing anthropocentrism, of humbly learning from ancient cultures, etc.?)

In his project of 'overcoming' metaphysics, Heidegger fully endorses this Nietzschean dismissal of quick and easy exits from metaphysics: the only real way to break the metaphysical closure is to 'pass through it' in its most dangerous form, to endure the pain of metaphysical nihilism at its most extreme, which means that one should reject as futile all false sedatives, all direct attempts to suspend the mad vicious cycle of modern technology by means of a return to premodern traditional Wisdom (from Christianity to Oriental thought), all attempts to reduce the threat of modern technology to the effect of some ontic social wrong (capitalist exploitation, patriarchal domination, 'mechanicist paradigm' . . .). These attempts are not only ineffectual: the true problem with them is that, on a deeper level, they incite the evil they are fighting even further. An excellent example here is the ecological crisis: the moment we reduce it to disturbances provoked by our excessive technological exploitation of nature, we silently already surmise that the solution is to rely again on technological innovations: new 'green' technology, *more efficient and global in its control of natural processes and human resources*. . . . Every concrete ecological concern and project to change technology in order to improve the state of our natural surroundings is thus devalued as relying on the very source of the trouble.

For Heidegger, the true problem is not ecological crisis in its ontic dimension, including a possible global catastrophe (hole in the ozone layer, melting of the ice caps, etc.), but the technological mode of relating to entities around us – this true crisis will confront us even more radically if the expected catastrophe does *not* occur; that is, if humankind does succeed in technologically 'mastering' the critical situation. . . . For that reason, Heidegger also denies philosophical relevance to the standard liberal problematic of the tension between 'open' and 'closed' societies, between the 'normal' functioning of the democratic capitalist system, with its respect for human rights and freedoms, and its (Fascist or Communist) totalitarian 'excesses'. Implicitly, at least, Heidegger devalues the effort to constrain the system – to maintain its 'human face', to compel it to respect the basic rules of democracy and freedom, to provide for human solidarity, to prevent its sliding into totalitarian excess – as an escape from the inner truth of the system that becomes perceptible in such excesses: such half-hearted efforts to keep the system in check are the worst way to remain within its horizon. One should recall here the key strategic role of the signifier 'hysteria' in the modern 'radical' political discourse, up to the Bolsheviks, who dismissed as 'hysterics' their opponents who groaned about the need for democratic values, the totalitarian threat to humanity, and so on. Along the same lines, Heidegger also denounces liberal-humanitarian demands for 'capitalism with a human face' as the unwillingness to confront the epochal truth in all its unbearable radicality. The parallel with the Bolsheviks is absolutely pertinent: what Heidegger shares with revolutionary Marxists is the notion that the system's truth emerges in its excess – that is to say, for Heidegger, as well as for Marxists, Fascism is not a simple aberration of the 'normal' development of capitalism but the necessary outcome of its inner dynamics.

Here, however, complications arise: on closer inspection, it soon becomes clear that Heidegger's argumentative strategy is twofold. On the one hand, he rejects every concern for democracy and human rights as a purely ontic affair unworthy of proper philosophical ontological questioning – democracy, Fascism, Communism, they all amount to the same with regard to the epochal Destiny of the West; on the other hand, his insistence that he is not convinced that democracy is the political form which best suits the essence of technology[6] none the less suggests that there is *another* political form which suits this ontological essence better – for some time, Heidegger thought he had found it in the Fascist 'total mobilization' (but, significantly, never in Communism, which always remains for him epochally the same as Americanism . . .). Heidegger, of course, emphasizes again and again how the ontological dimension of Nazism is not to be equated with Nazism as an ontic ideologico-political order; in the well-known passage from *An Introduction to Metaphysics*, for example, he repudiates the Nazi biologist race ideology as something that totally misses the 'inner greatness' of the Nazi movement, which lies in the encounter between modern man and technology.[7] None the less, the fact remains that Heidegger *never* speaks of the 'inner greatness' of, say, liberal democracy – as if liberal democracy is just that, a superficial world-view with no underlying dimension of assuming one's epochal Destiny. . . .[8]

Apropos of this precise point, I myself run into my first trouble with Heidegger (since I began as a Heideggerian – my first published book was on Heidegger and language). When, in my youth, I was bombarded by the official Communist philosophers' stories of Heidegger's Nazi engagement, they left me rather cold; I was definitely more on the side of the Yugoslav Heideggerians. All of a sudden, however, I became aware of how these Yugoslav Heideggerians were doing exactly the same thing with respect to the Yugoslav ideology of self-management as Heidegger himself did with respect to Nazism: in ex-Yugoslavia, Heideggerians entertained the same ambiguously assertive relationship towards Socialist self-management, the official ideology of the Communist regime – in their eyes, the essence of self-management was the very essence of modern man, which is why the philosophical notion of self-management suits the ontological essence of our epoch, while the standard political ideology of the regime misses this 'inner greatness' of self-management . . . Heideggerians are thus eternally in search of a positive, ontic political system that would come closest to the epochal ontological truth, a strategy which inevitably leads to error (which, of course, is always acknowledged only retroactively, *post factum*, after the disastrous outcome of one's engagement).

As Heidegger himself put it, those who came closest to the ontological Truth are condemned to err at the ontic level . . . err about what? Precisely about the line of separation between ontic and ontological. The paradox not to be underestimated is that the very philosopher who focused his interest on the enigma of ontological difference – who warned again and again against the metaphysical mistake of conferring ontological dignity on some ontic content (God as the highest Entity, for example) – fell into the trap of conferring on Nazism the ontological dignity of suiting the essence of modern man. The standard defence of Heidegger against the reproach of his Nazi past consists of two points: not only was his Nazi engagement a simple personal error (a 'stupidity [*Dummheit*]', as Heidegger himself put it) in no way inherently related to his philosophical project; the main counter-argument is that it is Heidegger's own philosophy that enables us to discern the true epochal roots of modern totalitarianism. However, what remains unthought here is the hidden complicity between the ontological indifference towards concrete social systems (capitalism, Fascism, Communism), in so far as they all belong to the same horizon of modern technology, and the secret privileging of a concrete sociopolitical model (Nazism with Heidegger, Communism with some 'Heideggerian Marxists') as closer to the ontological truth of our epoch.

Here one should avoid the trap that caught Heidegger's defenders, who dismissed Heidegger's Nazi engagement as a simple anomaly, a fall into the ontic level, in blatant contradiction to his thought, which teaches us not to confuse ontological horizon with ontic choices (as we have already seen, Heidegger is at his strongest when he demonstrates how, on a deeper structural level, ecological, conservative, and so on, oppositions to the modern universe of technology are already embedded in the horizon of what they purport to reject: the ecological critique of the technological exploitation of nature ultimately leads to a more 'environmentally sound' technology, etc.). Heidegger did not engage in the Nazi political project 'in spite of' his ontological philosophical approach, but *because of* it; this engagement was not 'beneath' his philosophical level – on the contrary, if one is to understand Heidegger, the key point is to grasp the complicity (in Hegelese: 'speculative identity') between the elevation above ontic concerns and the passionate 'ontic' Nazi political engagement.

One can now see the ideological trap that caught Heidegger: when he criticizes Nazi racism on behalf of the true 'inner greatness' of the Nazi movement, he repeats the elementary ideological gesture of maintaining an inner distance towards the ideological text – of claiming that there is something more beneath it, a non-ideological kernel: ideology exerts its hold over us by means of this very insistence that the Cause we adhere to is not 'merely' ideological. So where is the trap? When the disappointed Heidegger turns away from active engagement in the Nazi movement, he does so because the Nazi movement did not maintain the level of its 'inner greatness', but legitimized itself with inadequate (racial) ideology. In other words, what he expected from it was that it should legitimize itself through direct awareness of its 'inner greatness'. And the problem lies in this very expectation that a political movement that will directly refer to its historico-ontological foundation is possible. This expectation, however, is in itself profoundly metaphysical, in so far as it fails to recognize that the gap separating the direct ideological legitimization of a movement from its 'inner greatness' (its historico-ontological essence) is *constitutive*, a positive condition of its 'functioning'. To use the terms of the later Heidegger, ontological insight necessarily entails ontic blindness and error, and vice versa – that is to say, in order to be 'effective' at the ontic level, one must disregard the ontological horizon of one's activity. (In this sense, Heidegger emphasizes that 'science doesn't think' and that, far from being its limitation, this inability is the very motor of scientific progress.) In other words, what Heidegger seems unable to endorse is a concrete political engagement that would *accept* its necessary, constitutive blindness – as if the moment we acknowledge the gap separating the awareness of the ontological horizon from ontic engagement, any ontic engagement is depreciated, loses its authentic dignity.

Another aspect of the same problem is the passage from ready-at-hand to present-at-hand in *Being and Time*. Heidegger takes as the starting point the active immersion in its surroundings of a finite engaged agent who relates to objects around it as to something ready-at-hand; the impassive perception of objects as present-at-hand arises gradually from this engagement when things 'malfunction' in different ways, and is therefore a derivative mode of presence. Heidegger's point, of course, is that the proper ontological description of the way *Dasein* is in the world has to abandon the modern Cartesian duality of values and facts: the notion that the subject encounters present-at-hand objects on to which he then projects his aims, and exploits them accordingly, falsifies the proper state of things: the fact that engaged immersion in the world is primordial, and that all other modes of the presence of objects are derived from it.

On closer examination, however, the picture becomes somewhat blurred and more complex. The problem with *Being and Time* is how to co-ordinate the series of pairs of oppositions: authentic existence versus *das Man*; anxiety versus immersion in worldly activity; true philosophical thought versus traditional ontology; dispersed modern society versus the People assuming its historic Destiny. . . . The pairs in this series do not simply overlap: when a premodern artisan or farmer, following his traditional way of life, is immersed in his daily involvement with ready-at-hand objects that are included in his world, this immersion is definitely not the same as the *das Man* of the modern city-dweller. (This is why, in his notorious 'Why should we remain in the province?', Heidegger himself reports that when he was uncertain whether to accept the invitation to go to teach in Berlin, he asked his friend, a hard-working local farmer, who just silently shook his head – Heidegger immediately accepted this as the authentic answer to his predicament.) Is it not, therefore, that, in contrast to these two opposed modes of immersion – the authentic involvement with the ready-at-hand and the modern letting oneself go with the flow of *das Man* – there are also two opposed modes of acquiring a distance: the shattering existential experience of anxiety, which extraneates us from the traditional immersion in our way of life, and the theoretical distance of the neutral observer who, as if from outside, perceives the world in 'representations'? It seems as if this 'authentic' tension between the immersion of 'being-in-the-world' and its suspension in anxiety is redoubled by the 'inauthentic' pair of *das Man* and traditional metaphysical ontology. So we have four positions: the tension in everyday life between authentic 'being-in-the-world' and *das Man*, as well as the tension between the two modes of extracting ourselves from the everyday run of things, authentic existential resoluteness and the traditional metaphysical ontology – does not this give us a kind of Heideggerian semiotic square?

Heidegger is not interested in the (Hegelian) problem of legitimizing norms that regulate our immersion in the everyday life-world: he oscillates between direct (pre-reflexive) immersion in daily life and the abyss of the disintegration of this framework (his version of encountering 'absolute negativity').[9] He is acutely aware of how our everyday life is grounded on some fragile decision – how, although we are irreducibly thrown into a contingent situation, this does not mean that we are simply determined by it, caught in it like an animal: the original human condition is that of being out of joint, of abyss and excess, and any involvement in the daily life habitat relies on an act of resolute acceptance of it. Daily habitat and excess are not simply opposed: the habitat itself is 'chosen' in an 'excessive' gesture of groundless decision. This act of violent imposition is the 'third term' that undermines the alternative of fully fitting into a life-world context and of abstract decontextualized Reason: it consists in the violent gesture of breaking out of the finite context, the gesture which is not yet 'stabilized' in the position of neutral universality characteristic of the observing Reason, but remains a kind of 'universality-in-becoming', to put it in Kierkegaardese. The 'specifically human' dimension is thus neither that of the engaged agent caught in the finite life-world context, nor that of universal Reason exempted from the life-world, but the very discord, the 'vanishing mediator', between the two.

Heidegger's name for this act of violent imposition, *Ent-Wurf*, indicates the fundamental fantasy by means of which the subject 'makes sense of' – acquires the co-ordinates of – the situation into which he is thrown [*geworfen*], in which he finds himself, disorientated and lost.[10] What is problematic here is that Heidegger uses the notion of *Geworfenheit*, 'thrownness', into a finite contingent situation, and then of *Entwurf*, the act of authentically choosing one's way, on two levels whose relationship is not thought out: the individual and the collective one. On the individual level, the authentic encounter with death, which is 'always only mine', enables me to project my future in an authentic act of choice; but then, a community is also determined as being thrown into a contingent situation within which it must choose–assume its destiny. Heidegger passes from the individual to the societal level by means of the notion of *repetition*: 'The authentic repetition of a possibility of existence that has been – the possibility that *Dasein* may choose its hero – is grounded existentially in anticipatory resoluteness.'[11] The background here is unmistakably Kierke-gaardian: a true Christian community is grounded in the fact that each of its members has to repeat the mode of existence freely assumed by Christ, their hero.

This passage from the 'thrown projection' of the individual *Dasein* who, in an act of anticipatory decision, achieves an authentic mode of being, 'freely chooses his fate,' to a human community of a People which also, in a collective act of anticipatory decision *qua* repetition of a past possibility, authentically assumes its historial Destiny, is not phenomeno-logically grounded in an adequate way. The *medium* of collective (societal) being-there is not properly deployed: what Heidegger seems to be missing is simply that which Hegel designated as 'objective Spirit', the symbolic big Other, the 'objectified' domain of symbolic mandates, and so on, which is *not yet* the 'impersonal' *das Man*, but also *no longer* the premodern immersion in a traditional way of life. This illegitimate short circuit between individual and collective level is at the root of Heidegger's 'Fascist temptation'; at this point, the implicit politicization of *Being and Time* is at its strongest: does not the opposition between the modern anonymous dispersed society of *das Man*, with people busy following their everyday preoccupations, and the People authentically assuming its Destiny, reson-ate with the opposition between the decadent modern 'Americanized' civilization of frenetic false activity and the conservative 'authentic' response to it?

This is not to claim that Heidegger's notion of historical repetition as coinciding with authentic anticipatory projection is not an exemplary case of analysis. The key point not to be missed in Heidegger's analysis of historicity proper is the interconnection of the three temporal extases of time: when he speaks of 'thrown projection', this does not simply mean that a finite agent finds itself in a situation that limits its options; that it then analyses the potentialities allowed for by this finite situation, by its condition, chooses the possibility which best fits its interests and assumes it as its project. The point is that the future has a primacy: to be able to discern the possibilities opened up by the tradition into which an agent is thrown, one must already acknowledge one's engagement in a project – that is to say, the movement of repetition, as it were, retroactively reveals (and thus fully actualizes) that which it repeats.

For this reason, Heidegger's 'decision', in the precise sense of anticipatory resoluteness [*Ent-Schlossenheit*], has the status of a *forced choice*: the Heideggerian decision *qua* repetition is not a 'free choice' in the usual sense of the term. (Such a notion of freely choosing between alternative possibilities is utterly foreign to Heidegger; he dismisses it as belonging to superficial Americanized liberal individualism.) Rather, it is fundamentally the choice of 'freely assuming' one's imposed destiny. This paradox, necessary if one is to avoid the vulgar liberal notion of freedom of choice, indicates the theological problematic of *predestination* and *Grace*: a true decision/choice (not a choice between a series of objects leaving my subjective position intact, but the fundamental choice by means of which I 'choose myself') presupposes that I assume a passive attitude of 'letting myself be chosen' – in short, *free choice and Grace are strictly equivalent*; or, as Deleuze put it, we really choose only when we are *chosen*: 'Ne choisit bien, ne choisit effectivement que celui qui est choisi.'[12]

To dispel the notion that we are dealing here with an obscurantist-theological problematic, let us evoke a more telling leftist example of proletarian class interpellation: when a subject recognizes himself as a proletarian revolutionary, when he freely assumes and identifies with the task of revolution, he recognizes himself as being chosen by History to accomplish this task. In general, the Althusserian notion of ideological interpellation involves the situation of 'forced choice' by means of which the subject emerges out of the act of freely choosing the inevitable – that is, in which she/he is given the freedom of choice on condition that she/he makes the right choice: when an individual is addressed by an interpellation, she/he is 'invited to play a role in such a way that the invitation appears to have already been answered by the subject before it was proposed, but at the same time the invitation could be refused'.[13] Therein lies the ideological act of recognition, in which I recognize myself as 'always-already' that as which I am interpellated: in recognizing myself as X, I freely assume/choose the fact that I always-already was X. When, say, I am accused of a crime and agree to defend myself, I *presuppose myself* as a free agent legally responsible for my acts.

In her Internet discussion with Ernesto Laclau, Judith Butler made a nice Hegelian point about decision: it is not only that no decision is taken in an absolute void, that every decision is contextualized, is a decision-in-context, but contexts themselves:

> are in some ways produced by decisions, that is, there is a certain redoubling of decision-making. . . . There is first the decision to mark or delimit the context in which a decision [on what kinds of differences ought not to be included in a given polity] will be made, and then there is the marking off of certain kinds of differences as inadmissible.

The undecidability here is radical: one can never reach a 'pure' context prior to a decision; every context is 'always-already' retroactively constituted by a decision (as with reasons to do something, which are always at least minimally retroactively posited by the act of decision they ground – only once we decide to believe do reasons to believe become convincing to us, not vice versa). Another aspect of this same point is that not only is there no decision without exclusion (i.e. every decision precludes a series of possibilities), but also the act of decision itself is made possible by some kind of exclusion: something must be excluded in order for us to become beings which make decisions.

Is not the Lacanian notion of 'forced choice' a way to explain this paradox? Does not the primordial 'exclusion' which grounds decision (i.e. choice) indicate that the choice is, at a certain radically fundamental level, forced – that I have a (free) choice only on condition that I make the proper choice – so that, at this level, one encounters a paradoxical choice which overlaps with its meta-choice: I am told what I must choose freely. . . . Far from being a sign of 'pathological (or politically "totalitarian") distortion', this level of 'forced choice' is precisely what the psychotic position *lacks*: the psychotic subject acts as if he has a truly free choice 'all the way along'.

So, before we dismiss Heidegger's description of anticipatory decision as freely assuming one's destiny as a coded description of a conservative pseudo-revolution, we should stop for a moment and recall Fredric Jameson's assertion that a true Leftist is in a way much closer to today's neo-conservative communitarian than he is to a liberal democrat: he fully endorses the conservative criticism of liberal democracy and agrees with the conservative on practically everything *except the essential*, except a sometimes tiny feature which, none the less, changes everything. As for Heidegger's notion of authentic choice as a repetition, the parallel with Benjamin's notion of revolution as repetition, elucidated in his 'Theses on the Philosophy of History',[14] is striking: here also, revolution is conceptualized as a repetition that realizes the hidden possibility of the past, so that a proper view of the past (the one that perceives the past not as a closed set of facts but as open, as involving a possibility that failed, or was repressed, in its actuality) opens only from the standpoint of an agent engaged in a present situation. The present revolution, in its attempt to liberate the working class, also retroactively redeems all failed past attempts at liberation – that is to say, the point of view of a present agent engaged in a revolutionary project suddenly makes visible what the objectivist/positivist historiography, constrained to facticity, is by definition blind to: the hidden potentialities of liberation that were crushed by the victorious march of the forces of domination.

Read in this way, the appropriation of the past through its repetition in an anticipatory decision that enacts a project – this identification of fate and freedom, of assuming one's Destiny as the highest (albeit forced) free choice – does *not* involve a simple Nietzschean point that even the most neutral description of the past serves the present purposes of some power-political project. One must insist here on the opposition between the appropriation of the past from the standpoint of those who rule (the narrative of past history as the evolution leading to and legitimating their triumph) and the appropriation of that which, in the past, remained its utopian and failed ('repressed') potentiality. What Heidegger's description lacks is thus – to put it in a direct and somewhat crude way – insight into the radically *antagonistic* nature of every hitherto communal way of life.

Heidegger's ontology is thus in fact 'political' (to refer to the title of Bourdieu's book on Heidegger): his endeavour to break through traditional ontology, and to assert as the key to the 'sense of being' man's decision to adopt a 'project' by means of which he actively assumes his 'thrownness' into a finite historical situation, locates the historico-political act of decision in the very heart of ontology itself: the very choice of the historical form of *Dasein* is in a sense 'political', it consists in an abyssal decision not grounded in any universal ontological structure. Thus the standard Habermasian liberal argumentation which locates the source of Heidegger's Fascist temptation in his 'irrational' decisionism, in his rejection of any universal rational-normative criteria for political activity, completely misses the point: what this criticism rejects as proto-Fascist decisionism is simply the basic condition of the *political*. In a perverted way, Heidegger's Nazi engagement was therefore a 'step in the right direction', a step towards openly admitting and fully assuming the consequences of the lack of ontological guarantee, of the abyss of human freedom:[15] as Alain Badiou put it, in Heidegger's eyes the Nazi 'revolution' was formally indistinguishable from the authentic politico-historical 'event'. Or – to put it in another way – Heidegger's political engagement was a kind of *passage à l'acte* in the Real that bears witness to the fact that he refused to go to the end in the Symbolic – to think out the theoretical consequences of his breakthrough in *Being and Time*.

The standard story about Heidegger is that he accomplished his *Kehre* (turn) after becoming aware of how the original project of *Being and Time* leads back to transcendental subjectivism: owing to the unreflected remainder of subjectivism (decisionism, etc.), Heidegger let himself be seduced into his Nazi engagement; when, however, he became aware of how he had 'burnt his fingers' with it, he cleared up the remainders of subjectivism and developed the idea of the historical-epochal character of Being itself. . . . One is tempted to invert this standard story: there is a kind of 'vanishing mediator' between Heidegger I and Heidegger II, a position of radicalized subjectivity coinciding with its opposite – that is, reduced to an empty gesture, the impossible *intersection* between the 'decisionism' of Heidegger I and his late 'fatalism' (the event of Being 'takes place' in man, who serves as its shepherd . . .). Far from being the 'practical consequence' of this radicalized subjectivity, Heidegger's Nazi engagement was a desperate attempt to *avoid* it. . . . In other words, what Heidegger later dismissed as the remainder of the subjectivist transcendental approach in *Being and Time* is what he should have stuck to. Heidegger's ultimate failure is not that he remained stuck in the horizon of transcendental subjectivity, but that he abandoned this horizon all too quickly, before thinking out all its inherent possibilities. Nazism was not a political expression of the 'nihilist, demoniac potential of modern subjectivity' but, rather, its exact opposite: a desperate attempt to avoid this potential.

This logic of the 'missing link' is often present in the history of thought, from Schelling to the Frankfurt School. In the case of Schelling, we have the almost unbearable tension of his *Weltalter* drafts, their ultimate failure; Schelling's late philosophy, which follows the *Weltalter*, effectively resolves this unbearable tension, but in the wrong way – by losing the very dimension that was most productive in it. We encounter the same procedure of 'false resolution' in the way Habermas's project relates to Adorno's and Horkheimer's 'dialectic of Enlightenment'. The latter is also a self-defeating project, a gigantic failure; and, again, what Habermas does is to resolve the unbearable tension of the 'dialectic of Enlightenment' by introducing a distinction, a kind of 'division of labour', between the two dimensions, production and symbolic interaction (in a strict homology with Schelling, who dissolves the tension of the *Weltalter* by introducing the distinction between 'negative' and 'positive' philosophy). Our point is that Heidegger's late 'thought of Being' enacts an analogous false resolution of the inherent deadlock of the original project of *Being and Time*.[16]

Why Did *Being and Time* Remain Unfinished?

Why is Heidegger's *Kant and the Problem of Metaphysics*[17] crucial here? Let us recall the simple fact that *Being and Time*, as we know it, is a fragment: what Heidegger published as the book consists of the first two sections of the first part; the project proved impossible to realize, and what came out of this failure, what (to use good old structuralist jargon) filled in the lack of the missing final part of *Being and Time*, was the abundance of Heidegger's writings after the famous *Kehre*. Our point, of course, is not simply to imagine the finished version of *Being and Time*: the impediment that stopped Heidegger was inherent. On closer examination, the situation is more complex. On the one hand – at least at manuscript level – the entire project of *Being and Time was* accomplished: not only do we have *Kant and the Problem of Metaphysics*, which encompasses the first section of the projected Part II, but Heidegger's lectures at Marburg in 1927 (published later as *The Basic Problems of Phenomenology*) do loosely cover precisely the remaining sections of the original *Being and Time* project (time as the horizon of the question of being; the Cartesian *cogito* and the Aristotelian conception of time as the planned sections two and three of the second part), so that, if we put these three published volumes together, we do get a rough realized version of the entire *Being and Time* project. Furthermore, perhaps even more enigmatic is the fact that although the published version of *Being and Time* does not cover even the complete first part of the entire project, but only its first two sections (section three, the exposition of time as the transcendental horizon for the question of being, is missing), it somehow strikes us as 'complete', as an organic Whole, as if nothing is really missing. What we are dealing with here is thus the opposite of the standard notion of 'closure' that conceals or 'sutures' the persisting openness (inconclusiveness): with *Being and Time*, it is rather as if Heidegger's insistence that the published book is just a fragment conceals the fact that the book is closed, finished. The concluding chapters (on historicity) cannot but strike us as artificially added, as if to add to the closure a hastily concocted attempt to designate another dimension (that of collective forms of historicity), for which there is no proper place in the original project. . . .[18]

If the published *Being and Time* were to cover the entire Part I of the original project, one could still somehow justify this perception of wholeness. (We did get the entire 'systematic' part; what is missing is merely the 'historic' part, the interpretation of·the three key moments in the history of Western metaphysics – Aristotle, Descartes, Kant – whose radicalized 'repetition' is Heidegger's own analytic of *Dasein*.) Obviously, the inherent impediment, the barrier preventing the completion of the project, already affects the last section of Part I. If we leave aside the problem of non-publication of the texts (lecture notes) covering the remaining two sections of Part II (does it have something to do with the enigmatic status of imagination in Aristotle, as demonstrated by Castoriadis, the status that explodes the ontological edifice? or with the same implicit anti-ontological thrust of the Cartesian *cogito* as the first announcement of the 'night of the world'?), the enigma is: why was Heidegger unable to accomplish his very systematic exploration of time as the horizon of Being? The standard, 'official' answer is well known: because it became clear to him that the approach of *Being and Time* was still too metaphysical/transcendental, 'methodological', in proceeding from *Dasein* to the question of Being, instead of directly approaching the temporal Disclosure of Being as that which sustains the unique status of *Dasein* among all entities. But what if there was another deadlock, another kind of abyss, that Heidegger encountered – and withdrew from – at this point? We therefore want to argue against the 'official' version of this impediment (that Heidegger became aware of how the project of *Being and Time* was still caught in the transcendental-subjectivist procedure of first establishing the 'conditions of possibility' of the sense of Being via the analysis of *Dasein*): what Heidegger actually encountered in his pursuit of *Being and Time* was the abyss of radical subjectivity announced in Kantian transcendental imagination, and he recoiled from this abyss into his thought of the historicity of Being.

This criticism of Heidegger does not seem at all new: it has already been made by, among others, Cornelius Castoriadis, who argues that the

Kantian notion of imagination (as that which undermines the standard 'closed' ontological image of the Cosmos) is announced already in a unique passage of *De Anima* (III, 7 and 8), where Aristotle claims: 'never does the soul think without phantasm', and develops this further into a kind of 'Aristotelian Schematism' (every abstract notion – say, of a triangle – has to be accompanied in our thought by a sensible, although not bodily, phantasmic representation – when we think of a triangle, we have in our mind an image of a concrete triangle).[19] Aristotle even announces the Kantian notion of time as the unsurpassable horizon of our experience when he asserts: 'it is not possible to think without time what is not in time' (*On Memory*, 449–50) – without finding a kind of figuration in something temporal; for example, that which 'endures forever'. Castoriadis opposes this notion of imagination to the standard one which otherwise prevails both in *De Anima* and in the entire subsequent metaphysical tradition: this radical notion of imagination is neither passive-receptive nor conceptual – that is to say, it cannot be properly placed ontologically, since it indicates a gap in the very ontological edifice of Being. Castoriadis thus seems fully justified in his claim:

> with respect to the 'recoiling' Heidegger imputes to Kant when faced with the 'bottomless abyss' opened up by the discovery of the transcendental imagination, it is Heidegger himself who in effect 'recoils' after writing his book on Kant. A new forgetting, covering-over, and effacement of the question of the imagination intervenes, for no further traces of the question will be found in any of his subsequent writings; there is a suppression of what this question unsettles for every ontology (and for every 'thinking of Being').[20]

Castoriadis also draws political consequences from this: it is Heidegger's recoiling from the abyss of imagination that justifies his acceptance of 'totalitarian' political closure, while the abyss of imagination provides the philosophical foundation for the democratic opening – the notion of society as grounded in a collective act of historical imagination: 'A full recognition of the radical imagination is possible only if it goes hand in hand with the discovery of the other dimension of the radical imaginary, the social-historical imaginary, instituting society as source of ontological creation deploying itself as history.'[21] However, Castoriadis's notion of imagination remains within the existentialist horizon of man as the being who projects his 'essence' in the act of imagination transcending all positive Being. So, before we pass the final judgement on it, it would be appropriate to take a closer look at the contours of imagination in Kant himself.

The mystery of transcendental imagination *qua* spontaneity lies in the fact that it cannot be properly located with regard to the couple of Phenomenal and Noumenal. Kant himself is caught here in a deadly impasse and/or ambiguity. On the one hand, he conceives of transcendental freedom ('spontaneity') as *noumenal*: as phenomenal entities, we are caught in the web of causal connections, while our freedom (the fact that, as moral subjects, we are free, self-originating agents) indicates the noumenal dimension. In this way, Kant solves the dynamic antinomies of reason: both propositions can be true – that is to say, since all phenomena are causally linked, man, as a phenomenal entity, is not free; as a noumenal entity, however, man can act morally as a free agent. . . . What blurs this clear picture is Kant's own insight into the catastrophic consequences of our direct access to the noumenal sphere: if this were to happen, men would *lose* their moral freedom and/or transcendental spontaneity; they would turn into lifeless puppets. That is to say: in a subchapter of his *Critique of Practical Reason* mysteriously entitled 'Of the Wise Adaptation of Man's Cognitive Faculties to His Practical Vocation', he answers the question of what would happen to us if we were to gain access to the noumenal domain, to Things in themselves:

> . . . instead of the conflict which now the moral disposition has to wage with inclinations and in which, after some defeats, moral strength of mind may be gradually won, God and eternity in their awful majesty would stand unceasingly before our eyes. . . . Thus most actions conforming to the law would be done from fear, few would be done from hope, none from duty. The moral worth of actions, on which alone the worth of the person and even of the world depends in the eyes of supreme wisdom, would not exist at all. The conduct of man, so long as his nature remained as it is now, would be changed into mere mechanism, where, as in a puppet show, everything would gesticulate well but no life would be found in the figures.[22]

Transcendental freedom and/or spontaneity itself is thus in a sense phenomenal: it occurs only in so far as the noumenal sphere is not accessible to the subject. This in-between – neither phenomenal nor noumenal, but the gap which separates the two and, in a way, precedes them – 'is' the subject, so that the fact that Subject cannot be reduced to Substance means precisely that transcendental Freedom, although it is not phenomenal (i.e. although it breaks up the chain of causality to which all phenomena are submitted) – that is, although it cannot be reduced to an effect unaware of its true noumenal causes (I 'feel free' only because I am blinded to the causality which determines my 'free' acts) – is also not noumenal, but would vanish in the case of the subject's direct access to the noumenal order. This impossibility of locating transcendental freedom/ spontaneity with regard to the couple phenomenal/noumenal explains why[23] Kant was at such a loss, and got involved in a series of inconsistencies in his efforts to determine the exact ontological status of transcendental spontaneity. And the mystery of transcendental imagination ultimately coincides with the mystery of this abyss of freedom.

Heidegger's great achievement was that he clearly perceived this Kantian deadlock, linking it to Kant's unwillingness to draw all the consequences from the finitude of the transcendental subject: Kant's 'regression' into traditional metaphysics occurs the moment he interprets the spontaneity of transcendental apperception as the proof that the subject has a noumenal side which is not subject to the causal constraints binding all phenomena. The finitude of the Kantian subject does not amount to the standard sceptical assertion of the unreliable and delusive character of human knowledge (man can never penetrate the mystery of the highest reality, since his knowledge is limited to ephemeral sensible phenomena . . .); it involves a much more radical stance: the very dimension which, from within the horizon of his finite temporal experience, appears to the subject as the trace of the inaccessible noumenal Beyond, is already marked by the horizon of finitude – it designates the way the noumenal Beyond *appears to the subject within his finite temporal experience*.

The radical consequence of all this for the relationship between temporality and eternity is that temporality is not a deficient mode of eternity: on the contrary, it is 'eternity' itself that has to be conceived as a specific modification of the subject's temporal (self-)experience. This means that the true split is no longer between the phenomenal (the domain of temporal and/or sensible experience) and the noumenal; rather, it runs down the middle of the noumenal itself, in the guise of the split between the way the noumenal In-itself *appears to the subject* and its 'impossible' In-itself *sans phrase*, *tout court*, without reference to the subject. God, the Supreme Being Who gives body to the Idea of the highest Good, of course, designates a noumenal entity (one cannot conceive of it in a consistent way as an object of our temporal experience). However, it designates a noumenal entity in the mode of 'For-us' – that is, it designates the way a finite rational entity (man) has to represent to itself the noumenal supreme Being; or, to put it in phenomenological terms, although God *qua* Supreme Being can never be a phenomenon in the sense of an object of sensible temporal experience, it is none the less a 'phenomenon' in a more radical sense of something that is meaningful only as an entity which *appears* to a finite being endowed with consciousness and/or the capacity for freedom. Perhaps, if we approach the divinity too closely, this sublime quality of supreme Goodness turns into an excruciating Monstrosity.

Here, Heidegger is fully justified in his ferocious aversion to Cassirer's reading of Kant during their famous Davos debate in 1929.[24] Cassirer simply contrasts the temporal finitude of the human condition (at this level, human beings are empirical entities whose behaviour can be explained by different sets of causal links) with the freedom of man *qua* ethical agent: in its symbolic activity, humanity gradually constructs the universe of values and meanings that cannot be reduced to (or explained via a reference to) the domain of facts and their interrelations – this universe of Values and Meanings posited by man's symbolic activity is the modern version of Plato's realm of eternal Ideas: that is to say, in it, a dimension different from that of the dynamic circuit of life, of generation and corruption, breaks through and comes into existence – a dimension which, although it does not exist outside the actual human life-world, is in itself 'immortal' and 'eternal'. In his capacity as 'symbolic animal', man transcends the confines of finitude and temporality. . . . Against this distinction, Heidegger demonstrates how the 'immortality' and 'eternity' of the symbolic system of Values and Meanings, irreducible to the level of empirically given positive facts, can emerge only as part of the existence of a finite and mortal being who is able to relate to his finitude as such: 'immortal' beings do not engage in symbolic activity, since, for them, the gap between fact and Value disappears. The key question, unanswered by Cassirer, is therefore: what is the specific structure of the *temporality* of human existence, so that it allows for the emergence of *meaning* – that is to say, so that a human being is able to experience his existence as embedded in a meaningful Whole?

One can see clearly, now, why Heidegger focuses on transcendental *imagination*: the unique character of imagination lies in the fact that it undermines the opposition between receptivity/finitude (of man as an empirical being caught in the phenomenal causal network) and spontaneity (i.e. the self-originating activity of man as a free agent, bearer of noumenal freedom): imagination is simultaneously receptive and positing, 'passive' (in it, we are affected by sensible images) and 'active' (the subject himself freely gives birth to these images, so that this affection is self-affection). And Heidegger's emphasis is on how spontaneity itself can be conceived only through this unity with an irreducible element of passive receptivity that characterizes human finitude: if the subject were to succeed in getting rid of receptivity and gaining direct access to the noumenal in itself, he would lose the very 'spontaneity' of his existence. . . . The deadlock of Kant is thus condensed in his misreading (or false identification) of the spontaneity of transcendental freedom as noumenal: transcendental spontaneity is precisely something that cannot be conceived of as noumenal.

The Trouble with Transcendental Imagination

Our next step should be to focus on the fundamental ambiguity of Kant's notion of imagination. As is well known, Kant distinguishes between the synthetic activity of the understanding [*synthesis intellectualis*] and the synthesis of the manifold of sensuous intuition which, while also absolutely 'spontaneous' (productive, free, not subject to empirical laws of association), none the less remains at the level of intuition, bringing the sensuous manifold together without already involving the activity of Understanding – this second synthesis is the *transcendental synthesis of imagination*. In discussing this distinction, interpreters usually focus on the dense and ambiguous last section of Chapter 1 of the First Division of the Transcendental Logic ('Of the Pure Conceptions of the Understanding, or Categories'), which, after defining synthesis as 'the process of joining different representations to each other, and of comprehending their diversity in one cognition',[25] goes on to claim that synthesis is:

the mere operation of the imagination – a blind but indispensable function of the soul, without which we should have no cognition whatever, but of the working of which we are seldom even conscious. But to reduce this synthesis to conceptions is a function of the understanding, by means of which we attain to cognition, in the proper meaning of the term.[26]

In this way, we obtain a three-step process that brings us to cognition proper:

The first thing which must be given to us in order to achieve the *a priori* cognition of all objects, is the diversity of the pure intuition; the synthesis of this diversity by means of the imagination is the second; but this gives, as yet, no cognition. The conceptions which give unity to this pure synthesis . . . furnish the third requisite for the cognition of an object, and these conceptions are given by the understanding.[27]

However, in so far as 'pure synthesis, represented generally, gives us the pure conception of the understanding',[28] the ambiguity is clearly discernible: is 'synthesis, generally speaking . . . the mere operation of imagination',[29] with Understanding as a secondary capacity intervening after imagination has already done its work, or is it that 'pure synthesis, represented generally, gives us the pure conception of the understanding', so that the synthesis of imagination is merely the application of the synthetic power of understanding on a lower, more primitive, precognitive level? Or, to put it in the terms of genus and species: is the force of imagination the impenetrable ultimate mystery of transcendental spontaneity, the root of subjectivity, the encompassing genus out of which grows understanding as its discursive cognitive specification, or is the encompassing genus understanding itself, with imagination as a kind of shadow cast retroactively by understanding on to the lower level of intuition – or, to put it in Hegelese, is the synthesis of imagination the underdeveloped 'In-itself' of a force posited 'as such', 'for itself', in Understanding? The point of Heidegger's reading is that one should determine the synthesis of imagination as the fundamental dimension at the root of discursive understanding, which should thus be analysed independently of the categories of Understanding – Kant recoiled from this radical step, and reduced imagination to a mere mediating force between the pure sensuous manifold of intuition and the cognitive synthetic activity of Understanding.

In contrast to this approach, we are tempted to emphasize a different aspect: the fact that Kant's notion of imagination silently passes over a crucial 'negative' feature of imagination: obsessed as he is with the endeavour to synthesize, to bring together the dispersed manifold given in intuition, Kant passes over in silence the opposite power of imagination emphasized later by Hegel – namely, imagination *qua* the 'activity of dissolution', which treats as a separate entity what has effective existence only as a part of some organic Whole. This negative power also comprises Understanding and Imagination, as is clear if we read two crucial passages from Hegel together. The first, less known, is from his manuscripts of *Jenaer Realphilosophie*, about the 'night of the world':

> The human being is this night, this empty nothing, that contains everything in its simplicity – an unending wealth of many representations, images, of which none belongs to him – or which are not present. This night, the interior of nature, that exists here – pure self – in phantasmagorical representations, is night all around it, in which here shoots a bloody head – there another white

ghastly apparition, suddenly here before it, and just so disappears. One catches sight of this night when one looks human beings in the eye – into a night that becomes awful.[30]

What better description could one offer of the power of imagination in its negative, disruptive, decomposing aspect, as the power that disperses continuous reality into a confused multitude of 'partial objects', spectral apparitions of what in reality is effective only as part of a larger organism? Ultimately, imagination stands for the capacity of our mind to dismember what immediate perception puts together, to 'abstract' not a common notion but a certain feature from other features. To 'imagine' means to imagine a partial object without its body, a colour without shape, a shape without a body: 'here a bloody head – there another white ghastly apparition'. This 'night of the world' is thus transcendental imagination at its most elementary and violent – the unrestrained reign of the violence of imagination, of its 'empty freedom' which dissolves every objective link, every connection grounded in the thing itself: 'For itself is here the arbitrary freedom – to tear up the images and to reconnect them without any constraint.'[31] The other passage – universally known, often quoted and interpreted – is from the Preface to the Phenomenology:

To break an idea up into its original elements is to return to its moments, which at least do not have the form of the given idea, but rather constitute the immediate property of the self. This analysis, to be sure, only arrives at thoughts which are themselves familiar, fixed, and inert determinations. But what is thus separated and non-actual is an essential moment; for it is only because the concrete does divide itself, and make itself into something non-actual, that it is self-moving. The activity of dissolution is the power and work of the Understanding, the most astonishing and mightiest of powers, or rather the absolute power. The circle that remains self-enclosed and, like substance, holds its moments together, is an immediate relationship, one therefore which has nothing astonishing about it. But that an accident as such, detached from what circumscribes it, what is bound and is actual only in its context with others, should attain an existence of its own and a separate freedom – this is the tremendous power of the negative; it is the energy of thought, of the pure 'I'. Death, if that is what we want to call this non-actuality, is of all things the most dreadful, and to hold fast what is dead requires the greatest strength. Lacking strength, Beauty hates the Understanding for asking her what it cannot do. But the life of Spirit is not the life that shrinks from death and keeps itself untouched by devastation, but rather the life that endures it and maintains itself in it. It wins its truth only when, in utter dismemberment, it finds itself. It is this power, not as something positive, which closes its eyes to the negative, as when we say of something that it is nothing or is false, and then, having done with it, turn away and pass on to something else; on the contrary, Spirit is this power only by looking the negative in the face, and tarrying with it. This tarrying with the negative is the magical power that converts it into being. This power is identical with what we earlier called the Subject. . . .[32]

Here, Hegel praises *not*, as one would expect, speculative Reason, but *Understanding* as the mightiest power in the world, as the infinite power of 'falsity', of tearing apart and treating as separate what naturally belongs together. Is this not a precise description of the basic negative gesture of – let us risk the term – 'pre-synthetic imagination', its destructive power of undermining every organic unity? So, although the two quoted passages[33] seem to speak of opposite phenomena (the first of the pre-rational/pre-discursive confused immersion in the purely subjective Interior; the second of the abstract discursive activity of Understanding, which decomposes every 'depth' of organic unity into detached elements), they are thus to be read together: both refer to the 'mightiest of powers', the power of disrupting the unity of the Real, violently installing the domain of *membra disjecta*, of *phenomena* in the most radical sense of the term. The 'night' of the 'pure self', in which dismembered and disconnected 'phantasmagorical representations' appear and vanish, is the most elementary manifestation of the power of negativity by means of which 'an accident as such, detached from what circumscribes it, what is bound and is actual only in its context with others, . . . attain[s] an existence of its own and a separate freedom'. Kant, in his *Critique of Pure Reason*, elaborates the notion of 'transcendental imagination' as the mysterious, unfathomable root of all subjective activity, as a 'spontaneous' capacity to connect sensible impressions that precedes rational synthesis of sensible data through a priori categories. What if, in the two quoted passages, Hegel is indicating a kind of even more mysterious *obverse* of the synthetic imagination, an even more primordial power of 'pre-synthetic imagination', of *tearing apart* sensible elements out of their context, of *dismembering* the immediate experience of an organic Whole? It would therefore be too hasty to identify this 'night of the world' with the Void of the mystic experience: it designates, rather, its exact opposite, that is, the primordial Big Bang, the violent self-contrast by means of which the balance and inner peace of the Void of which mystics speak are perturbed, thrown out of joint.

If there is some truth in Heidegger's contention that Kant retreated from the abyss of imagination, his retreat thus concerns, above all, his refusal to bring to light Imagination in its negative/disruptive aspect, as the force of tearing the continuous fabric of intuition apart. Kant is too quick in automatically assuming that the multitude of intuition is directly given, so that the bulk of the subject's activity is then constrained to bringing this multitude together, to organizing it into an interconnected Whole, from the most primitive synthesis of imagination, through the synthetic activity of the categories of Understanding, up to the regulative Idea of Reason, the impossible task of uniting our entire experience of the universe into a rational organic structure. What Kant neglects is the fact that the primordial form of imagination is the exact opposite of this synthetic activity: imagination enables us to tear the texture of reality apart, to treat as effectively existing something that is merely a component of a living Whole.

How, then, does the opposition between imagination and understanding relate to that between synthesis and analysis (in the sense of disrupting, decomposing, the primordial immediate unity of intuition)? This relation can be conceived as working both ways: one can determine imagination as the spontaneous synthesis of the sensuous manifold into a perception of unified objects and processes, which are then torn apart, decomposed, analysed by discursive understanding; or one can determine imagination as the primordial power of decomposition, of tearing-apart, while the role of understanding is then to bring together these *membra disjecta* into a new rational Whole. In both cases, the continuity between imagination and understanding is disrupted: there is an inherent antagonism between the two – it is either Understanding that heals the wound inflicted by imagination, synthesizing its *membra disjecta*, or Understanding mortifies, tears the spontaneous synthetic unity of imagination into bits and pieces.

At this point, a naive question is quite appropriate: which of the two axes, of the two relations, is more fundamental? The underlying structure here, of course, is that of a vicious cycle or mutual implication: 'the wound can be healed only by the spear that inflicted it' – that is to say, the multitude that the synthesis of imagination endeavours to bring together is already the result of imagination itself, of its disruptive power. This mutual implication none the less gives precedence to the 'negative', disruptive aspect of imagination – not only for the obvious common-sense reason that elements must first be dismembered in order to open up the space for the endeavour to bring them together again, but for a more radical reason: because of the subject's irreducible finitude, the very endeavour of 'synthesis' is always minimally 'violent' and disruptive. That is to say, the unity the subject endeavours to impose on the sensuous multitude via its synthetic activity is always erratic, eccentric, unbalanced, 'unsound', something that is externally and violently imposed on to the multitude, never a simple impassive act of discerning the inherent subterranean connections between the *membra disjecta*. In this precise sense, every synthetic unity is based on an act of 'repression', and therefore generates some indivisible remainder: it imposes as unifying feature some 'unilateral' moment that 'breaches the symmetry'. This is what, in the domain of cinematic art, Eisenstein's concept of 'intellectual montage' seems to aim at: intellectual activity brings together bits and pieces torn by the power of imagination from their proper context, violently recomposing them into a new unity that gives birth to an unexpected new meaning.

Kant's break with the previous rationalist/empiricist problematic can thus be located precisely: in contrast to this problematic, he no longer accepts some pre-synthetic zero-ground elements worked upon by our mind – there is no neutral elementary stuff (like elementary sensory 'ideas' in Locke) which is then composed by our mind – that is, the synthetic activity of our mind *is always-already at work*, even in our most elementary contact with 'reality'.[34] The pre-synthetic Real, its pure, not-yet-fashioned 'multitude' not yet synthesized by a minimum of transcendental imagination, is, *stricto sensu, impossible*: a level that must be retroactively presupposed, but can never actually be *encountered*. Our (Hegelian) point, however, is that this mythical/impossible starting point, the presupposition of imagination, is already the product, the result, of the imagination's disruptive activity. In short, the mythic, inaccessible zero-level of pure multitude not yet affected/fashioned by imagination is nothing but *pure imagination itself*, imagination at its most violent, as the activity of disrupting the continuity of the inertia of the pre-symbolic 'natural' Real. This pre-synthetic 'multitude' is what Hegel describes as the 'night of the world', as the 'unruliness' of the subject's abyssal freedom which violently explodes reality into a dispersed floating of *membra disjecta*. It is thus crucial to 'close the circle': we never exit the circle of imagination, since the very zero-level mythic presupposition of synthetic imagination, the 'stuff' on which it works, is imagination itself at its purest and most violent, imagination in its negative, disruptive aspect.[35]

The Passage through Madness

Hegel explicitly posits this 'night of the world' as pre-ontological: the symbolic order, the universe of the Word, *logos*, emerges only when this inwardness of the pure self 'must enter also into existence, become an object, oppose itself to this innerness to be external; return to being. This is language as name-giving power. . . . Through the name the object as individual entity is born out of the I.'[36] Consequently, what one should bear in mind is that, for the object to be 'born out of the I', it is necessary, as it were, to start with a clean slate – to erase the entirety of reality in so far as it is *not yet* 'born out of the I' by passing through the 'night of the world'. This, finally, brings us to *madness* as a philosophical notion inherent to the very concept of subjectivity. Schelling's basic insight – whereby, prior to its assertion as the medium of rational Word, the subject is the pure 'night of the Self', the 'infinite lack of being', the violent gesture of contraction that negates every being outside itself – also forms the core of Hegel's notion of madness: when Hegel determines madness as withdrawal from the actual world, the closing of the soul into itself, its 'contraction', the cutting-off of its links with external reality, he all too quickly conceives of this withdrawal as a 'regression' to the level of the 'animal soul' still embedded in its natural surroundings and determined by the rhythm of nature (night and day, etc.). Does not this withdrawal, on the contrary, designate the severing of the links with the *Umwelt*, the end of the subject's immersion in its immediate natural surroundings; and is it not, as such, the founding gesture of 'humanization'? Was not this withdrawal-into-self accomplished by Descartes in his universal doubt and reduction to *cogito*, which, as Derrida pointed out in his 'Cogito and the History of Madness',[37] also involves a passage through the moment of radical madness?

Here we must be careful not to miss the way Hegel's break with the Enlightenment tradition can be discerned in the reversal of the very metaphor of the subject: the subject is no longer the Light of Reason opposed to the non-transparent, impenetrable Stuff (of Nature, Tradition . . .); his very core, the gesture that opens up the space for the Light of *Logos*, is absolute negativity, the 'night of the world', the point of utter madness in which phantasmagorical apparitions of 'partial objects' wander aimlessly. Consequently, there is no subjectivity without this gesture of withdrawal; that is why Hegel is fully justified in inverting the standard question of how the fall–regression into madness is possible: the real question is, rather, how the subject is able to climb out of madness and reach 'normality'. That is to say: the withdrawal-into-self, the cutting-off of the links to the environs, is followed by the construction of a symbolic universe which the subject projects on to reality as a kind of substitute-formation, destined to recompense us for the loss of the imme-diate, pre-symbolic Real. However, as Freud himself asserted in his analysis of Daniel Paul Schreber, is not the manufacturing of a substitute-formation, which recompenses the subject for the loss of reality, the most succinct definition of paranoiac construction as the subject's attempt to cure himself of the disintegration of his universe?

In short, the ontological necessity of 'madness' lies in the fact that it is not possible to pass directly from the purely 'animal soul' immersed in its natural life-world to 'normal' subjectivity dwelling in its symbolic universe. The 'vanishing mediator' between the two is the 'mad' gesture of radical withdrawal from reality which opens up the space for its symbolic (re)constitution. Hegel already emphasized the radical ambiguity of the statement 'What I think, the product of my thought, is objectively true.' This statement is a speculative proposition that expresses simultaneously the 'lowest', the erratic attitude of the madman caught in his self-enclosed universe, unable to relate to reality, *and* the 'highest', the truth of speculative idealism, the identity of thought and being. If, therefore, in this precise sense – as Lacan put it – normality itself is a mode, a subspecies of psychosis – that is, if the difference between 'normality' and madness is inherent to madness – of what, then, does this difference between the 'mad' (paranoiac) construction and the 'normal' (social) construction of reality consist? Is 'normality' ultimately merely a more 'mediated' form of madness? Or, as Schelling put it, is normal Reason merely 'regulated madness'?

Does not Hegel's brief description – 'here shoots a bloody head, there another white ghastly apparition' – chime perfectly with Lacan's notion of the 'dismembered body' [*le corps morcelé*]? What Hegel calls the 'night of the world' (the phantasmagorical, pre-symbolic domain of partial drives) is an undeniable component of the subject's most radical self-experience, exemplified, among others, by Hieronymus Bosch's celebrated paintings. In a way, the entire psychoanalytic experience focuses on the traces of the traumatic passage from this 'night of the world' into our 'daily' universe of *logos*. The tension between the narrative form and the 'death drive', as the withdrawal-into-self constitutive of the subject, is thus the missing link that has to be presupposed if we are to account for the passage from 'natural' to 'symbolic' surroundings.

The key point is thus that the passage from 'nature' to 'culture' is not direct, that one cannot account for it within a continuous evolutionary narrative: something has to intervene between the two, a kind of 'vanishing mediator', which is neither Nature nor Culture – this In-between is silently presupposed in all evolutionary narratives. We are not idealists: this In-between is not the spark of *logos* magically conferred on *Homo sapiens*, enabling him to form his supplementary virtual symbolic surroundings, but precisely something that, although it is also no longer nature, is not yet *logos*, and has to be 'repressed' by *logos* – the Freudian name for this In-between, of course, is the death drive. Speaking of this In-between, it is interesting to note how philosophical narratives of the 'birth of man' are always compelled to presuppose such a moment in human (pre)history when (what will become) man is no longer a mere animal and simultaneously not yet a 'being of language', bound by symbolic Law; a moment of thoroughly 'perverted', 'denaturalized', 'derailed' nature which is not yet culture. In his pedagogical writings, Kant emphasized that the human animal needs disciplinary pressure in order to tame an uncanny 'unruliness' that seems to be inherent in human nature – a wild, unconstrained propensity to insist stubbornly on one's own will, cost what it may. Because of this 'unruliness' the human animal needs a Master to discipline him: discipline targets this 'unruliness', not the animal nature in man:

> It is discipline which prevents man from being turned aside by his animal impulses from humanity, his appointed end. Discipline, for instance, must restrain him from venturing wildly and rashly into danger. Discipline, thus, is merely negative, its action being to counteract man's natural unruliness. The positive part of education is instruction.
>
> Unruliness consists in independence of law. By discipline men are placed in subjection to the laws of mankind, and brought to feel their constraint. This, however, must be accomplished early. Children, for instance, are first sent to school, not so much with the object of their learning something, but rather that they may become used to sitting still and doing exactly as they are told. . . .
>
> The love of freedom is naturally so strong in man that when once he has grown accustomed to freedom, he will sacrifice everything for its sake. . . . Owing to his natural love of freedom it is necessary that man should have his natural roughness smoothed down; with animals, their instinct renders this unnecessary.[38]

Everything is in this marvellous text: from the Foucauldian motif of disciplinary micro-practice as preceding any positive instruction, to the Althusserian equation of the free subject with his subjection to the Law.

However, its fundamental ambiguity is no less discernible: on the one hand, Kant seems to conceive discipline as the procedure that makes the human animal free, delivering it from the hold of natural instincts; on the other, it is clear that what discipline targets is not directly man's animal nature but his excessive love of freedom, his natural 'unruliness', which goes far beyond obeying animal instincts – in this 'unruliness', another, properly noumenal dimension violently emerges, a dimension that suspends man's enchainment in the phenomenal network of natural causality. The story of morality is thus not the standard story of nature versus culture, of the moral Law constraining our natural 'pathological' pleasure-seeking propensities – on the contrary, the struggle is between the moral Law and *unnatural* violent 'unruliness', and, in this struggle, man's natural propensities are, rather, on the side of moral Law against the excess of 'unruliness' that threatens his well-being (since man 'has grown accustomed to freedom, he will sacrifice everything for its sake', including his well-being!). In Hegel's *Lectures on the Philosophy of World History*, a similar role is played by the reference to 'negroes': significantly, Hegel deals with 'negroes' before history proper (which starts with ancient China), in the section entitled 'The Natural Context or the Geographical Basis of World History': 'negroes' stand for the human spirit in its 'state of nature'; they are described as perverted, monstrous children, simultaneously naive and extremely corrupted – that is to say, living in the prelapsarian state of innocence and, precisely as such, the most cruel barbarians; part of nature and yet thoroughly denaturalized; ruthlessly manipulating nature through primitive sorcery, yet simultaneously terrified by raging natural forces; mindlessly brave cowards. . . .[39]

In a closer reading, one should link the problem of imagination as transcendental spontaneity to its point of failure announced in the two forms of the Sublime: these two forms are precisely the two modes of imagination's failure to accomplish its synthetic activity. Jacob Rogozinski drew attention to the way a kind of elementary violence is already at work in pure reason, in the most elementary synthesis of imagination (memory, retention, temporality). That is to say: what Kant fails to appreciate is the extent to which this synthesis constitutive of 'normal' reality is – in an unheard-of and simultaneously most fundamental sense – already 'violent', in so far as it consists in an order imposed by the subject's synthetic activity on the heterogeneous disarray of impressions.[40] Let us add that this violence of synthesis is perhaps already an answer to the more fundamental violence of dismemberment, of tearing the natural continuity of experience apart. If the synthesis of imagination were to succeed without a gap, we would obtain perfect self-sufficient and self-enclosed auto-affection. However, the synthesis of imagination necessarily fails; it gets caught in an inconsistency in two different ways:

- first, in an inherent way, through the imbalance between apprehension and comprehension, which generates the mathematical sublime: synthetic comprehension is not able to 'catch up' with the magnitude of the apprehended perceptions with which the subject is bombarded, and it is this very failure of synthesis that reveals its violent nature;

- then, in an external way, through the intervention of the (moral) Law that announces another dimension, that of the noumenal: the (moral) Law is necessarily experienced by the subject as a violent intrusion disturbing the smooth self-sufficient run of the auto-affection of his imagination.

In these two cases of the violence that emerges as a kind of answer to the preceding violence of the transcendental imagination itself, we thus encounter the matrix of mathematical and dynamic antinomies. This is the exact locus at which the antagonism between (philosophical) materialism and idealism is discernible in Kant's philosophy: it concerns the question of primacy in the relationship between the two antinomies. Idealism gives priority to the dynamic antinomy, to the way the suprasensible Law transcends and/or suspends from the outside the phenomenal causal chain: from this perspective, phenomenal inconsistency is merely the way in which the noumenal Beyond inscribes itself into the phenomenal domain. Materialism, in contrast, gives priority to mathematical antinomy, to the inherent inconsistency of the phenomenal domain: the ultimate outcome of mathematical antinomy is the domain of an 'inconsistent All', of a multitude that lacks the ontological consistency of 'reality'. From this perspective, the dynamic antinomy itself appears as an attempt to resolve the inherent deadlock of mathematical antinomy by transposing it into the coexistence of two distinct orders, the phenomenal and the noumenal. In other words, mathematical antinomy (i.e. the inherent failure or collapse of imagination) 'dissolves' phenomenal reality in the direction of the monstrous Real, while dynamic antinomy transcends phenomenal reality in the direction of the symbolic Law – it 'saves phenomena' by providing a kind of external guarantee of the phenomenal domain.[41]

As Lenin had already emphasized, the history of philosophy consists of an incessant, repetitive tracing of the difference between materialism and idealism; what one has to add is that, as a rule, this line of demarcation does not run where one would obviously expect it to run – often, the materialist choice hinges on how we decide between seemingly secondary alternatives. According to the predominant philosophical cliché, the last vestige of Kant's materialism is to be sought in his insistence on the Thing-in-itself, the external Other that forever resists being dissolved in the subject's activity of reflexive (self-)positing. Thus Fichte, in his rejection of the Kantian Thing-in-itself – that is to say, in his notion of the absolute act of the subject's self-positing – eliminates the last trace of materialism from Kant's edifice, opening up the way for Hegel's 'panlogicist' reduction of all reality to an externalization of the absolute subject's notional self-mediation . . . Contrary to this predominant cliché, incorrectly sustained by Lenin himself, Kant's 'materialism' consists, rather, in *asserting the primacy of mathematical antinomy*, and in conceiving dynamic antinomy as secondary, as an attempt to 'save phenomena' through the noumenal Law as their constitutive exception.

In other words, it is only too easy to locate the greatest effort and scope of imagination – and, simultaneously, its ultimate failure – in its inability to make the noumenal dimension present (therein lies the lesson of the Sublime: the attempt to represent the noumenal – i.e. to fill the gap between the noumenal and the imagined phenomenal – fails, so that imagination can reveal the noumenal dimension only in a negative way, via its failure, as that which eludes even the greatest effort of imagination). Prior to this experience of gap and failure, 'imagination' is already a name for the violent gesture that opens up and sustains the very gap between the noumenal and the phenomenal. The true problem is not how to bridge the gap separating the two but, rather, how this gap came to emerge in the first place.

Thus Heidegger was right, in a way, in his emphasis on transcendental imagination as preceding and grounding the dimension of the constitutive categories of Understanding, and this same priority holds even for the Sublime as the impossible scheme of the Ideas of Reason. The gesture to be accomplished here is simply to invert and/or displace the standard notion, according to which sublime phenomena, by their very failure, bear witness in a negative way to another dimension, that of the noumenal dimension of Reason. Rather, it is the other way round: the Sublime, in its extreme, in its approaching the Monstrous, indicates an abyss which is already concealed, 'gentrified', by the Ideas of Reason. In other words, it is not that, in the experience of the Sublime, imagination fails properly to schematize/temporalize the suprasensible dimension of Reason; rather, it is that the regulative Ideas of Reason are ultimately nothing but a secondary endeavour to cover up, to sustain the abyss of the Monstrous announced in the failure of transcendental imagination.

To clarify this point further, one should introduce here the distinction between scheme and symbol: scheme offers a direct, sensible presentation of a notion of Understanding; while a symbol retains a distance, merely indicating something beyond it. The persistence in time is thus an adequate *scheme* of the category of substance; while Beauty, a beautiful object, is – as Kant puts it – the 'symbol of the Good', that is, not a scheme, but a symbolic representation of the Good as an Idea of Reason, not a category of Understanding. And things become complicated here with the Sublime: the Sublime is not a symbol of the Good; so, in a way, it is closer to the scheme, it stands for an effort of imagination to 'schematize' the Idea of Reason. However, it is a strange case of a failed schematism, of a scheme that succeeds through its very failure. Because of this success-in-failure, the Sublime involves a strange mixture of pleasure and pain: it is a pleasure provided by the very experience of pain, of the painful failure of imagination, of the painful gap between apprehension and comprehension. Do we not encounter here again the Freudian/Lacanian paradox of *jouissance* 'beyond the pleasure principle', as pleasure-in-pain – of *das Ding* which can be experienced only in a negative way – whose contours can be discerned only negatively, as the contours of an invisible void? Similarly, is not the (moral) Law itself a sublime Thing, in so far as it also elicits the painful sentiment of humiliation, of self-debasement, mixed with a profound satisfaction that the subject has done his duty?

What we approach in the first, negative, painful time of the experience of the Sublime is what Kant refers to as the 'chaotic aggregate', as 'stepmotherly nature', nature as a cruel mother not subject to any Law. As Rogozinski has demonstrated, this notion of 'chaotic aggregate' as *das Ungeheure* (the Monstrous) plays the same role as 'diabolical Evil' in the Kantian ethics: a hypothesis necessarily evoked but then instantly revoked, 'domesticated'. This reference to the feminine is by no means accidental and neutral. As is well known, in his Analytics of the Sublime in the *Critique of Judgement* Kant evokes as the most sublime of all statements the inscription on the temple of Isis (the divine Mother Nature): 'I am all that is, that was and that will be, and no mortal will ever raise my veil.' As the temporal description clearly indicates, we are dealing here with Nature in its impossible totality, with Nature as the totality of phenomena which can never be accessible to our finite experience. A couple of years later, however, in 'Your Great Master', his polemics against those who want or pretend to reveal the secret beneath the veil, Kant gives a masculine twist to the secret behind the veil: 'The hidden Goddess in front of whom . . . we fall on our knees, is none other than the moral Law in ourselves.'[42] Here, literally, woman (the primordial Mother Nature) appears as 'one of the Names-of-the-Father'(Lacan): her true secret is the paternal moral Law. We are dealing here not with the totality of phenomena but with what is beyond phenomena, the noumenal Law. Of course, these two versions of what is behind the veil refer to the two modes of the Sublime (mathematical/dynamic), and to the two corresponding types of antinomies of reason. There are thus two conclusions to be drawn:

1. Kant himself, albeit implicitly, did already sexualize the two antinomies, in so far as he linked the totality of phenomena generating the first (mathematical) type of antinomies to the 'feminine' principle of the monstrous pure chaotic multitude, and the second (dynamic) type of antinomies to the 'masculine' principle of the moral Law.

2. The shift of pain into pleasure in the experience of the Sublime is also implicitly sexualized; it occurs when we become aware of how, beneath the horror of the chaotic aggregate of phenomena, there is the moral Law – that is, it involves the 'magic' shift from the feminine monstrosity to the masculine Law.

Again, everything hinges here on where we put the accent: is – in the idealist option – the monstrosity of the chaotic aggregate of phenomena just the extreme of our imagination, which still fails to convey the proper noumenal dimension of the moral Law? Or – the materialist option – is it the other way round, and is the moral Law itself, in its very sublime quality, 'the last veil covering the Monstrous', the (already minimally 'gentrified', domesticated) way we, finite subjects, are able to perceive (and endure) the unimaginable Thing?

The Violence of Imagination

So when Kant endeavours to move beyond the domain of imagination and to articulate suprasensible Rational Ideas as what accounts for human dignity, Heidegger interprets this move as a 'retreat' from the abyss of imagination. Heidegger is right in so far as Kant is in effect trying to ground imagination in a system of Rational Ideas whose status is noumenal. But is this the only way to break out of the closure of self-affection that constitutes synthetic imagination? What if it is the very insistence on synthetic imagination as the unsurpassable horizon of the appearance/disclosure of being which, by retaining us within the closure of temporal auto-affection, screens the abyss of the unimaginable which is *not eo ipso* the metaphysical dimension of noumena? That is to say: when Kant claims that, without the minimal synthesis of transcendental imagination, there would be no 'phenomena' in the proper sense of the term, only 'a blind play of representations, that is to say, less than a dream', does he not thereby evoke the monstrous 'chaotic aggregate', the 'not-yet-world', the pre-ontological *chora*, which forms the background of the experience of the Sublime?

The experience of the Sublime reaches the very border of this 'chaotic aggregate' of the senses in order to retreat from it into the suprasensible dimension of the noumenal Law. Is not the Monstrous which is explicitly rendered thematic in the dialectics of the Sublime in the third *Critique* thus already at work at the very heart of the transcendental aesthetics in the first *Critique*? Is not the transcendental imagination (in its synthetic function) already a defence against this chaotic aggregate? Are not the spectral appearances of partial objects mentioned by Hegel in the quoted passage about the 'night of the world' precisely such a pre-synthetic, pre-ontological 'blind play of representations', which is 'less than a dream'? The wager of the Kantian Sublime is that another synthesis, not that of the ontological synthesis accomplished by the temporal self-affection of transcendental imagination, can save us from this abyss of the failure of imagination.

The violence of imagination in the Sublime is twofold: it is the violence *of* imagination itself (our senses are stretched to their utmost and bombarded with images of extreme chaos), as well as the violence *done to* imagination by Reason (which compels our faculty of imagination to exert all its powers and then to fail miserably, since it is unable to comprehend Reason). Every imagination is already violent in itself, in the guise of the tension between apprehension [*Auffassung*] and comprehension [*Zusammenfassung*]: the second can never fully catch up with the first. Consequently, temporality itself, 'as such', involves a gap between the apprehension of the dispersed multitude and the synthetic act of the comprehension of the unity of this multitude. Our faculty of imagination fails to achieve this unity when the object is too large – that is, in the case of the 'mathematical sublime': 'there is not enough time', there are too many units for us to accomplish their synthesis. This 'not-enough-time' is not a secondary deficiency, it appertains to the very notion of time – that is, 'there is time' only in so far as 'there is not enough time', temporality *as such* is sustained by the gap between apprehension and comprehension: a being able to close this gap and fully to comprehend the apprehended multitude would be a noumenal *archetypus intellectus* no longer constrained by the limitations of temporality. This violence of the synthesis of comprehension is then followed by the violence of the synthesis of retention which endeavours to counteract ·the flow of time, to retain what runs away, to resist the temporal drainage.

Rogozinski's conclusion regarding this twofold gap and/or violence (of comprehension over apprehension, of retention over the flow of time) is that time itself and the transcendental imagination in its synthetic activity of auto-affection are not directly the same, since the second already exerts a *violence* on the pure temporal dispersal – without this violence, reality itself would not retain its minimal ontological consistency. Transcendental schematism thus designates the procedure by which, already at the level of pre-discursive, purely intuitive temporal experience, the pure pre-synthetic temporal dispersal is violently subordinated to the synthetic activity of the subject, whose definitive form is the application of the discursive categories of Understanding to intuition. Schematism forges our temporal experience into a homogeneous linear succession in which past and future are subordinated to the present (which retains the past and announces the future): what transcendental schematism prevents us from thinking is precisely the paradox of *creatio ex nihilo*.

In schematized time, nothing really *new* can emerge – everything is always-already there, and merely deploys its inherent potential.[43] The Sublime, on the contrary, marks the moment at which something emerges out of Nothing – something new that cannot be accounted for by reference to the pre-existing network of circumstances. We are dealing here with another temporality, the temporality of freedom, of a radical rupture in the chain of (natural and/or social) causality. . . . When, for example, does the experience of the Sublime occur in politics? When, 'against their better judgement', people disregard the balance sheet of profits and losses and 'risk freedom'; at that moment, something that, literally, cannot be 'accounted for' in the terms of 'circumstances' miraculously 'becomes possible'. . . .[44] The feeling of the Sublime is aroused by an Event that momentarily suspends the network of symbolic causality.

In so far as freedom is the proper name for this suspension of causality, one is able here to throw a new light on the Hegelian definition of freedom as 'conceived necessity': the consequent notion of subjective idealism compels us to invert this thesis and to conceive of *necessity as (ultimately nothing but) conceived freedom*. The central tenet of Kant's transcendental idealism is that it is the subject's 'spontaneous' (i.e. radically *free*) act of transcendental apperception that changes the confused flow of sensations into 'reality', which obeys necessary laws. This point is even clearer in moral philosophy: when Kant claims that moral Law is the *ratio cognoscendi* of our transcendental freedom, is he not literally saying that necessity is conceived freedom? That is to say: the only way for us to get to know (to conceive of) our freedom is via the fact of the unbearable pressure of the moral Law, of its *necessity*, which enjoins us to act against the compulsion of our pathological impulses. At the most general level, one should posit that 'necessity' (the symbolic necessity that regulates our lives) relies on the abyssal free act of the subject, on his contingent decision, on the *point de capiton* that magically turns confusion into a new Order. Is not this freedom, which is not yet caught in the cobweb of necessity, the abyss of the 'night of the world'?

For this reason, Fichte's radicalization of Kant is consistent, not just a subjectivist eccentricity. Fichte was the first philosopher to focus on the uncanny contingency at the very heart of subjectivity: the Fichtean subject is not the overblown Ego = Ego as the absolute Origin of all reality, but a finite subject thrown, caught, in a contingent social situation forever eluding mastery.[45] The *Anstoss*, the primordial impulse that sets in motion the gradual self-limitation and self-determination of the initially void subject, is not merely a mechanical external impulse; it also indicates another subject who, in the abyss of its freedom, functions as the challenge [*Aufforderung*] compelling me to limit/specify my freedom, that is, to accomplish the passage from abstract egotist freedom to concrete freedom within the rational ethical universe – perhaps this intersubjective *Aufforderung* is not merely the secondary specification of the *Anstoss*, but its exemplary original case.

It is important to bear in mind the two primary meanings of *Anstoss* in German: check, obstacle, hindrance, something that *resists* the boundless expansion of our striving; *and* an impetus, a stimulus, something that incites our activity. *Anstoss* is not simply the obstacle the absolute I posits to itself in order to stimulate its activity – so that, by overcoming the self-posited obstacle, it asserts its creative power, like the games the proverbial perverted ascetic saint plays with himself by inventing ever new temptations and then, in successfully resisting them, confirming his strength. If the Kantian *Ding an sich* corresponds to the Freudian–Lacanian Thing, *Anstoss* is closer to *objet petit a*, to the primordial foreign body that 'sticks

in the throat' of the subject, to the object-cause of desire that *splits it up*.
Fichte himself defines *Anstoss* as the non-assimilable foreign body that
causes the subject to divide into the empty absolute subject and the finite
determinate subject, limited by the non-I. *Anstoss* thus designates the
moment of the 'run-in', the hazardous knock, the *encounter* of the Real in
the midst of the ideality of the absolute I: there is no subject without
Anstoss, without the collision with an element of irreducible facticity and
contingency – 'the I is supposed to encounter something foreign *within
itself*. The point is thus to acknowledge 'the presence, within the I itself,
of a realm of irreducible otherness, of absolute contingency and incom-
prehensibility. . . . Ultimately, not just Angelus Silesius's rose, but every
Anstoss whatsoever *ist ohne Warum.*'[46]

In clear contrast to the Kantian noumenal *Ding* that affects our senses,
Anstoss does not come from outside, it is *stricto sensu ex-timate*: a non-
assimilable foreign body at the very core of the subject – as Fichte himself
emphasizes, the paradox of *Anstoss* lies in the fact that it is simultaneously
'purely subjective' *and* not produced by the activity of the I. If *Anstoss* were
not 'purely subjective', if it were already the non-I, part of objectivity, we
would fall back into 'dogmatism' – that is to say, *Anstoss* would effectively
amount to no more than a shadowy remainder of the Kantian *Ding an
sich*, and would thus bear witness to Fichte's inconsequentiality (the usual
criticism of Fichte); if *Anstoss* were simply subjective, it would present a
case of the subject's hollow playing with itself, and we would never reach
the level of objective reality – that is, Fichte would effectively be a solipsist
(another common criticism of his philosophy). The crucial point is that
Anstoss sets in motion the constitution of 'reality': at the beginning is the
pure I with the non-assimilable foreign body at its heart; the subject
constitutes reality by assuming a distance towards the Real of the formless
Anstoss, and conferring on it the structure of objectivity.[47]

If Kant's *Ding an sich* is not Fichte's *Anstoss*, what is the difference
between them? Or – to put it in another way – where *do* we find in Kant
something that announces Fichte's *Anstoss*? One should not confuse
Kant's *Ding an sich* with the 'transcendental object', which (contrary to
some confused and misleading formulations found in Kant himself) is not
noumenal but the 'nothingness', the void of horizon of objectivity, of
that which stands against the (finite) subject, the minimal form of
resistance which is not yet any positive determinate object that the subject
encounters in the world – Kant uses the German expression *Dawider*,
what is 'out there opposing itself to us, standing against us'. This *Dawider*
is *not* the abyss of the Thing, it does not point to the dimension of the

unimaginable; it is, on the contrary, the very horizon of openness towards objectivity within which particular objects appear to a finite subject.

The Monstrous

Fichte was a philosopher of the primacy of practical over theoretical Reason; so we are now also in a position to show how our reading of Kant affects the Kantian approach to the ethical problematic. In his *Kant and the Problem of Metaphysics*, Heidegger endeavours to think the moral Law itself – that is, the problematic of practical Reason – according to the same model of the synthesis of imagination as pure auto-affection, as the unity of activity (spontaneity) and passivity (receptivity): in his moral experience, the subject submits himself to a Law that is not external but posited by himself, so that being affected by the Call of moral Law is the ultimate form of self-affection – in it, as well as in the Law that characterizes autonomous subjectivity, autonomy and receptivity coincide. This is the origin of all the paradoxes of Heidegger's reading: Heidegger first reduces temporality and Law to pure self-affection of the subject, then rejects them for this very reason – because they remain within the constraints of subjectivity. In short, Heidegger himself generates the 'subjectivist' reading of Kant to which he then refers in rejecting him. . . .

Heidegger's devaluation of Kant's practical philosophy in his *Kant and the Problem of Metaphysics* belongs in the long line of critics, from Heinrich Heine and Feuerbach to Adorno and Horkheimer in *Dialectic of Enlightenment*, who dismiss the *Critique of Practical Reason* as Kant's betrayal of the subversive anti-metaphysical potential of his *Critique of Pure Reason*: in his ethical thought, Kant asserts freedom and moral Law as that on account of which the finite subject (man) is not constrained to phenomenal experience – that is, as a window on the purely rational noumenal domain, beyond or outside time: literally the domain of meta-physics. The price Kant pays for this is that he has to limit the scope, the grounding role, of transcendental imagination and its movement of temporalization: the experience of freedom and moral Law is *not* rooted in temporal self-affection. According to Heidegger, the ultimate cause of this 'regression' into the metaphysical opposition between temporal and eternal lies in Kant's metaphysical notion of time as the linear succession of moments under the domination of the present: so, although Kant is compelled to invoke temporal determinations in his notion of the subject *qua* moral agent (morality involves the infinite temporal progress; only a finite being dwelling in time can be affected by the Call of Duty, etc.), he is ultimately able to conceive the fact of freedom only as something pointing to a domain outside time (to noumenal eternity), not as the extasis of another, more original, non-linear mode of temporality.

Is there no actual link between Kant's ethical duty and Heidegger's Call of Conscience? Heidegger's notion of the Call of Conscience is usually criticized for its formal decisionism: this Voice is purely formal, it tells *Dasein* to make an authentic choice without providing any concrete criteria enabling the subject to identify authentic choice. (The location of this Call is ex-timate in the Lacanian sense: as Heidegger emphasizes, this Call is not pronounced/uttered by *another Dasein* or divine Agent; it comes from outside, but is simultaneously something that emerges from Nowhere, since it is the voice of the very heart of *Dasein*, reminding it of its own unique potentiality.) Heidegger links this Call of Conscience to the motif of guilt, conceived as an a priori (existential) formal feature of *Dasein* as such: it is not a concrete guilt about some determinate act or non-act but the expression of the formal act that in the case of *Dasein*, owing to its finitude and thrownness, and at the same time its anticipatory-projecting opening towards the future, potentiality always and a priori outstrips the actualization of *Dasein*'s determinate existence. The usual point here is that Heidegger 'secularizes the Protestant notion of Sin as consubstantial with human existence as such', depriving it of its positive theological foundation by redefining it in a purely formal way.

Heidegger should none the less be defended here: this criticism is no better grounded than the standard criticism that the Marxist narrative of the Communist revolution leading to the classless society is a secularized version of the religious narrative of Fall and Salvation; in both cases, the answer should be: why shouldn't we turn the criticism around and claim that the latter, allegedly 'secularized' version provides the true version of which the religious narrative is merely a mystified and naive anticipation? Furthermore, do not these Heideggerian notions of Guilt and Call of Conscience rely on the paradigmatically modern tradition that stretches from Kantian ethics to the strict Freudian notion of superego? That is to say: the first thing to note is that the formal character of the Call of Conscience and universalized Guilt are strictly identical, two sides of the same coin: it is precisely because *Dasein* never receives any positive injunction from the Call of Conscience that it can never be sure of accomplishing its proper duty – that Guilt is consubstantial with it. What we are dealing with here is a reformulation of Kant's categorical impera-tive, which is also tautologically empty: it says that the subject should do his duty without specifying what this duty is, and thus shifts the burden of determining the content of duty wholly on to the subject.

Heidegger was thus fully justified when, a couple of years later (in his 1930 course on the essence of human freedom), he indulged in a brief attempt to save Kant's *Critique of Practical Reason* by interpreting the Kantian moral imperative in the terms of *Being and Time*, as the Call of Conscience that shatters and transports us from our immersion into *das Man*, into the inauthentic ontic morality of 'this is how *it is done*, how *one does it*': Kantian practical reason provides a glimpse into the abyss of freedom beyond (or, rather, beneath) the constraints of traditional metaphysical ontology. This reference to the *Critique of Practical Reason* is founded on an accurate insight into Kant's radical ethical revolution, which breaks with the metaphysical ethics of Supreme Good – and just as Heidegger retreated from the abyss of the unimaginable Monstrosity lurking in the Kantian problematic of transcendental imagination, so he also retreated from the Monstrosity discernible in the Kantian 'ethical formalism' when, after his *Kehre*, he no longer reserved an exceptional role for Kant. From the mid-1930s onwards, it is the Event of the Truth of Being, its (dis)closure, which provides the historial/epochal law/measure of what, in our everyday experience, can count as ethical injunction. Kant is thereby reduced to a figure in the line stretching from Plato's Idea of Supreme Good (which already subordinates Being to Supreme Good) to the modern nihilistic babble about 'values'; he even lays the ground for the modern turn from the notion of Good as inherent in the order of Being itself to the subjectivist notion of 'values' that human beings impose on 'objective' reality, so that his ethical revolution provides a key link in the line from Platonism to modern nihilism towards values. Kant was the first to assert the Will as the Will to Will: in all its goals, the Will basically wills *itself*, and therein lie the roots of nihilism. The autonomy of the moral Law means that this Law is *self-posited*: when my will follows its Call, it ultimately wills *itself*.[48]

Heidegger thus denies any truly subversive potential of the Kantian ethical revolution, of his assertion of Law as barred/empty, not determined by any positive content (it is upon this feature that Lacan grounds his thesis on Kant's practical philosophy as the starting point in the lineage culminating in Freud's invention of psychoanalysis). As Rogozinski demonstrated, what is crucial here is the fate of the triad Beautiful/ Sublime/Monstrous: Heidegger ignores the Sublime – that is, he links Beauty directly to the Monstrous (most evidently in his reading of Antigone in *An Introduction to Metaphysics*[49]): Beauty is the mode of apparition of the Monstrous; it designates one of the modalities of the Truth-Event that shatters our allegiance to the everyday run of things – that is, it derails our immersion in *das Man* (the way 'it is done'). This passing over the Sublime is directly linked to the insertion of Kant in the Platonic lineage of the Supreme Good – to Heidegger's dismissal of the Kantian ethical revolution: if the Beautiful is, as Kant put it, the symbol of the *Good*, then the Sublime is precisely the failed scheme of the ethical *Law*. The stakes in Heidegger's direct linking of the Beautiful to the Monstrous are thus higher than they may seem: the disappearance of the Sublime in Heidegger's reading of Kant is the obverse of his ignorance of the Kantian motif of the *pure form* of Law; the fact that the Kantian moral Law is 'empty', a pure form, radically affects the status of the Monstrous. How?

Heidegger, of course, thematizes the Monstrous (or rather, the Uncanny, *das Unheimliche*, as he translates the 'daemonic' from *Antigone*'s first great chorus): in his detailed reading of this chorus in *An Introduction to Metaphysics*, he deploys the contours of the overpowering violence of nature, of earth, as well as the violence of man who, by dwelling in language, throws the natural course of events 'off the rails' and exploits it for his own purposes. He insists repeatedly on the 'out-of-joint' character of man: not only is his fight against/with the powers of nature 'derailing'; the very institution of *polis*, of a communal order, is characterized as an act of violent imposition, as grounded in an abyssal decision. So Heidegger is well aware that every dwelling in the familiar everyday universe is grounded in a violent/monstrous act of resolutely deciding/assuming one's fate: that since man is primordially 'out of joint', the very imposition of a 'home [*heim*]', of a communal site of dwelling, *polis*, is *unheimlich*, reposes on an excessive/violent deed. The problem is that this domain of *Unheimliches* remains for him the very domain of the disclosure of historical shape of being, of a world, grounded in impenetrable earth, in which man historically dwells, of the tension between earth (natural surroundings) and the shape of man's communal being. And, in so far as the particular shape of historical being is 'beauty', one can see the precise sense in which, for Heidegger, Beauty and the Monstrous are co-dependent.

The Kantian/Lacanian Monstrous, however, involves another dimension: a dimension not-yet-worldly, ontological, the disclosure of a historical shape of communal destiny of being, but a pre-ontological universe of the 'night of the world' in which partial objects wander in a state preceding any synthesis, like that in Hieronymus Bosch's paintings (which are strictly correlative to the emergence of modern subjectivity). Kant himself opens up the domain of this uncanny pre-ontological spectrality, of the 'undead' apparitions, with his distinction between negative and infinite judgement.[50] This domain is not the old, premodern 'underground' as the dark, lower strata of the global cosmic order in which monstrous entities dwell, but something *stricto sensu* acosmic.

In other words, what Heidegger misses is the radical anti-ontological (or, rather, anti-cosmological) thrust of Kant's philosophy: against the neo-Kantian historico-culturalist or epistemological misreading of Kant, Heidegger is justified in emphasizing how Kant's *Critique of Pure Reason* provides the foundation of a new ontology of finitude and temporality; what he misses is that the antinomies of pure reason generated by Kant's insistence on the subject's finitude undermine the very notion of cosmos as a whole of the universe, as a meaningful hermeneutic totality of surroundings, as a *life-world* in which a historical people dwells. Or – to put it in yet another way – what Heidegger misses is the suspension of the dimension of the (being-in-the-)world, psychotic self-withdrawal, as the ultimate (im)possibility, as the most radical dimension of subjectivity, as that against which the violent synthetic imposition of a (New) Order – the Event of Historical Disclosure of Being – is the defence.

And this brings us back to the problematic of the Sublime which Heidegger left out in his reading of Kant: the Kantian notion of the Sublime is strictly correlative to this failure of ontology/cosmology; it designates the inability of transcendental imagination to bring about the closure of the horizon necessary for the notion of a cosmos. The Monstrous conceptualized by Kant in its different guises (from the chaotic aggregate of stepmotherly nature to the diabolical Evil) is thus wholly incompatible with the Monstrous of which Heidegger speaks: it is almost the exact obverse of the violent imposition of a new historical shape of Being; namely, the very gesture of the suspension of the dimension of World-Disclosure. And the ethical Law is empty/sublime precisely in so far as its 'primordially repressed' content is the abyss of the 'night of the world', the Monstrous of a spontaneity not yet bound by any Law – in Freudian terms: of death drive.

Kant with David Lynch

Kant's notion of the transcendental constitution of reality thus opens up a specific 'third domain', which is neither phenomenal nor noumenal but *stricto sensu* pre-ontological. In Derridean terms, we could designate it as spectrality; in Lacanian terms, it would be too quick and inappropriate to designate it as fantasy since, for Lacan, fantasy is on the side of reality – that is, it sustains the subject's 'sense of reality': when the phantasmic frame disintegrates, the subject undergoes a 'loss of reality' and starts to perceive reality as an 'unreal' nightmarish universe with no firm ontological foundation; this nightmarish universe is not 'pure fantasy' but, on the contrary, *that which remains of reality after reality is deprived of its support in fantasy.*

So when Schumann's *Carnival* – with its 'regression' to a dreamlike universe in which intercourse between 'real people' is replaced by a kind of masked ball where one never knows what or who is hidden beneath the mask laughing crazily at us: a machine, a slimy life-substance, or (undoubtedly the most horrifying) simply the 'real' double of the mask itself – sets to music Hoffmann's *Unheimliche*, what we obtain is not the 'universe of pure fantasy' but, rather, the unique artistic rendering of the *decomposition* of the fantasy-frame. The characters musically depicted in *Carnival* are like the ghastly apparitions strolling along the main street of Oslo in Munch's famous painting, pale-faced and with a frail, but strangely intense source of light within their eyes (signalling *gaze* as object replacing the looking eye): desubjectivized living dead, frail spectres deprived of their material substance. It is against this background that one should approach the Lacanian notion of 'traversing (going through) the fantasy': 'traversing the fantasy' precisely does *not* designate what this term suggests to a common-sensical approach: 'getting rid of the fantasies, of illusionary prejudices and misperceptions, which distort our view of reality, and finally learning to accept reality the way it actually is . . .'. In 'traversing the fantasy' we do not learn to suspend our phantasmagorical productions – on the contrary, we identify with the work of our 'imagination' even more radically, in all its inconsistency – that is to say, prior to its transformation into the phantasmic frame that guarantees our access to reality.[51]

At this 'zero-level', impossible to endure, we have only the pure void of subjectivity, confronted by a multitude of spectral 'partial objects' which, precisely, are exemplifications of the Lacanian *lamella*, the undead object-libido.[52] Or – to put it in yet another way – the death drive is *not* the pre-subjective noumenal Real itself, but the impossible moment of the 'birth of subjectivity', of the negative gesture of contraction/withdrawal that replaces reality with *membra disjecta*, with a series of organs as stand-ins for the 'immortal' libido. The monstrous Real concealed by the Ideas of Reason is not the noumenal, but this primordial space of *'wild' pre-synthetic imagination*, the impossible domain of transcendental freedom/ spontaneity at its purest, prior to its subordination to any self-imposed Law, the domain glimpsed momentarily in various 'extreme' points of post-Renaissance art, from Hieronymus Bosch to the Surrealists. This domain is imaginary, but not yet the Imaginary *qua* specular identification of the subject with a fixed image, that is, prior to the imaginary identification as formative of the ego. So the great implicit achievement of Kant is the assertion not of the gap between transcendentally constituted phenomenal reality and the transcendent noumenal domain, but of the 'vanishing mediator' between the two: if one brings his line of thought to its conclusion, one has to presuppose, between direct animality and human freedom subordinated to Law, the monstrosity of a pre-synthetic imagination 'run amok', generating spectral apparitions of partial objects. It is only at this level that, in the guise of the partial libido-objects, we encounter the impossible object correlative to the pure void of the subject's absolute spontaneity: these partial objects ('here a bloody head – there another white ghastly apparition') are the impossible forms in the guise of which the subject *qua* absolute spontaneity 'encounters itself among objects'.

As for Lacan, it is often noted that his classic account of imaginary identification already presupposes the gap to be filled by it, the horrifying experience of dispersed 'organs without a body', of *le corps morcelé*, of its *membra disjecta* freely floating around – it is at *this* level that we encounter the death drive at its most radical. And, again, it is *this* dimension of pre-phantasmic and pre-synthetic imagination from which Heidegger retreated when he abandoned the idea of maintaining Kant as the central point of reference in his development of the analytic of *Dasein*. Further-more, the same movement should be repeated at the level of intersubjectivity: the Heideggerian *Mit-Sein*, the fact that *Dasein*'s being-in-the-world always-already relates to other *Daseins*, is not the primary phenomenon. Prior to it, there is a relationship to another subject who is not yet properly 'subjectivized', a partner in a discursive situation, but one who remains the 'neighbour' as the ex-timate foreign body absolutely close to us.[53] For Freud and Lacan, 'neighbour' is definitely one of the names of *das Ungeheure*, of the Monstrous: what is at stake in the process of 'Oedipalization', the establishment of the rule of the paternal Law, is precisely the process of 'gentrifying' this monstrous otherness, transforming it into a partner within the horizon of discursive communication. Today, the artist who is actually obsessed with imagination in its monstrous pre-ontological dimension is David Lynch. After the release of *Eraserhead*, his first film, a strange rumour began to circulate to account for its traumatic impact:

> At the time, it was rumored that an ultra-low frequency drone in the film's soundtrack affected the viewer's subconscious mind. People said that although inaudible, this noise caused a feeling of unease, even nausea. This was over ten years ago and the name of the film was *Eraserhead*. Looking back on it now, one could say that David Lynch's first feature length film was such an intense experience audio-visually that people needed to invent explanations ... even to the point of hearing inaudible noises.[51]

The status of this voice which no one can perceive, but which none the less dominates us and produces material effects (feelings of unease and nausea), is *real–impossible* in the Lacanian sense of the term. It is crucial to distinguish this inaudible voice from the voice that is the object of the psychotic hallucination: in psychosis (paranoia), the 'impossible' voice is not only presupposed to exist and to exert its effectiveness; the subject actually purports to hear it. Another example of the same voice is found (unexpectedly, perhaps) in hunting: as is well known, hunters use a small metallic whistle to reach their dogs; owing to its high frequency, only dogs can hear it and react to it – which, of course, gives rise to the persistent myth that we humans unknowingly also hear this whistle (beneath the threshold of conscious perception) and obey it ... a perfect example of the paranoid notion that humans can be controlled by invisible/imperceptible media.

This notion is given a direct critico-ideological twist in John Carpenter's underrated film *They Live* (1988), in which a lonely drifter arrives in Los Angeles and discovers that our consumerist society is dominated by aliens, whose human disguises and subliminal advertising messages are visible only through special glasses: when we put these glasses on, we can perceive all around us injunctions ('Buy this!', 'Turn into this store!', etc.) which we otherwise notice and obey without being aware of them. Again, the charm of this idea lies in its very naivety: as if the surplus of an ideological mechanism over its visible presence is itself materialized on another, invisible level, so that, with special glasses on, we can literally 'see ideology'....[55]

At the level of speech itself, a gap forever separates what one is tempted to call proto-speech or 'speech-in-itself' from 'speech-for-itself', explicit symbolic registration. For example, today's sex psychologists tell us that even before a couple explicitly state their intention to go to bed together, everything is already decided at the level of innuendos, body language, exchange of glances.... The trap to be avoided here is the precipitate *ontologization* of this 'speech-in-itself', as if speech in fact pre-exists itself as a kind of fully-constituted 'speech before speech' – as if this 'speech *avant la lettre*' actually exists as another, more fundamental, fully constituted language, reducing normal, 'explicit' language to its secondary surface reflex, so that things are already truly decided before they are explicitly spoken about. What one should always bear in mind against this delusion is that this other proto-speech remains virtual: it becomes actual only when its scope is sealed, posited as such, in explicit Word. The best proof of this is the fact that this proto-language is irreducibly ambiguous and undecidable: it is 'pregnant with meaning', but with a kind of unspecified free-floating meaning waiting for the actual symbolization to confer on it a definitive spin.... In a famous passage from his letter to Lady Ottoline Morrell, in which he recalls the circumstances of his declaration of love to her, Bertrand Russell refers precisely to this gap that forever separates the ambiguous domain of proto-speech from the explicit act of symbolic assumption: 'I did not know I loved you till I heard myself telling you so – for one instant I thought "Good God, what have I said?" and then I knew it was the truth.'[56] And again, it is wrong to read this passage from In-itself to For-itself as if, deep in himself, Russell 'already knew that he loved her': this effect of always-already is strictly retroactive; its temporality is that of a *futur antérieur* – that is to say, Russell was not in love with her all the time without knowing it; rather, he *will have been* in love with her.

In the history of philosophy, the first to approach this uncanny pre-ontological, not-yet-symbolized texture of relations was none other than Plato himself, who, in his late dialogue *Timaeus*, feels compelled to pre-suppose a kind of matrix-receptacle of all determinate forms governed by its own contingent rules [*chora*] – it is crucial not to identify this *chora* too hastily with the Aristotelian matter [*hyle*]. However, it was the great break through of German Idealism to outline the precise contours of this pre-ontological dimension of the spectral Real, which precedes and eludes the ontological constitution of reality (in contrast to the standard cliché according to which German Idealists pleaded the 'pan-logicist' reduction of all reality to the product of the Notion's self-mediation). Kant was the first to detect this crack in the ontological edifice of reality: if (what we experience as) 'objective reality' is not simply given 'out there', waiting to be perceived by the subject, but an artificial composite constituted through the subject's active participation – that is, through the act of transcendental synthesis – then the question crops up sooner or later: what is the status of the uncanny X that *precedes* the transcendentally constituted reality? F.W.J. Schelling gave the most detailed account of this X in his notion of the Ground of Existence – of that which 'in God Himself is not yet God': the 'divine madness', the obscure pre-ontological domain of 'drives', the pre-logical Real that forever remains the elusive Ground of Reason that can never be grasped 'as such', merely glimpsed in the very gesture of its withdrawal. . . .[57] Although this dimension may appear to be utterly foreign to Hegel's 'absolute idealism', it was nevertheless Hegel himself who provided its most poignant description in the quoted passage from the *Jenaer Realphilosophie*: is not the pre-ontological space of 'the night of the world', in which 'here shoots a bloody head – there another white ghastly apparition, suddenly here before it, and just so disappears', the most succinct description of Lynch's universe?

This pre-ontological dimension is best discerned through the crucial Hegelian gesture of transposing epistemological limitation into ontological fault. That is to say: all Hegel does is, in a way, to supplement Kant's well-known motto of the transcendental constitution of reality ('the conditions of possibility of our knowledge are at the same time the conditions of possibility of the object of our knowledge') by its negative – the limitation of our knowledge (its failure to grasp the Whole of Being, the way our knowledge gets inexorably entangled in contradictions and inconsistencies) is simultaneously the limitation of the very object of our knowledge, that is, the gaps and voids in our knowledge of reality are simultaneously the gaps and voids in the 'real' ontological edifice itself. It may seem that here Hegel is the very opposite of Kant: does he not, in clear contrast to Kant's assertion that it is impossible to conceive of the universe as a Whole, deploy the last and most ambitious global ontological edifice of the totality of Being? This impression, however, is misleading: what it fails to take note of is the way the innermost 'motor' of the dialectical process is the interplay between epistemological obstacle and ontological deadlock. In the course of a dialectical reflexive turn, the subject is compelled to assume that the insufficiency of his knowledge with regard to reality signals the more radical insufficiency of reality itself (see the standard Marxist notion of the 'critique of ideology', whose basic premiss is that the 'inadequacy' of the ideologically distorted view of social reality is not a simple epistemological mistake, but simultaneously signals the much more troubling fact that something must be terribly wrong with our social reality itself – only a society which is 'wrong' in itself generates a 'wrong' awareness of itself). Hegel's point here is very precise: not only do the inherent inconsistencies and contradictions of our knowledge not prevent it from functioning as 'true' knowledge of reality, but there is 'reality' (in the most usual sense of 'hard external reality' as opposed to 'mere notions') only in so far as the domain of the Notion is alienated from itself, split, traversed by some radical deadlock, caught in some debilitating inconsistency.

To get an approximate idea of this dialectical vortex, let us recall the classic opposition of the two mutually exclusive notions of light: light as composed of particles and light as consisting of waves – the 'solution' of quantum physics (light is both at the same time) transposes this opposition into the 'thing itself', with the necessary result that 'objective reality' itself loses its full ontological status – that it turns into something that is ontologically incomplete, composed of entities whose status is ultimately virtual. Or think of the way the universe we reconstruct in our minds while reading a novel is full of 'holes', not fully constituted: when Conan Doyle describes Sherlock Holmes's flat, it is meaningless to ask exactly how many books there were on the shelves – the writer simply did not have a precise idea of it in his mind. What, however, if – on the level of symbolic meaning, at least – the same goes for *reality itself*? Abraham Lincoln's famous 'You can fool all the people some of the time, and some of the people all the time, but you cannot fool all the people all of the time' is logically ambiguous: does it mean that there are *some* people who can *always* be fooled, or that on every occasion *someone or other* is bound to be fooled? What, however, if it is wrong to ask 'What did Lincoln really mean?' Isn't the most probable solution to this enigma that Lincoln himself was not aware of the ambiguity – he simply wanted to make a witty point, and the phrase 'imposed itself on him' because 'it sounded good'? And what if such a situation in which one and the same *signifier* (here: the same line) 'sutures' the fundamental ambiguity and inconclusiveness which persists at the level of the signified content pertains also to what we call 'reality'? What if our social reality is 'symbolically constructed' also in this radical sense, so that in order to maintain the appearance of its consistency, an empty signifier (what Lacan called the Master-Signifier) has to cover up and conceal the ontological gap?

So the gap that forever separates the domain of (symbolically mediated, i.e. ontologically constituted) *reality* from the elusive and spectral *real* that precedes it is crucial: what psychoanalysis calls 'fantasy' is the endeavour to close this gap by (mis)perceiving the pre-ontological Real as simply *another*, 'more fundamental', level of reality – fantasy projects on to the pre-ontological Real the form of constituted reality (as in the Christian notion of another, suprasensible reality). The great merit of Lynch is that he resists this properly metaphysical temptation to close the gap between these pre-ontological phenomena and the level of reality. Apart from his primary visual procedure for conveying the spectral dimension of the Real (the excessive close-up on the depicted object, which renders it unreal), one should focus on the way Lynch plays with uncanny non-localizable sounds. The nightmare sequence of *The Elephant Man*, for example, is accompanied by a strange vibrating noise that seems to transgress the border separating interior from exterior: it is as if, in this noise, the extreme *externality* of a machine coincides with the utmost *intimacy* of the bodily interior, with the rhythm of the palpitating heart. Does not this coincidence of the very core of the subject's being, of his/her life-substance, with the externality of a machine, offer a perfect illustration of the Lacanian notion of *ex-timacy*?

On the level of speech, perhaps the best illustration of this gap is the scene in Lynch's *Dune* when, in his confrontation with the Emperor, the space guild representative utters unintelligible whispers transformed into articulate speech only by passing through a microphone – in Lacanian terms, through the medium of the big Other. In *Twin Peaks* as well, the dwarf in the Red Lodge speaks an incomprehensible, distorted English, rendered intelligible only with the help of subtitles, which assume here the role of the microphone, that is, the medium of the big Other. . . . In both cases, Lynch reveals the gap that forever separates pre-ontological proto-speech, this 'murmur of the Real', from the fully constituted *logos*.

This brings us to the fundamental feature of dialectical-materialist ontology: the minimal gap, the delay, which forever separates an event 'in itself' from its symbolic inscription/registration; this gap can be discerned in its different guises from quantum physics (according to which an event 'becomes itself', is fully actualized, only through its registration in its surroundings – that is, the moment its surroundings 'take note' of it) to the procedure of 'double take' in the classic Hollywood comedies (the victim of a fraud or an accident first perceives the event or the statement which means catastrophe to him calmly, even with irony, unaware of its consequences; then, after a minimal time lapse all of a sudden he shudders or stiffens – like the father who, upon learning that his unmarried innocent daughter is pregnant, first calmly remarks 'OK, what's the big deal?', and only later, after a couple of seconds, turns pale and starts to shout . . .). What we are dealing with here is – in Hegelese – the minimal gap between In-itself and For-itself; Derrida described this gap apropos of the notion of gift: as long as a gift is not recognized, it 'is' not fully a gift; the moment it is recognized, it is no longer a pure gift, since it is already caught in the cycle of exchange. Another exemplary case would be the tension in an emerging love relationship: we all know the charm of the situation just before the magic silence is broken – the two partners are already assured of their mutual attraction, erotic tension hangs in the air, the situation itself seems to be 'pregnant' with meaning, to precipitate itself towards the Word, to wait for the Word, to be in search of the Word which will name it – yet once the Word is pronounced, it never fully fits, it necessarily brings about the effect of disappointment, the charm is lost, every birth of meaning is an abortion. . . .

This paradox points towards the key feature of dialectical materialism which is most clearly perceptible in chaos theory and quantum physics (and which, perhaps, defines what we call 'postmodernism'): a cursory approach ignorant of details reveals (or even generates) the features which remain out of reach to a detailed, exceedingly close approach. As is well known, chaos theory was born out of the imperfection of the measuring apparatus: when the same data, repetitively processed by the same computer program, led to radically different results, scientists became aware that a difference in data too small to be noted can produce a gargantuan difference in the final outcome. . . . The same paradox is operative in the very foundation of quantum physics: the distance towards the 'thing itself' (the constitutive imprecision of our measuring, that is, the barrier of 'complementarity' which prevents us from simultaneously accomplishing different measurings) is *part of the 'thing itself'*, not merely our epistemological defect: that is, in order for (what we perceive as) 'reality' to appear, some of its features *have to remain 'unspecified'*.

Is not the gap between the level of quantum potentialities and the moment of 'registration' which confers actuality on it homologous in a way to the logic of 'double take' – to the gap between the event itself (a father being informed of his daughter's pregnancy) and its symbolic registration – the moment when the process 'appears to itself', is registered? Of crucial importance here is the difference between this dialectical-materialist notion of 'symbolic registration' which, 'after the fact', confers actuality on the fact in question, and the idealist equation *esse* = *percipi*: the act of (symbolic) registration, the 'second take', always comes after a minimal delay and remains forever incomplete, cursory, a gap separating it from the In-itself of the registered process – yet precisely as such, it is part of the 'thing itself', as if the 'thing' in question can fully realize its ontological status only by means of a minimal delay with regard to itself.

The paradox thus lies in the fact that *'false' appearance is comprised within the 'thing itself'*. And, incidentally, *therein* lies the dialectical 'unity of essence and appearance' completely missed by the textbook platitudes on how 'essence must appear', and so on: the approximate 'view from afar' which ignores all the details and limits itself to the 'mere appearance', is nearer the 'essence' than a close gaze; the 'essence' of a thing thus paradoxically constitutes itself through the very removal of the 'false' appearance from the Real in its immediacy.[58] We thus have three elements, not only essence and its appearing: first, there is reality; within it, there is the 'interface'-screen of appearances; finally, on this screen, 'essence' appears. The catch is thus that appearance is literally the appearing/emerging of the essence – that is, the only place for the essence to dwell. The standard Idealist reduction of reality as such, in its entirety, to the mere appearance of some hidden Essence falls short here: within the domain of 'reality' itself, a line must be drawn which separates 'raw' reality from the screen through which the hidden Essence of reality appears, so that if we take away this medium of appearance, we lose the very 'essence' which appears in it. . . .

Kant's Acosmism

From this vantage point, one can clearly see where Kant 'recoils' from the abyss of transcendental imagination. Remember his answer to the question of what would happen to us if we were to gain access to the noumenal domain, to Things-in-themselves: no wonder this vision of a man who turns into a lifeless puppet because of his direct insight into the monstrosity of the divine Being-in-itself provokes such an unease among the commentators on Kant (usually, it is either passed over in silence or dismissed as an uncanny, out-of-place body): what Kant delivers is no less than what one is tempted to call *the Kantian fundamental fantasy*, the Other Scene of freedom, of the spontaneous free agent, the Scene in which the free agent is turned into a lifeless puppet at the mercy of a perverse God.

Its lesson, of course, is that there is no active free agent without this phantasmic support, without this Other Scene in which he is totally manipulated by the Other. In short, the Kantian prohibition of direct access to the noumenal domain should be reformulated: what should remain inaccessible to us is not the noumenal Real, but our *fundamental fantasy* itself – the moment the subject comes too close to this phantasmic core, he loses the consistency of his existence.

So, for Kant, direct access to the noumenal domain would deprive us of the very 'spontaneity' that forms the core of transcendental freedom: it would turn us into lifeless automata or, to put it in today's terms, into computers, into 'thinking machines'. But is this conclusion really unavoidable? Is the status of consciousness basically that of freedom in a system of radical determinism? Are we free only in so far as we fail to recognize the causes determining us? To save us from this predicament, we should again displace the ontological obstacle into a positive ontological condition. That is to say: the mistake of the identification of (self-)consciousness with misrecognition, with an epistemological obstacle, is that it stealthily (re)introduces the standard, premodern, 'cosmological' notion of reality as a positive order of being: in such a fully constituted positive 'chain of being' there is, of course, no place for the subject, so the dimension of subjectivity can be conceived of only as something strictly co-dependent with the epistemological misrecognition of the true positivity of being. Consequently, the only way to account effectively for the status of (self-)consciousness is to assert *the ontological incompleteness of 'reality' itself*: there is 'reality' only in so far as there is an ontological gap, a crack, at its very heart – that is, a traumatic excess, a foreign body that cannot be integrated into it. This brings us back to the notion of the 'night of the world': in this momentary suspension of the positive order of reality, we confront the ontological gap because of which 'reality' is never a complete, self-enclosed, positive order of being. It is only this experience of the psychotic withdrawal from reality, of the absolute self-contraction, which accounts for the mysterious 'fact' of transcendental freedom – for a (self-)consciousness that is actually 'spontaneous', whose spontaneity is not an effect of misrecognition of some 'objective' process.

Only at this level are we able to appreciate Hegel's breathtaking achievement: far from regressing from Kant's criticism to pre-critical metaphysics expressing the rational structure of the cosmos, Hegel fully accepts (and draws the consequences from) the result of Kantian cosmological antinomies – there *is* no 'cosmos', the very notion of cosmos as the ontologically fully constituted positive totality is inconsistent. On that account, Hegel also rejects Kant's vision of a man who, because of his direct insight into the monstrosity of the divine Being-in-itself, would turn into a lifeless puppet: such a vision is meaningless and inconsistent, since, as we have already pointed out, it secretly reintroduces the ontologically fully constituted divine totality: a world conceived *only* as Substance, *not* also as Subject. For Hegel, the fantasy of such a transformation of man into a lifeless puppet-instrument of the monstrous divine Will (or whim), horrible as it may appear, already signals the retreat from the true monstrosity, which is that of the abyss of freedom, of the 'night of the world'. What Hegel does is thus to 'traverse' this fantasy by demonstrating its function of filling in the pre-ontological abyss of freedom – that is, by reconstituting the positive Scene in which the subject is inserted into a positive noumenal order.

That is our ultimate difference from Rogozinski: in the different answer to the question 'What lies beyond the synthetic imagination? What is this ultimate abyss?'. Rogozinski is in search of a non-violent, pre-synthetic, pre-imaginative unity-in-diversity, of a 'secret connection between things', a utopian Secret Harmony beyond phenomenal causal links, a mysterious Life of the Universe as the temporal–spatial non-violent unity of pure diversity, the enigma that bothered Kant in his last years (*Opus Posthumum*). From our perspective, however, this Secret Harmony is precisely the temptation to be resisted: the problem for us is how we are to conceive of the founding gesture of subjectivity, the 'passive violence', the negative act of (not yet imagination, but) abstraction, self-withdrawal into the 'night of the world'. This 'abstraction' is the abyss concealed by the ontological synthesis: by the transcendental imagination constitutive of reality – as such, it is the point of the mysterious emergence of transcendental 'spontaneity'.

The problem with Heidegger, therefore, is that he limits the analysis of schematism to transcendental analytics (to Understanding, to the categories constitutive of reality), neglecting to consider how the problematic of schematism re-emerges in the *Critique of Judgement*, where Kant conceives of the Sublime precisely as an attempt to *schematize* the Ideas of Reason themselves: the Sublime confronts us with the failure of imagination, with that which remains forever and a priori un-imaginable – and it is here that we encounter the subject *qua* the void of negativity. In short, it is precisely because of the limitation of Heidegger's analysis of schematism to transcendental analytics that he is unable to address the excessive dimension of subjectivity, its inherent madness.

From our perspective, the problem with Heidegger is thus, in the last analysis, the following one: the Lacanian reading enables us to unearth in Cartesian subjectivity its inherent tension between the moment of excess ('diabolical Evil' in Kant, the 'night of the world' in Hegel . . .) and the subsequent attempt to gentrify-domesticate-normalize this excess. Again and again, post-Cartesian philosophers are compelled, by the inherent logic of their philosophical project, to articulate a certain excessive moment of 'madness' inherent to *cogito*, which they then immediately endeavour to 'renormalize'. And the problem with Heidegger is that his notion of modern subjectivity does not seem to account for this inherent excess. In short, this notion simply does not 'cover' that aspect of *cogito* that leads Lacan to claim that *cogito* is the subject of the unconscious.

Or – to put it in yet another way – the paradoxical achievement of Lacan, which usually passes unnoticed even among his advocates, is that, on the very behalf of psychoanalysis, he returns to the Modern Age, 'decontextualized' rationalist notion of subject. That is to say: one of the clichés of today's American appropriation of Heidegger is to emphasize how he, along with Wittgenstein, Merleau-Ponty, and others, elaborated the conceptual framework that enables us to get rid of the rationalist notion of subject as an autonomous agent who, excluded from the world, processes data provided by the senses in a computer-like way. Heidegger's notion of 'being-in-the-world' indicates our irreducible and unsurpassable 'embeddedness' in a concrete and ultimately contingent life-world: we are always-already *in* the world, engaged in an existential project against a background that eludes our grasp and forever remains the opaque horizon into which we are 'thrown' as finite beings. And it is customary to interpret the opposition between consciousness and the Unconscious along the same lines: the disembodied Ego stands for rational consciousness, whereas the 'Unconscious' is synonymous with the opaque background that we can never fully master, since we are always-already part of it, caught in it.

Lacan, however, in an unprecedented gesture, claims the exact opposite: the Freudian 'Unconscious' has nothing whatsoever to do with the structurally necessary and irreducible opaqueness of the background, of the life-context in which we, the always-already engaged agents, are embedded; the 'Unconscious' is, rather, the disembodied rational machine that follows its path irrespective of the demands of the subject's life-world; it stands for the rational subject in so far as it is originally 'out of joint', in discord with its contextualized situation: the 'Unconscious' is the crack that makes the subject's primordial stance something other than 'being-in-the-world'.

In this way, one can also provide a new, unexpected solution to the old phenomenological problem of how the subject can disengage itself from its concrete life-world and (mis)perceive itself as a disembodied rational agent: this disengagement can occur only because there is from the very outset something in the subject that resists its full inclusion into its life-world context, and this 'something', of course, is the unconscious as the psychic machine which disregards the requirements of the 'reality principle'. This shows how, in the tension between our immersion in the world as engaged agents and the momentary collapse of this immersion in anxiety, there is no place for the Unconscious. The paradox is that once we throw out the Cartesian rational subject of self-consciousness, we lose the Unconscious.

Perhaps this is also the moment of truth in Husserl's resistance against embracing *Being and Time* – in his insistence that Heidegger misses the proper transcendental stance of phenomenological *ēpohē* and ultimately again conceives *Dasein* as a worldly entity: although this reproach *stricto sensu* misses its mark, it does express the apprehension of how, in Heidegger's notion of being-in-the-world, the point of 'madness' that characterizes the Cartesian subjectivity, the self-withdrawal of the *cogito* into itself, the eclipse of the world, disappears. . . . It is well known how Heidegger turned around the famous Kantian statement that the great scandal of philosophy is that the passage from our representations of objects to objects themselves was not properly proven. For Heidegger, the true scandal is that this passage is perceived as a problem at all, since the fundamental situation of *Dasein* as being-*in*-the-world, as always-already engaged with objects, renders the very formulation of such a 'problem' meaningless. From our perspective, however, the 'passage' (i.e. the subject's entry into the world, his or her constitution as an agent engaged in reality, into which she/he is thrown) is not only a legitimate problem, but even *the* problem of psychoanalysis.[59] In short, I intend to read Freud's statement that 'the Unconscious is outside time' against the background of Heidegger's thesis on temporality as the ontological horizon of the experience of Being: precisely in so far as it is 'outside time', the status of the Unconscious (drive) is (as Lacan put it in *Seminar XI*) 'pre-ontological'. The pre-ontological is the domain of the 'night of the world' in which the void of subjectivity is confronted by the spectral proto-reality of 'partial objects', bombarded with these apparitions of *le corps morcelé*. What we encounter here is the domain of pure, radical fantasy as pre-temporal spatiality.

Husserl's distinction between *eidetic* and *phenomenologico-transcendental*

reduction is crucial here: nothing is lost in the phenomenologico-
transcendental reduction, the entire flow of phenomena is retained, it is
only the subject's existential stance towards them that changes – instead
of accepting the flow of phenomena as indicating entities (objects and
states of things) that exist 'in themselves', out there in the world, the
phenomenological reduction 'derealizes' them, accepting them as the
pure non-substantial phenomenal flow (a shift that is perhaps close to
some versions of Buddhism). This 'disconnection' from reality is lost in
Heidegger's notion of *Dasein* as 'being [thrown] in the world'. On the
other hand, although Husserl's phenomenologico-transcendental reduction may appear to be the very opposite of the Kantian transcendental
dimension (the dimension of a priori conditions of experience), there is
none the less an unexpected link with Kant. In his unpublished manuscript 'Kant's Materialism', Paul de Man focused on the Kantian problematic of the Sublime as the locus of Kant's materialism:

> Kant's looking at the world just as one sees it [*wie man ihn sieht*] is an absolute,
> radical formalism that entertains no notion of reference or semiosis . . . the
> radical formalism that animates aesthetic judgment in the dynamics of the
> sublime is what is called materialism.

To put it in Heidegger's terms, the experience of the Sublime involves
the suspension of our engagement in the world, of our dealing with
objects as 'ready-at-hand', caught in a complex network of meanings and
uses which forms the texture of our life-world. De Man's paradoxical
claim thus counters the standard thesis according to which materialism is
to be located on the level of some positive and determinate content which
fills in the empty formal frame (in materialism, content generates and
determines the form, while idealism posits a formal a priori irreducible to
the content it embraces), as well as the level of the practical engagement
with objects as opposed to their passive contemplation. One is tempted to
supplement this paradox with another: Kant's materialism is ultimately *the
materialism of imagination*, of an *Einbildungskraft* which precedes every
ontologically constituted reality.

When we talk about the world we should, of course, bear in mind that
we are dealing with two distinct notions of it: (1) the traditional metaphysical notion of the world as the totality of all entities, the ordered 'Great
Chain of Being', within which man occupies a specific place as one of the
beings; (2) the properly Heideggerian phenomenologically grounded
notion of the world as the finite horizon of the disclosure of being, of the
way entities offer themselves to a historical *Dasein* that projects its future

against the background of being thrown into a concrete situation. (So when we encounter an object from the distant historical past – say, a medieval tool – what makes it 'past' is not its age as such but the fact that it is a trace of a world (of a historical mode of the disclosure of being, of an interconnected texture of significations and social practices) that is no longer directly 'ours'.

Now when we claim that Kant, in his antinomies of pure reason, undermined the (ontological validity of the) notion of the world, is not this claim limited to the traditional metaphysical notion of the world as the totality of all entities (which is effectively beyond the horizon of possible experience)? Furthermore, does not the notion of transcendental horizon (as opposed to noumenal transcendence) already point towards the Heideggerian notion of the world as the finite historical horizon of the disclosure of being, if only we purge it of its Cartesian physicalist connotations (categories of understanding as the conceptual framework of the scientific comprehension of representations of natural, present-at-hand objects) and transpose it into the horizon of meaning of a finite engaged agent? Perhaps one should add another notion of the world to the list: the premodern 'anthropocentric', but not yet subjective view of the world as cosmos, the finite ordered 'Great Chain of Being' with Earth in the centre, the stars above, the universe whose order bears witness to a deeper meaning, and so on. Although this ordered cosmos (reasserted today in various 'holistic' approaches) also differs radically from the properly modern, infinite meaningless 'silent universe' of void and atoms, it should not be confused with the phenomenological-transcendental notion of world as a horizon of meaning determining how entities are disclosed to a finite agent.

Does all this mean, then, that the Kantian destruction of the notion of the world via antinomies of pure reason does not affect world as the finite horizon of the disclosure of entities to an engaged agent? Our wager is that it does: the dimension designated by Freud as that of the Unconscious, of the death drive, and so on, is precisely the pre-ontological dimension that introduces a gap into one's engaged immersion in the world. Of course, Heidegger's name for the way the engaged agent's immersion in his world can be shattered is 'anxiety': one of the central motifs of *Being and Time* is that any concrete world-experience is ultimately contingent and, as such, always under threat; in contrast to an animal, *Dasein* never fully fits its surroundings; its immersion in its determinate Life-World is always precarious, and can be undermined by a sudden experience of its fragility and contingency. The key question, therefore, is: how does this shattering experience of anxiety, which extraneates *Dasein* to its immersion in its contingent way of life, relate to the experience of the 'night of the world', of the point of madness, of radical contraction, of self-withdrawal, as the founding gesture of subjectivity? How does the Heideggerian being-towards-death relate to the Freudian death drive? In contrast to some attempts to identify them (found in Lacan's work of the early 1950s), one should insist on their radical incompatibility: 'death drive' designates the 'undead' *lamella*, the 'immortal' insistence of drive that precedes the ontological disclosure of Being, whose finitude confronts a human being in the experience of 'being-towards-death'.

Notes

1. See Jacques Derrida, *De l'esprit. Heidegger et la question*, Paris: Galilée 1987.

2. See Reiner Schürmann, *Heidegger on Being and Acting*, Bloomington: Indiana University Press 1987.

3. See Theodor W. Adorno, *The Jargon of Authenticity*, London: New Left Books 1973.

4. See Jean-François Lyotard, *Heidegger et 'les Juifs'*, Paris: Galilée 1988.

5. '"Eating Well", or the Calculation of the Subject: An Interview with Jacques Derrida', in *Who Comes After the Subject*, ed. Eduardo Cadava, Peter Connor and Jean-Luc Nancy, New York: Routledge 1991, p. 104.

6. When, in his *Spiegel* interview, Heidegger was asked which political system is best accommodated to modern technology, he answered: 'I am not convinced that it is democracy' (*The Heidegger Controversy: A Critical Reader*, ed. Richard Wollin, Cambridge, MA: MIT Press 1993, p. 104).

7. 'The works that are being peddled about nowadays as the philosophy of National Socialism . . . have nothing whatever to do with the inner truth and greatness of this movement (namely the encounter between global technology and modern man).' (Martin Heidegger, *An Introduction to Metaphysics*, New Haven, CT: Yale University Press 1997, p. 199.)

8. With respect to the coupling of Stalinism and Fascism, Heidegger silently grants priority to Fascism – at this point, I differ from him and follow Alain Badiou (see Alain Badiou, *L'Éthique*, Paris: Hatier 1993), who claims that despite the horrors committed on its behalf (or, rather, on behalf of the specific form of these horrors), Stalinist Communism was inherently related to a Truth-Event (of the October Revolution); while Fascism was a pseudo-event, a lie in the guise of authenticity. See Chapter 2 of Slavoj Žižek, *The Plague of Fantasies*, London: Verso 1997.

9. See Robert Pippin, Idealism as Modernism, Cambridge: Cambridge University Press 1997, pp. 395–414.

10. I draw here on a conversation with Eric Santner.

11. Martin Heidegger, *Being and Time*, Albany, NY: SUNY Press 1996, p. 437.

12. Gilles Deleuze, *Image-temps*, Paris: Éditions de Minuit 1985, p. 232. To put it in another way: choice is always a meta-choice; it involves a choice to choose or not. Prostitution, for example, is a simple exchange: a man pays a woman for having sex with her. Marriage, on the other hand, involves two levels: in traditional marriage, with man as breadwinner, he *pays* the woman *much more* (maintains her as his wife) in order *not to have to pay her* (for sex). So, in the case of marriage for money, one can say that the husband pays the wife in order that

she should sell not only her body but also her soul – that she should pretend that she is giving herself to him out of love. Yet another way to put it would be to say that one pays a prostitute to have sex with her, whereas one's wife is a prostitute whom one has to pay even more if one *doesn't* have sex with her (since in this case she is not satisfied, and one has to appease her in another way, with generous gifts).

13. Mark Poster, *The Second Media Age*, Cambridge: Polity Press 1995, p. 81.

14. See Walter Benjamin, 'Theses on the Philosophy of History', in *Illuminations*, New York: Schocken Books 1969.

15. Fredric Jameson was already bang on target with his controversial claim that Heidegger's open political engagement in 1933, far from presenting a deplorable anomaly, is his only sympathetic public gesture.

16. One should also take into account here the level of style: Heidegger I is 'technical', 'non-musical', introducing new difficult technical distinctions, coining new terms, depriving ethically connoted categories of their concrete engagement, etc.; while Heidegger II is 'musical', abandoning strict conceptual distinctions for poetic mediations, replacing long systematic development of the line of thought (simply recall the use of paragraphs in Being and Time) with short, circular poetic ruminations. One should, of course, focus attention on what is excluded in both terms of this alternative: they are both 'deadly serious', one in a compulsory technical way, piling up newly coined terms to deal with conceptual distinctions; the other in poetic surrender to the mystery of Destiny. What is missing in both cases is *joyful irony*, the very fundamental feature of Nietzsche's style. (Remember how thoroughly and obviously Heidegger misses the profound irony and ambiguity of Nietzsche's seemingly brutal rejection of Wagner – in *The Case of Wagner* – when he praises this rejection as crucial for Nietzsche's maturation as a thinker.)

17. See Martin Heidegger, *Kant and the Problem of Metaphysics*, Bloomington: University of Indiana Press 1997.

18. On a more general level, it would be interesting to elaborate the concept of unfinished philosophical projects, from the early Hegel to Michel Foucault (whose first volume of the *History of Sexuality* announces a global project fundamentally different from what was later actually published as volumes II and III); this non-accomplishment is the obverse of the procedure of those philosophers (from Fichte to Husserl) who never got further than the establishment of the founding principles of their edifice – that is, who repeatedly (re)wrote the same grounding and/or introductory text.

19. See Cornelius Castoriadis, 'The Discovery of the Imagination', *Constellations*, vol. 1, no. 2 (October 1994).

20. Ibid., pp. 185–6.

21. Ibid., p. 212.

22. Immanuel Kant, *Critique of Practical Reason*, New York: Macmillan 1956, pp. 152–3.

23. As Robert Pippin demonstrated in Chapter 1 of *Idealism as Modernism*.

24. See 'Appendix V: Davos Disputation', in Heidegger, *Kant and the Problem of Metaphysics*, pp. 193–207.

25. Immanuel Kant, *Critique of Pure Reason*, London: Everyman's Library 1988, p. 78.

26. Ibid.

27. Ibid.

28. Ibid.

29. Ibid.

30. G.W.F. Hegel, 'Jenaer Realphilosophie', in *Frühe politische Systeme*, Frankfurt: Ullstein 1974, p. 204; translation quoted, from Donald Phillip Verene, *Hegel's Recollection*, Albany, NY: SUNY Press 1985, pp. 7–8.

31. Hegel, 'Jenaer Realphilosophie', pp. 204–5.

32. G.W.F. Hegel, *Phenomenology of Spirit*, trans. A.V. Miller, Oxford: Oxford University Press 1977, pp. 18–19.

33. To which I myself have referred repeatedly in almost all my books.

34. On this crucial point, see Zdravko Kobe, *Automaton transcendentale* I, Ljubljana: Analecta 1995.

35. Here, of course, we are repeating the reversal that Hegel accomplishes apropos Kant's Thing-in-itself: this pure presupposition of our – subjective – positing/mediation, this external Thing which affects us, but that is not yet worked through by the subject's reflexive activity, actually turns out to be its exact opposite: something purely posited, the result of the utmost effort of mental abstraction, a pure Thing-of-thought [*Gedankending*]. In the same way, the pre-synthetic real presupposition of imagination is already the product of imagination at its purest.

36. Hegel, 'Jenaer Realphilosophie', p. 206; trans. quoted from Verene, p. 8.

37. See Jacques Derrida, 'Cogito and the History of Madness', in *Writing and Difference*, Chicago: University of Chicago Press 1978.

38. *Kant on Education*, London: Kegan Paul, French, Trubner & Co. 1899, pp. 3–5.

39. See G.W.F. Hegel, *Lectures on the Philosophy of World History, Introduction: Reason in History*, Cambridge: Cambridge University Press 1975, pp. 176–90.

40. See Jacob Rogozinski, *Kanten*, Paris: Éditions Kimé 1996, pp. 124–30.

41. For a more detailed account of the connection between the Kantian antinomies and Lacan's paradoxes of non-All, see Chapter 2 of Slavoj Žižek, *Tarrying With the Negative*, Durham, NC: Duke University Press 1993.

42. Quoted from Rogozinski, *Kanten*, p. 118.

43. The great achievement of Schelling's notion of Past, Present and Future as the three 'ages' of the Absolute was to break the constraints of the Kantian temporal schematism, with its predominance of the Present: what Schelling makes thematic, in the guise of the abyss of the Real, are the contours of a Past that was never present, since it is past from the very beginning of time; complementary to it is the notion of a Future that will always remain 'to come', not just a deficient mode of the Present.

44. One is tempted to establish here a connection with Badiou's notion of the Truth-Event as the unforeseen emergence of something New that cannot be accounted for in terms of the network of existing causes. (See Chapter 3 below.)

45. See Daniel Breazeadale, 'Check or Checkmate? On the Finitude of the Fichtean Self', in *The Modern Subject. Conceptions of the Self in Classical German Philosophy*, ed. Karl Ameriks and Dieter Sturma, Albany, NY: SUNY Press 1995, pp. 87–114.

46. Ibid., p. 100.

47. What imposes itself here is the parallel between the Fichtean *Anstoss* and the Freudian–Lacanian schema of the relationship between the primordial *Ich* [*Ur-Ich*] and the object, the foreign body in its midst, which disturbs its narcissistic balance, setting in motion the long process of the gradual expulsion and structuration of this inner snag, through which (what we experience as) 'external, objective reality' is constituted (see Chapter 3 of Slavoj Žižek, *Enjoy Your Symptom!*, New York: Routledge 1993).

48. Rogozinski opposes to this reading another 'subterranean' tendency in Kant himself, according to which the Kantian categorical imperative stands for a Call of Otherness that not only involves its own temporality of finitude (a temporality that breaks the constraints of the linear succession of 'nows', since it is the temporality of the Events of Freedom, of ruptures that emerge *ex nihilo*), but is also a Law no longer grounded in a Will: like the Court's enigmatic Law in Kafka's *Trial*, the moral imperative is a Law that 'wants nothing from you'. In this fundamental *indifference* towards human affairs lies the ultimate enigma of the Law.

49. See Heidegger, *An Introduction to Metaphysics*, pp. 146–65.

50. See Chapter 3 of Žižek, *Tarrying With the Negative*.

51. So one should be very careful in defending the thesis that the fact that feminine subjectivity finds it easier to break the hold of fantasy, to 'traverse' its fundamental fantasy, than masculine subjectivity means that women entertain towards the universe of symbolic semblances/fictions the attitude of cynical distance ('I know that the phallus, symbolic phallic power, is a mere semblance, and the only thing that counts is the Real of *jouissance*' –

the well-known cliché about women as subjects who can easily 'see through' the spell of symbolic fictions, ideals, values, and focus on hard facts – sex, power . . . – that really count, and are the true desublimated support of sublime semblances): such a cynical distance does *not* amount to 'traversing the fantasy', since it implicitly reduces fantasy to the veil of illusions distorting our access to reality 'as it really is'. In contrast to the conclusion that imposes itself with false evidence, one should insist that the cynical subject is the one who is *least* delivered from the hold of fantasy.

52. For this notion of *lamella*, see Jacques Lacan, *The Four Fundamental Concepts of Psycho-Analysis*, New York: Norton 1979, pp. 197–8.

53. See, again, Chapter 3 of Žižek, *Tarrying With the Negative.*

54. Yuji Konno, 'Noise Floats, Night Falls', in *David Lynch: Paintings and Drawings*, Tokyo: Tokyo Museum of Contemporary Art 1991, p. 23.

55. Of course, the question remains open to what extent this paranoid notion is quite justified in the case of subliminal advertising.

56. Quoted from R.W. Clark, *The Life of Bertrand Russell*, London: Weidenfeld & Nicolson 1975, p. 176.

57. For a detailed account, see Slavoj Žižek, *The Indivisible Remainder. An Essay on Schelling and Related Matters*, London: Verso 1996.

58. The same holds for the Kantian moral Law: if one gets too close to it, its sublime grandeur suddenly changes into the horrifying abyss of the Thing threatening to swallow the subject.

59. From this standpoint, it is crucial to reread Husserl's late manuscripts on 'passive synthesis', published after his death in *Husserliana*, as pointing towards this domain that eludes Heidegger – from which, that is, Heidegger retreated. Perhaps the later Husserl was not exclusively immersed in a philosophical project rendered obsolete by the great break-through of *Being and Time*. . . . See Edmund Husserl, *Analysen zur passiven Synthesis*, Husserliana, vol. XI, The Hague: Martinus Nijhoff 1966.

2

The Hegelian Ticklish Subject

What Is 'Negation of Negation'?

Colin Wilson's *From Atlantis to the Sphinx*,[1] one in the endless series of New Age airport pocketbook variations on the theme of 'recovering the lost wisdom of the ancient world' (the book's subtitle), opposes in its concluding chapter two types of knowledge: the 'ancient' intuitive, encompassing one, which makes us experience directly the underlying rhythm of reality ('right-brain awareness'), and the modern knowledge of self-consciousness and rational dissection of reality ('left-brain awareness'). After all his high praise for the magic powers of ancient collective consciousness, the author acknowledges that although this type of knowledge had enormous advantages, 'it was essentially *limited.* It was too pleasant, too relaxed, and its achievements tended to be communal';[2] so it was necessary for human evolution to escape from this state to the more active attitude of rational technological domination. Today, of course, we are confronted by the prospect of reuniting the two halves and 'recovering the lost wisdom', combining it with modern achievements (the usual story of how modern science itself, in its most radical achievements – quantum physics, and so on – already points towards the self-sublation of the mechanistic view in the direction of the holistic universe dominated by a hidden pattern of the 'dance of life').

Here, however, Wilson's book takes an unexpected turn: how will this synthesis occur? Wilson is intelligent enough to reject both predominant views: the directly premodern one, according to which the history of the 'rationalist West' was a mere aberration, and we should simply return to the old wisdom; and the pseudo-Hegelian notion of a 'synthesis' that would somehow maintain the balance between the two spiritual principles, enabling us to keep the best of both worlds: to regain the lost Unity while maintaining the achievements based on its loss (technical progress, individualist dynamics, etc.). Against both these versions, Wilson emphasizes that the next stage, the overcoming of the limitation of the Western rationalist/individualist stance, must somehow emerge from within this Western stance. He locates its source in the force of imagination: the Western principle of self-consciousness and individuation also brought about a breathtaking rise in our capacity of imagination, and if we develop this capacity to its utmost, it will lead to a new level of collective consciousness, of *shared* imagination. So the surprising conclusion is that the longed-for next step in human evolution, the step beyond the alienation from nature and the universe as a Whole, 'has already happened. It has been happening for the past 3500 years. Now all we have to do is recognise it' (the last sentence in the book).[3]

So what happened 3,500 years ago – that is, around 2000 BC? The decline of the Old Kingdom of Egypt, the highest achievement of ancient wisdom, and the rise of the new, violent cultures out of which modern European consciousness arose – in short, the Fall itself, the fateful forgetting of the ancient wisdom which enabled us to maintain a direct contact with the 'dance of life'. If we take these statements literally, the unavoidable conclusion is that *the moment of the Fall (the forgetting of the ancient wisdom) coincides with its exact opposite, with the longed-for next step in evolution.* Here we have the properly Hegelian matrix of development: the Fall is already *in itself* its own self-sublation; the wound is already in itself its own healing, so that the perception that we are dealing with the Fall is ultimately a misperception, an effect of our skewed perspective – all we have to do is to accomplish the move from In-itself to For-itself: to change our perspective and recognize how the longed-for reversal is already operative in what is going on.

The inner logic of the movement from one stage to another is not that from one extreme, to the opposite extreme, and then to their higher unity; the second passage is, rather, simply the radicalization of the first. The problem with the 'Western mechanistic attitude' is not that it forgot-repressed the ancient holistic Wisdom, but that *it did not break with it thoroughly enough*: it continued to perceive the new universe (of discursive stance) from the perspective of the old one, of the 'ancient wisdom'; and of course, from this perspective the new universe cannot but appear as the catastrophic world which comes about 'after the Fall'. We rise again from the Fall not by undoing its effects, but in recognizing in the Fall itself the longed-for liberation.

In *States of Injury*,[4] Wendy Brown refers to the same logic of the dialectical process when she emphasizes how the first reaction of the oppressed to their oppression is that they imagine a world simply deprived of the Other that exerts oppression on them – women imagine a world *without men*; African-Americans a world *without whites*; workers a world *without capitalists*. . . . The mistake of such an attitude is not that it is 'too radical', that it wants to annihilate the Other instead of merely changing it; but, on the contrary, that it is not radical enough: it fails to examine the way the identity of its own position (that of a worker, a woman, an African-American . . .) is 'mediated' by the Other (there is no worker without a capitalist organizing the production process, etc.), so that if one is to get rid of the oppressive Other, one has substantially to transform the content of one's own position. That is also the fatal flaw of precipitate historicization: those who want 'free sexuality delivered of the Oedipal burden of guilt and anxiety' proceed in the same way as the worker who wants to survive *as a worker* without a capitalist; they also fail to take into account the way their own position is 'mediated' by the Other. The well-known Mead–Malinowski myth of the free, non-inhibited sexuality reigning in the South Pacific provides an exemplary case of such an 'abstract negation': it merely projects into the spatio–historical Other of 'primitive societies' the fantasy of a 'free sexuality' rooted in our own historical context. In this way, it is not 'historical' enough: it remains caught in the co-ordinates of one's own historical horizon precisely in its attempt to imagine a 'radical' Otherness – in short, anti-Oedipus is the ultimate Oedipal myth. . . .

This mistake tells us a lot about the Hegelian 'negation of negation': its matrix is not that of a loss and its recuperation, but simply that of a process of passage from state A to state B: the first, immediate 'negation' of A negates the position of A *while remaining within its symbolic confines*, so it must be followed by another negation, which then negates the very symbolic space common to A and its immediate negation (the reign of a religion is first subverted in the guise of a theological heresy; capitalism is first subverted in the name of the 'reign of Labour'). Here the gap that separates the negated system's 'real' death from its 'symbolic' death is crucial: the system has to die twice. The only time Marx uses the term 'negation of negation' in *Capital*, apropos of the 'expropriation of expropriators' in socialism, he has in mind precisely such a two-stage process. The (mythical) starting point is the state in which producers own their means of production; in the first stage, the process of expropriation takes place *within the frame of the private ownership of the means of production*, which means that the expropriation of the majority amounts to the appropriation and concentration of the ownership of the means of production in a small class (of capitalists); in the second stage, these expropriators are themselves expropriated, since the very form of private ownership is abolished. . . . What is of interest here is that, in Marx's eyes, *capitalism itself, in its very notion*, is conceived as a point of passage between the two more 'stable' modes of production: capitalism lives off the incomplete realization of its own project (the same point was later made by Deleuze, who emphasized that capitalism poses a limit to the very forces of 'deterritorialization' it itself unleashes).[5]

The same matrix of the Hegelian triad also structured the experience of the dissident struggle against Party rule; in Slovenia, this struggle proceeded in three stages. The first was the stage of inherent opposition, of criticizing the regime in the name of its own values: 'What we have is not true socialism, true socialist democracy!' This criticism was 'pre-Hegelian': it did not take into account the fact that the existing regime's failure to realize its notion signalled the insufficiency of this notion itself); for this reason, the regime's answer to this criticism was, strictly speaking, correct: it was abstract; it displayed the position of the Beautiful Soul unable to perceive in the reality it criticizes the only historically possible realization of the ideals it advocates against this reality.

The moment the opposition accepted this truth, it passed to the next, second stage: to construct the space of autonomous 'civil society' conceived of as external to the sphere of political power. Now the attitude was: we do not want power, we just want the autonomous space outside the domain of political power in which we can articulate our artistic, civil rights, spiritual, and so on, interests, criticize power and reflect on its limitations, without endeavouring to supplant it. Again, of course, the regime's fundamental criticism of this attitude ('Your indifference towards power is false and hypocritical – what you are really after *is* power') was correct, and the passage to the last, third, stage was thus to summon up our courage and, instead of hypocritically asserting that our hands were clean, that we did not want power, to reverse our position and emphatically agree with power's criticism: 'Yes, we *do* want power, and why shouldn't we? Why should it be reserved for you?'

In the first two stages, we encounter the split between knowledge and truth: the position of the regime's proponents was false, yet there was some truth in their criticism, while the opposition was hypocritical (although this hypocrisy was conditioned by the constraints imposed by the regime itself, so that in the hypocrisy of its opposition the regime received the truth about the falsity of its own discourse); in the third stage, hypocrisy was finally on the side of the regime itself. That is to say: when the dissidents finally acknowledged that they were after power, the

liberal, 'civilized' Party members criticized them for a brutal lust for power
– of course, this criticism was pure hypocrisy, since it was enunciated by
those who in fact *did* (still) hold absolute power. The other key feature
was that what actually mattered in the first two stages was *the form itself*: as
for the content, the positive criticism of the existing power was irrelevant
(much of the time it was the rejection of the emerging market reforms
which then played directly into the hands of the Party hardliners) – the
whole point was its place of enunciation, the fact that criticism was
formulated *from outside*. In the next stage, that of autonomous civil society,
this outside became only 'for itself', that is, the key dimension was again
purely formal, that of limiting the power to the political domain in the
restricted sense of the term. Only in the third stage did form and content
coincide.

The logic of the passage from In-itself to For-itself is crucial here. When
a lover drops his/her partner, it is always traumatic for the abandoned
subject to learn about the third person who caused the break; is it not
even worse, however, if the partner learns that *there was nobody*, that the
partner dropped him/her for no external reason? In such situations, is
the infamous 'third person' the cause on account of which the lover
dropped his/her erstwhile partner, or did this third person merely serve
as a pretext, giving body to the discontent in the liaison which was already
there? 'In itself', the liaison was over before the lover encountered a new
partner, but this fact became 'for itself', turned into the awareness that
the liaison was over, only through encountering a new partner. So, in a
sense, the new partner is a 'negative magnitude', giving body to the
discontent in the relationship – precisely as such, however, she/he is
necessary if this discontent is to become 'for itself', if it is to actualize
itself. The passage from In-itself to For-itself thus involves the logic of
repetition: when a thing becomes 'for itself', nothing actually changes in
it; it just repeatedly asserts ('re-marks') what it already was in itself.[6]
'Negation of negation' is thus nothing but repetition at its purest: in the
first move, a certain gesture is accomplished and fails; then, in the second
move, this same gesture is simply *repeated*. Reason is nothing but the
repetition of Understanding that deprives it of the excess baggage of
suprasensible irrational Beyond, just as Christ is not opposed to Adam but
merely the second Adam.

The self-referentiality of this passage is best captured by W.C. Fields's
great one-liner which provides his own version of Hegel's dictum that the
secrets of the Egyptians were secrets also for the Egyptians themselves: *you
can deceive only a crook*; that is, your deception will succeed only if it

mobilizes and manipulates the victim's own propensity to cheat. This paradox is confirmed by every successful swindler: the way to do it properly is to depict for the prospective victim the opportunity of making a quick fortune in a semi-legal way, so that the victim, aroused by your offer of deceiving a third party, does not notice the true catch that will turn *him* into a sucker . . . or, to put it in Hegelese, your – the crook's – external reflection on the victim is already an inherent reflective determination of the victim himself. In my 'negation' – deception of the nonexistent third victim – I effectively 'negate myself', the deceiver himself is deceived (in a kind of mocking reversal of the 'redemption of the redeemer' from Wagner's *Parsifal*).

This, then, is how the Hegelian 'cunning of Reason' works: it counts on the egotistic/deceitful impetuses in its victims – that is to say, the Hegelian 'Reason in History' is like the proverbial American con-artist who swindles his victims by manipulating their own sneaky features. There definitely is a kind of poetic justice in this reversal: the subject, as it were, receives from the swindler his own message in its true/inverted form – that is, he is not the victim of the external dark machinations of the true swindler but, rather, the victim of his own crookedness. Yet another example of the same reversal is provided by the way the outright *moralization of politics* necessarily ends up in its very opposite: in the no less radical *politicization of morals*. Those who directly translate the political antagonism in which they participate into moral terms (the struggle of Good and Evil, of honesty against corruption) are sooner or later compelled to perform the political instrumentalization of the domain of morals: to subordinate their moral assessments to the actual needs of their political struggle – 'I support X because he is morally good' imperceptibly drifts into 'X must be good because I support him'. Analogously, the leftist direct politicization of sexuality ('the personal is political', that is, the notion of sexuality as the arena for the political power struggle) unavoidably changes into the sexualization of politics (the direct grounding of political oppression in the fact of sexual difference, which sooner or later ends up in some version of the New Age transformation of politics into the struggle between Feminine and Masculine Principles . . .).

The Dialectical Anamorphosis

The last two examples clearly display how Hegel's behest to conceive the Absolute 'not only as Substance, but also as Subject' denotes the exact opposite of what it seems to mean (the absolute Subject's 'swallowing' – integrating – the entire substantial content through its activity of mediation): does not Hegel's *Phenomenology of Spirit* tell us again and again the same story of the repeated failure of the subject's endeavour to realize his project in social Substance, to impose his vision on the social universe – the story of how the 'big Other', the social substance, again and again thwarts his project and turns it upside-down? Lacan can thus be at least partially excused for his slip in confounding two separate 'figures of consciousness' from *Phenomenology* (the 'Law of the Heart' and the 'Beautiful Soul'); what they share is the same matrix which, perhaps even more than the 'Unhappy Consciousness', condenses the basic operation of *Phenomenology*: in both cases, the subject endeavours to assert his particular righteous attitude, but the actual social perception of his attitude is the exact opposite of his self-perception – for the social Substance, the subject's righteousness equals crime.

An obvious counter-argument imposes itself here: in the course of the phenomenological process, we are still dealing with a subject who is caught in his narcissistic limited frame, and therefore has to pay the price for it by his ultimate demise; the actual universal subject emerges only at the end of the process, and is no longer opposed to substance but truly encompasses it. . . . The properly Hegelian answer to this criticism is that *there simply is no such 'absolute subject'*, since the Hegelian subject is *nothing but* the very movement of unilateral self-deception, of the *hubris* of positing oneself in one's exclusive particularity, which necessarily turns against itself and ends in self-negation. 'Substance as Subject' means precisely that this movement of self-deception, by means of which a particular aspect posits itself as the universal principle, is not external to Substance but constitutive of it.

For this reason, the Hegelian 'negation of negation' is not the magic return to identity which follows the painful experience of splitting and alienation, but the very revenge of the decentred Other against the subject's presumption: the first negation consists in the subject's move against the social Substance (in his 'criminal' act which disturbs the substantial balance), and the subsequent 'negation of negation' is nothing but the *revenge of the Substance* (for instance, in psychoanalysis, 'negation' is the subject's repression into the unconscious of some substantial content of his being, while the 'negation of negation' is the return of the repressed). To refer again to the well-worn example of the Beautiful Soul: 'negation' is the Beautiful Soul's critical attitude towards its social surroundings, and the 'negation of negation' is the insight into how the Beautiful Soul itself depends on – and thus fully participates in – the wicked universe it purports to reject. 'Negation of negation' presupposes no magic reversal; it simply signals the unavoidable displacement or thwartedness of the subject's teleological activity. For that reason, insistence on the way in which negation of negation can also fail, on how the splitting can also not be followed by the 'return to Self', therefore misses the mark: negation of negation *is* the very logical matrix of the necessary failure of the subject's project – that is to say, a negation without its self-relating negation would be precisely the *successful* realization of the subject's teleological activity.

This crucial aspect could also be clarified via reference to one of the most important aspects of David Lynch's revolution in cinema: in contrast to the entire history of cinema, in which one dominant subjective perspective organizes the narrative space (in *film noir*, for example, the perspective of the hero himself, whose voice-over comments on the action), Lynch endeavours to present multiple points of view. In *Dune*, he applies a procedure (unfairly dismissed by many critics as a recourse to a non-filmic naivety bordering on the ridiculous) of using a *multiple* voice-over commentary on the action which, in addition, does not speak from an imagined future place (the hero remembering past events in a flashback), but is contemporaneous with the event on which it comments, expressing the subject's doubts, anxieties, and so on. The hero's voice-over does not encompass the depicted situation, but is itself embedded in it, is a part of it, expresses the subject's engagement in it.

No wonder, then, that this procedure strikes today's spectator as ridiculous – it is uncannily close to another staple Hollywood gesture: when a person on screen hears or sees something which takes him aback (as stupid, unbelievable, etc.), his gaze usually stiffens, he inclines his head slightly and looks directly into the camera, accompanying it with 'What?' or some similar remark – if the scene occurs in a television series, this gesture is as a rule accompanied by canned laughter, as was regularly the case in *I Love Lucy*. This idiotic gesture signals the reflexive moment of registration: the actors' direct immersion in their narrative reality is momentarily perturbed; the actor, as it were, extracts himself from the narrative context and assumes the position of an observer of his own predicament. . . . In both cases, in *Dune* and in *I Love Lucy*, this apparently innocent procedure threatens the very foundation of the standard onto-logical edifice; it inscribes a subjective point of view into the very heart of 'objective reality'. In other words, it undermines the opposition between naive objectivism and transcendental subjectivism: we have neither the 'objective reality' that is given in advance, with a multitude of subjective perspectives providing distorted views of it, nor its transcendental counter-point, the unified Subject who encompasses and constitutes the whole of reality; what we have is the paradox of multiple subjects who are *included* in reality, embedded in it, and whose perspectives on reality are none the less constitutive of it. What Lynch is striving to illustrate is the ambiguous and uncanny status of subjective illusion which, precisely as an illusion (a distorted view of reality), constitutes reality: if we subtract from reality the illusory perspective on it, we lose reality itself.

On a philosophical level, this delicate distinction allows us to grasp Hegel's break with Kantian idealism. Hegel, of course, learned the lesson of Kant's transcendental idealism (there is no reality prior to a subject's 'positing' activity); however, he refused to elevate the subject into a neutral-universal agent who directly constitutes reality. To put it in Kantian terms: while he admitted that there is no reality without the subject, Hegel insisted that *subjectivity is inherently 'pathological'* (biased, limited to a distorting, unbalanced perspective on the Whole). Hegel's achievement was thus *to combine*, in an unprecedented way, *the ontologically constitutive character of the subject's activity with the subject's irreducible pathological bias*: when these two features are thought together, conceived as co-dependent, we obtain the notion of a *pathological bias constitutive of 'reality' itself*.

The Lacanian name for this pathological bias constitutive of reality is, of course, *anamorphosis*. What does anamorphosis actually amount to, say, in Holbein's *Ambassadors*? A part of the perceived scene is distorted in such a way that it acquires its proper contours only from the specific viewpoint from which the remaining reality is blurred: when we clearly perceive the stain as a skull, and thus reach the point of 'the Spirit is a bone', the rest of reality is no longer discernible. We thus become aware that reality already involves our gaze, that this gaze is *included* in the scene we are observing, that this scene already 'regards us' in the precise sense in which, in Kafka's *The Trial*, the door of the Law is there only for the 'man from the country'. One can again discern the tiny, imperceptible, but none the less crucial gap that forever separates Lacan from the standard Idealist notion of 'subjective constitution' (according to which reality *as such*, the whole of it, is 'anamorphotic' in the general sense of *esse = percipi*, of 'being there' only for the subject's gaze): Lacan's notion of the blind spot in reality *introduces anamorphic distortion into reality itself.* The fact that reality is there for the subject only *must be inscribed in reality itself in the guise of an anamorphic stain* – this stain stands for the gaze of the Other, for the gaze *qua* object. In other words, the anamorphic stain corrects the standard 'subjective idealism' by rendering the gap between the eye and the gaze: the perceiving subject is always-already gazed at from a point that eludes his eyes.

3, 4, 5

The Hegelian notion of 'Substance as Subject' is as a rule identified with the triadic form of the dialectical process: 'the Substance is Subject' means that it is a self-developing entity, externalizing itself, positing its Otherness, and then reuniting itself with it. . . . In contrast to this commonplace, one could assert that the actual dimension of subjectivity is discernible precisely in the deadlocks of triplicity, in those places where Hegel oscillates and proposes a form of quadruplicity, even of quintuplicity. How pertinent, then, is the form of triad, that is, the infamous tripartite 'rhythm' of the Hegelian process? Although they may appear purely formal in the worst sense of the term, these considerations immediately confront us with the innermost tension and instability of the Hegelian system as the system of *subjectivity*.

Let us take as the starting point the well-known passage from the concluding 'methodological' remarks of his greater *Logic*, in which Hegel himself speaks of triplicity *or* quadruplicity: the middle moment of a process, between the starting immediacy and the concluding mediated immediacy – that is to say, the moment of *negation* – can be counted twice, as immediate negation and/or as self-relating negation, so that the entire process consists of three or four moments. In his philosophy of nature, Hegel seems to give a positive ontological grounding to this formal alternative when he asserts that the basic form of the spirit is triplicity and that of nature is quadruplicity: since nature is the kingdom of externality, each of the logical moments has to acquire separated positive existence in it. (In so far as, in Hegel's standard male-dominated perspective, man and woman are related as culture and nature, one is even tempted to claim that Hegel's allocation of quadruplicity to nature points towards the traditional opposition of 3 and 4 as the 'masculine' and 'feminine' numbers in oriental thought.[7])

There is, however, another, much more substantial and pertinent exemplification of the logic of quadruplicity. The Idea, the kingdom of Logic, of pure conceptual determinations, of 'God prior to the act of Creation', can be negated in two ways: in the guise of Nature as well as in the guise of the finite Spirit. Nature is the immediate negation of the Idea; it stands for the Idea in its indifferent spatial externality. Quite distinct from it is the finite Spirit, active subjectivity, which asserts its infinite right and opposes itself to the Universal, disturbing its organic balance, subordinating the interest of the Whole to its egotism; this negation is self-related, it is 'Evil', the moment of Fall (in contrast to Nature's innocence). The paradox of this second negation is that it is more radical, the moment of infinite pain, self-alienation; but, for that very reason, closer to Reconciliation: since, in the case of the finite Self, the Fall from Totality is self-related, posited as such, it is also present as the longing for reunification with the lost Totality. . . . Vittorio Hösle's idea is that the moment of Reconciliation which should then follow that of the finite spirit is none other than the 'objective' Spirit, in which the two divided moments, nature and finite spirit, are reconciled: the totality of intersubjective *Sittlichkeit* as man's 'second nature'.[8] The entire system could thus be composed of four moments: the logical Idea, its immediate externalization in Nature, its abstract 'return to itself' in the finite subject opposed to Nature, and the fourth moment, ethical Substance, 'second nature', as the reconciliation between Nature and finite Spirit. According to Hösle, Hegel's insistence on Triad against quadruplicity hinges on his failure properly to grasp the logic of intersubjectivity as opposed to the monadic Subject and its dialectical movement towards the Object.

These problems overdetermine Hegel's oscillation between different overall structures of his Logic, as well as between different correlations between Logic itself and the *Realphilosophie*. In his Logic, the triadic articulation of Being–Essence–Notion overlaps strangely with the dyadic split into 'objective logic' (Being and Essence) and the 'subjective logic' of the Notion – in clear contrast to the overall articulation of the dialectical process in which subjectivity comes second and stands for the moment of split, negativity, loss. For Hösle, who is quite justified in emphasizing how games with 'alternative histories', with possible different versions of Hegel's system, are deeply productive, the symptomatic weak point, the point of failure that betrays the problematic nature of 'subjective logic' as the concluding moment of the entire Logic, is the passage from its first part to 'objectivity', which throws us back to structures which properly belong to the domain of Essence (causal mechanisms), to the philosophy of Nature (chemism, organism) or to the philosophy of finite spirit (external teleology). Hegel *has to* accomplish this gesture of 'externalizing' the subjective logic proper into objectivity, so that he can then propose as the third moment the absolute Idea, the synthesis of subjective logic with objectivity.

It would thus have been much more consistent to posit 'subjective logic' (notion–judgement–syllogism) as the *second* part of an overall triadic structure, and to add to 'subjective logic' proper (the first part of the logic of Notion) a third logic, a synthesis of 'objective' logic (which describes the categorial structure of pre-subjective reality from Being through Essence, concluding in the notion of Actuality, of Substance as *causa sui* and its passage into subject) and of 'subjective' logic (which describes the categorial structure of the finite subject's reasoning – it is precisely here that we find the content of traditional 'logic'). This third logic would describe the categorial structure of 'second nature', of spiritual Substance as the unity of objective and subjective moment – that is, it would define the categorial structure of *inter*subjectivity. And – one is tempted to add, in an anachronistic prolepsis – in so far as Lacan defines the symbolic order as neither objective nor subjective, but precisely as the order of intersubjectivity, is not the perfect candidate for this third logic of intersubjectivity the psychoanalytic 'logic of the signifier' that deploys the strange structure of the subject's relationship to the Other *qua* his symbolic Substance, the space in which he interacts with other subjects? Do we not already possess fragments of this logic in a multitude of domains and guises: the logical structure of atomic physics, which includes in its structure subjectivity (the position of the observer, the passage from quantum virtuality to actual existence); the 'autopoiesis' of life, which already displays an internal teleology; Lacan's notion of 'logical time'; up to Hegel's own intersubjective dialectic of Crime (against the ethical Substance) and its Pardon, the Criminal's reconciliation with the estranged Community, in which Habermas discerned the model of the intersubjective communicational process?

However, we still have to face the question of whether the social Substance is effectively the accomplished reconciliation between Nature and finite Spirit: is it not that a gap forever persists between the 'first' nature and the 'second'? Is not the 'second nature' a precarious state of balance that can be destroyed at any moment, either by an external contingency (the proverbial comet hitting the Earth) or by humanity's self-destruction through war or ecological catastrophe? Furthermore, is not the object of psychoanalysis precisely this gap between first and second nature – the insecure position of a human subject who, after losing his footing in the first nature, can never feel fully at ease in the second: what Freud called *das Unbehagen in der Kultur*, the different way the subject's passage from first to second nature can go wrong (psychosis, neurosis . . .)? There is thus a core that resists the subject's full reconciliation with his second nature: the Freudian name for this kernel is drive, the Hegelian name for it is 'abstract negativity' (or, in the more poetic terms of the young Hegel, the 'night of the world'). Is this not why Hegel insists on the necessity of war which, from time to time, must allow the subject to regain the taste for abstract negativity and shake off his full immersion in the concrete totality of the social Substance *qua* his 'second nature'?

Because of this gap, the overall structure of Logic should, rather, have been *quadruple*: 'objective logic' (describing the categorial structures of pre-subjective reality) and 'subjective logic' (describing the structure of the finite subject's reasoning, from notion to syllogism) should be followed by 'intersubjective logic', and, furthermore (since the intersubjective Substance still does not fill the gap between itself and objectivity, between first and second nature), 'absolute logic'. In Lacanian terms, intersubjective logic is the logic of the signifier dealing with the structure of *desire*, while absolute logic is the logic of the Real, the logic of *drive*. And in fact, at the conclusion of his Logic, in his search for a synthesis between the Idea of the True and the Idea of the Good, Hegel seems to describe the central paradox of drive: the solution of the tension between passivity (contemplation of the True) and activity (effort to realize the Good) is for the subject to grasp the fact that, in his ethical effort, he is not striving in vain to realize an impossible Ideal, but is realizing something that is already actual through his very repeated efforts to realize it. Is this not the paradox later defined by Lacan in his distinction between the drive's *aim* and *goal* (the drive's true aim is realized in its very repeated failure to realize its goal)?

With regard to the relationship between Logic itself and *Realphilosophie*, Hösle again points out how their parallel is never perfect and stable: in the standard form of Hegel's system (Logic–Nature–Spirit), the triad of Logic (Being–Essence–Notion) is not adequately reflected in the mere duality of *Realphilosophie* (Nature–Spirit); if, however, we transform *Realphilosophie* into the triad of Nature – finite Spirit – objective/naturalized Spirit, the overall structure of the system is no longer a triad, but becomes quadruple. So we have either the overall triad, but without the perfect parallel between Logic and *Realphilosophie*, or the perfect triadic parallel, but with the overall dyadic split between Logic and *Realphilosophie* . . .

And – I am further tempted to add – this failure of Hegel to accomplish, in an additional turn of the screw, the reconciliation of the Spirit *qua* 'return to itself' of the Idea from Nature with Nature itself, can also be discerned in his reductionist notion of sexuality. That is to say, Hegel conceives the 'culturalization' of sexuality as its simple 'sublation' into the civilized, socio-symbolic form of marriage. Hegel treats sexuality in his philosophy of nature as a mere natural foundation and presupposition of human society, in which natural copulation is 'sublated' in the spiritual link of marriage, biological procreation is 'sublated' in symbolic descendancy marked by the family Name, and so on. Although Hegel is, of course, well aware that this 'sublation' also affects and changes the form of satisfying natural needs (copulation is preceded by the process of seduction; it is usually done in the missionary position and not *a tergo*, as with animals, etc.), he leaves out of consideration the way this symbolic-cultural 'sublation' not only changes the form of satisfying natural needs, but somehow affects their very substance: in a sexual obsession like courtly love, the ultimate aim, satisfaction itself, is disconnected from its natural ground; it changes into a lethal passion that persists beyond the natural cycle of need and its satisfaction.

The point is not only that humans have sex in a more cultivated way (or, of course, in an incomparably more cruel way) than animals, but that they are able to elevate sexuality into an absolute Aim to which they subordinate their entire life – Hegal seems to ignore this change of the biological need to copulate into sexual drive as a properly 'metaphysical passion'. Let us take Tristan and Isolde: where, in Hegel's system, is the place for this deadly passion, for this will to drown oneself in the night of *jouissance*, to leave behind the daily universe of symbolic obligations – for this unconditional drive which is neither Culture nor Nature? Although this passion strives to suspend the domain of Culture (of symbolic obligations, etc.), it clearly has nothing to do with a return to instinctual Nature – rather, it involves the most radical perversion of the natural instinct, so that, paradoxically, it is the very recourse to the order of Culture that enables us to escape the deadly vortex of this 'unnatural' passion, and to regain the pacifying natural balance of instinctual needs in their symbolized form.[9] To put it in yet another way: what Hegel leaves out of consideration is the fact that 'there is no sexual relationship': culture not only confers a cultivated form on sexuality, but thoroughly derails it, so that the only way for a human being to be able to 'do it', to enjoy it, is to rely on some 'perverse' idiosyncratic phantasmic scenario – the ultimate human perversion is that *so-called 'natural' instinctual sexual satisfaction needs a cultural prosthesis, some kind of symbolic crutch, in order to remain operative.* It is only at this level, in the 'perverse' culturalization of the sexual impetus itself, that we obtain the actual 'reconciliation' of Nature and Culture.[10]

Along these lines, one can also account for the 'secret' of the actual bipartite structure of Hegel's *Phenomenology*: the logical counterpart to the two parts into which the development of *Phenomenology* evidently falls – the 'synchronous' triad Consciousness–Selfconsciousness–Reason and the 'historical' triad Spirit–Religion–Philosophy (i.e. Absolute Knowing) – is the duality in early Hegel (up to the Jena years) of Logic *and* Metaphysics as the two parts of 'pure' philosophy, which is then followed by *Realphilosophie* (corresponding to the later philosophy of Nature and of Spirit). The distinction between Logic and Metaphysics proper fits the distinction between subjective reflexive Reason, to which only the finite reality caught in the network of relations/mediations is accessible, and the human Spirit in so far as it grasps (or, rather, directly identifies with) the Absolute itself beyond all reflexive oppositions (of subject and object, of thought and being, of reason itself and intuition . . .). This distinction, of course, remains Schellingian: Hegel 'became Hegel' when he accepted that there is no Absolute *beyond* or *above* the reflexive oppositions and contradictions of the Finite – the Absolute is *nothing but* the movement of self-sublation of these finite determinations; it is not beyond reflection, but absolute reflection itself. Once Hegel gained this insight, the distinction between Logic and Metaphysics had to collapse: Logic itself had to be identified with 'Metaphysics', with the philosophical science of the inherent categorial network that determines every conceivable form of reality.

What we have here is the paradigmatic case of dialectical 'progress': we pass from Logic (dealing with external reflexive oppositions, with reasoning as opposed to its object, Being) to Metaphysics (directly describing the structure of the Absolute) not by any kind of 'progress', of a major transmutation of Logic, but by becoming aware of how what we (mis)perceived as a mere *organon*, introductory tools, preparatory step, to our grasping the Absolute – that is, to Metaphysics proper – *already describes* the structure of the Absolute. In other words, we fail to grasp the Absolute *precisely in so far as we continue to presuppose that, above and beyond the domain of our finite reflected reasoning, there is an Absolute to be grasped* – we actually overcome the limitation of external reflection by simply becoming aware of how this external reflection is inherent to the Absolute itself. *This* is Hegel's fundamental criticism of Kant: not that Kant fails to overcome the external reflection of Understanding, but that he still thinks that there is some Beyond which eludes its grasp. What Kant does not see is that his *Critique of Pure Reason*, as the critical 'prolegomena' to a future metaphysics, *already is* the only possible metaphysics.

Overlapping with this distinction is the distinction between 'Logic' in the (traditional Aristotelian) sense of *organon*, providing the conceptual tools that help us to grasp the ontological structure of reality (the rules of our formation of Notions and forms of judgement and reasoning), and 'Metaphysics' (which directly describes the ontological structure): the first triad of *Phenomenology* remains at the level of 'Logic', providing the phenomenal sequence of the different modes whereby the finite, isolated subject can grasp society; while the second triad directly describes the phenomenal sequence of the actual historical shapes/figurations of the Absolute itself. (The 'logic' of the early Hegel thus loosely fits the first part of the mature Hegel's 'subjective logic', which follows the 'objective' logic deploying the ontological structure of pre-subjective reality.) In this precise sense, one can argue with justification that Hegel's *Phenomenology* is a work of passage – that its structure still betrays traces of the early Hegel, especially in its fascination with the 'mad dance' of reflexivity, of dialectic reversals, as the (still) introductory prelude to the System proper, with its satisfied speculative self-deployment. In other words, *Phenomenology* is not yet 'truly Hegelian' precisely in so far as it still conceives of its role as that of the 'introduction' to the System proper (although simultaneously as its first part – that is the source of its ultimate unresolved ambiguity).

For Hegel, Reason is not another, 'higher' capacity than that of 'abstract' Understanding; what defines Understanding is the very illusion that, beyond it, there is another domain (either the ineffable Mystical or Reason) which eludes its discursive grasp. In short, to get from Understanding to Reason, one does not have to *add* anything, but, on the contrary, to *subtract* something: what Hegel calls 'Reason' is *Understanding itself*, bereft of the illusion that there is something Beyond it. This is why, in the direct choice between Understanding and Reason, one has first to choose Understanding: not in order to play the stupid game of self-blinding (the absolute subject first has to alienate itself, to posit external reality as independent of itself, in order to supersede/sublate this alienation by way of recognizing in it its own product . . .), but for the simple reason that *there is nothing outside or beyond Understanding*. First, we choose Understanding; then, in the second move, *we choose Understanding again*, only without anything in addition to it (i.e. without the illusion that there is another, 'higher' capacity beyond or beneath it, even if this 'higher' capacity is called Reason) – and this Understanding, deprived of the illusion that there is something beyond it, is Reason.

This enables us to throw some new light on the age-old question of the relationship between Kant and Hegel. Today's Kantians' most convincing answer to Hegel's criticism of Kant (as exemplified, say, in his detailed examination of the inconsistencies and displacements discernible in the 'moral view of the world' in *Phenomenology of Spirit*) is a simple: *so what?* What Hegel criticizes as inconsistencies (the fact that Kant's moral theory posits the *necessity* of ethical activity, while simultaneously making a true ethical act *impossible to accomplish*, etc.) *is* precisely the paradox of the authentic Kantian position. . . . The Hegelian answer to this would be: true, but Kant is not able to *acknowledge*, to *state openly*, these paradoxes that provide the very core of his philosophical edifice; and, far from *adding* anything to Kant (say, the 'higher' capacity of Reason that is able to move beyond the Kantian opposites of noumenal and phenomenal, of freedom and necessity, etc.), *Hegel's critique simply openly states and assumes the paradoxes constitutive of Kant's position*. It is enough to mention the relationship between Essence and its Appearing: Kant, of course, 'implicitly' already knows that the noumenal Essence beyond phenomenal reality is not simply a transcendent In-itself, but somehow has to *appear* within this very reality (see his well-known example of enthusiasm as a *sign* of noumenal Freedom: in the enthusiasm generated by the French Revolution in enlightened observers all around Europe, noumenal Freedom *appeared* as the belief in the possibility of a historical act which, as it were, starts *ex nihilo* – which suspends the chain of causal dependencies and realizes freedom); however, this ultimate identity of the noumenal with the appearance remained 'in itself' for Kant – within his edifice, it was not possible explicitly to state that noumenal Freedom is *nothing but* a rupture within phenomenal reality, the premonition of another dimension which *appears* within phenomenal reality.[11]

The *Speculative* Identity of Substance and Subject

So, to return to Hösle's basic criticism of Hegel: Hegel misses the need for the *second* Reconciliation between Nature and Spirit (*qua* Nature returned into itself from its externality), because he fails to deploy all the consequences of the fact that the movement of *Er-Innerung* (internalization of the external, of what is merely given as necessary-contingent) is strictly correlative to the opposite movement of externalization, of renewed 'naturalization'. Hegel, who always emphasizes the aspect of *Er-Innerung*, of the Spirit's 'return to itself' from the externality of Nature, does not sufficiently take into account the opposite movement of externalization – the fact that the Spirit which 'returns to itself from Nature' is still the finite Spirit abstractly opposed to Nature, and should as such, in yet another dialectical turn of the screw, be again reconciled with Nature. ... It seems, none the less that Hösle misses here the proper Hegelian move in which 'abstract' internalization (withdrawal to the Interior of thought) is accompanied by – is another aspect of – the assertion of the meaningless externality abstractly opposed to the subject. The classical political example, of course, is that of the Roman Empire, in which the subject withdraws from the *Sittlichkeit* of the Greek *polis* into abstract inner freedom and, *for that very reason*, externality asserts its right in the guise of the state power of the Empire experienced by the subject as an external power in which he no longer recognizes his ethical substance.

The most elementary form of the Spirit's externalization, of course, is *language*: as Hegel emphasizes again and again, our inner experience can shed the traces of external senses and acquire the form of a pure thought only by again becoming externalized in a meaningless sign – we *think* only in *words*, in language. The same goes for *customs* in general: customs form the necessary background, the space of our social freedom. And the same goes for the social Substance itself, for the positive order of *Sittlichkeit*, the Lacanian 'big Other', which is precisely our 'second nature': 'objective spirit', the spirit's renewed naturalization and/or externalization.[12]

In an approach to Hegel which, with its emphasis on historical dialectic as the only aspect of Hegel worth saving, is the very opposite of Hösle's systematic reconstruction, Charles Taylor also endeavours to deploy the inner inconsistency of the Hegelian logic of externalization of the Idea. According to Taylor,[13] the Hegelian Spirit has two embodiments: it posits its presupposition, its conditions of existence, *and* it expresses itself in its bodily exterior. In the case of the Absolute Spirit, the two embodiments coincide, while in the case of man *qua* finite being, the two are forever separated – that is to say, man is always embedded in a set of conditions of existence which he cannot ever fully 'internalize', transform into an expression of his subjectivity – there is always an element of contingent externality which persists.

The first association here, of course, is Schelling: the point of Schelling's distinction between Divine Existence and its insurmountable Ground is that the gap that forever separates expression from external conditions of existence holds also for the Absolute Subject, for God

Himself – God Himself is embedded in a set of conditions which forever remain an impenetrable Other. For this reason, Schelling is the enigmatic 'vanishing mediator' between absolute Idealism and post-Hegelian historicism. This passage from Idealism to historicism is perhaps best expressed by the famous statement from the beginning of Marx's *Eighteenth Brumaire* about how men create history, but not out of nothing or in the conditions they have chosen themselves – they create history in the conditions which were found and imposed on them. Here there is a clear contrast with (a certain image of) Hegelian Idealism, in which the absolute Idea acts as the Subject that posits its entire content and thus actualizes itself only out of itself, relying on no external contingent presuppositions – that is, it is not bound by the confines of temporality–contingency–finitude. However, what comes in between absolute Idealism and post-Idealist historicism is the unique position of Schelling as the 'vanishing mediator': Schelling retains the Absolute as Subject (i.e. he speaks of God, not of man), but he none the less *applies to Him the fundamental postulate of temporality–contingency–finitude*, so that what he ultimately asserts is that God created the universe, but not out of nothing – He created it in the conditions which were found and imposed on Him (these 'conditions', of course, are the unfathomable Real of the Ground of God, that which in God Himself is not yet God).[14]

Taylor's mistake here is that he redoubles the notion of subject into human subjectivity (finite, caught in the gap between presupposition and expression) and a spectral monster called 'Absolute Subject', the Spirit [*Geist*], God – or, as Taylor calls it (in a thoroughly un-Hegelian fashion) 'cosmic spirit', whose mere 'vehicle' is the (self-)consciousness of the finite human subject. We thus finish with a split between two subjects, the infinite absolute Subject and the finite human subject, instead of the properly dialectical speculative identity between the infinite Substance and the Subject as the agent of finitude/appearance/split – 'Substance is Subject' means that the split which separates Subject from Substance, from the inaccessible In-itself beyond phenomenal reality, is inherent to the Substance itself. In other words, the key point is to read Hegel's proposition 'Substance is Subject' not as a direct assertion of identity, but as an example (perhaps *the* example) of 'infinite judgement', like 'the Spirit is a bone'. The point is not that the Substance (the ultimate foundation of all entities, the Absolute) is not a pre-subjective Ground but a Subject, an agent of self-differentiation, which posits its otherness and then reappropriates it, and so on: 'Subject' stands for the non-substantial agency of phenomenalization, appearance, 'illusion', split, finitude, Understanding, and so on, and to conceive Substance as Subject means precisely that split, phenomenalization, and so forth, are inherent to the life of the Absolute itself. There is no 'absolute Subject' – subject 'as such' is relative, caught in self-division, and it is *as such* that the Subject is inherent to the Substance.

In contrast to this *speculative* identity of Substance and Subject, the notion of their *direct* identity thus involves the redoubling of subjects, which again reduces subjectivity proper to an accident ('vehicle') of the substantial Absolute, of an Other who speaks 'through' finite human subjects. This also opens up the false, pseudo-Hegelian notion of a dialectical process in which its Subject ('cosmic spirit') posits its external-ity, alienates itself from itself, in order to regain its integrity on a higher level: the misleading presupposition at work here is that the Subject of the process is somehow given from the outset, not engendered by the very process of the Substance's splitting.

Another way to make the same point is with regard to the two different ways of reading the situation of the subject confronted with the unfath-omable excess of a Thing which eludes his reflexive symbolic grasp. The 'substantialist' way to read it is simply to claim that our (finite subject's) capacity to grasp the Object we are confronting always and a priori surpasses us: there is something in the object that forever resists being translated into our conceptual network (the point about the 'preponder-ance of the objective' made regularly by Adorno in his *Negative Dialectics*). Of what, however, does this excess consist? What if what eludes our grasp, what is 'in the object more than the object itself', are the traces of what, in past history, this 'object' (say, a historical situation the subject endeav-ours to analyse) *might have* become, but failed to do so? To grasp a historical situation 'in its becoming' (as Kierkegaard would have put it) is not to perceive it as a positive set of features ('the way things actually are'), but to discern in it the traces of failed 'emancipatory' attempts at liberation. (Here I am, of course, alluding to Walter Benjamin's notion of the revolutionary gaze which perceives the actual revolutionary act as the redemptive repetition of past failed emancipatory attempts.) In this case, however, the 'preponderance of the objective', that which eludes our grasp in the Thing, is no longer the excess of its positive content over our cognitive capacities but, on the contrary, its *lack*, that is, the traces of *failures*, the *absences* inscribed in its positive existence: to grasp the October Revolution 'in its becoming' means to discern the tremendous emancipa-tory potential that was simultaneously aroused and crushed by its historical actuality. Consequently, this excess/lack is not the part of the 'objective' that is in excess of the subject's cognitive capacities: rather it consists of the traces of the subject himself (his crushed hopes and desires) in the object, so that what is properly 'unfathomable' in the object is the objective counterpart/correlative of the innermost kernel of the subject's own desire.

The Hegelian Forced Choice

These paradoxes provide a clue to the Hegelian opposition between 'concrete' and 'abstract' universality. Hegel was the first to elaborate the properly modern notion of *individualization through secondary identification*. At the beginning, the subject is immersed in a particular life-form into which he was born (family, local community); the only way for him to tear himself away from his primordial 'organic' community, to cut his links with it and assert himself as an 'autonomous individual', is to shift his fundamental allegiance, to recognize the substance of his being in another, secondary community, which is universal and, simultaneously 'artificial'; no longer 'spontaneous' but 'mediated,' sustained by the activity of independent free subjects (nation versus local community; profession in the modern sense – job in a large anonymous company – versus the 'personalized' relationship between an apprentice and his master-artisan; the academic community of knowledge versus the traditional wisdom passed from generation to generation; etc., up to a mother who relies more on child-care manuals than on parental advice). This shift from primary to secondary identification does not involve a direct loss of primary identifications: what happens is that primary identifications undergo a kind of transubstantiation; they start to function as the form of appearance of the universal secondary identification (say, precisely by being a good member of my family, I thereby contribute to the proper functioning of my nation-state). Therein lies the Hegelian difference between 'abstract' and 'concrete' universality: the universal secondary identification remains 'abstract' in so far as it is directly opposed to the particular forms of primary identification – that is, in so far as it compels the subject to renounce his primary identifications; it becomes 'concrete' when it reintegrates primary identifications, transforming them into the modes of appearance of the secondary identification.

This tension between 'abstract' and 'concrete' universality is clearly discernible in the precarious social status of the early Christian Church:

on the one hand, there was the zealotry of the radical groups which saw no way of combining the true Christian attitude with the existing space of predominant social relations, and thus posed a serious threat to the social order; on the other hand, there were the attempts to reconcile Christianity with the existing structure of domination, so that you could participate in social life, occupy your determinate place in it (as a servant, peasant, artisan, feudal lord . . .) and remain a good Christian – accomplishing your determinate social role was not only seen as compatible with being a Christian, it was even perceived as a specific way of fulfilling the universal duty of being a Christian.

On a first approach, things thus seem clear and unambiguous: the philosopher of abstract universality is Kant (and, in Kant's steps, Fichte): in Kant's philosophy, the Universal (the moral Law) functions as the abstract *Sollen*, that which 'ought to be' and which, as such, possesses a terrorist/subversive potential – the Universal stands for an impossible/ unconditional demand, whose power of negativity is destined to under-mine any concrete totality; against this tradition of abstract/negative universality opposed to its particular content, Hegel emphasizes how true universality is actualized in the series of concrete determinations per-ceived by the abstract point of view of Understanding as the obstacle to the full realization of the Universal (say, the universal moral Duty is actualized, becomes effective, through the concrete wealth of particular human passions and strivings devalued by Kant as 'pathological' obstacles).

However, are things really so simple? In order not to misread the properly Hegelian flavour of the opposition between abstract and con-crete universality, one should 'crossbreed' it with another opposition, that between positive Universality as a mere impassive/neutral medium of the coexistence of its particular content (the 'mute universality' of a species defined by what all members of the species have in common), and Universality in its actual existence, which is *individuality*, the assertion of the subject as unique and irreducible to the particular concrete totality into which he is inserted. In Kierkegaardese, this difference is the one between the positive Being of the Universal and universality-in-becoming: the obverse of the Universal as the pacifying neutral medium/container of its particular content is the Universal as the power of negativity that undermines the fixity of every particular constellation, and this power comes into existence in the guise of the individual's absolute egotist self-contraction, his negation of all determinate content. The dimension of Universality becomes actual (or, in Hegelese, 'for itself') only by 'entering into existence' *as universal*, that is, by opposing itself to all its particular content, by entering into a 'negative relationship' with its particular content.

With regard to the opposition between abstract and concrete Universality, this means that the only way towards a truly 'concrete' universality leads through the full assertion of the radical negativity by means of which the universal negates its entire particular content: despite misleading appearances, it is the 'mute universality' of the neutral container of the particular content which is the predominant form of abstract universality. In other words, the only way for a Universality to become 'concrete' is to stop being a neutral-abstract medium of its particular content, and to *include itself among its particular subspecies*. What this means is that, paradoxically, the first step towards 'concrete universality' is the radical negation of the entire particular content: only through such a negation does the Universal gain existence, become visible 'as such'. Here let us recall Hegel's analysis of phrenology, which closes the chapter on 'Observing Reason' in his *Phenomenology*: Hegel resorts to an explicit phallic metaphor in order to explain the opposition of the two possible readings of the proposition 'the Spirit is a bone' (the vulgar-materialist 'reductionist' reading – the shape of our skull actually and directly determines the features of our mind – and the speculative reading – the spirit is strong enough to assert its identity with the most utterly inert stuff, and to 'sublate' it – that is to say, even the most utterly inert stuff cannot escape the Spirit's power of mediation). The vulgar-materialist reading is like the approach which sees in the phallus only the organ of urination, while the speculative reading is also able to discern in it the much higher function of insemination (i.e. precisely 'conception' as the biological anticipation of *concept*).

On a first approach, we are dealing here with the well-known elementary movement of *Aufhebung* ('sublation'): you must go through the lowest in order once more to reach the highest, the lost totality (you must lose the immediate reality in the self-contraction of the 'night of the world' in order to regain it as 'posited', mediated by the symbolic activity of the subject; you must renounce the immediate organic Whole and submit yourself to the mortifying activity of abstract Understanding in order to regain the lost totality at a higher, 'mediated' level, as the totality of Reason). This move thus seems to offer itself as an ideal target of the standard criticism: yes, of course Hegel recognizes the horror of the psychotic self-contraction and its 'loss of reality', yes, he acknowledges the need for abstract dismemberment, but only as a step, a detour on the triumphant path which, according to the inexorable dialectical necessity, leads us back to the reconstituted organic Whole. . . . Our contention is that such a reading *misses the point* of Hegel's argumentation:

> The *depth* which the Spirit brings forth from within – but only as far as its picture-thinking consciousness where it lets it remain – and the *ignorance* of this consciousness about what it really is saying, are the same conjunction of the high and the low which, in the living being, Nature naively expresses when it combines the organ of its highest fulfilment, the organ of generation, with the organ of urination. The infinite judgement, *qua* infinite, would be the fulfilment of life that comprehends itself; the consciousness of the infinite judgement that remains at the level of picture-thinking behaves as urination.[15]

A close reading of this passage makes it clear that Hegel's point is *not* that, in contrast to the vulgar empiricist mind which sees only urination, the proper speculative attitude has to choose insemination. The paradox is that *the direct choice of insemination is the infallible way to miss it*: it is not possible to choose the 'true meaning' directly – that is to say, one *has* to begin by making the 'wrong' choice (of urination): the true speculative meaning emerges only through repeated reading, as the after-effect (or by-product) of the first, 'wrong' reading.[16]

The same goes for social life, in which the direct choice of the 'concrete universality' of a particular ethical life-world can end only in a regression to premodern organic society which denies the infinite right of subjectivity as the fundamental feature of modernity. Since the subject-citizen of a modern state can no longer accept his immersion in some particular social role that confers on him a determinate place within the organic social Whole, the only way to the rational totality of the modern state leads through the horror of revolutionary Terror: one should ruthlessly tear up the constraints of premodern organic 'concrete universality', and fully assert the infinite right of subjectivity in its abstract negativity. In other words, the point of Hegel's deservedly famous analysis of the revolutionary Terror in his *Phenomenology* is not the rather obvious insight into how the revolutionary project involved the unilateral direct assertion of abstract Universal Reason, and was as such doomed to perish in self-destructive fury, since it was unable to organize the transposition of its revolutionary energy into a concrete stable and differentiated social order; Hegel's point, rather, is the enigma of why, despite the fact that revolutionary Terror was a historical deadlock, we have to pass through it in order to attain the modern rational state. . . . We can now see here how wrong were the late-nineteenth-century conservative British Hegelians

(Bradley and others), who interpreted the social logic of Hegel's concrete universality as demanding the identification of each individual with his/her specific post within the defined and hierarchical Whole of the global social body – this, precisely, is what the modern notion of subjectivity precludes.

In other words, 'to conceive the Absolute not only as Substance, but also as Subject' means that when we are confronted with the radical choice between the organic Whole and the 'madness' of the unilateral feature which throws the Whole out of joint and into damaging imbalance, this choice has the structure of a forced choice – that is to say, one has to choose unilateral 'madness' against the organic Whole. So when one is confronted by the choice between the premodern organic social Body and the revolutionary Terror which unleashes the destructive force of abstract negativity, *one has to choose Terror* – only in this way can one create the terrain for the new post-revolutionary reconciliation between the demands of social Order and the abstract freedom of the individual. The monstrosity of the revolutionary Terror is an absolutely indispensable 'vanishing mediator' – this outburst of radical negativity which undermined the old established order; cleared the slate, as it were, for the new rational order of the modern State.[17] The same holds for the couple *Sittlichkeit/Moralität*: for the opposition between the subject's immersion in his concrete social life-world and his abstract individualist/universal moral opposition to this concrete inherited universe; in this choice, one has to choose *Moralität*, that is, the act of the individual who, on behalf of a larger universality, undermines the determinate positive order of *mores* which defines his society (Socrates versus the concrete totality of the Greek city; Christ versus the concrete totality of Jews). Hegel is fully aware that the positive form in which this abstract universality gains actual existence is that of extreme violence: the obverse of the inner peace of Universality is the destructive fury towards all particular content, that is to say, the universality 'in becoming' is the very opposite of the peaceful neutral medium of all particular content – only in this way can universality become 'for itself'; only in this way can 'progress' take place.

One can thus precisely determine the moment when 'Hegel became Hegel': only when he renounced the aesthetic/Greek vision of the organic social totality of *Sittlichkeit* (which found its most articulate expression in the posthumously published *System der Sittlichkeit* [1802–03], a text which definitely points towards what was later developed as the 'organic' proto-Fascist corporate-organicist notion of society) – that is to say, when he became fully aware that the only path to true concrete totality is that in every direct choice between abstract negativity and a concrete Whole, the subject has to choose abstract negativity. This shift is most clearly detectable in young Hegel's oscillation in his appreciation of Christianity: Hegel 'becomes Hegel' when he fully endorses the disruptive 'abstractly negative' *skandalon* of Christ's emergence – when, that is, when he renounces the nostalgic hope of a return to a new version of Greek *mores* as a solution to the problems of modernity.

In this sense, the mature Hegelian 'reconciliation' remains utterly ambiguous: it designates the reconciliation of a split (the healing of the wound of the social body), as well as the reconciliation *with* this split as the necessary price of individual freedom. With regard to politics, one is thus tempted to turn around the standard myth of the young 'revolutionary' Hegel who, in his later years, betrayed his subversive origins and became the state philosopher praising the existing order as the embodiment of Reason, as the 'actually existing God': rather, it was the young Hegel whose 'revolutionary' project – from today's perspective, at least – announced the Fascist 'aestheticization of the political,' the establishment of a new organic Order that abolishes modern individuality; while 'Hegel became Hegel' through his insistence on the unavoidable assertion of the 'infinite right of the individual' – on how the road to 'concrete universality' leads only through the full assertion of 'abstract negativity'.

Another way to discern this passage from pre-Hegelian Hegel to 'Hegel who became Hegel' is via a small but significant change in the social structure. In *System der Sittlichkeit*, society is subdivided into three estates, each involving a specific ethical stance: the peasantry with the attitude of pre-reflexive thrust, immersion into substance; entrepreneurs, the bourgeois class, with their reflected attitude of individual competition and achievement (civil society proper, industry, exchange); the aristocracy, the universal class, which runs political life and goes to war, ready to risk their lives when necessary. Significantly, after Hegel 'became Hegel', the universal class is no longer the aristocracy (as landlords, they are included in the peasantry), but the enlightened state bureaucracy. The key point of this change is that now, not only the aristocracy but everybody, any individual from any class, can be mobilized and has to go to war: absolute negativity, the risk of death which dissolves all fixed attachments to a determinate content, is no longer the privilege of a specific class, but becomes a universal right/obligation of every citizen. Above and beyond his specific place within the social body, every citizen thus participates in abstract/absolute negativity: no individual is completely delimited by what reduces him to his particular place within the social edifice.[18]

This is why, in the passage from his Introduction to *Phenomenology* quoted at length in Chapter 1, Hegel hails *Understanding* (*not* Reason!), its infinite power to disrupt any organic link, to treat as separated what originally belongs together and has actual existence only as part of its concrete context: here 'Understanding' is another name for what we have called 'pre-synthetic imagination', for imagination's power to dissipate any organic Whole, the power that precedes the *synthesis* of imagination whose highest expression is *logos* (as Heidegger liked to point out, in old Greek, *legein* also means 'to collect, to gather'). This is why those who advocate the subject's willing submission to and acceptance of his/her proper place within the concrete totality of the substantial Order are as far from Hegel as could be: the very existence of subjectivity involves the 'false', 'abstract' choice of Evil, of Crime – that is, an excessive 'unilateral' gesture which throws the harmonious Order of the Whole out of balance: why? Because such an arbitrary choice of something trivial and insubstan-tial, such an exercise of utter caprice based on no good reason ('I want it because I want it!'), is, paradoxically, the only way for the Universal to assert itself 'for itself', against all determinate particular content.

This entry into the existence of the Universal 'as such,' in contradistinc-tion to all determinate content, this violent unilateral endorsement of some 'abstract' feature, which tears it out of its concrete life-context and thus involves the mortification of the organic Whole of Life, is the moment of the actualization of Subject against the balanced substantial Order. The fear that the Hegelian dialectical movement will generate a negativity 'too strong' to be reinserted into the circle of dialectical mediation is thus deeply misplaced: the fact that 'Substance is [also to be conceived of as] Subject' means that this explosion of the organic Unity is what *always happens* in the course of the dialectical process, and the new 'mediated' Unity which comes afterwards in no way signals a return 'at a higher level' to the lost initial Unity – in the newly reinstated 'mediated' totality, we are dealing with a *substantially different* Unity, a Unity grounded on the disruptive power of negativity, a Unity in which *this negativity itself assumes positive existence.*

Perhaps this is the source of the unresolved tension that ends Hegel's *Logic*, the tension between Life and Knowledge as the two paradigms of the absolute Idea: in Life, the Particular is still submerged in the Universal – that is to say, Life is a dynamic system in which the Universal reproduces itself through the incessant process of the emerging and passing off of its particular moments, a system kept alive by the very perpetual dynamics of the self-movement of its constituents; however, such a system, in which the Universal is the Power that expresses itself in the incessant production of the wealth of its particular moments, remains a 'dynamized substance', it does not yet involve subjectivity proper. In Taylor's terms (not quite adequate), we are dealing here with the opposition between the 'expressivist'/productive aspect of the Absolute (Life as a *causa sui* that reproduces and 'expresses' itself through the infinite process of the generation and corruption of its moments) and its 'cognitive' aspect (the Absolute that actualizes itself only through its full self-knowledge) – how are we to reconcile the two?

The first paradox is that activity is on the side of Substance (the 'expressivist' generative Power) and passivity on the side of Subject (the subject *qua* consciousness 'passively' takes into account what takes place): Substance is *praxis*, active intervention; while Subject is *theoria*, passive intuition. What we have here is the opposition of *Sein* and *Sollen*, of the True and the Good; however, contrary to the standard way of conceptualizing this opposition (the Spinozan passive intuition of Substance versus the Fichtean active Subject who spontaneously and autonomously posits the entire objective content), Hegel connects the four terms in a crisscross way: expressive productivity is on the side of the Spinozan Substance which permanently realizes the Good by actively shaping reality; while the Subject's fundamental attitude is that of Knowing – the Subject endeavours to establish what is True, to discern the contours of objectivity.

Hegel's solution as a German Idealist, of course, is a knowledge which is 'spontaneous,' – that is, in itself a *praxis* generative of its object, but *not* in the (Fichtean) sense of 'intellectual intuition', of a knowledge directly productive of its objects, and not even in the somewhat weaker Kantian sense of knowledge as transcendentally constitutive of its objects. One is even tempted to say that Hegel opts for precisely the opposite solution: at the level of substantial content, 'everything has already taken place', so that knowledge merely takes it into account – that is to say, it is a purely formal act which registers the state of things; precisely as such, however – as the purely formal gesture of 'taking into account' what 'in itself' is already there – knowledge is 'performative', and brings about the actualization of the Absolute. So we are *not* dealing with a new version of the mystical Union in which the subject's activity overlaps with the activity of the Absolute–God itself – in which the subject experiences himself as the 'vehicle of the Absolute' (in his greatest activity he is passive, since it is the Absolute who is effectively active through him); such a mystical Union remains the summit of Schelling's 'dynamized Spinozism'. Hegel's point is, rather, the opposite one: *in my greatest passivity, I am already active* – that is to say, the very passive 'withdrawal' by means of which the thought 'secedes', 'splits off' from its object, acquires a distance, violently tears itself off 'the flow of things', assuming the stance of an 'external observer'; this non-act is *its highest act*, the infinite Power which introduces a gap into the self-enclosed Whole of Substance.

The same problem confronts us in the guise of the opposition between 'positing' and 'external' reflection from the beginning of Book II of Hegel's *Logic*. Positing reflection is 'ontological', it conceptualizes the Essence as the productive/generative power that 'posits' the wealth of appearances; external reflection, in contrast, is 'epistemological', it stands for the subject's reflexive penetration of the object of knowledge – for his effort to discern, behind the veil of phenomena, the contours of their underlying rational structure (their Essence).[19] The fundamental deadlock of the entire 'logic of Essence' is that these two aspects, the 'ontological' and the 'epistemological', can never be fully synchronized: no solution can resolve the oscillation between the two poles – either the appearance is reduced to something that is 'merely subjective' ('the Essence of things is an inaccessible In Itself, what I can contemplate is merely their illusive appearance'), or the Essence itself becomes subjectivized ('the hidden Essence is ultimately the subject's rational construct, the result of his conceptual work' – just think of contemporary subparticle physics, in which the last constituents of reality have the status of a highly abstract hypothesis – of a pure rational presupposition that we shall never encounter outside the theoretical network, in our everyday experience). Again, this tension is resolved not by the inclusion of external reflection into the overall structure of the Absolute's self-positing activity, as a mediating moment of split and externality, but by the opposite assertion of the direct 'ontological' status of the 'externality' of reflection itself – every positive and determinate ontological entity can emerge 'as such' only in so far as the Absolute is 'external to itself', in so far as a gap prevents its full ontological actualization.[20]

'Concrete Universality'

We can now see in what precise sense Hegel's logic remains 'transcendental' in the strict Kantian sense – that is, in what sense its notional network is not merely formal, but constitutive of reality itself, whose categorial structure it describes. What sets in motion the dialectical progress in Hegel's *Logic* is the inherent tension in the status of every determinate/

limited category: each concept is simultaneously *necessary* (i.e. indispensable if we are to conceive reality, its underlying ontological structure) and *impossible* (i.e. self-refuting, inconsistent: the moment we fully and consequently 'apply' it to reality, it disintegrates and/or turns into its opposite). This notional tension/'contradiction' is simultaneously the ultimate *spiritus movens* of 'reality' itself: far from signalling the failure of our thought to grasp reality, the inherent inconsistency of our notional apparatus is the ultimate proof that our thought is not merely a logical game we play, but is able to reach reality itself, expressing its inherent structuring principle.

What accounts for this paradoxical overlapping of necessity and impossibility is, of course, the notion of the self-relating Universality grounded in its constitutive exception. Why are five-cent coins larger than ten-cent coins; why this exception to the general rule according to which volume follows value? Karel van het Reve, the famous Dutch linguist, literary scientist and Popperian criticist of psychoanalysis and deconstruction, has formulated the logic of rule and its exception in the guise of what he ironically calls 'Reve's Conjecture':[21] in the domain of symbolic rules, Popper's logic of falsification has to be *inverted* – that is to say, far from falsifying the rule, the exception one has to search for *confirms* it. Besides enumerating examples from a multitude of symbolic, rule-regulated, activities (in chess, we have *rocade* as the exception, a move that violates the fundamental logic of other possible moves; in card games, there is often an exceptional lower combination that can overrule the highest one; etc.), Reve focuses on linguistics: in grammar, a particular exception is needed in order to reveal (and thus to make us sensitive to) the universal rule that we otherwise follow: 'A rule cannot exist if there is no exception against which it can distinguish itself.'[22] These exceptions are usually dismissed as so-called *deponentia*, 'irrational' irregularities due either to the influence of some neighbouring foreign language or to remainders of earlier linguistic forms. In Latin, for example, when a verb form ends in *-or*, it usually designates a passive form: *laudo* is 'I praise', *laudor* 'I am praised', and so on – however, surprisingly, *loquor* is not 'I am spoken' but 'I speak'!

In Hegelese, such exceptions are necessary if rules are to become 'for-themselves', not merely a natural 'in-itself' – that is, if they are to be 'noted', perceived 'as such'.[23] For this reason, any attempt to account for these exceptions and/or violations by invoking the influence of neighbouring tongues or past forms of the same tongue is insufficient: such causal connections are undoubtedly 'historically accurate'; in order for them to become *effective,* however, they have to fulfil some inherent need in the *present* system (as with the unfortunate 'remainders of the bourgeois past' evoked in the ex-Communist countries as an excuse for all the woes of the Socialist present; as if these 'remainders' did not play a necessary role in – and were not kept alive by – the inconsistency of that very Socialist present). Examples abound here: bourgeois utilitarian society needs an aristocracy as the exception to reveal its basic utilitarian stance, and so on; up to *erection* (of the penis), which can serve as the proof and sign of potency precisely on account of the immanent danger of failure: of the prospect that it will *not* occur.[24]

There are three main versions of the relationship between the Universal and its particular content.

1. The standard notion of neutral universality, indifferent to its particular content: the Cartesian *cogito* is the neutral thinking substance, common to all humans, indifferent to gender, and as such the philosophical foundation of the political equality of the sexes. From this perspective, the fact that, in descriptions of *cogito* in modern philosophy, one actually finds a predominance of male features is ultimately an inconsistency due to historical circumstances: with Descartes, Kant, Hegel, and others, *cogito* remained an 'unfinished project'; its consequences were not thought out to the end. (When post-Cartesians like Malebranche, for example, repeated that women cannot think clearly and are much more susceptible than men to the impressions of their senses, they were simply following the prejudices of the social reality of their times.)

2. The standard Marxist or critico-ideological 'symptomatic' reading, which not only discerns beneath the universality of *cogito* the predominance of certain male features ('*cogito* effectively stands for the white upper-class male patriarchal individual'), but, in its strongest version, even claims that *the very gesture of universalization, of obliterating particular differences – the* form *of abstract universality as such – is not gender-neutral, but inherently 'masculine',* since it defines the modern male attitude of domination and manipulation, so that sexual difference does not only stand for the difference of the two species of the human genus, but involves two different modes of the functioning of the very relationship between the Universal and the Particular.

3. There is, however, a third version, elaborated in detail by Ernesto Laclau:[25] the Universal is empty, yet precisely as such always-already filled in, that is, hegemonized by some contingent, particular content that acts

as its stand-in – in short, each Universal is the battleground on which the multitude of particular contents fight for hegemony. (If *cogito* silently privileges men as opposed to women, this is not an eternal fact inscribed in its very nature, but something that can be changed through hegemonic struggle.) The distinction between this third version and the first is that the third version allows for no content of the Universal which would be effectively neutral and, as such, common to all its species (we can never define any features which are common to all humans in absolutely the same modality): all positive content of the Universal is the contingent result of hegemonic struggle – in itself, the Universal is absolutely empty.

In accepting this third position, one should insist on the *cut* in the particular substantial content by means of which a Universal establishes itself. That is to say: the paradox of the proper Hegelian notion of the Universal is that it is not the neutral frame of the multitude of particular contents, but inherently divisive, splitting up its particular content: the Universal always asserts itself in the guise of some particular content which claims to embody it directly, excluding all other content as merely particular.

What, then, is Hegelian 'concrete universality', if it involves such a radical cut – if it is *not* the organic articulation of a Whole in which each element plays its unique, particular but irreplaceable part? Perhaps a reference to music could be of some help here; let us take the concept of a *violin concerto* – when, in what way, do we treat it as an actual 'concrete universality'? When we do not subdivide it simply into its particular forms (the Classical violin concerto, the great Romantic concertos from Mendelssohn via Tchaikovsky to Sibelius, etc.), but conceive its 'species' or 'stages' as so many attempts to grasp – to determine, to give a form to, to struggle with – the very universality of the concept. It is already deeply significant that Mozart's violin concertos are a bit of a failure (at least measured against his high standards, and compared with his piano concertos) – no wonder his most popular piece for violin and concerto is his *Sinfonia concertante*, which is a strange kind of animal (the violin is not yet allowed to assume an autonomous role against the orchestra, so we are dealing with a symphony in a 'concerting' mode, not with a violin concerto proper).

The reason for this probably lies in the fact, emphasized by Adorno, that the violin, much more than the piano, is the ultimate musical instrument and expression of subjectivity: a concerto for solo violin, with its interaction between violin and orchestra, thus provides perhaps the ultimate musical endeavour to express what German Idealism called the interaction between Subject and Substance; Mozart's failure bears witness to the fact that his universe was not yet that of radical assertion of subjectivity, which occurred only with Beethoven. With Beethoven's one violin concerto, however, things again became rather problematic: he was accused, not unfairly, of accentuating the main melodic line in the first movement in an excessively repetitive way that borders on musical *kitsch* – in short, the balance between violin and orchestra, between Subject and Substance, is already disturbed by the subjective excess. The proper counterpoint to this excess is then (again the one) violin concerto of Brahms, which was quite appropriately characterized as the 'concerto *against* the violin': it is the massive symphonic weight of the orchestra which ultimately engulfs the solo voice of the violin, fighting and squashing its expressive thrust, reducing it to one among the elements of the symphonic texture. Perhaps the last link in this development was Bartók's 'concerto for orchestra' (that is, only for orchestra, with no single instrument being allowed to stand out as the bearer of a solo voice), a true counterpoint to Schumann's 'concert without orchestra' (the most accurate formula of his slide into madness, i.e. into psychotic seclusion gradually bereft of the support in the 'big Other', the substantial symbolic order). What all these examples have in common is that each of them is not just a particular case of the universal concept of 'violin concerto', but a desperate attempt to hammer out a position with regard to the very universality of this concept: each time, this universal concept is 'disturbed' in a specific way – disavowed, turned around, thrown off by the excessive emphasis on one of its poles. In short, there never has been a violin concerto that fully 'realized its concept' (a dialogue engendering a productive tension and reconciliation between violin and orchestra, Subject and Substance): every time some invisible hindrance prevents the concept's fulfilment. (This inherent hindrance preventing the immediate actualization of the concept is another name for the Lacanian Real.) Here we have an example of Hegelian 'concrete universality': a process or a sequence of particular attempts that do not simply exemplify the neutral universal notion but struggle with it, give a specific twist to it – the Universal is thus fully engaged in the process of its particular exemplification; that is to say, these particular cases in a way, decide the fate of the universal notion itself.[26]

To those who still remember Althusser's anti-Hegelian elaboration of the notion of *overdetermination* as the key category of the Marxist dialectic, it will come as no surprise that Althusser's polemics against Hegel's notion of universality is misdirected: the feature that Althusser emphasized as the main characteristic of overdetermination (in each particular constellation, the universality in question is 'overdetermined', given a specific flavour or spin, by the unique set of concrete conditions – that is to say, in the Marxist dialectic, *the exception is the rule*; we never encounter the appropriate embodiment of universality as such) is the very fundamental feature of Hegelian concrete universality. So it is not enough to claim that concrete universality is articulated into a texture of particular constellations, of situations in which a specific content hegemonizes the universal notion; one should also bear in mind that all these particular exemplifications of the universality in question are branded by the sign of their ultimate failure: each of the historical figures of the violin concerto is above all the *failure* to actualize the 'notion' of the violin concerto fully and adequately. The Hegelian 'concrete universality' thus involves the Real of some central impossibility: universality is 'concrete', structured as a texture of particular figurations, precisely because it is forever prevented from acquiring a figure that would be adequate to its notion. This is why – as Hegel puts it – the Universal genus is always *one of its own species*: there is universality only in so far as there is a gap, a hole, in the midst of the particular content of the universality in question, that is, in so far as, among the species of a genus, there is always one species missing: namely, the species that would adequately embody the genus itself.

'Rather than want nothing . . .'

The notion that best illustrates the necessity of a 'false' ('unilateral', 'abstract') choice in the course of a dialectical process is that of 'stubborn attachment'; this thoroughly ambiguous notion is operative throughout Hegel's *Phenomenology*. On the one hand, it stands for the pathological attachment to some particular content (interest, object, pleasure . . .) scorned by the moralistic judging conscience. Hegel is far from simply condemning such an attachment: he emphasizes again and again that such an attachment is the ontological a priori of an *act* – the hero's (active subject's) act by means of which he disturbs the balance of the socio-ethical totality of *mores* is always and necessarily experienced by his community as a crime. On the other hand, a far more perilous 'stubborn attachment' is that of the inactive judging subject who remains pathologically attached to his abstract moral standards and, on behalf of them, condemns every act as criminal: such a stubborn clinging to abstract moral standards, which could legitimize us to pass judgement on every active subjectivity, is the ultimate form of Evil.

As for the tension between ethnic particularity and universalism, 'stubborn attachment' describes simultaneously the subject's clinging to his particular ethnic identity, which he is not ready to abandon under any circumstances, and a direct reference to abstract universality as that which remains the same, the unchangeable stable framework in the universal change of all particular content. The properly dialectical paradox, of course, is that if the subject is to extract himself from the substantial content of his particular ethnic totality, he can do so only by clinging to some radically contingent idiosyncratic content. For that reason, 'stubborn attachment' is simultaneously the resistance to change–mediation–universalization *and* the very operator of this change: when, irrespective of circumstances, I stubbornly attach myself to some accidental particular feature to which I am bound by no inner necessity, this 'pathological' attachment enables me to disengage myself from immersion in my particular life-context. That is what Hegel calls the 'infinite right of subjectivity': to risk everything, my entire substantial content, for the sake of some trifling, idiosyncratic feature that matters more to me than anything else. The paradox, therefore, lies in the fact that I can arrive at the Universal-for-itself only through a stubborn attachment to some contingent particular content, which functions as a 'negative magnitude', as something wholly indifferent in itself whose meaning resides entirely in the fact that it gives body to the subject's arbitrary will ('I want this because I want it!', and the more trifling this content, the more my will is asserted . . .). This idiosyncratic feature, of course, is in itself contingent and unimportant: a metonymy of void, of nothingness – willing this X is a way of 'willing Nothingness'.

The immediate opposite of 'stubborn attachment' as the supreme expression of the subject's obstinate self-will is, of course, *discipline.* The notion of the formative power of discipline (precisely in its 'traumatic' dimension of obeying a blind meaningless 'mechanical' ritual) was crucial for the Hegelian notion of subjectivity. In his *Gymnasialreden,* delivered at the end of the school year when he was head of the Nuremberg Gymnasium, Hegel insisted on the necessity of mechanical drill in military service, and on learning Latin. The strange status of Latin is of special interest: why did Latin, not Greek, become the *lingua franca* of the West? Greek is the mythical 'language of origins', endowed with full meaning; while Latin is 'mechanical', second-hand, a language of imitation in which the original wealth of meaning was lost (as Heidegger emphasizes again and again) – so it is all the more significant that Latin, not Greek, became the universal medium of Western civilization.[27] Why?

It is not merely that this mechanical drill, the capacity to obey meaningless rules, provides the ground for later meaningful autonomous spiritual activity (one must first learn, get accustomed to, the rules of grammar and social etiquette, in order to be able to indulge freely in 'higher' creative activity) and is thus subsequently 'sublated [aufgehoben]', reduced to a mere invisible Ground for a higher activity. The crucial point is, rather, that without this radical externalization, this sacrifice of all inner substantial spiritual content, the subject remains embedded in his Substance, and cannot emerge as pure self-relating negativity – the true speculative meaning of the meaningless external drill resides in the radical abandonment of all 'inner' substantial content of my spiritual life; it is only through such an abandonment that I emerge as the pure subject of enunciation, no longer attached to any positive order, rooted in any particular life-world. So, like Foucault, Hegel insists on a close link between discipline and subjectivization, although he gives it a slightly different twist: the subject produced by disciplinary practices is not 'the soul as the prison of the body', but – if I may risk this formulation – precisely a soulless subject, a subject deprived of the depth of his 'soul'.[28]

Hegel's point is thus the very opposite of what is usually attributed to him: the 'mechanical' activity of meaningless drill and blind obedience can never be fully sublated into the 'higher' spiritual exercise of Sense – not because of the irreducible remainder of material inertia but, on the contrary, precisely to guarantee the autonomy of the subject with regard to his substantial content: the complete 'sublation' of mechanical drill into Spiritual content (in Lacanese: of the symbolic machine into Meaning) would equal the subject's complete immersion in Substance. In so far as meaningless mechanical drill compels the subject to distance himself from every substantial content, the subject has from time to time to be shaken out of his self-complacent immersion in the substantial totality of Meaning, and confronted with the void of pure negativity – that, according to Hegel, is the role of war, which he considers necessary precisely in so far as it involves a meaningless sacrifice and destruction that undermines the complacency of our daily routine. And, again, Hegel has to be supplemented here with Lacan: what makes the subject endure this meaningless drill of self-discipline is the surplus-enjoyment produced by it. In other words, the supplement of meaningless drill to the spiritual totality is none other than the supplement of *objet petit a* to the field of Meaning: it bears witness to the fact that Hegel was no 'semantic idealist', that he was well aware of how the very domain of Meaning can never achieve closure and ground itself in a self-referential circle – it has to rely on an 'indivisible remainder' of *jouissance* provided by blind mechanical exercise. This is also, *par excellence*, the case of religion in relation to philosophical reasoning: is not prayer the 'highest' example of mechanical-repetitive activity destined to provide its own satisfaction – that is, enjoyment – as Hegel himself emphasizes in his *Lectures on the Philosophy of Religion*?

The advantage of Hegel's account of disciplinary practices over Foucault's is that Hegel, as it were, provides the transcendental genesis of discipline by answering the question: how and why does (that which will become) the subject (the Althusserian 'individual') willingly subject itself to the formative discipline of Power? How and why does it let itself be caught in it? Hegel's answer, of course, is the fear of Death, the absolute Master: since my bodily existence is subject to natural corruption, and since I cannot get rid of the body and thoroughly negate it, the only thing I can do is embody negativity: instead of directly negating my body, I live my bodily existence as the permanent negativization, subordination, mortification, disciplining, of the body. . . . The life of formative discipline – what Hegel calls *Bildung* – is thus an endeavour to neutralize the excessive life-substance in me, to live my actual life as if I am already dead, to ward off desire which 'makes me feel alive'. The positive figure of the Master who effectively oppresses me is ultimately a stand-in for the radical negativity of Death, the absolute Master – this explains the deadlock of the obsessional neurotic who organizes his entire life as the expectation of the moment when his Master will die, so that he will then finally be able to become fully alive, to 'enjoy life'; when the obsessional's Master actually dies, the impact of his death is, of course, exactly the opposite: the obsessional is confronted with the void of Death, the absolute Master, which was lurking beneath the actual Master.

What Hegel already hints at, and Lacan elaborates, is how this renunciation of the body, of bodily pleasures, produces a pleasure of its own – which is precisely what Lacan calls surplus-enjoyment. The fundamental 'perversion' of the human libidinal economy is that when some pleasurable activity is prohibited and 'repressed', we do not simply get a life of strict obedience to the Law deprived of all pleasures – the exercise of the Law itself becomes libidinally cathected, so that the prohibitory activity itself provides a pleasure of its own. Apropos of the ascetic, for example, Hegel emphasizes how his endless mortification of his body becomes a source of perverse excessive enjoyment: the very renunciation of libidinal satisfaction becomes an autonomous source of satisfaction, and this is the 'bribe' which makes the servant accept his servitude.[29]

The key problem is thus the uncanny possibility of the dialectical reversal of *negating the body* into *embodied negation*, of repressing a libidinal urge into obtaining libidinal satisfaction from this very act of repression. This mystery is that of *masochism*: how can the very violent denial and repudiation of erotic satisfaction become eroticized? How can libidinal investment not only detach itself from its direct goal, but even shift from it to the very activity opposing this goal? The Freudian name for this original 'detachability' of the erotic impulse from its 'natural' object, for this original possibility of the erotic impulse shifting its attachment from one object to another, is, of course, none other than *death drive*. In order to account for the nihilistic denial of the assertive will to life, Nietzsche, in *On the Genealogy of Morals*, introduced the well-known distinction between not willing at all and willing Nothing itself: nihilistic hatred of life is 'a revolt against the most fundamental presuppositions of life; yet it is and remains a will! ... rather than want nothing, man even wants nothingness.'[30] Here one should recall that Lacan (who otherwise ignores Nietzsche) implicitly refers to the same distinction in his definition of hysterical anorexia: the anorexic subject does not simply refuse food and not eat; rather, she *eats Nothing itself*. For Lacan, human desire (in contrast to animal instinct) is always, constitutively, mediated by reference to Nothingness: the true object-cause of desire (as opposed to the objects that satisfy our needs) is, by definition, a 'metonymy of lack', a stand-in for Nothingness. (Which is why, for Lacan, *objet petit a* as the object-cause of desire is the originally lost object: it is not only that we desire it in so far as it is lost – this object is nothing but a loss positivized.)[31]

So we are back at the problematic of 'stubborn attachment', since it is absolutely crucial to bear in mind the co-dependence between detachability from any determinate content and excessive attachment to a particular object that makes us indifferent to all other objects – such an object is what Lacan, following Kant, calls 'negative magnitude', that is, an object which, in its very positive presence, acts as a stand-in for the void of Nothingness (or for the abyss of the impossible Thing), so that *wanting this particular object, maintaining one's 'stubborn attachment' to it come what may, is the very concrete form of 'wanting Nothingness'*. Excess and lack of attachment thus *stricto sensu* coincide, since excessive attachment to a particular contingent object is the very operator of lethal dis-attachment: to take a rather pathetic example, Tristan's unconditional, excessive attachment to Isolde (and vice versa) was the very form of his dis-attachment, of

his cutting-off of all his links with the world and immersion into Nothingness. (A beautiful woman as the image of death is a standard feature of
male phantasmic space.)

One can see how this paradox perfectly fits Lacan's notion of sublimation as the elevation of some particular positive object to 'the dignity of
the Thing': the subject becomes excessively attached to an object in so far
as this object starts to function as a stand-in for Nothingness. Here,
Nietzsche on the one hand, and Freud and Lacan on the other, part
company: what Nietzsche denounces as the 'nihilistic' gesture to counteract life-asserting instincts, Freud and Lacan conceive as the very basic
structure of human drive as opposed to natural instincts. In other words,
what Nietzsche cannot accept is the radical dimension of the death drive
– the fact that the excess of the Will over a mere self-contended satisfaction is always mediated by the 'nihilistic' stubborn attachment to Nothingness. The death drive is not merely a direct nihilistic opposition to any
life-asserting attachment; rather, it is the very formal structure of the
reference to Nothingness that enables us to overcome the stupid self-
contended life-rhythm, in order to become 'passionately attached' to
some Cause – be it love, art, knowledge or politics – for which we are
ready to risk everything. In this precise sense, it is meaningless to talk
about the sublimation of drives, since drive as such involves the structure
of sublimation: we pass from instinct to drive when, instead of aiming
directly at the goal that would satisfy us, satisfaction is brought about by
circulating around the void, by repeatedly missing the object which is the
stand-in for the central void. So, when a subject desires a series of positive
objects, the thing to do is to distinguish between objects which are actually
desired as particular objects, and *the* object which is desired as the stand-
in for Nothingness: which functions as a 'negative magnitude' in the
Kantian sense of the term.

'Include me out!'

As for this Nietzschean difference between 'willing nothing (not willing
anything at all)' and 'willing Nothingness itself', one should read it against
the background of Lacan's distinction, elaborated apropos of Ernst Kris's
case of 'pathological' self-accusation of plagiarism, between 'stealing
nothing (in the simple sense of "not stealing anything")' and 'stealing
Nothingness itself': when the patient – an intellectual obsessed with the
notion that he is constantly stealing ideas from his colleagues – is proved

by the analyst (Kris) not, in reality, to have stolen anything, this does not yet prove that he is simply innocent. What the patient is actually stealing is 'nothing' itself, just as an anorexic is not simply eating nothing (in the sense of 'not eating anything') but, rather, *eating Nothingness itself*. . . . What, exactly, do these passages, so often referred to, mean? Darian Leader[32] linked this case to another in which a patient evokes the anecdote of a man suspected by his employer of stealing something: as he leaves the factory where he works every evening, his wheelbarrow is searched systematically – nothing is found, until at last it is understood that he is stealing wheelbarrows themselves. . . . Along the same lines, as Lacan emphasizes, when Kris's patient displays his obsession with the 'pathological' feeling of plagiarizing, the crucial point is not to take this self-accusation at face value, and endeavour to prove to the patient that in reality he is not stealing anything from his colleagues – what the patient (as well as his analyst) fails to see is that 'the real plagiarism is in the form of the object itself, in the fact that for this man something can only have a value if it belongs to someone else':[33] the patient's apprehension that everything he possesses is stolen conceals the profound satisfaction – *jouissance* – he derives from the very fact of *not* having anything that truly belongs to him – that is truly 'his'.

On the level of desire, this attitude of stealing means that desire is always the desire of the Other, never immediately 'mine' (I desire an object only in so far as it is desired by the Other) – so the only way for me authentically to 'desire' is to reject all positive objects of desire, and desire Nothingness itself (again, in all the senses of this term, up to desiring that specific form of Nothingness which is desire itself – for this reason, human desire is always desire to desire, desire to be the object of the Other's desire). Again, we can easily see the homology with Nietzsche: a Will can be a 'Will to Will', a willing which wants willing itself, only in so far as it is a Will which actively wills Nothingness. (Another well-known form of this reversal is the characterization of Romantic lovers as actually being in love not with the beloved person, but with Love itself.)

Crucial here is the self-reflexive turn by means of which the (symbolic) form itself is counted among its elements: to Will the Will itself is to Will nothing, just as to steal the wheelbarrow itself (the very form–container of stolen goods) is to steal Nothingness itself (the void which potentially contains stolen goods). This 'nothing' ultimately stands for the subject itself – that is, it is the empty signifier without signified, which represents the subject. Thus the subject is not directly included in the symbolic order: it is included as the very point at which signification breaks down.

Sam Goldwyn's famous retort when he was confronted with an unaccept-able business proposition, 'Include me out!', perfectly expresses this intermediate status of the subject's relationship to the symbolic order, between direct inclusion and direct exclusion: the signifier which 'repre-sents the subject for other signifiers' is the empty signifier, the 'signifier without signified', the signifier by means of (in the guise of) which 'nothing (the subject) is counted as something' – in this signifier, the subject is not simply included into the signifier's network; rather, his very exclusion from it (signalled by the fact that there is no signified to this signifier) is 'included' in it, marked, registered by it.

This situation is the same as that of the well-known childish nonsense also often quoted by Lacan: "I have three brothers, Ernest, Paul and myself' – the third term, 'myself', designates the way the subject is simultaneously included in the series (as 'myself'), and excluded from it (as the absent 'subject of the enunciation' who has three brothers, including himself) – that is to say, this term, precisely, 'includes me out'. Thus reflexivity sustains the gap between the subject of the enunciation and the subject of the statement/enunciated: when – to take the old notorious Freudian example – the patient says: 'I do not know who that [person in my dream] was, but it was *not* my mother!', the enigma is: why did he deny something that nobody suggested to him? In other words, the real message of the patient's 'It was *not* my mother!' lies not in its enunciated content, but in the very fact that this message was uttered at all – the real message consists in the very act of delivering this message (like a person who, when nobody is accusing him of theft, already vehemently defends himself: 'I did *not* steal it!' – why does he defend himself, when nobody was even thinking of accusing him?). The fact that the message was delivered at all is thus like the wheelbarrow which should be 'excluded in' the content rather than 'included out' of it: it tells us a lot, providing the crucial element with regard to the content (theft).

This formula, 'include me out', provides the most succinct definition of the *obsessional's* subjective attitude. That is to say: what is the goal of the obsessional attitude? To achieve the position of a pure invisible mediator – that is, to play, in intersubjective relations, the role of what, in chemistry, one calls a 'catalyst': the substance which speeds up, or even sets in motion, a process of chemical reaction without itself changing or being affected in any way. From my personal experience, I recall the catastrophic consequences of one of my benevolent interventions. I was sleeping in a friend's apartment in a room in which my friend, an analyst, received his patients; close to this room was another room in which another analyst also received patients. So once, in the middle of the day, I returned briefly to the apartment to leave a package there; since voices told me that the other analyst was receiving patients in his room, I tiptoed silently into my room and put the package into a chest. While I was doing this, I noticed a book on the table which did not belong there; I also saw a gap in the bookshelves where this book obviously fitted – so, unable to resist the compulsive temptation, I put the book back in its proper place, then tiptoed out of the apartment. Later I learned from my friend that by doing this, by simply putting an object back in its proper place, I had caused the analyst from the adjacent room to have a nervous breakdown. The book I found on the table was to be returned by this analyst to the friend in whose room I was sleeping. Just before I arrived, this analyst entered my room and, since he was late and a patient was already waiting for him, just threw the book on the table. Immediately after I left, the patient had to go to the toilet, so the analyst used the opportunity of the short break to enter my room again and put the book back in its proper place – one can imagine his shock when he noticed that *the book was already back in its proper place on the shelf*! Only two or three minutes passed between his two visits to the room, and he had not heard noises (since I tiptoed in and out), so he was convinced that he himself must have put the book there. However, since he clearly remembered at the same time that only a short while ago he had just thrown the book on the table, he thought he was having hallucinations and losing control over his acts – even my friend, to whom the analyst later told the story, thought the latter was losing his mind. . . .

Something similar happens in the Coen brothers' excellent film *Blood Simple*: the private investigator, hired by the jealous husband to kill his wife and her lover, kills the husband himself instead. Afterwards, the lover who stumbles on the dead husband thinks that his mistress (the wife) committed the crime, and erases its traces; the wife, on the other hand, also wrongly assumes that her lover did it – a set of unexpected complications arises from the couple's unawareness that another agent has intervened in the situation. . . . This, then, is the unattainable ideal towards which the obsessional neurotic strives: to be 'included' (to intervene in a situation), but in the mode of 'out', of an invisible mediator/intercessor who is never properly counted, included, among the elements of the situation.

In *Sleeping with the Enemy*, Julia Roberts escapes from her pathological sadistic husband and assumes a new identity in a small Iowa town; in his efforts to track her down, the husband locates her blind old mother and approaches her in a nursing home – in order to trap her into revealing her daughter's whereabouts to him, he poses as a police detective who, aware of the fact that the husband is a pathological killer, wants to warn Julia Roberts that her husband is on her tracks, and to protect her from his merciless revenge. The husband thus uses the very effort to protect Julia Roberts against his fury as a means of tracking her down and taking his revenge – by including himself in the series of those trying to protect Julia Roberts, he 'includes himself out' as to what he effectively is. . . . A similar inversion provides what is probably the best solution to the subgenre of the 'locked-room mystery' (a murder which 'couldn't occur', since it took place in a hermetically isolated place), in which John Dickson Carr specialized: the murderer is the very person who discovers the murder – he starts shouting 'Murder! Murder!', inducing the person to be murdered to unlock the door of his room, and *then* quickly murdering him – since the murderer was the one who 'discovered' the murder, nobody suspects *him* . . . again, here the murderer is 'included out' from the series of those trying to solve the crime. (This logic, of course, is that of the thief himself shouting 'Catch a thief!' – including himself out from the set of potential thieves.)

In both these cases, the mistake of those concerned is that in their search for the dangerous murderer, they forget to include in the series of suspects the wheelbarrow itself – that is, those engaged in the effort to solve or prevent the crime. Again, the link between the 'impossible' inscription of subjectivity into the series and the empty form (of the 'signifier without signified') is crucial here: the series is 'subjectivized' when and only when one of its elements is an empty element – that is, an element which inscribes in the series its very formal principle: this element does not simply 'mean nothing'; rather, it 'means Nothingness itself' and, as such, represents the subject.

We are therefore back at the mystery of *reflection*, of the self-referential reflexive turn that is consubstantial with subjectivity. Repression first emerges as an attempt to *regulate desires* considered 'illicit' by the predominant socio-symbolic order; however, this power of repression can maintain itself in the psychic economy only if it is sustained by the *desire for regulation* – if, that is, the very formal activity of regulation/repression/subjection becomes libidinally invested and turns into an autonomous source of libidinal satisfaction. This satisfaction provided by the very regulatory activity, this desire for regulation, plays exactly the same structural role as the wheelbarrow in the story quoted by Leader: we can closely inspect all the desires the subject endeavours to regulate, but we get the key to the specific mode of his subjective stance only if we 'include out' the desire for regulation itself. . . .

This reflexive reversal is hysteria at its most elementary: the reversal of the impossibility of satisfying a desire into the desire for the desire to remain unsatisfied (and thus turn into a 'reflected' desire, a 'desire *to desire*'). Perhaps that is the limitation of Kant's philosophy: not in its formalism as such but, rather, in the fact that Kant was not able and/or ready to *count/include the form into content, as part of the content*. On a first approach, it may seem that, precisely, Kant *was* able to do so: is not the mysterious fact that, in a moral agent, the pure *form* of moral Law *can* act as the motive, the motivational force, of practical activity the key point of his ethical theory? Here, however, one should introduce the Hegelian distinction between 'in itself' and 'for itself': Kant does accomplish this step (of 'including out' the form into content itself) *in itself*, not yet *for itself* – that is, he is not ready to embrace all the consequences of this 'inclusion out' of the form into content, and continues to treat form as 'pure form', abstractly opposed to its content (which is why, in his formulations, he constantly 'regresses' to the standard notion of a man split between the universal Call of Duty and the wealth of pathological egotistic impulses). In a way, Hegel is much closer to Kant than he may appear to be: what often creates a difference between the two is the barely perceptible gap that separates the In-itself from the For-itself.

Towards a Materialist Theory of Grace

Hegelian 'concrete universality' is thus much more paradoxical than it may appear: it has nothing whatsoever to do with any kind of aesthetic organic totality, since it reflexively 'includes out' the very excess and/or gap that forever spoils such a totality – the irreducible and ultimately unaccountable gap between a series and its excess, between the Whole and the One of its exception, is the very *terrain* of 'concrete universality'. For this reason, the true politico-philosophical heirs of Hegel are not authors who endeavour to rectify the excesses of modernity via the return to some new form of organic substantial Order (like the communitarians) but, rather, authors who fully endorse the political logic of the excess constitutive of every established Order. The exemplary case, of course, is Carl Schmitt's decisionist claim that the rule of law ultimately hinges on an abyssal act of violence (violent imposition) grounded only in itself:

every positive statute to which this act refers in order to legitimize itself is self-referentially posited by this act itself.[34]

The basic paradox of Schmitt's position is that his very polemics against liberal-democratic formalism inexorably get caught in the formalist trap. Schmitt targets the utilitarian-enlightened grounding of the political in some presupposed set of neutral-universal norms or strategic rules which (should) regulate the interplay of individual interests (either in the guise of legal normativism *à la* Kelsen, or in the guise of economic utilitarianism): it is not possible to pass directly from a pure normative order to the actuality of social life – the necessary mediator between the two is an act of Will, a decision, grounded only in itself, which *imposes* a certain order or legal hermeneutics (reading of abstract rules). Any normative order, taken in itself, remains stuck in abstract formalism; it cannot bridge the gap that separates it from actual life. However – and this is the core of Schmitt's argumentation – the decision which bridges this gap is not a decision for some concrete order, but primarily the decision for the formal principle of order as such. The concrete content of the imposed order is arbitrary, dependent on the Sovereign's will, left to historical contingency – the *principle of order*, the *Dass-Sein* of Order, has priority over its concrete content, over its *Was-Sein*. That is the main feature of modern conservativism, which sharply distinguishes it from every kind of traditionalism: modern conservativism, even more than liberalism, assumes the lesson of the dissolution of the traditional set of values and/or authorities – there is no longer any positive content which could be presupposed as the universally accepted frame of reference. (Hobbes was the first explicitly to posit this distinction between the principle of order and any concrete order.) The paradox thus lies in the fact that the only way to oppose legal normative formalism is to revert to decisionist formalism – there is no way of escaping formalism within the horizon of modernity.

And does not this gap also provide the implicit political background for Lacan's logic of the universal and its constitutive exception? It is easy to translate Schmitt's critique of liberalism into Lacanese: what liberalism misrecognizes is the constitutive role of the exceptional/excessive Master-Signifier. This reference to Lacan also enables us to account for the necessary ambiguity of Schmitt's notion of exception: it stands simultaneously for the intrusion of the Real (of the pure contingency that perturbs the universe of symbolic *automaton*) *and* for the gesture of the Sovereign who (violently, without foundation in the symbolic norm) imposes a symbolic normative order: in Lacanese, it stands for *objet petit a* as well as for S_1, the Master-Signifier.

This double nature of the foundational act is clearly discernible in religion: Christ calls on his followers to obey and respect their superiors in accordance with established customs *and* to hate and disobey them, that is, to cut all human links with them: 'If anyone comes to me and does not hate his father and his mother, his wife and children, his brothers and sisters – yes, even his own life – he cannot be my disciple'(Luke 14: 26). Do we not encounter here Christ's own 'religious suspension of the ethical'? The universe of established ethical norms (*mores*, the substance of social life) is reasserted, but only in so far as it is 'mediated' by Christ's authority: first, we have to accomplish the gesture of radical negativity and reject everything that is most precious to us; later, we get it back, but as an expression of Christ's will, mediated by it (the way a Sovereign relates to positive laws involves the same paradox: a Sovereign compels us to respect laws precisely in so far as he is the point of the suspension of laws). When Christ claims that he did not come to undermine the Old Law, but merely to fulfil it, one has to read into this 'fulfilment' the full ambiguity of the Derridean supplement: *the very act of fulfilling the Law undermines its direct authority*. In this precise sense, 'Love Is the Fulfilment of the Law'(Romans 13: 10): love accomplishes what the Law (Commandments) aims at, but this very accomplishment simultaneously involves the suspension of the Law. The notion of belief which fits this paradox of authority was elaborated by Kierkegaard; this is why, for him, *religion is eminently modern*: the traditional universe is ethical, while the Religious involves a radical disruption of the Old Ways – true religion is a crazy wager on the Impossible we have to make once we lose support in tradition.

What is properly modern in Schmitt's notion of exception is thus the violent gesture of asserting the independence of the abyssal act of free decision from its positive content. What is 'Modern' is the gap between the act of decision and its content – the perception that what really matters is the act as such, independent of its content (or 'ordering', independent of the positive determinate order). The paradox (which grounds so-called 'conservative modernism') is thus that the innermost possibility of modernism is asserted in the guise of its apparent opposite, of the return to an unconditional authority that cannot be grounded in positive reasons. Consequently, the properly modern God is the God of predestination, a kind of Schmittian politician who draws the line of separation between Us and Them, Friends and Enemies, the Delivered and the Damned, *by means of a purely formal, abyssal act of decision, without any grounds in the actual properties and acts of concerned humans* (since they were not yet even born). In traditional Catholicism, salvation depends on earthly good deeds; in the logic of Protestant predestination, earthly deeds and fortunes (wealth) are at best an ambiguous *sign* of the fact that the subject is already redeemed through the inscrutable divine act – that is, he is not saved *because* he is rich or did good deeds, he accomplishes good deeds or is rich *because* he is saved. . . . Crucial here is the shift from act to sign: from the perspective of predestination, a deed becomes a *sign* of the predestined divine decision.

The epistemological version of this voluntarist decisionism was asserted by Descartes (in his *Reply to the Six Objections*), apropos of the most elementary mathematical truths: 'God did not will the three angles of a triangle to be equal to two right angles because he knew that they could not be otherwise. On the contrary, it is because he willed the three angles of a triangle to be necessarily equal to two right angles that this is true and cannot be otherwise.' The best proof of how this gap, once asserted, cannot be denied, is provided by Malebranche, who opposed this 'modernist' assertion of the primacy of Will over Reason, since he was not ready to accept as the ultimate Ground of the world 'a certain absolute decree, without reason' (as Leibniz put it in his 'On the Philosophy of Descartes'): however, this rejection in no way entailed a return to the premodern identification of God with the rational harmonious order of the universe in which Truth coincides with Supreme Good.[35]

Malebranche begins by extending the rational necessity followed by God in His acts from Nature to Grace: not only is Nature a gigantic Cartesian mechanism which, in its movement, obeys simple laws; the same holds for Grace itself, whose distribution follows universal laws that are indifferent towards individuals. It may well happen that – as with rain which, obeying the blind laws of Nature, can fall on barren land, leaving the carefully cultivated field nearby dry; or with the proverbial brick from a roof, which can hit the head of a virtuous person and miss a criminal walking nearby – Grace can also hit the worst offender or hypocrite, and miss a virtuous man. Why? Because, more than the happiness of worthless individuals, God values the simplicity and order of the structure of the entire universe: the cruel and undeserved fate of virtuous individuals is the price to be paid if the universe is to be governed by simple universal laws. The Malebranchian God is thus uncannily close to the God in the memoirs of Daniel Paul Schreber: a cruel and indifferent God who emphatically does *not* 'understand' our individual secrets and dreams, an Egoist who loves Himself more than His creatures and whose blind universal Will inevitably, without any qualms, tramples down individual flowers:

> The general laws which diffuse grace in our hearts, thus find nothing in our wills which determine their efficacy – just as the general laws which govern the rains are not based on the dispositions of the places where it rains. For whether the grounds be fallow or whether they be cultivated, it rains indifferently in all places, both in the deserts and in the sea.[36]

Why, then, did God create the world in the first place? For the sake of Christ's arrival – in order, that is, for the world to be delivered by Christ. Here Malebranche inverts 'God so loved the world, that he gave his only son' into 'It would be unworthy of God to love the world, if this work were not inseparable from his son'. From this inversion, Malebranche is not afraid to draw the only logical, albeit morbid, conclusion that God the Father 'never had a more agreeable sight than that of his only son fastened to the cross to re-establish order in the universe'.[37] As such, Christ is the occasional cause of Grace: in contrast to God the Father, Christ the Son dispenses Grace with regard to individual merits, but since he is constrained by the finite horizon of a human soul, he acts and makes his choices following his particular will, and is prone to mistakes.

Malebranche thus gives a theological twist to the standard Cartesian epistemological occasionalism: for him, occasionalism is not only or primarily a theory of perception and volition (we do not see bodies, 'we see all things in God'; our mind is not capable of directly moving even the smallest body), but also the theory of Salvation, since the human soul of Christ is the occasional cause of the distribution of Grace to particular persons. Here Malebranche relies on a homology with the domain of Nature in which, if we are to explain event X, we need general laws that regulate physical processes as well as the texture of prior particular events which, in accordance with general laws, generate event X – general laws become effective only through the texture of particular existences that actualize them. In a similar way, God the Father sustains the general laws of Grace, while Christ acts as its occasional cause and determines who will acutally be touched by Grace.[38] In this way, Malebranche endeavours to avoid the two extremes: before the Fall, God did plan to provide Grace to all men (in contrast to Calvinism, which advocates predestination – selection of the few – before the Fall); because of Adam's Fall, however, sin is universal; all men deserve to be lost, and in order to redeem the world, God sent His Son, Christ, so that it is Christ alone who can furnish the occasion for Grace to be distributed. However, Christ's soul was human and, as such, prone to human limitations; his thoughts were 'accompanied by certain desires' with regard to people he encountered; he was perplexed and intrigued by some, repelled by others – so he distributed Grace unevenly, giving it to a sinner or withholding it from a virtuous person.

So Malebranche is unable to avoid the discrepancy between Grace and virtue: God's general will operates on a universal level and distributes Grace according to simple Cartesian laws which, from an individual perspective, necessarily appear unjust and tainted by cruel indifference. Malebranche denies the notion of a God who has in mind me in my particularity, a God who acts with a particular will to help me, to answer my prayer; Christ, on the other hand, does act with a *volonté particulière*, but because of his human limitations his distribution of Grace is irregular and unjust, pathologically twisted. . . . Does this not bring us back to Hegel, to his thesis on how *abstract universality coincides with arbitrary subjectivity*? The relationship between the general laws of Grace and Christ's particular occasional causes is that of *speculative identity*: abstract general laws realize themselves in the guise of their opposite, in contingent particular whims of a subject's (Christ's) disposition – as in the Hegelian civil society of the market, in which the universal anonymous law realizes itself through the contingent interaction of subjective particular interests.[39]

A question arises here: why this detour through Adam's Fall and the arrival of Christ; why does God not distribute Grace directly and abundantly to all men through His *volonté générale*? *On account of His Narcissism*: God created the world for His Glory – that is, so that the world would be redeemed through Christ's sacrifice. The opponents of Malebranche, of course, were quick to draw from this the unavoidable uncanny conclusion: *all* men had to be damned so that Christ was able to redeem *some* of them – or, as Bossuet put it: 'we would all be saved, if we had no Saviour'.[40] This paradox is the key to Malebranche's series of strange reversals of the established theological clichés: Adam had to fall, corruption was necessary in order to make Christ's arrival possible; at no time was God happier than when He was observing Christ's suffering on the Cross. . . . In what, then, consists the role of freedom within the confines of strict occasionalism? Malebranche is not afraid to draw the radical conclusion: at the level of content, everything is decided '*en nous sans nous*'[41] – that is to say, we are mechanisms; God prompts us, produces feelings and movements in us; we are completely ruled by motives. The margin of freedom lies only in the subject's capacity to withhold or grant his consent from or to a motive – freedom is the power 'which the soul has, to suspend or to give its consent to motives, which naturally follow interesting perceptions'.[42] What, then, happens in an act of (human) freedom? Malebranche's answer is radical and consistent: 'Nothing. . . . The only thing we do is stop ourselves, put ourselves at rest.' This is 'an immanent act which produces nothing physical in our substances',[43] 'an act which does nothing and which makes the general cause [God] do nothing'.[44] Freedom as our consent to motives is thus purely reflexive: everything is effectively decided *en nous sans nous*; the subject merely provides his formal consent. Is not this reduction of freedom to the 'nothing' of an empty gesture the 'truth' of the Hegelian Absolute Subject?

Notes

1. Colin Wilson, *From Atlantis to the Sphinx*, London: Virgin Books 1997.
2. Ibid., p. 352.
3. Ibid., p. 354.
4. See Wendy Brown, *States of Injury*, Stanford, CA : Stanford University Press 1996, p. 36.
5. The matrix of the notorious 'Hegelian triad' is provided by the two shifts in the relationship between headache and sex. In the good old pre-feminist days, the sexually subdued wife was supposed to reject the husband's or man's advances with: 'Not tonight, darling, I've got a headache!' In the sexually liberated 1970s, when it became acceptable for women to play the active role in instigating sex, it was usually the man who used the same excuse to stall a woman's advances: 'I don't want to do it tonight, I've got a headache!' In the therapeutic 1980s and 1990s, however, women again use a headache as an argument, but for the opposite purpose: 'I've got a headache, so let's do it (to refresh me)!' (Perhaps, between the second and third phases, one should insert another brief stage of absolute negativity in which the two partners simply agree that since they both have a headache, they shouldn't do it . . .)
6. For this reason, *la traversée du fantasme* in psychoanalytic treatment is double – that is, there are two *traversées*, and analysis proper fills in the distance 'in between the two *traversées*'. The first *traversée* is the breakdown of the phantasmic support of the analysand's everyday existence, which sustained his demand to enter psychoanalysis: something must go awry, the pattern of his everyday life must disintegrate, otherwise analysis remains empty chatter with no radical subjective consequences. The point of preliminary talks is to establish if this elementary condition for real analysis is fulfilled. Then one works towards 'going through' the fantasy. This gap is, again, the gap between In-itself and For-itself: the first traversing is 'In-itself', and only the second is 'For-itself'.
7. However, the oscillation is not only that between triplicity or quadruplicity: historical dialectics often seems to point towards quintuplicity. In Hegel's *Phenomenology*, the ideal triad of Western history would be the Greek *Sittlichkeit* – the world of immediate ethical substantiality and organic unity – its alienation in the medieval universe, culminating in modern utilitarianism, and the final reconciliation of the ethical Substance with free individuality in the modern rational State; however, in each of the two passages (from substantial unity to its alienation, and from utter alienation to reconciliation) an uncanny intermediate moment

intervenes: between Greek substantial unity and medieval alienation there is the Roman epoch of abstract individualism (in which, although the Greek substantial ethical unity is already lost, alienation *has not yet occurred* – the Romans did not yet conceive of their real world as a mere reflection of the transcendent Deity); between utilitarian civil society and the modern rational State there is the brief epoch of Absolute Freedom, the traumatic Terror of the Revolution (which already supersedes alienation, but in an immediate way, and thus, instead of bringing about true reconciliation, ends up in utter self-destructive fury). The interesting point is that a homologous shift of triplicity to quintuplicity via the intrusion of the two intermediate stages seems also to disturb the standard historical materialist triad of pre-class tribal society, 'alienated' class societies, and approaching post-class socialist society: 'Oriental Despotism' intervenes between pre-class tribal society and classic slave society, then reintervenes again in the guise of the despotic Stalinist State between capitalism and 'authentic' socialism.

8. See Vittorio Hösle, *Hegels System: Der Idealismus der Subjektivität und das Problem der Intersubjektivität*, vols 1 and 2, Hamburg: Felix Meiner Verlag 1988.

9. Another indicator of Hegel's failure seems to be the way he treats madness in his 'Anthropology': he reduces the withdrawal from the public social universe that characterizes madness to the regression to 'animal soul', missing the obvious point that the 'night of the world' to which we return in psychosis is not the animal universe but, rather the radical negation, suspension, of the living being's immersion in its natural surroundings. See para. 408 in *Hegel's Philosophy of Mind*, Oxford: Clarendon Press 1992.

10. The standard argument of the Catholic Church against contraception (according to which sex, deprived of the higher goal of procreation, is reduced to animal fornication) thus obviously misses the point: is it not precisely sex in the service of procreation – i.e. biological reproduction – that is animal? Is it not specifically human that sexual activity can detach itself from its 'natural' goal and turn into an end-in-itself? Or, to put it in male-chauvinist terms: is it possible to imagine the opposition between 'whore' and 'mother' in the animal universe? From the standpoint of nature, 'Spirit' designates a meaningless expenditure, a *zielgehemmtes* instinct – that is, an instinct thwarted as to its 'natural' goal, and thereby caught in the endless repetitive movement of drive. If – as Lacan emphasized again and again – the symbolic gesture *par excellence* is an empty and/or interrupted gesture, a gesture meant not to be accomplished, then sexuality 'humanizes' itself by cutting its links with the natural movement of procreation.

11. The trickiest procedure in interpreting great texts of the philosophical tradition is the precise positioning of a thesis or notion which the author ferociously rejects: at these points, the question to be asked is always 'Is the author simply rejecting another's notion, or is he actually *introducing* this idea in the very guise of its rejection?'. Take Kant's rejection of the notion of 'diabolical Evil' (Evil elevated into moral Duty, i.e. accomplished not out of 'pathological' motivation, but just 'for its own sake'): is not Kant here *rejecting a notion the conceptual space for which was opened up only by his own philosophical system* – that is to say, is he not battling with the innermost consequence, the unbearable excess, of *his own* philosophy? (To make an unexpected comparison, is he not behaving a little bit like the proverbial wife who accuses her husband's best friend of making advances to her, thereby betraying her own disavowed sexual desire for him?) One of the matrixes of 'progress' in the history of philosophy is that a later philosopher, a pupil of the first one, openly assumes and fully articulates the notion which his teacher actually introduced in the guise of polemical rejection – as was the case with Schelling, with his theory of evil, in relation to Kant.

12. This externality of the *symbolic* order should furthermore be opposed to the externality of the *peu de réalité*, of an asinine positive element in which the big Other itself must embody itself in order to acquire full actuality: 'the Spirit is a bone', the State as a rational totality becomes actual in the body of the Monarch, and so on. The role of the King (Monarch) in Hegel's rational State is thus what Edgar Allan Poe called the 'imp of perversity': when a criminal succeeds in wholly obliterating the traces of his crime – when there are no

symptomatic 'returns of the repressed', no 'clues' that betray the presence of the Other Scene of crime – that is, when he is in no danger of being discovered, when the camouflage of rationalization works perfectly – the criminal feels an irresistible urge to display his crime publicly, to shout out the truth about his horrible deed. Is it not the same with the Hegelian deduction of the monarchy? Just when the social edifice attains the accomplished rationality of a perfectly organized State, this rationality is paid for by the necessity to supplement it by – to posit at its head – the thoroughly 'irrational' element of the hereditary monarch who is *immediately*, in his nature (i.e. due to his biological descendency), what he is 'in culture', in terms of his symbolic title.

13. See Charles Taylor, *Hegel*, Cambridge, MA: Cambridge University Press 1975, p. 92.

14. Recall the standard cynical designation of someone as 'a relative genius' – one is a genius or not; 'genius' is not an attribute that allows levels of amplification. In the same way, Schelling qualifies God as 'relatively Absolute': He is the absolute Master and Creator, but His absolute power is none the less qualified, limited by what is not yet God in Him.

15. G.W.F. Hegel, *Phenomenology of Spirit*, Oxford: Oxford University Press 1977, p. 210. In the accompanying footnote, the translator (A.V. Miller) draws attention to the passage from Hegel's *Philosophy of Nature* in which he asserts the same identity: 'In many animals the organs of excretion and the genitals, the highest and lowest parts in the animal organization, ar intimately connected: just as speech and kissing, on the one hand, and eating, drinking and spitting, on the other, are all done with the mouth.'

16. I owe this precise point to Mladen Dolar; see 'The Phrenology of Spirit', in *Supposing the Subject*, ed. Joan Copjec, London: Verso 1994.

There is a clear parallel between this necessity to make the wrong choice in order to reach the proper result (to choose 'urination' in order to reach 'insemination'), and the structure of the Russian joke from Socialist times on Rabinovitch, who wants to emigrate from the Soviet Union for two reasons: 'First, I fear that if the socialist order disintegrates, all the blame for the Communist crimes will be put on us, the Jews.' To the state bureaucrat's exclamation 'But nothing will ever change in the Soviet Union! Socialism is here to stay for ever!', Rabinovitch calmly answers: 'That's my second reason!' Here also, the only way to reach the true reason is via the wrong first reason.

17. To put it in Ernesto Laclau's terms of antagonism versus the structure of differences: for Hegel, every system of differences – every positive social structure – is based on an antagonistic struggle, and war is the return of the antagonistic logic of 'Us versus Them' which forever threatens every structure of differences.

18. Perhaps the problem with this triadic articulation of the social edifice is that Hegel tries to compress into a synchronous order three different global principles of social organization: (1) the premodern peasant/feudal principle, which, in feudalism, structures the whole of society (artisans themselves are organized into guilds and estates, they do not function in a free market; State power itself is paternalistic, involving a naive pre-reflexive trust of its subjects in the King's divine right to rule); (2) the modern market-liberal principle of civil society, which also determines the way peasant life functions (with agriculture itself organized as a branch of industrial production) and the political superstructure (the State reduced to a 'police state', the 'night watchman' guaranteeing the legal and police/political conditions of civil life); (3) the planned state-socialist logic in which the State bureaucracy, as the universal class, also endeavours to run the entire production, including agriculture (no wonder the biggest effort of Stalinism, as the supreme expression of this tendency, was to crush the peasantry, with its naive-trusting pre-reflexive attitude).

Can these three principles be effectively 'mediated' into a complete and stable 'syllogism of Society'? The problem is that each of them is split from within, involved in an antagonistic tension that introduces the properly *political* dimension: the archaic organic order can turn into Fascist populist violence against 'Them'; liberalism is split between a conservative *laissez-faire* attitude and an activist stance of *égaliberté*; state socialism generates a reaction in the guise of grass-roots spontaneous self-organization. Do not these three principles therefore need (or involve) a fourth principle: that, precisely, of the *political as such*, of social antagonism, of democratic destabilization of the articulated social body, a principle which, from time to time, finds expression in different forms of 'spontaneous' or 'direct' democracy (like workers' councils in the revolutionary turmoil at the end of World War I, or democratic 'forums' in the disintegration of Socialism)? For a more detailed account of this notion of the political, see Chapter 4 below.

19. One should bear in mind that all categories of reflection directly involve reference to the knowing subject: say, the difference between appearance and essence exists only for the gaze of the subject to whom only the appearance is directly accessible, who then endeavours to penetrate the underlying essence hidden beneath the veil. See Taylor, *Hegel*, pp. 257–9.

20. This point is also crucial for the proper understanding of the difference that separates Hegel from Schelling: as long as Hegel remained committed to Schelling's critique of Kantian–Fichtean subjectivism, he – as it were – backed insemination against urination, that is, the direct choice of the concrete totality against the abstract subjective division. Hegel 'became Hegel' the moment he became aware that every choice between Totality and abstract subjectivity which disbands Totality's concrete organic link is ultimately a forced choice in which the subject is compelled to choose *himself* – that is, the 'unilateral' disruptive violence which 'is' the subject.

21. See Karel van het Reve, 'Reves Vermutung', in *Dr Freud and Sherlock Holmes*, Hamburg: Fischer Verlag 1994, pp. 140–51.

22. Ibid., p. 149.

23. Lacan has something of the same order in mind when he posits the correlation between the universal 'phallic function' and its constitutive exception.

24. Another example: how does a couple come to the decision to marry, to enter a permanent, symbolically asserted relationship? Usually, the decision is *not* taken when the two partners, after a period of trial and deliberation, finally ascertain the harmonious nature of their respective needs and character features; rather, after some small conflict that disturbs the bliss of their common life, the partners become aware of the insignificance of this conflict – of how the bond between them is infinitely stronger than this annoyance. It is thus the very disturbing detail which forces me to become aware of the depth of my attachment.

25. See Ernesto Laclau, *Emancipation(s)*, London: Verso 1996.

26. Perhaps the best formulation of this vertiginous abyss in which the Universal is caught in the Hegelian dialectical process is provided by Jean-Luc Nancy in his *Hegel. L'inquiétude du négatif*, Paris: Hachette 1997.

27. See Renata Salecl, *The Spoils of Freedom*, London: Routledge 1994, p. 136.

28. Within the domain of language, Hegel makes the same point by means of his notion of 'mechanical memory'. See Chapter 2 of Slavoj Žižek, *The Metastases of Enjoyment*, London: Verso 1994.

29. Judith Butler claims that when he deals with the structure of religious sacrificial labour, Hegel abandons its dialectical subversion, which would consist in pointing out how the sacrificial renunciation is false in so far as it produces a satisfaction of its own, a pleasure-in-pain (or, to put it in Lacanian terms, the undermining of the enunciated content via reference to its position of enunciation: I inflict pain on myself, but at the level of the subjective position of enunciation I experience this pain as excessively pleasurable). According to Butler, in the case of sacrificial religious labour, pain and satisfaction are externally opposed; what makes me endure pain, or even inflict it on myself, is not the direct perverse satisfaction I get out of it, but the belief that the more I suffer here, on this earth, the more I will be compensated, the more satisfaction I will get, in the Beyond, after my death. (See Judith Butler, *The Psychic Life of Power*, Stanford, CA: Stanford University Press 1997, p. 44.) Is this, however, in fact Hegel's position? Is not Hegel well aware that the promised pleasure of the Beyond is a mere mask for the pleasure I derive here and now from imagining this future reward?

30. Friedrich Nietzsche, *On the Genealogy of Morals*, New York: Vintage 1989, p. 163.

31. And is this not connected to the logical distinction between external and internal negation? The basic procedure of Stalinist paranoia was to read external negation as internal: the people's indifference towards constructing Socialism (not wanting to do it) was read as active plotting against it (wanting not to do it, i.e. opposing it). One can thus say that the space of the death drive is this very gap between external and internal negation, between wanting nothing and actively wanting Nothingness.

32. See Darian Leader, *Promises Lovers Make When It Gets Late*, London: Faber & Faber 1997, pp. 49–66.

33. Ibid., p. 56.

34. See Carl Schmitt, *Political Theology: Four Chapters on the Concept of Sovereignty*, Cambridge, MA: MIT Press 1988.

35. See Miran Božovič, 'Malebranche's Occasionalism, or, Philosophy in the Garden of Eden', in *Cogito and the Unconscious*, ed. Slavoj Žižek, Durham, NC: Duke University Press 1998.

36. Nicolas Malebranche, *Treatise on Nature and Grace*, Oxford: Clarendon Press 1992, pp. 140–41.

37. Nicolas Malebranche, *Traité de morale*, Paris: Garnier–Flammarion 1995, p. 41.

38. Malebranche's use of the term 'occasionalism' is thus highly idiosyncratic in that it combines this meaning (the need for a particular cause to supplement the universal law) with a different meaning which refers to the (lack of a direct) relationship between the two substances: since there is no direct connection between body and soul – since a body cannot directly act upon a soul (and vice versa), the co-ordination between the two (the fact that when I think about raising my hand, my hand actually goes up) must be guaranteed by God's general will. In this second case, an occasional cause (say, my intention to raise my hand) does not have to rely only on general laws in order to connect with other objects of the same order (my other intentions and thoughts): the divine general laws also have to sustain the co-ordination between two totally independent series of particular events, the 'mental' and 'bodily' series.

39. One should be attentive here to the implicit dialectic of the Universal and its exception: the Universal is merely potential, 'prelapsarian', and it realizes itself via the Fall, in the guise of the contingently distributed particular Grace.

40. See also Fenelon's version: 'it is precisely because we have a Saviour that so many souls perish' ('Réfutations du système du Père Malebranche', in *Œuvres de Fenelon*, Paris: Chez Lefevre 1835, ch. 36).

41. Nicolas Malebranche, *Entretiens sur la métaphysique*, Paris: Vrin 1984, p. 117.

42. Nicolas Malebranche, *Recherche de la vérité*, Paris: Galerie de la Sorbonne 1991, p. 428.

43. Ibid., p. 431.

44. Ibid.

PART II

The Split Universality

3

The Politics of Truth, or, Alain Badiou as a Reader of St Paul

'The beginning is the negation of that which begins with it'[1] – Schelling's statement applies perfectly to the itinerary of the four contemporary political philosophers who began as Althusserians and then elaborated their own distinctive position by distancing themselves from their starting point. The cases that immediately spring to mind are, of course, those of Étienne Balibar and Jacques Rancière.

Back in the 1960s, Balibar was Althusser's favoured pupil and privileged collaborator; all his work in the last decade, however, is sustained by a kind of avoidance of (and silence about) the name 'Althusser' (significantly, his key essay on Althusser bears the title '*Tais-toi, Althusser!*': 'Shut up [remain silent], Althusser!'). In a revealing commemorative essay, Balibar describes the last phase of Althusser's theoretical activity (even prior to his unfortunate mental health problems) as a systematic pursuit of (or exercise in) self-destruction, as if Althusser was caught in the vortex of a systematic undermining and subverting of his own previous theoretical propositions. Against the background of this debris of the Althusserian theoretical edifice, Balibar painfully endeavours to formulate his own position, not always in a fully consistent way, often combining the standard Althusserian references (Spinoza) with references to Althusser's archenemies (note the growing importance of Hegel in Balibar's recent essays).

Rancière, who also began as a strict Althusserian (with a contribution to *Lire le Capital*), then (in *La leçon d'Althusser*), accomplished a violent gesture of distancing, which enabled him to follow his own path, focusing on what he perceived as the main negative aspect of Althusser's thought: his theoreticist elitism, his insistence on the gap forever separating the universe of scientific cognition from that of ideological (mis)recognition in which the common masses are immersed. Against this stance, which allows theoreticians to 'speak for' the masses, to know the truth about them, Rancière endeavours again and again to elaborate the contours of those magic, violently poetic moments of subjectivization in which the excluded ('lower classes') put forward their claim to speak for themselves, to effect a change in the global perception of the social space so that their claims have a legitimate place in it.

In a more mediated way, the same also holds for Ernesto Laclau and Alain Badiou. Laclau's first book (*Politics and Ideology in Marxist Theory*) was still strongly Althusserian (the notion of ideological interpellation plays a central role in it); his further development, especially in *Hegemony and Socialist Strategy* (written with Chantal Mouffe), could be read as a kind of 'postmodernist' or 'deconstructionist' displacement of the Althusserian edifice: the distinction between science and ideology collapses, since the notion of ideology is universalized as the struggle for hegemony that rends the very heart of every social formation, accounting for its fragile identity and, simultaneously, forever preventing its closure; the notion of the subject is reconceptualized as the very operator of hegemony. Finally, there is the strange case of Alain Badiou. Is not Badiou also intimately related to Althusser, not only on the level of his personal intellectual biography (he began as a member of the Lacano–Althusserian legendary *Cahiers pour l'Analyse* group in the 1960s; his first booklet was published in Althusser's *Théorie* series) but also on the inherent theoretical level: his opposition of knowledge (related to the positive order of Being) and truth (related to the Event that springs from the void in the midst of being) seems to reverse the Althusserian opposition of science and ideology: Badiou's 'knowledge' is closer to (a positivist notion of) science, while his description of the Truth-Event bears an uncanny resemblance to Althusserian 'ideological interpellation'.

The Truth-Event . . .

The axis of Badiou's theoretical edifice is – as the title of his main work indicates – the gap between Being and Event.[2] 'Being' stands for the positive ontological order accessible to Knowledge, for the infinite multitude of what 'presents itself' in our experience, categorized in genuses and species in accordance with its properties. According to Badiou, the only proper science of Being-as-Being is mathematics – his first paradoxical conclusion is thus to insist on the gap that separates philosophy from ontology: ontology is mathematical science, not philosophy, which involves a different dimension. Badiou provides an elaborated analysis of Being. At the bottom, as it were, is the presentation of the pure multiple, the not yet symbolically structured multitude of experience, that which is given; this multitude is not a multitude of 'Ones', since counting has not yet taken place. Badiou calls any particular consistent multitude (French society; modern art . . .) a 'situation'; a situation is structured, and it is its structure that allows us to 'count [the situation] as One'. Here, however, the first cracks in the ontological edifice of Being already appear: for us to 'count [the situation] as One', the 'reduplication' proper to the symbolization (symbolic inscription) of a situation must be at work: that is, in order for a situation to be 'counted as One', its structure must always-already be a meta-structure that designates it as one (i.e. the signified structure of the situation must be redoubled in the symbolic network of signifiers). When a situation is thus 'counted as One', identified by its symbolic structure, we have the 'state of the situation'. Here Badiou is playing on the ambiguity of the term state: 'state of things' as well as State (in the political sense) – there is no 'state of society' without a 'state' in which the structure of society is re-presented/redoubled.

This symbolic *reduplicatio* already involves the minimal dialectic of Void and Excess. The pure multiple of Being is not yet a multitude of Ones, since, as we have just seen, to have One, the pure multiple must be 'counted as One'; from the standpoint of the state of a situation, the preceding multiple can only appear as *nothing*, so nothing is the 'proper name of Being as Being' prior to its symbolization. The Void is the central category of ontology from Democritus' atomism onwards: 'atoms' are nothing but configurations of the Void. The excess correlative to this Void takes two forms. On the one hand, each state of things involves at least one excessive element which, although it clearly belongs to the situation, is not 'counted' by it, properly included in it (the 'non-integrated' rabble in a social situation, etc.): this element is presented, but not re-presented. On the other hand, there is the excess of re-presentation over presentation: the agency that brings about the passage from situation to its state (State in society) is always in excess with regard to what it structures: State power is necessarily 'excessive', it never simply and transparently re-presents society (the impossible liberal dream of a state reduced to the service of civil society), but acts as a violent intervention in what it re-presents.

This, then, is the structure of Being. From time to time, however, in a wholly contingent, unpredictable way, out of reach for Knowledge of Being, an Event takes place that belongs to a wholly different dimension

– that, precisely, of non-Being. Let us take French society in the late eighteenth century: the state of society, its strata, economic, political, ideological conflicts, and so on, are accessible to knowledge. However, no amount of Knowledge will enable us to predict or account for the properly unaccountable Event called the 'French Revolution'. In this precise sense, the Event emerges *ex nihilo*: if it cannot be accounted for in terms of the situation, this does not mean that it is simply an intervention from Outside or Beyond – it attaches itself precisely to the Void of every situation, to its inherent inconsistency and/or its excess. The Event is the Truth of the situation that makes visible/legible what the 'official' situation had to 'repress', but it is also always localized – that is to say, the Truth is always the Truth *of* a specific situation. The French Revolution, for example, is the Event which makes visible/legible the excesses and inconsistencies, the 'lie', of the *ancien régime*; and it is the Truth *of* the *ancien régime* situation, localized, attached to it. An Event thus involves its own series of determinations: the Event itself; its naming (the designation 'French Revolution' is not an objective categorizing but part of the Event itself, the way its followers perceived and symbolized their activity); its ultimate Goal (the society of fully realized emancipation, of freedom–equality–fraternity); its 'operator' (the political movements struggling for the Revolution; and, last but not least, its *subject*, the agent who, on behalf of the Truth-Event, intervenes in the historical multiple of the situation and discerns/identifies in it signs–effects of the Event. What defines the subject is his *fidelity* to the Event: the subject comes *after* the Event and persists in discerning its traces within his situation.

The subject is thus, for Badiou, a finite contingent emergence: not only is Truth not 'subjective' in the sense of being subordinated to his whims, but the subject himself 'serves the Truth' that transcends him; he is never fully adequate to the infinite order of Truth, since the subject always has to operate within a finite multiple of a situation in which he discerns the signs of Truth. To make this crucial point clear, let us take the example of the Christian religion (which perhaps provides *the* example of a Truth-Event): the Event is Christ's incarnation and death; its ultimate Goal is the Last Judgement, the final Redemption; its 'operator' in the multiple of the historical situation is the Church; its 'subject' is the corpus of believers who intervene in their situation on behalf of the Truth-Event, searching in it for signs of God. (Or, to take the example of love: when I fall passionately in love, I become 'subjectivized' by remaining faithful to this Event and following it in my life.)

Today, however, when even the most radical intellectual succumbs to the compulsion to distance himself from Communism, it seems more appropriate to reassert the October Revolution as an Event of Truth defined against the opportunistic leftist 'fools' and conservative 'knaves'. The October Revolution also allows us to identify clearly three ways of betraying the Truth-Event: simple disavowal, the attempt to follow old patterns as if nothing had happened, just a minor disturbance (the reaction of 'utilitarian' liberal democracy); false imitation of the Event of Truth (the Fascist staging of the conservative revolution as a pseudo-event); and a direct 'ontologicization' of the Event of Truth, its reduction to a new positive order of being (Stalinism).[3] Here one can readily grasp the gap that separates Badiou from deconstructionist fictionalism: his radical opposition to the notion of a 'multitude of truths' (or, rather, 'truth-effects'). Truth is contingent; it hinges on a concrete historical situation; it is the truth *of* this situation, but in every concrete and contingent historical situation there is *one and only one* Truth which, once articulated, spoken out, functions as the index of itself and of the falsity of the field subverted by it.

When Badiou speaks of 'this symptomal torsion of being which is a truth in the always-total texture of knowledges',[4] every term has its weight. The texture of Knowledge is, by definition, always total – that is, for Knowledge of Being, there is no excess; excess and lack of a situation are visible only from the standpoint of the Event, not from the standpoint of the knowing servants of the State. From within this standpoint, of course, one sees 'problems', but they are automatically reduced to 'local', marginal difficulties, to contingent errors – what Truth does is to reveal that (what Knowledge misperceives as) marginal malfunctionings and points of failure are a structural necessity. Crucial for the Event is thus the elevation of an empirical obstacle into a transcendental limitation. With regard to the *ancien régime*, what the Truth-Event reveals is how injustices are not marginal malfunctionings but pertain to the very structure of the system which is in its essence, as such, 'corrupt'. Such an entity – which, misperceived by the system as a local 'abnormality', effectively condenses the global 'abnormality' of the system as such, in its entirety – is what, in the Freudo–Marxian tradition, is called the *symptom*: in psychoanalysis, lapses, dreams, compulsive formations and acts, and so on, are 'symptomal torsions' that make accessible the subject's Truth, inaccessible to Knowledge, which sees them as mere malfunctionings; in Marxism, economic crisis is such a 'symptomal torsion'.

Here Badiou is clearly and radically opposed to the postmodern anti-Platonic thrust whose basic dogma is that the era when it was still possible to base a political movement on a direct reference to some eternal metaphysical or transcendental truth is definitely over: the experience of our century proves that such a reference to some metaphysical a priori can lead only to catastrophic 'totalitarian' social consequences. For this reason, the only solution is to accept that we live in a new era deprived of metaphysical certainties, in an era of contingency and conjectures, in a 'risk society' in which politics is a matter of *phronesis*, of strategic judgements and dialogue, not of applying fundamental cognitive insights. . . . What Badiou is aiming at, against this postmodern *doxa*, is precisely the resuscitation of the *politics of (universal) Truth* in today's conditions of global contingency. Thus Badiou rehabilitates, in the modern conditions of multiplicity and contingency, not only philosophy but the properly *meta-physical* dimension: the infinite Truth is 'eternal' and *meta-* with regard to the temporal process of Being; it is a flash of another dimension transcending the positivity of Being.

The latest version of the disavowal of Truth is provided by the New Age opposition to the *hubris* of so-called Cartesian subjectivity and its mechanicist dominating attitude towards nature. According to the New Age cliché, the original sin of modern Western civilization (as, indeed, of the Judaeo-Christian tradition) is man's *hubris*, his arrogant assumption that he occupies the central place in the universe and/or that he is endowed with the divine right to dominate all other beings and exploit them for his profit. This *hubris*, which disturbs the rightful balance of cosmic powers, sooner or later forces Nature to re-establish that balance: today's ecological, social and psychic crisis is interpreted as the universe's justified answer to man's presumption. Our only solution thus lies in the shift of the global paradigm, in adopting the new holistic attitude in which we will humbly assume our constrained place in the global Order of Being. . . .

In contrast to this cliché, one should assert the excess of subjectivity (what Hegel called the 'night of the world') as the only hope of redemption: true evil lies not in the excess of subjectivity as such, but in its 'ontologization', in its reinscription into some global cosmic framework. Already in de Sade, excessive cruelty is ontologically 'covered' by the order of Nature as the 'Supreme Being of Evil'; both Nazism and Stalinism involved the reference to some global Order of Being (in the case of Stalinism, the dialectical organization of the movement of matter).

True arrogance is thus the very opposite of the acceptance of the *hubris* of subjectivity: it lies in false humility – that is to say, it emerges when the subject pretends to speak and act on behalf of the Global Cosmic Order, posing as its humble instrument. In contrast to this false humility, the entire Western stance was anti-global: not only does Christianity involve reference to a higher Truth which cuts into and disturbs the old pagan order of Cosmos expressed in profound Wisdoms; even Plato's Idealism itself can be qualified as the first clear elaboration of the idea that the global cosmic 'Chain of Being' is not 'all there is', that there is another Order (of Ideas) which suspends the validity of the Order of Being.

One of Badiou's great theses is that the pure multiple lacks the dignity of the proper object of thought: from Stalin to Derrida, philosophical common sense has always insisted on infinite complexity (everything is interconnected; reality is so complex that it is accessible to us only in approximations . . .). Badiou implicitly condemns deconstructionism itself as the latest version of this common-sense motif of infinite complexity. Among the advocates of 'anti-essentialist' postmodern identity politics, for example, one often encounters the insistence that there is no 'woman in general', there are only white middle-class women, black single mothers, lesbians, and so on. One should reject such 'insights' as banalities unworthy of being objects of thought. The problem of philosophical thought lies precisely in how the universality of 'woman' emerges out of this endless multitude. Thus, one can also rehabilitate the Hegelian difference between bad (spurious) and proper infinity: the first refers to common-sense infinite complexity; the second concerns the infinity of an Event, which, precisely, transcends the 'infinite complexity' of its context. In exactly the same way one can distinguish between historicism and historicity proper: historicism refers to the set of economic, political, cultural, and so on, circumstances whose complex interaction allows us to account for the Event to be explained, while historicity proper involves the specific temporality of the Event and its aftermath, the span between the Event and its final End (between Christ's death and the Last Judgement, between Revolution and Communism, between falling in love and the accomplished bliss of living together . . .).

Perhaps the gap separating Badiou from the standard postmodern deconstructionist political theorists is ultimately created by the fact that the latter remain within the confines of the pessimistic wisdom of the failed encounter: is not the ultimate deconstructionist lesson that every enthusiastic encounter with the Real Thing, every pathetic identification of a positive empirical Event with it, is a delusive semblance sustained by the short circuit between a contingent positive element and the preceding universal Void? In it, we momentarily succumb to the illusion that the promise of impossible Fullness is actually realized – that, to paraphrase Derrida, democracy is no longer merely *à venir* but has actually arrived; from this, deconstructionists draw the conclusion that the principal ethico-political duty is to maintain the gap between the Void of the central impossibility and every positive content giving body to it – that is, never fully to succumb to the enthusiasm of hasty identification of a positive Event with the redemptive Promise that is always 'to come'. In this deconstructionist stance, admiration for the Revolution in its utopian enthusiastic aspect goes hand in hand with the conservative melancholic insight that enthusiasm inevitably turns into its opposite, into the worst terror, the moment we endeavour to transpose it into the positive structuring principle of social reality.

It may seem that Badiou remains within this framework: does not he also warn against the *désastre* of the revolutionary temptation to confound the Truth-Event with the order of Being: of the attempt to 'ontologize' Truth into the ontological principle of the order of Being? However, things are more complex: Badiou's position is that although the universal Order has the status of a semblance, from time to time, in a contingent and unpredictable way, a 'miracle' can happen in the guise of a Truth-Event that deservedly shames a postmodernist sceptic. What he has in mind is a very precise political experience. For example, in France, during the first Mitterrand government in the early 1980s, all well-meaning Leftists were sceptical about Minister of Justice Robert Badinter's intention to abolish the death penalty and introduce other progressive reforms of the penal code. Their stance was 'Yes, of course we support him; but is the situation yet ripe for it? Will the people, terrified by the rising crime rate, be willing to swallow it? Isn't this a case of idealistic obstinacy that can only weaken our government, and do us more harm than good?'. Badinter simply ignored the catastrophic predictions of the opinion polls, and persisted – with the surprising result that, all of a sudden, it was the majority of the people who changed their minds and started to support him.

A similar event happened in Italy in the mid 1970s, when there was a referendum on divorce. In private, the Left, even the Communists – who, of course, supported the right to divorce – were sceptical about the outcome, fearing that the majority of people were not yet mature enough, that they would be frightened by the intense Catholic propaganda depicting abandoned children and mothers, and so on. To the great surprise of everyone, however, the referendum was a great setback for the Church and the Right, since a considerable majority of 60 per cent voted for the right to divorce. Events like this do occur in politics, and they are authentic Events belying shameful 'post-ideological realism': they are not momentary enthusiastic outbursts occasionally disturbing the usual depressive/conformist/utilitarian run of things, only to be followed by an inexorable sobering disillusionment 'the morning after'; on the contrary, they are the moment of Truth in the overall structure of deception and lure. The fundamental lesson of postmodernist politics is that *there is no Event*, that 'nothing really happens', that the Truth-Event is a passing, illusory short circuit, a false identification to be dispelled sooner or later by the reassertion of difference or, at best, the fleeting promise of the Redemption-to-come, towards which we have to maintain a proper distance in order to avoid catastrophic 'totalitarian' consequences; against this structural scepticism, Badiou is fully justified in insisting that – to use the term with its full theological weight – *miracles do happen. . . .*[5]

. . . and Its Undecidability

We can now see the sense in which the Truth-Event is 'undecidable': it is undecidable from the standpoint of the System, of the ontological 'state of things'. An Event is thus circular in the sense that its identification is possible only from the standpoint of what Badiou calls 'an *interpreting intervention*'[6] – if, that is, one speaks from a subjectively engaged position, or – to put it more formally – if one includes in the designated situation the act of naming itself: the chaotic events in France at the end of the eighteenth century can be identified as the 'French Revolution' only for those who accept the 'wager' that such an Event exists. Badiou formally defines *intervention* as 'every procedure by means of which a multiple is recognized as an event'[7] – so 'it will remain forever doubtful if there was an event at all, except for the intervenor. [*l'intervenant*] who decided that he belonged to the situation'.[8] Fidelity to the Event designates the continuous effort of traversing the field of knowledge from the standpoint of Event, intervening in it, searching for the signs of Truth. Along these lines, Badiou also interprets the Pauline triad of Faith, Hope and Love: Faith is faith in the Event (the belief that the Event – Christ's rising from the dead – really took place); Hope is the hope that the final reconciliation announced by the Event (the Last Judgement) will actually occur; Love is the patient struggle for this to happen, that is, the long and arduous work to assert one's fidelity to the Event.

Badiou calls the language that endeavours to name the Truth-Event the 'subject-language'. This language is meaningless from the standpoint of Knowledge, which judges propositions with regard to their referent within the domain of positive being (or with regard to the proper functioning of speech within the established symbolic order): when the subject-language speaks of Christian redemption, revolutionary emancipation, love, and so on, Knowledge dismisses all this as empty phrases lacking any proper referent ('political-messianic jargon', 'poetic hermeticism', etc.). Let us imagine a person in love describing the features of his beloved to his friend: the friend, who is not in love with the same person, will simply find this enthusiastic description meaningless; he will not get 'the point' of it. . . . In short, subject-language involves the logic of the shibboleth, of a difference which is visible only from within, not from without. This, however, in no way means that the subject-language involves another, 'deeper' reference to a hidden true content: it is, rather, that the subject-language, 'derails' or 'unsettles' the standard use of language with its established meanings, and leaves the reference 'empty' – with the 'wager' that this void will be filled when the Goal is reached, when Truth actualizes itself as a new situation (God's kingdom on earth; the emancipated society . . .). The naming of the Truth-Event is 'empty' precisely in so far as it refers to the fullness yet to come.

The undecidability of the Event thus means that an Event does not possess any ontological guarantee: it cannot be reduced to (or deduced, generated from) a (previous) Situation: it emerges 'out of nothing' (the Nothing which was the ontological truth of this previous situation). Thus there is no neutral gaze of knowledge that could discern the Event in its effects: a Decision is always-already here – that is, one can discern the signs of an Event in the Situation only from a previous Decision for Truth, just as in Jansenist theology, in which divine miracles are legible as such only to those who have already decided for Faith. A neutral historicist gaze will never see in the French Revolution a series of traces of the Event called the 'French Revolution', merely a multitude of occurrences caught in the network of social determinations; to an external gaze, Love is merely a succession of psychic and physiological states. . . . (Perhaps this was the negative achievement that brought such fame to François Furet: did not his main impact derive from his de-eventualization of the French Revolution, in adopting an external perspective towards it and turning it into a succession of complex specific historical facts?) The engaged observer perceives positive historical occurrences as parts of the Event of the French Revolution only to the extent that he observes them from the unique engaged standpoint of Revolution – as Badiou puts it, an Event is self-referential in that *it includes its own designation*: the symbolic designation 'French Revolution' is part of the designated content itself, since, if we subtract this designation, the described content turns into a multitude of positive occurrences available to knowledge. In this precise sense, an Event involves subjectivity: the engaged 'subjective perspective' on the Event is part of the Event itself.[9]

The difference between veracity (the accuracy–adequacy of knowledge) and Truth is crucial here. Let us take the Marxist thesis that all history is the history of class struggle: this thesis already presupposes engaged subjectivity – that is to say, only from this slant does the whole of history appear as such; only from this 'interested' standpoint can one discern traces of the class struggle in the entire social edifice, up to the products of the highest culture. The answer to the obvious counter-argument (this very fact proves that we are dealing with a distorted view, not with the true state of things) is that it is the allegedly 'objective', 'impartial' gaze that is not in fact neutral but already partial – that is, the gaze of the winners, of the ruling classes. (No wonder the motto of right-wing historical revisionists is 'Let's approach the topic of the Holocaust in a cool, objective way; let's put it in its context, let's inspect the facts . . .') A theorist of the Communist revolution is not someone who, after establishing by means of objective study that the future belongs to the working class, decides to take its side and to bet on the winner: the engaged view permeates his theory from the very outset.

Within the Marxist tradition, this notion of partiality as not only not an obstacle to but a positive condition of Truth was most clearly articulated by Georg Lukács in his early work *History and Class Consciousness*, and in a more directly messianic, proto-religious mode by Walter Benjamin in 'Theses on the Philosophy of History': 'truth' emerges when a victim, from his present catastrophic position, gains a sudden insight into the entire past as a series of catastrophes that led to his current predicament. So, when we read a text on Truth, we should be careful not to confuse the level of Knowledge with the level of Truth. For example, although Marx himself used 'proletariat' as synonymous with 'the working class' normally, one can none the less discern in his work a clear tendency to conceive 'the working class' as a descriptive term belonging to the domain of Knowledge (the object of 'neutral' sociological study, a social stratum subdivided into components, etc.); whereas 'proletariat' designates the operator of Truth, that is, the engaged agent of the revolutionary struggle.

Furthermore, the status of the pure multiple and its Void is also undecidable and purely 'intermediary': we never encounter it 'now', since it is always recognized as such retroactively, through the act of Decision that dissolves it – that is, by means of which we already pass over it. For example, Nazism as a pseudo-Event conceives of itself as the Decision for social Harmony and Order against the Chaos of modern liberal-Jewish-class-warfare society – however, modern society never perceives itself in the first person as fundamentally 'chaotic', it perceives 'chaos' (or 'disorder' or 'degeneration') as a limited, contingent deadlock, a temporary crisis – modern society appears as fundamentally 'chaotic' only from the standpoint of the Decision for Order, that is, once the Decision *is already made*. One should therefore resist the retroactive illusion according to which Decision *follows* the insight into the open undecidability of the situation: it is only the Decision itself that reveals the previous State as 'undecidable'. Prior to Decision, we inhabit a Situation which is enclosed in its horizon; from within this horizon, the Void constitutive of this Situation is by definition invisible; that is to say, undecidability is reduced to – and appears as – a marginal disturbance of the global System. After the Decision, undecidability is over, since we inhabit the new domain of Truth. The gesture that closes/decides the Situation (again) thus absolutely coincides with the gesture that (retroactively) opens it up.

The Event is thus the Void of an invisible line separating one closure from another: prior to it, the Situation was closed; that is, from within its horizon, (what will become) the Event necessarily appears as *skandalon*, as an undecidable, chaotic intrusion that has no place in the State of the Situation (or, to put it in mathematical terms, that is 'supernumerary'); once the Event takes place and is assumed as such, the very previous Situation appears as undecidable Chaos. For an established political Order, the revolutionary turmoil that threatens to overthrow it is a chaotic dislocation, while from the viewpoint of the Revolution, *ancien régime* itself is a name for disorder, for an impenetrable and ultimately 'irrational' despotism. Here Badiou is clearly opposed to the Derridean ethics of openness to the Event in its unpredictable alterity: such an emphasis on unpredictable Alterity as the ultimate horizon remains within the confines of a Situation, and serves only to defer or block the Decision – it involves us in the 'postmodernist' indefinite oscillation of 'how do we know this truly is the Event, not just another semblance of the Event?'

How *are* we to draw a demarcation line between a true Event and its semblance? Is not Badiou compelled to rely here on a 'metaphysical' opposition between Truth and its semblance? Again, the answer involves the way an Event relates to the Situation whose Truth it articulates: Nazism was a pseudo-Event and the October Revolution was an authentic Event, because only the latter related to the very foundations of the Situation of capitalist order, effectively undermining those foundations, in contrast to Nazism, which staged a pseudo-Event precisely in order to *save* the capitalist order. The Nazi strategy was 'to change things so that, at their most fundamental, they can remain the same'.

We all remember the famous scene from Bob Fosse's *Cabaret*, which takes place in the early 1930s, in a small country inn near Berlin: a boy (in Nazi uniform, as we learn in the course of the song) starts to sing a sorrowful elegiac song about the Fatherland, which should give Germans a sign that tomorrow belongs to them, and so on; the crowd gradually joins him, and everyone, including a group of decadent nightlifers from Berlin, is impressed by its emotional impact. . . . This scene is often evoked by pseudo-intellectuals as the moment when they 'finally grasped what Nazism was about, how it worked'. One is tempted to add that they are right, but for the wrong reasons: it is not the pathos of patriotic engagement *as such* that is 'Fascist'. What actually prepares the ground for Fascism is the very liberal suspicion and denunciation of every form of unconditional engagement, of devotion to a Cause, as potentially 'totalitarian' fanaticism – that is to say, the problem lies in the very complicity of the atmosphere of incapacitating cynical decadent self-enjoyment with the Fascist Event, with the Decision which purports to (re)introduce Order into this Chaos. In other words, what is false about the Nazi ideological machine is not the rhetoric of Decision as such (of the Event that puts an end to decadent impotence, etc.), but – on the contrary – the fact that the Nazi 'Event' is aestheticized theatre, a faked event effectively unable to put an end to the decadent crippling impasse. It is in this precise sense that the common reaction to the Nazi song from *Cabaret* is right for the wrong reasons: what it fails to perceive is how our former cynical pleasure in decadent cabaret songs about money and sexual promiscuity created the background that made us susceptible to the impact of the Nazi song.

So how are an Event and its naming related? Badiou rejects Kant's reading of the Event of the French Revolution, the reading which locates the crucial effect of the Revolution in the sublime feeling of enthusiasm that the revolutionary events in Paris set in motion in passive observers across Europe, not directly involved in the event itself, and then opposes this sublime effect (the assertion of our belief in the progress of man's Reason and Freedom) to the grim reality of the Revolution itself (Kant readily concedes that horrible things took place in France: the Revolution often served as the catalyst for the outburst of the lowest destructive passions of the wild mob). Badiou sarcastically remarks that such an aestheticization of the Revolution admired from a safe distance by passive observers goes hand in hand with the utmost loathing for the actual revolutionaries themselves. (Do we not again encounter here the tension between the Sublime and the Monstrous [*das Ungeheure*]: what appears from a proper distance to be the Sublime cause of enthusiasm turns into the figure of monstrous Evil, once we approach it too closely and get directly involved in it?)

Against this Kantian celebration of the sublime effect on passive observers, Badiou insists on the immanence of the Truth-Event: the Truth-Event is Truth in itself for its agents themselves, not for external observers. On a first approach, it may appear that Kant's position is more 'Lacanian' here: is not the Truth of an Event a priori decentred with regard to the Event itself; does it not depend on the mode of its inscription into the big Other (personified here by enlightened public opinion), which is always, a priori, deferred? Is not what is properly unthinkable precisely a Truth that would directly know itself as Truth? Is not the delay of comprehension constitutive (therein lies the Hegelian materialist lesson: the Owl of Minerva flies only at dusk)? Furthermore, if a Truth-Event is radically immanent, how are we to distinguish Truth from its simulacrum? Is it not only the reference to the decentred big Other that enables us to draw this distinction?

Badiou none the less provides a precise criterion for this distinction in the way an Event relates to its conditions, to the 'situation' out of which it arose: a true Event emerges out of the 'void' of the situation; it is attached to its *élément surnuméraire*: to the symptomatic element that has no proper place in the situation, although it belongs to it, while the simulacrum of an Event disavows the symptom. For this reason, the Leninist October Revolution remains an Event, since it relates to the 'class struggle' as the symptomatic torsion of its situation, while the Nazi movement is a simulacrum, a disavowal of the trauma of class struggle. . . . The difference lies not in the inherent qualities of the Event itself, but in its place – in the way it relates to the situation out of which it emerged. As for the external gaze that bears witness to the Truth of the Event, this gaze is able to discern that Truth only in so far as it is the gaze of the individuals who are already engaged on its behalf: there is no neutral enlightened public opinion to be impressed by the Event, since Truth is discernible only for the potential members of the new Community of 'believers', for their engaged gaze.

In this way, we can paradoxically retain both distance *and* engagement:

in the case of Christianity, the Event (Crucifixion) becomes a Truth-Event 'after the fact', that is, when it leads to the constitution of the group of believers, of the engaged Community held together by fidelity to the Event. There is thus a difference between an Event and its naming: an Event is the traumatic encounter with the Real (Christ's death; the historic shock of revolution; etc.), while its naming is the inscription of the Event into the language (Christian doctrine, revolutionary consciousness). In Lacanese, an Event is *objet petit a*, while naming is the new signifier that establishes what Rimbaud calls the New Order, the new readability of the situation based on Decision (in the Marxist revolutionary perspective, the entire prior history becomes a history of class struggle, of defeated emancipatory striving).

Truth and Ideology

From this brief description one can already get a presentiment of what one is tempted to call, in all naivety, the intuitive power of Badiou's notion of the subject: it effectively describes the experience each of us has when he or she is subjectively fully engaged in some Cause which is 'his or her own': in those precious moments, am I not 'fully a subject'? But does not this very feature make it *ideological?* That is to say, the first thing that strikes the eye of anyone who is versed in the history of French Marxism is how Badiou's notion of the Truth-Event is uncannily close to Althusser's notion of ideological interpellation. Furthermore, is it not significant that Badiou's ultimate example of the Event is *religion* (Christianity from St Paul to Pascal) as the prototype of *ideology*, and that this event, precisely, does *not* fit any of the four *génériques* of the event he enumerates (love, art, science, politics)?[10]

So, perhaps, if we take Badiou's thought itself as a 'situation' of Being, subdivided into four *génériques*, (Christian) religion itself is his 'symptomal torsion', the element that belongs to the domain of Truth without being one of its acknowledged parts or subspecies? This seems to indicate that the Truth-Event consists in the elementary ideological gesture of interpellating individuals (parts of a 'situation' of Being) into subjects (bearers/followers of Truth). One is tempted to go even a step further: the paradigmatic example of the Truth-Event is not only religion in general but, specifically, *Christian* religion centred on the Event of Christ's arrival and death (as Kierkegaard had already pointed out, Christianity inverts the standard metaphysical relationship between Eternity and Time: in a way, Eternity itself hinges on the temporal Event of Christ). So perhaps Badiou can also be read as the last great author in the French tradition of Catholic dogmaticists from Pascal and Malebranche on (we need only recall that two of his key references are Pascal and Claudel). For years the parallel between revolutionary Marxism and Messianic Christianity was a common topic among liberal critics like Bertrand Russell, who dismissed Marxism as a secularized version of Messianic religious ideology; Badiou, in contrast (following a line from the later Engels to Fredric Jameson), fully endorses this homology.

This reading is further confirmed by Badiou's passionate defence of St Paul as the one who articulated the Christian Truth-Event – Christ's Resurrection – as the 'universal singular' (a singular event that interpellates individuals into subjects universally, irrespectively of their race, sex, social class . . .) and the conditions of the followers' fidelity to it.[11] Of course, here Badiou is well aware that today, in our era of modern science, one can no longer accept the fable of the miracle of Resurrection as the form of the Truth-Event. Although the Truth-Event does designate the occurrence of something which, from within the horizon of the predominant order of Knowledge, appears impossible (think of the laughter with which the Greek philosophers greeted St Paul's assertion of Christ's Resurrection on his visit to Athens), today, any location of the Truth-Event at the level of supernatural miracles necessarily entails regression into obscurantism, since the event of Science is irreducible and cannot be undone. Today, one can accept as the Truth-Event, as the intrusion of the traumatic Real that shatters the predominant symbolic texture, only occurrences which take place in a universe compatible with scientific knowledge, even if they move at its borders and question its presuppositions – the 'sites' of the Event today are scientific discovery itself, the political act, artistic invention, the psychoanalytic confrontation with love. . . .

That is the problem with Graham Greene's drama The Potting Shed, which endeavours to resuscitate the Christian version of the shattering impact of the impossible Real: the life of the family of a great positivist philosopher who dedicated his whole effort to fighting religious superstitions is thoroughly shattered by an unexpected miracle: his son, the object of the philosopher's greatest love, is mortally ill and already proclaimed dead when, miraculously, he is brought back to life by means of what, evidently, cannot be anything but a direct intervention of Divine Grace. The story is told in retrospect from the standpoint of a family friend who, after the philosopher's death, writes his biography and is puzzled by an enigma in the latter's life: why, a couple of years before his death, did the philosopher suddenly stop writing; why did he lose his will to live, as if his life was suddenly deprived of meaning, and enter a period of resignation, passively awaiting his death? Interviewing the surviving family members, he soon discovers that there is a dark family secret nobody wants to talk about, until, finally, one of the family breaks down and confesses to him that the shattering secret is the miraculous resuscitation of the philosopher's son, which rendered his entire theoretical work, his lifelong engagement, meaningless.... Intriguing as it is, such a story cannot effectively engage us today.

Apropos of St Paul, Badiou tackles the problem of locating his position with regard to the four *génériques* that generate effective truths (science, politics, art, love) – that is, with regard to the fact that (today, at least) Christianity, based on a fabulous event of Resurrection, cannot be counted as an effective Truth-Event, but merely as its semblance. His proposed solution is that St Paul is the anti-philosophical *theoretician of the formal conditions of the truth-procedure*; what he provides is the first detailed articulation of how fidelity to a Truth-Event operates in its universal dimension: the excessive, *surnuméraire* Real of a Truth-Event ('Resurrection') that emerges by Grace (i.e. cannot be accounted for in the terms of the constituents of the given situation) sets in motion, in the subjects who recognize themselves in its call, the militant 'work of Love', that is, the struggle to disseminate, with persistent fidelity, this Truth in its universal scope, as concerning everyone. So although St Paul's particular message is no longer operative for us, the very terms in which he formulates the operative mode of the Christian religion do possess a universal scope as relevant for every Truth-Event: every Truth-Event leads to a kind of 'Resurrection,' – through fidelity to it and a labour of Love on its behalf, one enters another dimension irreducible to mere *service des biens*, to the smooth running of affairs in the domain of Being, the domain of Immortality, of Life unencumbered by death.... None the less, the problem remains of how it was possible for the first and still most pertinent description of the mode of operation of the fidelity to a Truth-Event to occur apropos of a Truth-Event that is a mere semblance, not an actual Truth.

From a Hegelian standpoint there is a deep necessity in this, confirmed by the fact that in our century the philosopher who provided the definitive description of an authentic political *act* (Heidegger in *Being and Time*) was seduced by a political act that was undoubtedly a fake, not an actual Truth-Event (Nazism). So it is as if, if one is to express the formal structure of fidelity to the Truth-Event, one has to do it apropos of an Event that is merely its own semblance. Perhaps the lesson of all this is more radical than it appears: what if what Badiou calls the Truth-Event *is*, at its most radical, a purely formal act of decision, not only not based on an actual truth, but ultimately *indifferent* to the precise status (actual or fictitious) of the Truth-Event it refers to? What if we are dealing here with an inherent key component of the Truth-Event – what if the true fidelity to the Event is 'dogmatic' in the precise sense of unconditional Faith, of an attitude which does not ask for good reasons and which, for that very reason, cannot be refuted by any 'argumentation'?

So, back to our main line of argument: Badiou defines as 'generic' the multiple within a situation that has no particular properties, reference to which would enable us to classify it as its subspecies: the 'generic' multiple belongs to the situation, but is not properly included in it as its subspecies (the 'rabble' in Hegel's philosophy of law, for example). A multiple element/part of the situation which does not fit into it, which sticks out, is generic precisely in so far as it directly gives body to the being of the situation as such. It subverts the situation by directly embodying its universality. And, with regard to Badiou's own classification of generic procedures in four species (politics, art, science, love), does not religious ideology occupy precisely this generic place? It is none of them, yet precisely as such it gives body to the generic as such.[12]

Is not this identity of the Truth-Event and ideology further confirmed by *futur antérieur* as the specific temporality of generic procedures? Starting from the naming of the Event (Christ's death, Revolution), generic procedure searches for its signs in the multitude with a view to the final goal that will bring full plenitude (the Last Judgement, Communism, or, in Mallarmé, *le Livre*). Generic procedures thus involve a temporal loop: fidelity to the Event enables them to judge the historic multiple from the standpoint of plenitude to come, but the arrival of this plenitude already involves the subjective act of Decision – or, in Pascalian, the 'wager' on it. Are we thus not close to what Laclau describes as hegemony? Let us take the democratic-egalitarian political Event: reference to the Democratic Revolution enables us to read history as a continuous democratic struggle aiming at total emancipation; the present situation is experienced as fundamentally 'dislocated', 'out of joint' (the corruption of the *ancien régime*, class society, fallen terrestrial life) with regard to the promise of a redeemed future. For the language-subject, 'now' is always a time of antagonism, split between the corrupt 'state of things' and the promise of Truth.

So, again, is not Badiou's notion of the Truth-Event uncannily close to Althusser's notion of (ideological) interpellation? Isn't the process Badiou is describing that of an individual interpellated into a subject by a Cause? (Significantly, in order to describe the formal structure of fidelity to the Truth-Event, he uses the same example as Althusser in his description of the process of interpellation.) Is not the circular relationship between the Event and the subject (the subject serves the Event in his fidelity, but the Event itself is visible as such only to an already engaged subject) the very circle of ideology? Prior to constraining the notion of the subject to ideology – to identifying the subject as such as ideological – Althusser entertained for a short time the idea of the four modalities of subjectivity: the ideological subject, the subject in art, the subject of the Unconscious, the subject of science. Is there not a clear parallel between Badiou's four generics of truth (love, art, science, politics) and these four modalities of subjectivity (where love corresponds to the subject of the Unconscious, the topic of psychoanalysis, and politics, of course, to the subject of ideology)? The paradox is thus that Badiou's opposition of knowledge and truth seems to turn exactly around Althusser's opposition of ideology and science: 'non-authentic' knowledge is limited to the positive order of Being, blind to its structural void, to its symptomal torsion; while the engaged Truth that subjectivizes provides authentic insight into a situation.

St Paul with Badiou

According to a deep – albeit unexpected – logic, the topic of Pauline Christianity is also crucial for Badiou's confrontation with psychoanalysis. When Badiou adamantly opposes the 'morbid obsession with death', when he opposes the Truth-Event to the death drive, and so on, he is at his weakest, succumbing to the *temptation of the non-thought*. It is symptomatic that Badiou is compelled to identify the liberal-democratic *service des biens*, the smooth running of things in the positivity of Being where 'nothing actually happens', with the 'morbid obsession with death'. Although one can easily see the element of truth in this equation (mere *service des biens*, deprived of the dimension of Truth, far from being able to function as 'healthy' everyday life, not bothered by 'eternal' questions, necessarily regresses into nihilistic morbidity – as Christians would put it, there is true Life only in Christ, and life outside the Event of Christ sooner or later turns into its opposite, a morbid decadence; when we dedicate our life to excessive pleasures, these very pleasures are sooner or later spoiled), one should none the less insist here on what Lacan calls the space or distance *between the two deaths*: to put it in Badiou's Christian terms, in order to be able to open oneself up to the life of true Eternity, one has to suspend one's attachment to 'this' life and enter the domain of *ate*, the domain between the two deaths, the domain of the 'undead'.

This point is worthy of more detailed examination, since it condenses the gap that separates Badiou from Lacan and psychoanalysis in general. Badiou, of course, is also well aware of the opposition of two deaths (and two Lives): when St Paul opposes Life and Death (Spirit is Life, while Flesh brings Death), this opposition of Life and Death has nothing to do with the biological opposition of life and death as parts of the cycle of generation and corruption, or with the standard Platonic opposition of Soul and Body: for St Paul, 'Life' and 'Death', Spirit and Flesh, designate two subjective stances, two ways to live one's life. So when St Paul speaks of Death and Resurrection – rising into the eternal Life in Christ – this has nothing to do with biological life and death but, rather, provides the co-ordinates of the two fundamental 'existential attitudes' (to use this modern term anachronistically). This leads Badiou to a specific interpretation of Christianity which *radically dissociates Death and Resurrection*: they are not the same, they are not even dialectically interconnected in the sense of gaining access to eternal Life by paying the price of suffering which redeems us from our sins. For Badiou, Christ's death on the Cross simply signals that 'God became man', that eternal Truth is something immanent to human life, accessible to every human being. The message of the fact that God had to became man and to die (to suffer the fate of all flesh) in order to resurrect is that Eternal Life is something accessible to humanity, to all men as finite mortal beings: each of us can be touched by the Grace of the Truth-Event and enter the domain of Eternal Life. Here Badiou is openly anti-Hegelian: there is no dialectics of Life and Death, in the sense of the Truth-Event of Resurrection emerging as the magic reversal of negativity into positivity when we are fully ready to 'tarry with the negative', to assume our mortality and suffering at its most radical. The Truth-Event is simply a radically New Beginning; it designates the violent, traumatic and contingent intrusion of another dimension not 'mediated' by the domain of terrestrial finitude and corruption.

One must thus avoid the pitfalls of the morbid masochist morality that perceives suffering as inherently redeeming: this morality remains within the confines of the Law (which demands from us a price for the admission to Eternal Life), and is thus not yet at the level of the properly Christian notion of Love. As Badiou puts it, Christ's death is not in itself the Truth-Event, it simply prepares the site for the Event (Resurrection) by asserting the identity of God and Man – the fact that the infinite dimension of Immortal Truth is also accessible to a human finite mortal; what ultimately matters is only the Resurrection of the dead (i.e. human-mortal) Christ, signalling that each human being can be redeemed and can enter the domain of Eternal Life, that is, participate in the Truth-Event.

Therein lies the message of Christianity: the positivity of Being, the Order of the cosmos regulated by its Laws, which is the domain of finitude and mortality (from the standpoint of the cosmos, of the totality of positive Being, we are merely particular beings determined by our specific place in the global order – the Law is ultimately another name for the Order of cosmic Justice, which allocates to each of us his or her proper place), is not 'all there is'; there is another dimension, the dimension of True Life in Love, accessible to all of us through Divine Grace, so that we can all participate in it. Christian Revelation is thus an example (although probably *the* example) of how we, human beings, are not constrained to the positivity of Being; of how, from time to time, in a contingent and unpredictable way, a Truth-Event can occur that opens up to us the possibility of participating in Another Life by remaining faithful to the Truth-Event. The interesting thing to note is how Badiou here turns around the standard opposition of the Law as universal and Grace (or charisma) as particular, the idea that we are all subjected to the universal Divine Law, whereas only some of us are touched by Grace, and can thus be redeemed: in Badiou's reading of St Paul, on the contrary, it is Law itself which, 'universal' as it may appear, is ultimately 'particularist' (a legal order always imposes specific duties and rights on us, it is always a Law defining a specific community at the expense of excluding the members of other ethnic, etc., communities), while Divine Grace is truly universal, that is, non-exclusive, addressing all humans independently of their race, sex, social status, and so on.

We thus have two lives, the finite biological life and the infinite Life of participating in the Truth-Event of Resurrection. Correspondingly, there are also two deaths: the biological death and Death in the sense of succumbing to the 'way of all flesh'. How does St Paul determine this opposition of Life and Death as the two subjective, existential attitudes? Here we touch the crux of Badiou's argument, which also directly concerns psychoanalysis: for Badiou, the opposition of Death and Life overlaps with the opposition of Law and Love. For St Paul, succumbing to the temptations of the flesh does not simply mean indulging in unbridled terrestrial conquests (the search for pleasures, power, wealth . . .) irrespective of the Law (of moral prohibitions). On the contrary, his central tenet, elaborated in what is probably the (deservedly) most famous passage in his writings, Chapter 7, verse 7, in the Epistle to the Romans, is that there is no Sin prior to or independent of the Law: what comes before it is a simple innocent prelapsarian life forever lost to us mortal human beings. The universe we live in, *our* 'way of all flesh', is the universe in which Sin and Law, desire and its prohibition, are inextricably intertwined: it is the very act of Prohibition that gives rise to the desire for its transgression, that is, fixes our desire on the prohibited object:

> What then should we say? That the law is sin? By no means! Yet, if it had not been for the law, I would not have known sin, I would not have known what it is to covet if the law had not said, 'You shall not covet.' But sin, seizing an opportunity in the commandment, produces in me all kinds of covetousness. Apart from the law sin lies dead. I was once alive apart from the law, but when the commandment came, sin revived and I died, and the very commandment that promised life proved to be death to me. For sin, seizing an opportunity in the commandment, deceived me and through it killed me. . . . I do not understand my own actions. For I do not do what I want, but I do the very thing I hate. Now if I do what I do not want, I agree that the law is good. But in fact it is no longer I that do it, but sin that dwells within me. For I know that nothing good dwells within me, that is, in my flesh. I can will what is right, but I cannot do it.[13]

This passage, of course, must be seen in its context: in the whole of this part of the Epistle, the problem St Paul struggles with is how to avoid the trap of *perversion*, that is, of a Law that generates its transgression, since it needs it in order to assert itself as Law. For example, in Romans 3: 5–8, St Paul fires off a barrage of desperate questions:

> But if our injustice serves to confirm the justice of God, what should we say? That God is unjust to inflict wrath on us? . . . But if through my falsehood God's truthfulness abounds to his glory, why am I still being condemned as a sinner? And why not say (as some people slander us by saying that we say) 'Let us do evil so that good may come'?

This 'Let us do evil so that good may come [from it]' is the most succinct definition of the short circuit of the perverse position. Does this make God a closet pervert who brings about our fall so that He may then redeem us through His sacrifice, or – to quote Romans 11: 11 – 'have they stumbled so as to fall', that is, did we stumble (become involved in Sin, in the 'way of all flesh') because God needed our Fall as part of His plan of ultimate Redemption? If this is how things are, then the answer to the question 'Should we continue to sin in order that grace may abound?'(Romans 6: 1) is affirmative: it is only and precisely by indulging in Sin that we enable God to play His part as our Saviour. But St Paul's entire effort is to break out of this vicious cycle in which the prohibitive Law and its transgression generate and support each other.

In his *Philosophical Notebooks*, Lenin made the well-known statement that everyone who aims at really understanding Marx's *Capital* should read the whole of Hegel's *Logic* in detail. He then did it himself, supplementing quotes from Hegel with hundreds of ' *sics*' and marginal comments like: 'The first part of this sentence contains an ingenious dialectical insight; the second part is theological rubbish!' A task awaiting true Lacanian dialectical materialists is to repeat the same gesture with St Paul, since, again, everyone who aims at really understanding Lacan's *Écrits* should read the entire text of Romans and Corinthians in detail: one cannot wait for a Lacanian volume of *Theological Notebooks*, with quotes accompanied by hundreds of ' *sics*' and comments like: 'The first part of this sentence provides the deepest insight into Lacanian ethics, while the second part is just theological rubbish!' . . .[14]

So, back to the long quote from Romans: the direct result of the intervention of the Law is thus that it *divides* the subject and introduces a morbid confusion between life and death: the subject is divided between (conscious) obedience to the Law and (unconscious) desire for its transgression generated by the legal prohibition itself. It is not I, the subject, who transgress the Law, it is non-subjectivized 'Sin' itself, the sinful impulses in which I do not recognize myself, and which I even hate. Because of this split, my (conscious) Self is ultimately experienced as 'dead', as deprived of living impetus; while 'life', ecstatic affirmation of living energy, can appear only in the guise of 'Sin', of a transgression that gives rise to a morbid sense of guilt. My actual life-impulse, my desire, appears to me as a foreign automatism that persists in following its path independently of my conscious Will and intentions. St Paul's problem is thus not the standard morbid moralistic one (how to crush transgressive impulses, how finally to purify myself of sinful urges), but its exact opposite: how can I break out of this vicious cycle of the Law and desire, of the Prohibition and its transgression, within which I can assert my living passions only in the guise of their opposite, as a morbid death drive? How would it be possible for me to experience my life-impulse not as a foreign automatism, as a blind 'compulsion to repeat' making me transgress the Law, with the unacknowledged complicity of the Law itself, but as a fully subjectivized, positive 'Yes!' to my Life?

Here St Paul and Badiou seem fully to endorse Hegel's point that there is Evil only for the gaze that perceives something as Evil: it is the Law itself that not only opens up and sustains the domain of Sin, of sinful urges to transgress it, but also finds a perverse and morbid satisfaction in making us feel guilty about it. The ultimate result of the rule of the Law thus consists of all the well-known twists and paradoxes of the superego: I can enjoy only if I feel guilty about it, which means that, in a self-reflexive turn, I can take pleasure *in* feeling guilty; I can find enjoyment in punishing myself for sinful thoughts; and so on. So when Badiou speaks of the 'morbid fascination of the death drive', and so forth, he is not resorting to general platitudes, but referring to a very precise 'Pauline' reading of the psychoanalytic notions he uses: the entire complex entanglement of Law and desire – not only illicit sinful desires that go against the Law, but this morbid intertwining of life and death in which the 'dead' letter of the Law perverts my enjoyment of life itself, changing it into a fascination with death; this perverted universe in which the ascetic who flagellates himself on behalf of the Law enjoys more intensely than the person who takes innocent pleasure in earthly delights – is what St Paul designates as 'the way of the Flesh' as opposed to 'the way of the Spirit': 'Flesh' is not flesh as opposed to the Law, but flesh as an excessive self-torturing, mortifying morbid fascination *begotten by the Law* (see Romans 5: 20: 'law came in, with the result that the trespass multiplied').

As Badiou emphasizes, here St Paul is unexpectedly close to his great detractor Nietzsche, whose problem was also how to break away from the vicious cycle of the self-mortifying morbid denial of Life: for him the Christian 'way of the Spirit' is precisely the magic break, the New Beginning that delivers us from this debilitating morbid deadlock and enables us to open ourselves to the Eternal Life of Love without Sin (i.e. Law and the guilt the Law induces). In other words, it is as if St Paul himself has answered Dostoevsky's infamous 'If there is no God, everything is permitted!' in advance – for St Paul, *precisely since there* is *the God of Love, everything* is *permitted to the Christian believer* – that is to say, the Law which regulates and prohibits certain acts is suspended. For a Christian believer, the fact that he does not do certain things is based not on prohibitions (which then generate the transgressive desire to indulge precisely in these things) but in the positive, affirmative attitude of Love, which renders meaningless the accomplishment of acts which bear witness to the fact that I am not free, but still dominated by an external force:

' "All things are lawful for me", but not all things are beneficial. "All things are lawful for me", but I will not be dominated by anything.' (I Corinthians 7: 12 – 'All things are lawful for me' is often translated also as 'Nothing is prohibited to me'!) This rupture with the universe of the Law and its transgression is most clearly articulated in a very provoking 'analogy from marriage':

> Do you not know, brothers and sisters – for I am speaking to those who know the law – that the law is binding on a person only during that person's lifetime? Thus a married woman is bound by the law to her husband as long as he lives; but if her husband dies, she is discharged from the law concerning the husband. Accordingly, she will be called an adulteress if she lives with another man while her husband is alive. But if her husband dies, she is free from the law, and if she marries another man, she is not an adulteress.
>
> In the same way, my friends, you have died to the law through the body of Christ, so that you may belong to another, to him who has been raised from the dead in order that we may bear fruit for God. While we were living in the flesh, our sinful passions, aroused by the law, were at work in our members to bear fruit for death. But now we are discharged from the law, dead to that which held us captive. (Romans 7: 1–6)

To become a true Christian and embrace Love, one should thus 'die to the law', to break up the vicious cycle of 'sinful passions, aroused by the law'. As Lacan would have put it, one has to undergo the second, symbolic death, which involves the suspension of the big Other, the symbolic Law that hitherto dominated and regulated our lives. So the crucial point is that we have *two* 'divisions of the subject' which should not be confused. On the one hand, we have the division of the subject of the Law between his conscious Ego, which adheres to the letter of the Law, and his decentred desire which, operating 'automatically', against the subject's conscious will, compels him to 'do what he hates', to transgress the Law and indulge in illicit *jouissance*. On the other hand, we have the more radical division between this entire domain of the Law/desire, of the prohibition generating its transgression, and the properly Christian way of Love which marks a New Beginning, breaking out of the deadlock of Law and its transgression.

Between the Two Deaths

What stance does the Lacanian 'divided subject' adopt towards these two divisions? It may appear that the answer is simple and straightforward: psychoanalysis is *the* theory that conceptualizes, brings into daylight, the paradoxical structure of the first division. Is not Badiou's description of the intertwining of Law and desire full of implicit (sometimes even explicit) references to and paraphrases of Lacan? Is not the ultimate domain of psychoanalysis the connection between the symbolic Law and desire? Is not the multitude of perverse satisfactions the very form in which the connection between Law and desire is realized? Is not the Lacanian division of the subject the division that concerns precisely the subject's relationship to the symbolic Law? Furthermore, is not the ultimate confirmation of this Lacan's 'Kant avec Sade', which directly posits the Sadeian universe of morbid perversion as the 'truth' of the most radical assertion of the moral weight of symbolic Law in human history (Kantian ethics)? (The ironic point not to be missed here is that Foucault conceives of psychoanalysis as the final chain in the link that began with the Christian confessional mode of sexuality, irreducibly linking it to Law and guilt, while – at least in Badiou's reading – St Paul, the founding figure of Christianity, does the exact opposite: he endeavours to *break* the morbid link between Law and desire. . . .) However, the crucial point for psychoanalysis here is: does psychoanalysis remain within the confines of this 'morbid' masochistic obsession with death, of the perverse intermingling of Life and Death which characterizes the dialectics of the prohibitory Law that generates the desire for its transgression? Perhaps the best way to answer this question is to start with the fact that Lacan himself also focuses on the same passage from St Paul in his elaboration of the link between Law and desire, referring to the Thing as the impossible object of *jouissance* accessible only via the prohibitory Law, as its transgression. This passage should be quoted in full:

> Is the Law the Thing? Certainly not. Yet I can only know of the Thing by means of the Law. In effect, I would not have had the idea to covet it if the Law hadn't said: 'Thou shalt not covet it.' But the Thing finds a way by producing in me all kinds of covetousness thanks to the commandment, for without the Law the Thing is dead. But even without the Law, I was once alive. But when the commandment appeared, the Thing flared up, returned once again, and I met my death. And for me, the commandment that was supposed to lead to life

turned out to lead to death, for the Thing found a way and thanks to the commandment seduced me; through it I came to desire death.

I believe that for a little while now some of you at least have begun to suspect that it is no longer I who have been speaking. In fact, with one small change, namely, 'Thing' for 'sin', this is the speech of Saint Paul on the subject of the relations between the law and the sin in the Epistle to the Romans, Chapter 7, paragraph 7.

... The relationship between the Thing and the Law could not be better defined than in these terms. . . . The dialectical relationship between desire and the Law causes our desire to flare up only in relation to the Law, through which it becomes the desire for death. It is only because of the Law that sin . . . takes on an excessive, hyperbolic character. Freud's discovery – the ethics of psychoanalysis – does it leave us clinging to that dialectic?[15]

The crucial thing here is the last phrase, which clearly indicates that, for Lacan, there *is* 'a way of discovering the relationship to *das Ding* somewhere beyond the Law'[16] – the whole point of the ethics of psychoanalysis is to formulate the possibility of a relationship that avoids the pitfalls of the superego inculpation that accounts for the 'morbid' enjoyment of sin, while simultaneously avoiding what Kant called *Schwärmerei*, the obscurantist claim to give voice to (and thus to legitimize one's position by a reference to) a spiritual illumination, a direct insight into the impossible Real Thing. When Lacan formulates his maxim of psychoanalytic ethics, '*ne pas céder sur son désir*', that is, 'don't compromise, don't give way on your desire', the desire involved here is no longer the transgressive desire generated by the prohibitory Law, and thus involved in a 'morbid' dialectic with the Law; rather, it is fidelity to one's desire itself that is elevated to the level of ethical duty, so that '*ne pas céder sur son désir*' is ultimately another way of saying 'Do your duty!'[17]

It would therefore be tempting to risk a Badiouian–Pauline reading of the end of psychoanalysis, determining it as a New Beginning, a symbolic 'rebirth' – the radical restructuring of the analysand's subjectivity in such a way that the vicious cycle of the superego is suspended, left behind. Does not Lacan himself provide a number of hints that the end of analysis opens up the domain of *Love beyond Law*, using the very Pauline terms to which Badiou refers? Nevertheless, Lacan's way is not that of St Paul or Badiou: psychoanalysis is not 'psychosynthesis'; it does not already *posit* a 'new harmony', a new Truth-Event; it – as it were – merely wipes the slate clean for one. However, this 'merely' should be put in quotation marks, because it is Lacan's contention that, in this negative gesture of 'wiping the slate clean', something (a void) is confronted which is already 'sutured' with the arrival of a new Truth-Event. For Lacan, negativity, a negative gesture of withdrawal, precedes any positive gesture of enthusiastic identification with a Cause: negativity functions as the condition of (im)possibility of the enthusiastic identification – that is to say, it lays the ground, opens up space for it, but is simultaneously obfuscated by it and undermines it. For this reason, Lacan implicitly changes the balance between Death and Resurrection in favour of Death: what 'Death' stands for at its most radical is not merely the passing of earthly life, but the 'night of the world', the self-withdrawal, the absolute contraction of subjectivity, the severing of its links with 'reality' – *this* is the 'wiping the slate clean' that opens up the domain of the symbolic New Beginning, of the emergence of the 'New Harmony' sustained by a newly emerged Master-Signifier.

Here, Lacan parts company with St Paul and Badiou: God not only is but always-already was dead – that is to say, after Freud, one cannot directly have faith in a Truth-Event; every such Event ultimately remains a semblance obfuscating a preceding Void whose Freudian name is *death drive*. So Lacan differs from Badiou in the determination of the exact status of this domain beyond the rule of the Law. That is to say: like Lacan, Badiou delineates the contours of a domain beyond the Order of Being, beyond the politics of *service des biens*, beyond the 'morbid' superego connection between Law and its transgressive desire. For Lacan, however, the Freudian topic of the death drive cannot be accounted for in the terms of this connection: the 'death drive' is *not* the outcome of the morbid confusion of Life and Death caused by the intervention of the symbolic Law. For Lacan, the uncanny domain beyond the Order of Being is what he calls the domain 'between the two deaths', the pre-ontological domain of monstrous spectral apparitions, the domain that is 'immortal', yet not in the Badiouian sense of the immortality of participating in Truth, but in the sense of what Lacan calls *lamella*, of the monstrous 'undead' object-libido.[18]

This domain, in which Oedipus (or King Lear, to take another exemplary case) finds himself after the Fall, when his symbolic destiny is fulfilled, is for Lacan the proper domain 'beyond the Law'. That is to say: in his reading of the Oedipus myth, the early Lacan already focuses on what the usual version of the 'Oedipus complex' leaves out: the first figure of what is 'beyond Oedipus', which is *Oedipus himself* after he has fulfilled his destiny to the bitter end, the horrifying figure of Oedipus at Colonnus, this embittered old man with his thoroughly uncompromising attitude, cursing everyone around him. . . . Does not this figure of Oedipus at

Colonnus confront us with the inherent deadlock, the impossibility of *jouissance*, concealed by its Prohibition? Was he not the one who transgressed the Prohibition and paid the price by having to assume this impossibility? To illustrate the position of Oedipus at Colonnus, Lacan compares it to that of the unfortunate Mr Valdemar in Poe's famous story, the person who, via hypnosis, is put to death and then reawakened, imploring the people who observe the horrible experiment: 'For God's sake! – quick! – quick! – put me to sleep – or, quick! – waken me! quick! – I SAY TO YOU THAT I AM DEAD!' When he is awakened, Mr Valdemar:

> is no more than a disgusting liquefaction, something for which no language has a name, the naked apparition, pure, simple, brutal, of this figure which is impossible to gaze at face on, which hovers in the background of all the imaginings of human destiny, which is beyond all qualification, and for which the word carrion is completely inadequate, the complete collapse of this species of swelling that is life – the bubble bursts and dissolves down into inanimate putrid liquid.
>
> That is what happens in the case of Oedipus. As everything right from the start of the tragedy goes to show, Oedipus is nothing more than the scum of the earth, the refuse, the residue, a thing empty of any plausible appearance.[19]

It is clear that we are dealing here with the domain 'in between the two deaths', the symbolic and the real: the ultimate object of horror is the sudden emergence of this 'life beyond death' later (in *Seminar XI*) theorized by Lacan as *lamella*, the undead-indestructible object, Life deprived of support in the symbolic order. This, perhaps, is connected with today's phenomenon of cyberspace: the more our (experience of) reality is 'virtualized', changed into a screen-phenomenon encountered on an interface, the more the 'indivisible remainder' that resists being integrated into the interface appears as the horrifying remainder of undead Life – no wonder images of such a formless 'undead' substance of Life abound in today's science-fiction horror narratives, from *Alien* on.

Let us recall the well-known scene from Terry Gilliam's *Brazil*, to which I have often referred – the scene in which the waiter in a high-class restaurant recommends to his customers the best suggestions from the day's menu ('Today, our tournedos is really special!', etc.). Yet what the customers get on making their choice is a dazzling colour photograph of the meal on a stand above the plate, and on the plate itself a loathsome, excremental, paste-like lump:[20] this split between the image of the food and the Real of its formless excremental remnant exemplifies perfectly the disintegration of reality into the ghostlike, substanceless appearance on an interface and the raw stuff of the remainder of the Real – the obsession with this remainder is the price we have to pay for the suspension of the paternal Prohibition/Law that sustains and guarantees our access to reality. And of course, Lacan's point is that if one fully exploits the potentials opened up by our existence as *parlêtres* ('beings of language'), one sooner or later finds oneself in this horrifying in-between state – the threatening possibility of this occurrence looms over each of us.

This 'indivisible remainder', this formless stain of the 'little piece of the Real' that 'is' Oedipus after the fulfilment of his symbolic Destiny, is the direct embodiment of what Lacan calls *plus-de-jouir*, the 'surplus-enjoyment', the excess that cannot be accounted for by any symbolic idealization. When Lacan uses the term *plus-de-jouir*, he is, of course, playing on the ambiguity of the French expression ('excess of enjoyment' as well as 'no longer any enjoyment'); following this model, one is tempted to speak here of this formless 'indivisible remainder' that is Oedipus after the fulfilment of his Destiny as a case of *plus d'homme* – he is 'excessively human', he has lived the 'human condition' to the bitter end, realizing its most fundamental possibility; and, for that very reason, he is in a way 'no longer human', and turns into an 'inhuman monster', bound by no human laws or considerations. . . . As Lacan emphasizes, there are two main ways of coping with this 'remainder': traditional humanism disavows it, avoids confronting it, covers it up with idealizations, concealing it with noble images of Humanity; on the other hand, the ruthless and boundless capitalist economy puts this excess/remainder to use, manipulating it in order to keep its productive machinery in perpetual motion (as one usually puts it, there is no desire, no depravity, too low to be exploited for capitalist profiteering).

At this point, when Oedipus is reduced to the 'scum of humanity', we again encounter the ambiguous relationship (or, in Hegelese, the speculative identity) between the lowest and the highest, between the excremental scum and the sacred: after his utter dejection, all of a sudden, messengers from different cities vie for Oedipus's favours, asking him to bless their hometown with his presence, to which the embittered Oedipus answers with the famous line: 'Am I to be counted as something [according to some readings: as a man] only now, when I am reduced to nothing [when I am no longer human]?' Does not this line reveal the elementary matrix of subjectivity: you become 'something' (you are counted as a subject) only after going through the zero-point, after being deprived of all the 'pathological' (in the Kantian sense of empirical, contingent) features that support your identity, and thus reduced to 'nothing' – 'a Nothingness counted as Something' is the most concise formula of the Lacanian 'barred' subject (s).[21]

One could say that Martin Luther was the first great antihumanist: modern subjectivity is announced not in the Renaissance humanist celebration of man as the 'crown of creation', that is, in the tradition of Erasmus and others (to whom Luther cannot but appear as a 'barbarian'), but, rather, in Luther's famous statement that man is the excrement that fell out of God's anus. Modern subjectivity has nothing to do with the notion of man as the highest creature in the 'Great Chain of Being', as the final point of the evolution of the universe: modern subjectivity emerges when the subject perceives himself as 'out of joint', as *excluded* from the 'order of things', from the positive order of entities. For that reason, the ontic equivalent of the modern subject is inherently *excremental*: there is no subjectivity proper without the notion that at a different level, from another perspective, I am a mere piece of shit. For Marx, the emergence of working-class subjectivity is strictly co-dependent on the fact that the worker is compelled to sell the very substance of his being (his creative power) as a commodity on the market – that is, to reduce the *agalma*, the treasure, the precious core of his being, to an object that can be bought for money: there is no subjectivity without the reduction of the subject's positive-substantial being to a disposable 'piece of shit'. In this case of correlation between Cartesian subjectivity and its excremental objectal counterpart, we are not dealing merely with an example of what Foucault called the empirico-transcendental couple that characterizes modern anthropology, but rather, with the split between the subject of the enunciation and the subject of the enunciated:[22] if the Cartesian subject is to emerge at the level of the enunciation, he must be reduced to the 'almost-nothing' of disposable excrement at the level of the enunciated content.

What Badiou does not take into account can be best summarized by the fact that, in the Christian iconography, St Paul takes the place of Judas the Traitor among the twelve apostles – a case of metaphoric substitution if ever there was one. The key point is that St Paul was in a position to establish Christianity as an Institution, to formulate its universal Truth, precisely because he did *not* know Christ personally – as such he was excluded from the initiatory deadlock of those who were personally engaged with the Master; however, in order for this distance to become productive – that is, in order for his universal message to matter more than his person – Christ *had* to be betrayed. . . . To put it another way:

any idiot can bring about simple stupid miracles like walking on water or making food fall down from heaven – the true miracle, as Hegel put it, is that of the universal thought, and it took St Paul to perform it, that is, to translate the idiosyncratic Christ-Event into the form of universal thought.

The Lacanian Subject

What, then, is the subject here? The subject is strictly correlative with the ontological gap between the universal and the particular – with ontological undecidability, with the fact that it is not possible to derive Hegemony or Truth directly from the given positive ontological set: the 'subject' is the *act*, the *decision* by means of which we pass from the positivity of the given multitude to the Truth-Event and/or to Hegemony. This precarious status of the subject relies on the Kantian anti-cosmological insight that reality is 'non-all', ontologically not fully constituted, so it needs the supplement of the subject's contingent gesture to obtain a semblance of ontological consistency. 'Subject' is not a name for the gap of freedom and contingency that infringes upon the positive ontological order, active in its interstices; rather, 'subject' is the contingency that grounds the very positive ontological order, that is, the 'vanishing mediator' whose self-effacing gesture transforms the pre-ontological chaotic multitude into the semblance of a positive 'objective' order of reality. In this precise sense, every ontology is 'political': based on a disavowed contingent 'subjective' act of decision.[23] So Kant was right: the very idea of the universe, of the All of reality, as a totality which exists in itself, has to be rejected as a paralogism – that is to say, what looks like an *epistemological limitation* of our capacity to grasp reality (the fact that we are forever perceiving reality from our finite temporal standpoint) is the positive *ontological condition* of reality itself.

Here, however, one should avoid the fatal trap of conceiving the subject as the act, the gesture, which intervenes afterwards in order to fill in the ontological gap, and insist on the irreducible vicious cycle of subjectivity: 'the wound is healed only by the spear which smote it', that is, the subject 'is' the very gap filled in by the gesture of subjectivization (which, in Laclau, establishes a new hegemony; which, in Rancière, gives voice to the 'part of no part'; which, in Badiou, assumes fidelity to the Truth-Event; etc.). In short, the Lacanian answer to the question asked (and answered in a negative way) by such different philosophers as Althusser, Derrida and Badiou – 'Can the gap, the opening, the Void which precedes the

gesture of subjectivization, still be called "subject"?' – is an emphatic 'Yes!'
– the subject is both at the same time, the ontological gap (the 'night of
the world', the madness of radical self-withdrawal) as well as the gesture
of subjectivization which, by means of a short circuit between the Universal and the Particular, heals the wound of this gap (in Lacanese: the
gesture of the Master which establishes a 'new harmony'). *'Subjectivity' is a
name for this irreducible circularity, for a power which does not fight an external
resisting force (say, the inertia of the given substantial order), but an obstacle that
is absolutely inherent, which ultimately 'is' the subject itself.*[24] In other words,
the subject's very endeavour to fill in the gap retroactively sustains and
generates this gap.

The 'death drive' is thus the constitutive obverse of every emphatic
assertion of Truth irreducible to the positive order of Being: the negative
gesture that clears a space for creative sublimation. The fact that sublimation presupposes the death drive means that when we are enthusiastically
transfixed by a sublime object, this object is a 'mask of death', a veil that
covers up the primordial ontological Void – as Nietzsche would have put
it: to will this sublime object effectively amounts to willing a Nothingness.[25]
That is the difference between Lacan and Badiou: Lacan insists on the
primacy of the (negative) *act* over the (positive) establishment of a 'new
harmony' via the intervention of some new Master-Signifier; while for
Badiou, the different facets of negativity (ethical catastrophes) are
reduced to so many versions of the 'betrayal' of (or infidelity to, or denial
of) the positive Truth-Event.

This difference between Badiou and Lacan concerns precisely the status
of the subject: Badiou's main point is to avoid identifying the subject with
the constitutive Void of the structure – such an identification already
'ontologizes' the subject, albeit in a purely negative way – that is, it turns
the subject into an entity consubstantial with the structure, an entity that
belongs to the order of what is necessary and a priori ('no structure
without a subject'). To this Lacanian ontologization of the subject, Badiou
opposes its 'rarity', the local-contingent-fragile-passing emergence of subjectivity: when, in a contingent and unpredictable way, a Truth-Event takes
place, a subject is there to exert fidelity to the Event by discerning its
traces in a Situation whose Truth this Event is.[26] For Badiou, as well as for
Laclau, the subject is consubstantial with a contingent act of Decision;
while Lacan introduces the distinction between the subject and the
gesture of subjectivization: what Badiou and Laclau describe is the process
of subjectivization – the emphatic engagement, the assumption of fidelity
to the Event (or, in Laclau, the emphatic gesture of identifying empty

universality with some particular content that hegemonizes it), while the subject is the negative gesture of breaking out of the constraints of Being that opens up the space of possible subjectivization.

In Lacanese, the subject prior to subjectivization is the pure negativity of the death drive prior to its reversal into the identification with some new Master-Signifier.[27] Or – to put it in another way – Lacan's point is not that the subject is inscribed into the very ontological structure of the universe as its constitutive void, but that *'subject' designates the contingency of an Act that sustains the very ontological order of being*. 'Subject' does not open up a hole in the full order of Being: 'subject' is the contingent-excessive gesture that constitutes the very universal order of Being. The opposition between the subject *qua* ontological foundation of the order of Being and the subject *qua* contingent particular emergence is therefore false: the subject is the contingent emergence/act that sustains the very universal order of Being. The subject is not simply the excessive *hubris* through which a particular element disturbs the global order of Being by positing itself – a particular element – as its centre; the subject is, rather, the paradox of a particular element that sustains the very universal frame.

Lacan's notion of the act as real is thus opposed to both Laclau and Badiou. In Lacan, act is a purely *negative* category: to put it in Badiou's terms, it stands for the gesture of breaking out of the constraints of Being, for the reference to the Void at its core, *prior to filling this Void*. In this precise sense, the act involves the dimension of death drive that grounds a decision (to accomplish a hegemonic identification; to engage in a fidelity to a Truth), but cannot be reduced to it. The Lacanian death drive (a category Badiou adamantly opposes) is thus again a kind of 'vanishing mediator' between Being and Event: there is a 'negative' gesture constitutive of the subject which is then obfuscated in 'Being' (the established ontological order) and in fidelity to the Event.[28]

This minimal distance between the death drive and sublimation, between the negative gesture of suspension-withdrawal-contraction and the positive gesture of filling its void, is not just a theoretical distinction between the two aspects, which are inseparable in our actual experience: as we have already seen, the whole of Lacan's effort is precisely focused on those limit-experiences in which the subject finds himself confronted with the death drive at its purest, prior to its reversal into sublimation. Is not Lacan's analysis of Antigone focused on the moment when she finds herself in the state 'in between the two deaths', reduced to a living death, excluded from the symbolic domain?[29] Is this not similar to the uncanny figure of Oedipus at Colonnus who, after fulfilling his destiny, is also reduced to 'less than nothing', to a formless stain, the embodiment of some unspeakable horror? All these and other figures (from Shakespeare's King Lear to Claudel's Sygne de Coufontaine) are figures who find themselves in this void, trespassing the limit of 'humanity' and entering the domain which, in ancient Greek, was called *ate*, 'inhuman madness'. Here, Badiou pays the price for his proto-Platonic adherence to Truth and the Good: what remains beyond his reach, in his violent (and, on its own level, quite justified) polemics against the contemporary obsession with depoliticized 'radical Evil' (the Holocaust, etc.) and his insistence that the different facets of Evil are merely so many consequences of the betrayal of the Good (of the Truth-Event), is this domain 'beyond the Good', in which a human being encounters the death drive as the utmost limit of human experience, and pays the price by undergoing a radical 'subjective destitution', by being reduced to an excremental remainder. Lacan's point is that this limit-experience is the irreducible/ constitutive condition of the (im)possibility of the creative act of embracing a Truth-Event: it opens up and sustains the space for the Truth-Event, yet its excess always threatens to undermine it.

Classic onto-theology is focused on the triad of the True, the Beautiful and the Good. What Lacan does is to push these three notions to their limit, demonstrating that the Good is the mask of 'diabolical' Evil, that the Beautiful is the mask of the Ugly, of the disgusting horror of the Real, and that the True is the mask of the central Void around which every symbolic edifice is woven. In short, there is a domain 'beyond the Good' that is not simply everyday 'pathological' villainy, but the constitutive background of the Good itself, the terrifying ambiguous source of its power; there is a domain 'beyond the Beautiful' that is not simply the ugliness of ordinary everyday objects, but the constitutive background of Beauty itself, the Horror veiled by the fascinating presence of Beauty; there is a domain 'beyond Truth' that is not simply the everyday domain of lies, deceptions and falsities, but the Void that sustains the place in which one can only formulate symbolic fictions that we call 'truths'. If there is an ethico-political lesson of psychoanalysis, it consists in the insight into how the great calamities of our century (from the Holocaust to the Stalinist *désastre*) are not the result of our succumbing to the morbid attraction of this Beyond but, on the contrary, the result of our endeavour to avoid confronting it and to impose the direct rule of the Truth and/or Goodness.

The Master or the Analyst?

We are now in a position to provide a precise definition of the gap that separates Badiou from Lacan: for Badiou, what psychoanalysis provides is insight into the morbid intertwining of Life and Death, of Law and desire, an insight into the obscenity of the Law itself as the 'truth' of the thought and moral stance that limit themselves to the Order of Being and its discriminatory Laws; as such, psychoanalysis cannot properly render thematic the domain beyond the Law, that is, the mode of operation of fidelity to the Truth-Event – the psychoanalytic subject is the divided subject of the (symbolic) Law, *not* the subject divided between Law (which regulates the Order of Being) and Love (as fidelity to the Truth-Event). The logical consequence of this is that psychoanalysis, for Badiou, remains constrained to the field of Knowledge, unable to approach the properly positive dimension of Truth-processes: in the case of love, psychoanalysis reduces it to a sublimated expression of sexuality; in the case of science as well as art, psychoanalysis can only provide the subjective libidinal conditions of a scientific invention or a work of art, which are ultimately irrelevant to their truth-dimension – that an artist or a scientist was driven by his unresolved Oedipus complex or latent homosexuality, and so on; in the case of politics, psychoanalysis can conceive of collectivity only against the background of the *Totem and Taboo* or *Moses and Monotheism* problematic of primordial crime and guilt, and so on, unable to conceive a militant 'revolutionary' collective that is bound *not* by parental guilt but by the positive force of Love.

For Lacan, on the other hand, *a Truth-Event can operate only against the background of the traumatic encounter with the undead/monstrous Thing*: what are Badiou's four *génériques* – art, science, love, politics – if not four ways of reinscribing the encounter with the Real Thing on to the symbolic texture? In *art*, beauty is 'the last veil of the Monstrous'; far from being just another symbolic narrative, *science* is the endeavour to formulate the structure of the Real beneath the symbolic fiction; for the later Lacan, *love* is no longer merely the narcissistic screen obfuscating the truth of desire, but the way to 'gentrify' and come to terms with the traumatic drive; finally, militant *politics* is a way of putting to use the terrific force of Negativity in order to restructure our social affairs. . . . So Lacan is not a postmodernist cultural relativist: there definitely *is* a difference between an authentic Truth-Event and its semblance, and this difference lies in the fact that in a Truth-Event the void of the death drive, of radical negativity, a gap that momentarily suspends the Order of Being, continues to resonate.

This brings us back to the problem of human finitude: when Badiou dismisses the topic of human finitude, from Heideggerian 'being-towards-death' to Freudian 'death drive', as the morbid obsession with what makes man equal to and thus reduced to a mere animal – as the blindness to that properly meta-physical dimension that elevates man beyond the animal kingdom and allows him to 'gain immortality' by participating in a Truth-Event – his theoretical gesture involves a 'regression' to 'non-thought', to a naive traditional (pre-critical, pre-Kantian) opposition of two orders (the finitude of positive Being; the immortality of the Truth-Event) that remains blind to how the very space for the specific 'immortality' in which human beings can participate in the Truth-Event is opened up by man's unique relationship to his finitude and the possibility of death. As Heidegger conclusively demonstrated in his polemics against Cassirer's neo-Kantian reading of Kant, that is Kant's great philosophical revolution: it is the very finitude of the transcendental subject as constitutive of 'objective reality' that allows Kant to break out of the frame of traditional metaphysics, to reject the notion of the cosmos as the ordered Whole of Being: to posit that the order of Being, the field of transcendentally constituted reality, is in itself non-totalizable, cannot be coherently thought of as a Whole, since its existence is attached to finite subjectivity; the transcendental spontaneity of freedom thus emerges as a third domain, neither phenomenal reality nor the noumenal In-itself.[30]

The key point is that the 'immortality' of which Lacan speaks (that of the 'undead' *lamella*, the object that 'is' libido) can emerge only within the horizon of human finitude, as a formation that stands for and fills the ontological Void, the hole in the texture of reality opened up by the fact that reality is transcendentally constituted by the finite transcendental subject. (If the transcendental subject were not finite but infinite, we would be dealing not with transcendental constitution but with 'intellectual intuition' – with an intuition that directly creates what it perceives: a prerogative of the infinite Divine Being.) So the point is not to deny the specifically human mode of 'immortality' (that of participating in a Truth-Event sustaining a dimension irreducible to the constrained positive order of Being), but to bear in mind how this 'immortality' is based on the specific mode of human finitude. For Kant himself, the finitude of the transcendental subject is not a limitation of his freedom and transcendental spontaneity, but its positive condition: if a human subject were to gain direct access to the noumenal domain, he would change from a free subject into a lifeless puppet directly confronted with and dominated by the awesome Divine Power.

In short, against Badiou, one should insist that only to a finite/mortal being does the act (or Event) appear as a traumatic intrusion of the Real, as something that cannot be named directly: it is the very fact that man is split between mortality (a finite being destined to perish) and the capacity to participate in the Eternity of the Truth-Event which bears witness to the fact that we are dealing with a finite/mortal being. To a truly infinite/ immortal being, the act would be transparent, directly symbolized, the Real would coincide with the Symbolic – that is, in Badiou's terms, naming would be directly inscribed into, would coincide with, the Event itself, which would thus lose its traumatic character as the intrusion of the Real that is *innomable* (what cannot be named). Or – to put it in yet another way – the act (Event) can never be fully subjectivized, integrated into the symbolic universe, precisely in so far as the subject who is its agent is a finite/mortal entity. Is not a further proof of this point the fact that, for Badiou, Truth is always the Truth of a specific contingent situation, attached to it: eternity/immortality is thus always eternity/immortality *of* the given finite, specific contingent situation or condition?

Perhaps the gap that finally separates Badiou from Lacan can also be formulated in terms of the difference between the Hysteric and the Master. Badiou is interested in how to retain fidelity to the Truth-Event, how to formulate the universal symbolic framework that guarantees and accomplishes this fidelity, how to transmute the unique singularity of the Event into the constitutive gesture of a lasting symbolic edifice based on fidelity to the Event – that is to say, he is opposed to the false poetics of those who remain fascinated by the ineffable singularity of the Event and consider every naming of the Event as already a betrayal. For this reason, Badiou elevates the figure of the Master: the Master is the one who *names the Event* – who, by producing a new *point de capiton*, Master-Signifier, reconfigures the symbolic field via the reference to the new Event. Lacan, in contrast, following Freud, takes the side of the Hysteric who, precisely, questions and challenges the Master's naming of the Event – who, that is, on behalf of her very fidelity to the Event, insists on the gap between the Event and its symbolization/naming (in Lacanese, between *objet petit a* and the Master-Signifier). The Hysteric's question is simply: 'Why is that name the name of the Event?'

When, in his unpublished course of 1997/98, Badiou elaborated the four possible subjective stances towards the Truth-Event, he added as the fourth term to the triad of Master/Hysteric/University the position of the Mystic. The Master pretends to name, and thus directly translate into symbolic fidelity, the dimension of the act – that is, the defining feature of the Master's gesture is to change the act into a new Master-Signifier, to guarantee the continuity and consequences of the Event. In contrast to the Master, the Hysteric maintains the ambiguous attitude of division towards the act, insisting on the simultaneous necessity and impossibility (ultimate failure) of its symbolization: there was an Event, but each symbolization of the Event already betrays its true traumatic impact – that is to say, the Hysteric reacts to each symbolization of the Event with a '*ce n'est pas ça*', that's not *it*. In contrast to both of them, the perverse agent of University discourse disavows that there was the event of an act in the first place – with his chain of knowledge, he wants to reduce the consequences of the act to just another thing that can be explained away as part of the normal run of things; in other words, in contrast to the Master, who wants to ensure the continuity between the Event and its consequences, and the Hysteric, who insists on the gap that forever separates an Event from its (symbolic) consequences, University discourse aims at 'suturing' the field of consequences by explaining them away without any reference to the Event ('Love? It's nothing but the result of a series of occurrences in your neuronal network!', etc.).

The fourth attitude Badiou adds is that of the Mystic, which is the exact obverse of perverse University discourse: if the latter wants to isolate the symbolic chain of consequences from their founding Event, the Mystic wants to isolate the Event from the network of its symbolic consequences: he insists on the ineffability of the Event, and disregards its symbolic consequences. For the Mystic, what matters is the bliss of one's immersion in the Event, which obliterates the entire symbolic reality. Lacan, however, in contrast to Badiou, adds as the fourth term to the triad of Master, Hysteric and University pervert the discourse of the analyst: for him, mysticism is the isolated position of the psychotic immersed in his/her *jouissance* and, as such, not a discourse (a social link) at all. So the consistency of Lacan's entire edifice hinges on the fact that a fourth *discursive* position is possible, which is not that of a Master, that of the Hysteric, or that of the University. This position, while maintaining the gap between the Event and its symbolization, avoids the hysterical trap and, instead of being caught in the vicious cycle of permanent failure, affirms this gap as positive and productive: it asserts the Real of the Event as the 'generator', the generating core to be encircled repeatedly by the subject's symbolic productivity.

The political consequences of this reassertion of psychoanalysis in the face of Badiou's critique constitute the very opposite of the standard psychoanalytic scepticism about the final outcome of the revolutionary process (the well-known story of 'the revolutionary process has to go wrong and end up in a self-destructive fury because it is unaware of its own libidinal foundations, of the murderous aggressivity that sustains its idealism', etc.): we are tempted to claim, rather, that Badiou's resistance to psychoanalysis is part of his hidden Kantianism, which ultimately also leads him to oppose the full revolutionary *passage à l'acte*. That is to say: although Badiou is adamantly anti-Kantian and, in his political stances, radically leftist (rejecting outright not only parliamentary democracy, but also multiculturalist 'identity politics'), at a deeper level his distinction between the order of the positive Knowledge of Being and the wholly different Truth-Event remains Kantian: when he emphasizes how, from the standpoint of Knowledge, there simply is no Event – how, that is, the traces of the Event can be discerned as signs only by those who are already involved in support of the Event – does he not thereby repeat Kant's notion of signs that announce the noumenal fact of freedom without positively proving it (like enthusiasm for the French Revolution)?

Badiou's inconsistent pure multiple is Lacan's Real as *pas-tout*, that which a 'state of a situation' unifies, inscribes, accounts for, turns into a consistent structure, that X that precedes the Kantian transcendental synthesis. The transformation of the pure multiple into the state of things corresponds to Kant's transcendental synthesis constituting reality. The order of reality, in Kant, is threatened/limited in two ways:[31] by 'mathematical antinomies' – that is, by the inherent failure of transcendental synthesis, the gap between apprehension and comprehension, the delay between the latter and the former (in Badiou, the ontological Void and the correlative excess of presentation over re-presentation that threatens the normal functioning of a state of things) – and by 'dynamic antinomies' – that is, by the intervention of an entirely different order of noumenal ethical Goals of rational Freedom (in Badiou, the Truth-Event). And in Kant, as well as in Badiou, is not the space for freedom opened up by the excess and inconsistency of the ontological order?[32]

Badiou's Kantianism is discernible precisely in the way he limits the scope of Truth: although Truth is universal and necessary as the truth of a situation, none the less it cannot name the Whole of the situation, but can exist only as the infinite, incessant effort to discern in the situation the traces of the Truth-Event, exactly homologous with the Kantian infinite ethical effort. When Truth pretends to grasp/name the entire situation, we end up in the catastrophe of Stalinism or the Maoist Cultural

Revolution, with their thoroughgoing 'totalitarian' destructive rage. This *innomable* surplus, that which forever resists being named in a situation, is, for Badiou, precisely defined in each of the four 'generics' of Truth: community in politics, sexual *jouissance* in love, and so on. From the Lacanian perspective, however, this core that resists naming is structured in a 'fundamental fantasy' – that is, it is the core of *jouissance*, and an authentic act *does* intervene in this core. So – to put it succinctly – for Lacan, the authentic act itself in its negative dimension, the act as the Real of an 'object' preceding naming, is what is ultimately *innomable*. Here one can see the crucial weight of the Lacanian distinction between the act as object, as a negative gesture of discontinuity, and its naming in a positive Truth-procedure. For this reason, one should stick to Lacan's thesis that 'truth has the structure of a fiction': truth is condemned to remain a fiction precisely in so far as the *innomable* Real eludes its grasp.

Notes

1. F.W.J. Schelling, *Sämtliche Werke*, ed. K.F.A. Schelling, Stuttgart: Cotta 1856–61, vol. VIII, p. 600.

2. Alain Badiou, *L'être et l'événement*, Paris: Éditions du Seuil 1988.

3. To make this logic clearer, let us mention another of Badiou's examples of Truth-Event: the atonal revolution in music accomplished by the Second Viennese School (Schoenberg, Berg, Webern). Here, also, we have three ways of betraying this Event of Truth: the traditionalists' dismissal of the atonal revolution as an empty formal experiment, which allows them to continue to compose in the old ways, as if nothing had happened; the pseudo-modernist imitation of atonality; and the tendency to change atonal music into a new positive tradition.

4. Badiou, *L'être et l'événement*, p. 25.

5. In theory, perhaps the main indication of this suspension of Event is the notion and practice of 'cultural studies' as the predominant name for the all-encompassing approach to socio-symbolic products: the basic feature of cultural studies is that they are no longer able or ready to confront religious, scientific or philosophical works in terms of their inherent Truth, but reduce them to a product of historical circumstances, to an object of anthropologico-psychoanalytic interpretation.

6. Badiou, *L'être et l'événement*, p. 202.

7. Ibid., p. 224.

8. Ibid., p. 29.

9. Up to a point, one can also say that Knowledge is constative, while Truth is performative.

10. As Badiou perspicaciously notes, these four domains of the Truth-Event are today, in public discourse, more and more replaced by their fake doubles: we speak of 'culture' instead of art, of 'administration' instead of politics, of 'sex' instead of love, of 'know-how' or 'wisdom' instead of science: art is reduced to an expression/articulation of historically specific culture, love to an ideological dated form of sexuality; science is dismissed as a Western, falsely universalized form of practical knowledge on an equal footing with forms of

pre-scientific wisdom; politics (with all the passion or struggle that this notion involves) is reduced to an immature ideological version or forerunner of the art of social gestion. . . .

11. See Alain Badiou, *Saint Paul. La fondation de l'universalisme*, Paris: Presses Universitaires de France 1997.

12. Of course, Badiou simultaneously mobilizes the association of 'generic' with 'generating': it is this 'generic' element that enables us to 'generate' propositions of the subject-language in which Truth resonates.

13. Romans 7: 7 to 7: 18 (quoted from *The Holy Bible: New Revised Standard Version*, Nashville, TN: Thomas Nelson Publishers 1990).

14. For Badiou, St Paul's fundamental problem was that of the appropriate discourse: to assert authentic Christian universalism, St Paul has to break with Greek philosophical sophistry as well as with Jewish prophetic obscurantism, which is still the predominant discursive mode of the Gospels. Here, however, one should perhaps complicate the picture a little: maybe Christ's obscure parables in the Gospels are more subversive than they appear; maybe they are there precisely to perplex and frustrate the disciples who are unable to discern a clear meaning in them; maybe the well-known statement from Matthew 19: 12 – 'Let anyone accept [or, as it is also translated: understand] this who can' – is to be read literally, as a signal that the search for a deeper meaning is misleading; maybe they are to be taken like the parable of the Door of the Law in Kafka's *Trial*, submitted to an exasperating literal reading by the priest, a reading that yields no deeper meaning. So maybe these parables are not the remainder of the old Jewish prophetic discourse but, rather, its immanent mocking subversion. And, incidentally, isn't it striking that this 'Let anyone accept this who can' is pronounced by Christ regarding the problem of castration? Here is the full quote: 'Not everyone can accept/understand this teaching, but only those to whom it is given. For there are eunuchs who have been so from birth, and there are eunuchs who have been made eunuchs by others, and there are eunuchs for the sake of the kingdom of heaven. Let anyone accept/understand this who can' (Matthew 19: 11–12). What is ultimately ungraspable, beyond comprehension, is the fact of castration in its different modalities.

15. Jacques Lacan, *The Ethics of Psychoanalysis*, London: Routledge 1992, pp. 83–4.

16. Ibid., p. 84.

17. Another problem here is the status of the reference to Kant: in so far as Kant is conceived of as the philosopher of the Law in Badiou's Pauline sense, Lacan's 'Kant avec Sade' retains its full validity – that is, the status of the Kantian moral Law remains that of a superego-formation, so that its 'truth' is the Sadeian universe of morbid perversion. However, there is another way of conceptualizing the Kantian moral injunction which delivers it from superego constraints. (See Appendix III of Slavoj Žižek, *The Plague of Fantasies*, London: Verso 1997.)

18. See Jacques Lacan, *The Four Fundamental Concepts of Psycho-Analysis*, New York: Norton 1979, pp. 197–8.

19. Jacques Lacan, *The Seminar, Book II: The Ego in Freud's Theory and in the Technique of Psychoanalysis*, New York: Norton 1991, pp. 231–2.

20. This scene from *Brazil* is psychotic, since it involves the disappearance of the Symbolic – that is to say, what happens in it is what Lacan describes as the psychotic torsion of the 'scheme L' of symbolic communication: symbolic reality falls apart into, on the one side, the pure Real of the excrement and, on the other, the pure Imaginary of the substanceless hallucinatory image. . . . (See Jacques Lacan, 'On a Question Preliminary to Any Possible Treatment of Psychosis', in *Écrits: A Selection*, New York: Norton 1977.) In short, what takes place in this scene is the dissolution of the Borromean knot in which, in the intricate interconnection between the three dimensions, each couple of them is linked through the third: when the efficiency of the Symbolic is suspended, the link between the other two dimensions (Imaginary and Real) that sustains our 'sense of reality' is cut.

21. The other famous quip of the embittered Oedipus is pronounced by the Chorus, which claims that the greatest boon granted to a mortal human being is not to be born at

all; the well-known comic rejoinder quoted by Freud and referred to by Lacan ('Unfortunately, that happens to scarcely one in a hundred thousand') takes on a new meaning today, in the midst of the heated debate about abortion: are not the aborted children in a sense those who *did* succeed in not being born?

22. See Lacan, *Écrits: A Selection*, p. 300.

23. That is the task of today's critique of ideology: to unearth, beneath any semblance of a 'reified' ontological order, its disavowed 'political' foundation: how it hinges on some excessive 'subjective' act.

24. Perhaps the first – and still unsurpassed – description of this paradox was provided by Fichte's notion of *Anstoss*, the 'obstacle/impetus' that sets in motion the subject's productive effort of 'positing' objective reality: this *Anstoss* is no longer the Kantian Thing-in-itself – an external stimulus affecting the subject from outside – but a core of contingency that is extimate: a foreign body at the very heart of the subject. Subjectivity is thus defined not by a struggle against the inertia of the opposed substantial order, but by an absolutely inherent tension. (See Chapter 1 above.)

25. Consequently, there is simply no place for the Freudian death drive in Badiou's pair of Being and Event: the death drive certainly interrupts the economy of the 'service of the Goods [*service des biens*]', the principle of the smooth running of affairs, which is the highest political principle of the Order of Being; on the other hand, Badiou is certainly right to emphasize that the emergence of the Truth-Event disavows the death drive. . . . In short, the death drive is the point that undermines Badiou's proto-Kantian ontological dualism between the Order of Being and the Event of Truth: it is a kind of 'vanishing mediator' between the two; it opens up a gap in the positivity of Being, a suspension in its smooth functioning, and it is this gap that can later be filled by the Truth-Event.

26. Alain Badiou, *L'être et l'événement*, pp. 472–4.

27. In his implicit polemics against Laclau and Lacan, Rancière makes the same point as Badiou: he emphasizes that politics is not a consequence of the incompleteness of the social subject – there is no ontological guarantee or foundation of politics in the a priori Void of Being, in the subject as constitutive Lack/Finitude/Incompleteness; one looks in vain for the philosophico-transcendental 'condition of possibility' of politics. The order of 'police' (the positive order of Being) is in itself full, there are no holes in it; it is only the political act itself, the gesture of political subjectivization, that adds to it the 'distance towards itself' and dislodges its self-identity . . . (see Jacques Rancière, *La mésentente*, Paris: Galilée 1995, pp. 43–67).

The Lacanian answer to this would be that here Rancière fetishizes the order of police, failing to recognize how this order itself relies on the excessive gesture of the Master, which is a stand-in for the political Lack – the 'gentrification', the positivization, of the properly political excess. In short, we do not have the full positivity of the police order perturbed from time to time by the heterogeneous intervention of political subjectivity: this positivity itself always-already relies on the (disavowal of some) excessive gesture of the Master. Or – to put it in yet another way – politics is not a *consequence* of the (pre-political) gap in the order of Being or non-coincidence of the social subject with itself: the fact that the social subject is never complete and self-identical means that the social being itself is always-already *based on* a (disavowed) gesture of politicization and, as such, thoroughly political.

28. This difference between Lacan and Badiou also has precise consequences for the appreciation of concrete political events. For Badiou, the disintegration of Eastern European Socialism was not a Truth-Event: apart from giving rise to a brief popular enthusiasm, the dissident ferment did not succeed in transforming itself into a stable movement of followers patiently engaged in the militant fidelity to the Event, but soon disintegrated, so that what we have today is either the return to vulgar liberal parliamentary capitalism or the advocacy of racist ethnic fundamentalism. However, if we accept the Lacanian distinction between the act as a negative gesture of saying 'No!', and its positive aftermath, locating the key dimension in the primordial negative gesture, then the process of disintegration did none the less

produce a true *act* in the guise of the enthusiastic mass movement of saying 'No!' to the Communist regime on behalf of authentic solidarity; this negative gesture counted more than its later failed positivization.

29. The case of Antigone, of course, is more complex, since she puts her life at stake and enters the domain 'in between the two deaths' *precisely in order to prevent her brother's second death*: to give him a proper funeral rite that will secure his eternalization in the symbolic order.

30. Another problem is that Kant often shrank from his own discovery, identifying freedom as noumenal (see Chapter 1 above).

31. Again, see Chapter 1 above.

32. Badiou's Kantianism can also be discerned in the way his political project gets caught in the quintessential Kantian paradox of 'spurious infinity' in our approach to the Ideal: for Badiou, the ultimate goal of political activity is to achieve presence without representation, that is, a situation no longer redoubled in its State; however, the political act itself in its essence is directed against the State; it is an intervention into the existing State that undermines its functioning – so it needs a pre-existing State in the same sense that one needs an enemy in order to assert oneself by fighting it.

4

Political Subjectivization and Its Vicissitudes

Badiou, Balibar, Rancière

As Fredric Jameson has often emphasized, the triad Traditionalism–Modernism–Postmodernism provides a logical matrix that can also be applied to a particular historical content. There are clearly three main readings of Nietzsche: traditional (the Nietzsche of the return to premodern aristocratic warrior values against decadent Judaeo-Christian modernity), modern (the Nietzsche of the hermeneutics of doubt and ironic self-probing), and postmodern (the Nietzsche of the play of appearances and differences). Does not the same hold for today's three main philosophico-political positions: the (traditionalist) *communitarians* (Taylor and others), the (modern) *universalists* (Rawls, Habermas), and the (postmodern) *'dispersionists'* (Lyotard and others)? What they all share is a *reduction of the political*, some version of *pre-political* ethics: there is no politics proper in a closed community ruled by a traditional set of values; universalists ground politics in a proceduralist a priori of discursive (or distributive) ethics; 'dispersionists' condemn politics as unifying, totalitarian, violent, and so on, and assume the position of ethical critics who reveal (or voice) the ethical Wrong or Evil committed by politics, without engaging in an alternative political project.[1]

Each of the three positions thus involves a pragmatic (performative) paradox of its own. The communitarians' problem is that in today's global society their position is a priori faked, marked by a split between enunciated and enunciation: they themselves do not speak from the particular position of a closed community, their position of enunciation is already universal (their mistake is thus the opposite of that of the universalist, who conceals the particular kernel of his alleged universality). The universalists' problem is that their universalism is always too narrow, grounded in an exception, in a gesture of exclusion (it represses the *différend*, does not even allow it to be properly formulated). And finally, the opposite problem of 'dispersionists' is that they are too all-inclusive: how do we pass from their 'ontological' assertion of multitude to ethics (of diversity, tolerance . . .)?[2]

Three contemporary French political philosophers (Alain Badiou, Étienne Balibar and Jacques Rancière) have formulated a kind of inherent self-criticism of these three positions – that is, each of them can be said to focus on the inherent split of the position in question:

- Is not Badiou the anti-communitarian communitarian? Does he not introduce a split in the notion of community, a split between positive communities grounded in the order of Being (nation-state, etc.), and the 'impossible' community-to-come grounded in fidelity to the Truth-Event, like the community of believers in Christ or the revolutionary community (or, one is tempted to add, the psychoanalytic community)?

- Is not Balibar the anti-Habermasian Habermasian, in so far as he accepts universality as the ultimate horizon of politics, but none the less focuses on the inherent split in the universal itself between (in Hegelese) an abstract and a concrete universal, between the concretely structured universal order and the infinite/unconditional universal demand of *égaliberté* which threatens to undermine it?

- Is not Rancière the anti-Lyotardian Lyotardian? By elaborating the gap between the positive global order (what he calls *la politique/police*) and political interventions which perturb this order and give word to *le tort* (to the Wrong, to those who are not included, whose statements are not comprehensible in the ruling political/police space), Rancière opts for a *political* mode of rebellion against the universal police/political order.

A fourth name should be added to this triad, a kind of constitutive exception to this series: the 'anti-Schmittian Schmittian' Ernesto Laclau (who works with Chantal Mouffe). Laclau acknowledges the fundamental, unsurpassable status of antagonism, yet instead of fetishizing it in a heroic warfare conflict, he inscribes it into the symbolic as the political logic of the struggle for hegemony. A series of obvious differences notwithstanding, the theoretical edifices of Laclau and Badiou are united by a deep homology. Against the Hegelian vision of the 'concrete universal', of the reconciliation between Universal and Particular (or between Being and

Event), which is still clearly discernible in Marx, they both start by asserting a constitutive and irreducible gap that undermines the self-enclosed consistency of the ontological edifice: for Laclau, this gap is the gap between the Particular and the empty Universal, which necessitates the operation of hegemony (or the gap between the differential structure of the positive social order – the logic of *differences* – and properly political antagonism, which involves the logic of *equivalence*); for Badiou, it is the gap between Being and Event (between the order of Being – structure, state of situation, knowledge – and the event of Truth, Truth as Event).

In both cases, the problem is how to break out of the self-enclosed field of ontology as a description of the positive universe; in both cases, the dimension which undermines the closure of ontology has an 'ethical' character – it concerns the contingent act of *decision* against the background of the 'undecidable' multiplicity of Being; consequently, both authors endeavour to conceptualize a new, post-Cartesian mode of *subjectivity* which cuts its links with ontology and hinges on a contingent act of decision. Both authors accomplish the return to a proto-Kantian formalism: they both elaborate a quasi-transcendental theory (of ideological hegemony or of Truth), which is destined to serve as the a priori framework for contingent empirical occurrences of hegemony or Truth. In both cases, however, this formal character of the theory is linked, by a kind of half-acknowledged umbilical cord, to a concrete and limited politico-historical constellation and practice (in Laclau, the post-Marxist strategy of the multitude of emancipatory struggles for recognition; in Badiou, the anti-State 'marginal' revolutionary politics in factories, on campuses, etc.).

The same goes for the other two authors. In the case of Rancière, his obvious paradigm is the 'spontaneous' rebellion of the proletarian masses (not the mythical Marxian proletariat as the Subject of History, but actual groups of exploited artisans, textile workers, working women and other 'ordinary' people) who reject the police frame defining their 'proper' place and, in a violent politico-poetic gesture, take the floor, start to speak for themselves. Balibar is more focused on the universe of 'civility', even decency: his problem is how, today, we are to maintain a civic space of dialogue in which we can articulate our demand for human rights; for that reason, Balibar resists the anti-State rhetorics of the New Left of the 1960s (the notion of the State as a mechanism of 'oppression' of people's initiatives) and emphasizes the role of the State as the (possible) guarantor of the space of civic discussion.

All these authors oscillate between proposing a neutral formal frame that describes the working of the political field, without implying any specific *prise de parti*, and the prevalence given to a particular leftist political practice. This tension was already clearly discernible in the work of Michel Foucault, who serves as the point of reference for most of these authors: his notion of Power is presented as a neutral tool that describes the way the entire field of existing power structures and resistances to them functions. Foucault liked to present himself as a detached positivist, laying bare the common mechanisms that underlie the activity of passionately opposed political agents; on the other hand, one cannot avoid the impression that Foucault is somehow passionately on the side of the 'oppressed', of those who are caught in the machinery of 'discipline and punishment', and aims to give them the chance to utter, to enable them to start to 'speak for themselves'. . . . Do we not find, on a different level, the same tension in Laclau? Laclau's notion of hegemony describes the universal mechanism of ideological 'cement' which binds any social body together, a notion that can analyse all possible sociopolitical orders, from Fascism to liberal democracy; on the other hand, Laclau none the less advocates a determinate political option, 'radical democracy'.[3]

Hegemony and Its Symptoms

So let us proceed like proper materialists, and begin with the exception to the series: with Laclau, whose proposition that today 'the realm of philosophy comes to an end and the realm of politics begins'[4] strangely echoes Marx's thesis on the passage from theoretical interpretation to revolutionary transformation. Although, of course, in Laclau this thesis has a different meaning, there is nevertheless a common thread: in both cases, any theoretical approach that endeavours to grasp and mirror adequately 'what is' (what Marx called the 'world-view') is denounced as something which, unbeknown to itself, relies on a contingent practical act – that is to say, in both cases the ultimate solution to philosophical problems is practice. For Marx, the philosophical problem of freedom finds its solution in the revolutionary establishment of a free society; while for Laclau, the breakdown of the traditional closed ontology reveals how features that we (mis)perceive as ontologically positive rely on an ethico-political decision that sustains the prevailing hegemony.

So what is hegemony? Those who still remember the good old days of Socialist Realism are well aware of the key role played by the notion of the 'typical' in its theoretical edifice: truly progressive Socialist literature should depict 'typical' heroes in 'typical' situations. Writers who, for example, presented a predominantly bleak picture of the Soviet reality were not accused simply of lying – the accusation was that they provided a distorted reflection of social reality by focusing on phenomena which were not 'typical', which were sad remainders of the past, instead of focusing on phenomena which were 'typical' in the precise sense of expressing the deeper underlying historical tendency of the progress towards Communism. A novel which presented a new Socialist type of man who dedicated his life to the happiness of all the people, of course, depicted a minority phenomenon (the majority of the people were not yet like that), but none the less a phenomenon which enabled us to identify the truly progressive forces active in the social situation.

Ridiculous as this notion of the 'typical' may sound, there is a grain of truth in it – it lies in the fact that each apparently universal ideological notion is always hegemonized by some particular content which colours its very universality and accounts for its efficiency. In the present rejection of the social welfare system by the New Right in the USA, for example, the very universal notion of the present welfare system as inefficient is contaminated by the more concrete representation of the notorious single African-American mother, as if social welfare were, in the last resort, a programme for single black mothers – the particular case of 'the single black mother' is silently conceived of as 'typical' of the universal notion of social welfare, and what is wrong with it. . . . The same goes for *every* universal ideological notion: one always has to look for the particular content which accounts for the specific efficiency of an ideological notion. In the case of the Moral Majority campaign against abortion, for example, the 'typical' case is the exact opposite of the (jobless) black mother: a successful and sexually promiscuous career woman who gives priority to her professional life over her 'natural' assignment of motherhood (in blatant contradiction to the facts, which tell us that the great majority of abortions occur in lower-class families with several children).

This specific 'twist', the particular content which is promulgated as 'typical' of the universal notion, is the element of fantasy, of the phantasmic background/support of the universal ideological notion – in Kant's terms, it plays the role of 'transcendental schematism', translating the empty universal notion into a notion which directly relates and applies to our 'actual experience'. As such, this phantasmic specification is by no means a mere insignificant illustration or exemplification: it is on this level of which particular content will count as 'typical' that ideological battles are won or lost. To go back to our example of abortion: the moment we perceive as 'typical' the case of abortion in a large lower-class family unable to cope economically with another child, the perspective changes radically. . . .[5]

'Single unemployed mother' is thus a *sinthome* in the strict Lacanian sense: a knot, a point at which all the lines of the predominant ideological argumentation (the return to family values, the rejection of the welfare state and its 'uncontrolled' spending, etc.) meet. For that reason, if we 'untie' this *sinthome*, the efficiency of its entire ideological edifice is suspended. We can see now in what sense the psychoanalytic *sinthome* is to be opposed to the medical symptom: the latter is a sign of some more fundamental process taking place on another level. When one claims, say, that fever is a symptom, the implication is that we should not cure only the symptom, but attack its causes directly. (Or, in social sciences, when one claims that adolescent violence is a symptom of the global crisis of values and the work ethic, the implication is that one should attack the problem 'at its root', by directly addressing problems of the family, employment, etc., not only by punishing the offenders.) The *sinthome*, in contrast, is not a 'mere symptom', but that which holds together the 'thing itself' – if one unties it, the 'thing itself' disintegrates. For that reason, psychoanalysis actually *does* cure by addressing the *sinthome* . . . .

This example makes it clear in what sense 'the universal results from a constitutive split in which the negation of a particular identity transforms this identity into the symbol of identity and fullness as such':[6] the Universal emerges within the Particular when some particular content starts to function as the stand-in for the absent Universal – that is to say, the universal is operative only through the split in the particular. A couple of years ago, the English yellow press focused on single mothers as the source of all the evils of modern society, from the budget crisis to juvenile delinquency – in this ideological space, the universality of the 'modern social Evil' was operative only through the split of the figure of 'single mother' into itself in its particularity and itself as the stand-in for the 'modern social Evil'. Owing to the contingent character of this link between the Universal and the particular content which functions as its stand-in (i.e. the fact that this link is the outcome of a *political* struggle for hegemony), the existence of the Universal always relies on an empty signifier: 'Politics is possible because the constitutive impossibility of society can only represent itself through the production of empty signifiers.'[7] Since 'society doesn't exist', its ultimate unity can be symbolized only in the guise of an empty signifier hegemonized by some particular content – the struggle for this content is the political struggle. In other words, politics exists because 'society doesn't exist': politics is the struggle for the content of the empty signifier which represents the impossibility of Society. The worn-out phrase 'the politics of the signifier' is thus fully justified: the order of signifier as such is political and, vice versa, there is no politics outside the order of the signifier. The space of politics is the gap between the series of 'ordinary' signifiers (S_2) and the empty Master-Signifier (S_1).

The only thing to add to Laclau's formulation is that his anti-Hegelian twist is perhaps, all too sudden:

> We are not dealing here with 'determinate negation' in the Hegelian sense: while the latter comes out of the apparent positivity of the concrete and 'circulates' through contents that are always determinate, our notion of negativity depends on the failure in the constitution of all determination.[8]

What, however, if the infamous 'Hegelian determinate negation' aims precisely at the fact that every particular formation involves a gap between the Universal and the Particular – or, in Hegelese, that a particular formation never coincides with its (universal) notion – and that it is this very gap that brings about its dialectical dissolution? Let us take the example of the State: there is always a gap between the notion of the State and its particular actualizations; Hegel's point here, however, is not that, in the course of the teleological process of history, positively existing, actual states are gradually approaching their notion, until finally, in the modern post-revolutionary state, actuality and notion overlap. Hegel's point, rather, is that the deficiency of actually existing, positive states with regard to their notion is grounded in an inherent deficiency of the very notion of the State; thus the split is inherent to the notion of the State – it should be reformulated as the split between the State *qua* the rational totality of social relations and the series of irreducible antagonisms which, *already on the level of the notion*, prevent this totality from fully actualizing itself (the split between State and civil society on account of which the unity of the State is ultimately always experienced by individuals as 'imposed from outside', so that individual subjects are never fully 'themselves' in the State, are never able fully to identify the Will of the State with their own). Again, Hegel's point here is not that the State which would fully fit its notion is impossible – it is possible; the catch is, rather, that *it is no longer a State, but a religious community*. What one should change is the notion of the State itself – that is, the very standard by means of which one measures the deficiency of actual states.

The struggle for ideologico-political hegemony is thus always the struggle for appropriation of the terms that are 'spontaneously' experienced as 'apolitical', as transcending political boundaries. No wonder the name of the strongest dissident opposition force in the former Eastern European countries was Solidarity: a signifier of the impossible fullness of society if ever there was one. It was as if, in those couple of years, what Laclau calls the logic of equivalence was brought almost to its extreme: 'Communists in power' served as *the* embodiment of non-society, of decay and corruption, magically uniting everyone against themselves, including disaffected 'honest Communists'. Conservative nationalists accused them of betraying Polish interests to the Soviet master; business-orientated individuals saw in them an obstacle to their unbridled capitalist activity; for the Catholic Church, Communists were amoral atheists; for the farmers, they represented the force of violent modernization which disrupted their way of life; for the artists and intellectuals, Communism was synonymous in their everyday experience with oppressive and stupid censorship; the workers saw themselves not only exploited by the Party bureaucracy but, even worse, humiliated by claims that this had been done on their behalf, in their own name; finally, disillusioned old Leftists perceived the regime as the betrayal of 'true Socialism'. The impossible *political* alliance between all these divergent and potentially antagonistic positions was possible only under the banner of a signifier which stood, as it were, on the very border which separates the political from the pre-political, and 'solidarity' was the perfect candidate for this role: it was politically operative as designating the 'simple' and 'fundamental' unity of human beings which should link them beyond all political differences.

Now, however, when this magic moment of universal solidarity is over, the signifier which, in some post-Socialist countries, is emerging as the signifier of what Laclau calls the 'absent fullness' of society is *honesty*: it forms the focus of the spontaneous ideology of 'ordinary people' caught in the economic-social turbulence in which hopes of a new fullness of Society which should follow the collapse of Socialism were cruelly betrayed, so that in their eyes, the 'old guard' (ex-Communists) and ex-dissidents who entered the ranks of power joined in exploiting them even more than before under the banner of democracy and freedom. . . . The battle for hegemony, of course, is now focused on the particular content which will give a spin to this signifier: what does 'honesty' mean? For a conservative, it means returning to traditional moral and religious values, as well as purging the social body of the remainders of the old regime; for a Leftist, social justice and resistance to rapid privatization; and so forth. The same measure – returning land to the Church, for example – is thus 'honest' from the conservative standpoint and 'dishonest' from the leftist standpoint – each position silently (re)defines 'honesty' to accommodate it to its own ideologico-political position. It would be wrong, however, to claim that the conflict is ultimately about different meanings of the term 'honesty': what gets lost in this 'semantic clarification' is that each position claims that *their honesty is the only 'true' honesty*: the struggle is not simply a struggle between different particular contents, it is a struggle inherent to the Universal itself.[9]

So how does a particular content succeed in displacing another content as a stand-in for the Universal? Laclau's answer is *readability*: in a concrete situation of post-Socialism, 'honesty' as the signifier of the absent fullness of Society will be hegemonized by the particular content which makes the everyday experience of engaged individuals more convincingly 'readable' – which enables them more effectively to organize their life-experience into a consistent narrative. Of course, 'readability' is not a neutral criterion, it depends on ideological struggle: the fact that, after the collapse of the standard bourgeois narrative in the Germany of the early 1930s, which was unable to account for the global crisis, Nazi anti-Semitism rendered this crisis 'more convincingly readable' than the socialist-revolutionary narrative is the contingent result of a series of overdetermined factors. Or, to put it in another way: this 'readability' does not imply a simple relationship of competition between a multitude of narratives/descriptions and the extra-discursive reality, where the narrative which is most 'adequate' with regard to reality wins: the relationship is circular and self-relating: the narrative already predetermines what we shall experience as 'reality'.

One is tempted to propose a way of simultaneously thinking of Laclau's notion of ideological universality as empty, as the frame within which different particular contents fight for hegemony, and the classic Marxist notion of ideological universality as 'false' (privileging a particular interest). Both of them bring into play the constitutive gap between the Universal and the Particular, albeit in a different way. For Laclau, this gap is the gap *between* the absent fullness of the Universal and a contingent particular content that acts as a stand-in for this absent fullness; for Marx, it is the gap *within* the (particular) content of the Universal, that is, the gap between the 'official' content of the Universal and its unacknowledged presuppositions, which involve a set of exclusions.

Let us take the classic example of human rights. The Marxist symptomal reading can convincingly demonstrate the particular content which gives the specific bourgeois ideological spin to the notion of human rights:

'universal human rights are in fact the right of white, male, private owners to exchange freely on the market, exploit workers and women, as well as exert political domination ...' – tendentially, at least, this approach considers the hidden 'pathological' spin to be constitutive of the very form of the Universal. Against this quick dismissal of the universal form itself as ideological (concealing an unacknowledged particular content), Laclau insists on the gap between the empty universality and its determinate content: the link between the empty universal notion of 'human rights' and its original particular content is contingent – that is to say, the moment they were formulated, 'human rights' started to function as an empty signifier whose concrete content could be contested and widened – what about the human rights of women, children, members of nonwhite races, criminals, madmen ...? Each of these supplementary gestures does not simply *apply* the notion of human rights to ever new domains (women, blacks ... can *also* vote, own property, actively participate in public life, etc.), but retroactively *redefines the very notion of human rights*.

Let us recall the gist of Marx's notion of exploitation: exploitation is not simply opposed to justice – Marx's point is not that workers are exploited because they are not paid the full value of their work. The central thesis of Marx's notion of 'surplus-value' is that *a worker is exploited even when he is 'fully paid'*; exploitation is thus not opposed to the 'just' equivalent exchange; it functions, rather, as its point of inherent exception – there is one commodity (the workforce) which is exploited precisely when it is 'paid its full value'. (The further point not to be missed is that the production of this *excess* is strictly equivalent to the *universalization* of the exchange-function: the moment the exchange-function is universalized – that is, the moment it becomes the structuring principle of the whole of economic life – the exception emerges, since at this point the workforce itself becomes a commodity exchanged on the market. Marx in effect announces here the Lacanian notion of the Universal which involves a constitutive exception.) The basic premiss of symptomal reading is thus that every ideological universality necessarily gives rise to a particular 'extimate' element, to an element which – precisely as an inherent, necessary product of the process designated by the universality – simultaneously undermines it: the symptom is an example which subverts the Universal whose example it is.[10]

The gap between the empty signifier and the multitude of particular contents which, in the fight for hegemony, endeavour to function as the representatives of this absent fullness, is thus *reflected within the Particular itself*, in the guise of the gap that separates the particular hegemonic

POLITICAL SUBJECTIVIZATION AND ITS VICISSITUDES 181

content of an ideological universality from the symptom that undermines
it (say, separates the bourgeois notion of 'just and equivalent exchange'
from the exchange between capital and workforce as the particular exchange
that involves exploitation precisely in so far as it is 'just' and 'equivalent').
We should therefore consider three, not just two, levels: the empty *Universal* ('justice'), the *particular* content which hegemonizes the empty
Universal ('just and equivalent exchange'), and the *individual*, the symptomatic excess which undermines this hegemonic content (exchange
between capital and workforce). One can see immediately in what sense
the individual is the dialectical unity of Universal and Particular: the
individual (the symptomatic excess) bears witness to the gap between
the Universal and the Particular: to the fact that the Universal is always
'false' in its concrete existence (hegemonized by some particular content
which involves a series of exclusions).

Let us make the same point from yet another perspective. Some years
ago, Quentin Skinner pointed out that a possible discussion between a
traditional liberal and a Marxist radical about the scope of the term
'political' involves more than the meaning of that term.[11] For the liberal,
the sphere of the political is restricted to a specific sphere of reaching
decisions which concern the administration of public affairs – not only
intimate (sexual) interests, but also art, science, even the economy, are
outside its scope. For the Marxist radical, of course, the political pervades
every sphere of our lives, from the social to the most intimate, and the
very perception of something as 'apolitical', 'private', and so on, is
grounded in a disavowed political decision. Both standard philosophical
versions, 'realist' and 'nominalist', fail to account for this struggle for
the Universal. According to the realist account, there is a 'true' content
of the notion of the political to be unearthed by a true theory, so that
once we gain access to this content, we can measure how close to it
different theories of the political have come. The nominalist account,
on the contrary, reduces the whole problem to the different nominal
definitions of the term: there is no real conflict; the two parties are simply
using the word 'political' in a different sense, conferring on it a different
scope.

What both accounts miss, what disappears in both of them, is the
antagonism, the struggle inscribed into the very heart of the 'thing itself'.
In the realist account, there is a true content of the universal notion to be
discovered, and the struggle is simply the conflict between different
erroneous readings of it – that is, it arises out of our misperception of the
true content. In the nominalist account, struggle again arises out of an

epistemological confusion, and is thus neutralized into a peaceful coexistence of the plurality of meanings. What gets lost in both cases is the fact that the struggle for hegemony (for the particular content which will function as the stand-in for the universality of the political) is groundless: the ultimate Real which cannot be further grounded in some ontological structure.

Here, however, one should add again that if the Marxist's operation is to be effective, it has to involve the symptomal reading of the liberal's position, which endeavours to demonstrate how the liberal's constriction of the scope of the 'political' has to disavow – to exclude violently – the political character of something which, *according to the liberal's own definition of the term*, should enter the scope of the political; and, furthermore, how *this very exclusion of something from the political is a political gesture par excellence.* The standard example: the liberal definition of 'private family life' as apolitical naturalizes – and/or changes into hierarchical relations grounded in pre-political psychological attitudes, in differences in human nature, in a priori cultural constants, and so on – a whole set of relations of subordination and exclusion that actually depend on political power relations.

Enter the Subject

How does *subjectivity* enter this process of hegemonic universalization? For Laclau, the 'subject' is the very agent which accomplishes the operation of hegemony – which sutures the Universal to a particular content. Although Laclau's and Badiou's notions of the subject seems to be very similar (in both cases, the subject is not a substantial agent but emerges in the course of an act of decision/choice that is not grounded in any pre-given factual Order), they are none the less separated by different stances towards 'deconstruction'.

Laclau's move is deconstructive – that is why, for him, the operation of hegemony in the course of which the subject emerges is the elementary matrix of ideology: hegemony involves a kind of structural short circuit between the Particular and the Universal, and the fragility of every hegemonic operation is grounded in the ultimately 'illusory' character of this short circuit; the task of theory is precisely to 'deconstruct' it, that is, to demonstrate how every hegemonic identification is inherently unstable, the contingent outcome of a struggle – in short, for Laclau, every hegemonic operation is ultimately 'ideological'. For Badiou, in contrast, a

Truth-Event is that which cannot be 'deconstructed', reduced to an effect of an intricate, overdetermined texture of 'traces'; here Badiou introduces the tension between the Necessity of a global situation and the contingent emergence of its Truth. For Badiou (in his anti-Platonic mode, despite his love of Plato), Necessity is a category of veracity, of the order of Being, while Truth is inherently contingent, it can occur or not. So if, against the deconstructionist and/or postmodern politics of 'undecidability' and 'semblance', Badiou – to paraphrase Saint-Just's well-known comment on 'happiness as a political factor' – wants to (re)assert *truth as a political factor*, this does not mean that he wants to return to the premodern grounding of politics in some eternal neutral order of Truth. For Badiou, *Truth itself is a theologico-political notion*: theological in so far as religious revelation is the unavowed paradigm of his notion of the Truth-Event; political because Truth is not a state to be perceived by means of a neutral intuition, but a matter of (ultimately political) engagement. Consequently, for Badiou, subjectivization designates the event of Truth that disrupts the closure of the hegemonic ideological domain and/or the existing social edifice (the Order of Being); while for Laclau, the gesture of subjectivization is the very gesture of establishing a (new) hegemony, and is as such the elementary gesture of ideology.[12]

In a way, everything seems to hinge on the relationship between Knowledge and Truth. Badiou limits Knowledge to a positive encyclopaedic grasp of Being which is, as such, blind to the dimension of Truth as Event: Knowledge knows only veracity (adequation), not Truth, which is 'subjective' (not in the standard sense of subjectivism, but linked to a 'wager', to a decision/choice which in a way transcends the subject, since the subject himself/herself is nothing but the activity of pursuing the consequences of the Decision). Is it not a fact, however, that every concrete, socially operative field of Knowledge presupposes a Truth-Event, since it is ultimately a kind of 'sedimentation' of an Event, its 'ontologization', so that the task of analysis is precisely to unearth the Event (the ethico-political decision) whose scandalous dimension always lurks behind 'domesticated' knowledge?[13] We can also see now the gap which separates Badiou from Laclau: for Badiou, an Event is a contingent rare occurrence within the global order of Being; while for Laclau (to put it in Badiou's terms), any Order of Being is itself always a 'sedimentation' of some past Event, a 'normalization' of a founding Event (for example, the Church as the Institution of Order is sedimented from the Event of Christ, say) – every positive ontological order already relies on a disavowed ethico-political decision.

Laclau and Badiou nevertheless share a hidden reference to Kant. That is to say, the ultimate *philosophical* question that lurks behind all this is that of Kantian formalism. The horizon of Laclau's central notion of hegemony is the constitutive gap between the Particular and the Universal: the Universal is never full; it is a priori empty, devoid of positive content; different particular contents strive to fill this gap, but every particular that succeeds in exerting the hegemonic function remains a temporary and contingent stand-in that is forever split between its particular content and the universality it represents.... Do we not encounter here the paradoxical logic of *desire* as constitutively *impossible*, sustained by a constitutive lack (the absent fullness of the empty signifier) that can never be supplied by any positive object, that is, by a constitutive 'out of joint' of the Particular with respect to the Universal ...? What, however, if this impossible desire to make up for the lack, to overcome the 'out of joint', is not the ultimate fact? What if, beyond (or, rather, beneath) it, one should presuppose not the fullness of a Foundation, but the *opposite* striving: an uncanny *active will to disrupt*? (It was Hegel who, apropos of Understanding, emphasized how, instead of complaining about the abstract, negative quality of Understanding, how Understanding replaces the immediate fullness of life with dry abstract categories, one should praise the infinite power of Understanding that is capable of tearing asunder what belongs together in nature, positing as separate what remains in reality joined together.) And is not the Freudian name for this active will to disrupt the *death drive*? In contrast to desire, which strives to regain the impossible balance between the Universal and the Particular – that is, for a particular content that would fill the gap between itself and the Universal – drive thus actively wills and sustains the gap between the Universal and the Particular.

Why Are Ruling Ideas Not the Ideas of Those Who Rule?

Our conclusion is thus that the ruling ideology, in order to be operative, has to incorporate a series of features in which the exploited/dominated majority will be able to recognize its authentic longings.[14] In short, every hegemonic universality has to incorporate *at least two* particular contents: the 'authentic' popular content and its 'distortion' by the relations of domination and exploitation. Of course Fascist ideology 'manipulates' authentic popular longing for a true community and social solidarity against fierce competition and exploitation; of course it 'distorts' the expression of this longing in order to legitimize the continuation of the relations of social domination and exploitation. In order to be able to achieve this effect, however, it none the less has to incorporate authentic popular longing. Ideological hegemony is thus not the case of some particular content directly filling in the void of the empty Universal; rather, the very form of ideological universality bears witness to the struggle between (at least) two particular contents: the 'popular' content expressing the secret longings of the dominated majority, and the specific content expressing the interests of the forces of domination.

One is tempted to refer here to the Freudian distinction between the latent dream-thought and the unconscious desire expressed in a dream: the two are not the same, since the unconscious desire articulates itself, inscribes itself, through the very 'working-through', translation, of the latent dream-thought into the explicit text of a dream. In the same way, there is nothing 'Fascist' ('reactionary', etc.) in the 'latent dream-thought' of the Fascist ideology (the longing for authentic community and social solidarity, etc.); what accounts for the properly Fascist character of the Fascist ideology is the way this 'latent dream-thought' is transformed/elaborated by the ideological 'dream-work' into the explicit ideological text which continues to legitimize social relations of exploitation and domination. And is it not the same with today's right-wing populism? Are not liberal critics too quick in dismissing the very values populism refers to as inherently 'fundamentalist' or 'proto-Fascist'?

Non-ideology (what Fredric Jameson calls the utopian moment present even in the most atrocious ideology) is thus absolutely indispensable: in a way, ideology is nothing but the form of appearance, the formal distortion/displacement, of non-ideology. To return to the worst imaginable case – was not Nazi anti-Semitism grounded in the utopian longing for an authentic community life, in the fully justified rejection of the irrationality of capitalist exploitation, and so on? Our point, again, is that it is theoretically and politically wrong to condemn the longing for authentic community life as such as 'proto-Fascist', to denounce it as a 'totalitarian fantasy' – to search for the possible 'roots' of Fascism in this very longing (the standard mistake of the liberal-individualist critique of Fascism): the non-ideological utopian character of this longing is to be fully asserted. What makes it 'ideological' is its articulation, the way this longing is functionalized as the legitimization of a very specific notion of capitalist exploitation (the result of Jewish influence, the predominance of financial over 'productive' capital, which tends towards a harmonious 'partnership' with workers . . .) and how to overcome it (by getting rid of the Jews, of course).

Crucial for a successful ideology is thus the tension *within* its particular content between the themes and motifs that belong to the 'oppressed' and those which belong to the 'oppressors': ruling ideas are *never* directly the ideas of the ruling class. Let us take what is arguably the ultimate example, Christianity – how did it become the ruling ideology? By incorporating a series of motifs and aspirations of the oppressed (truth is on the side of the suffering and humiliated; power corrupts . . .) and rearticulating them in such a way that they became compatible with the existing relations of domination. And the same holds even for Fascism. The fundamental ideological contradiction of Fascism is that between organicism and mechanicism: the corporatist-organic aestheticized vision of the Social Body *and* the extreme 'technologization', mobilization, destruction, wiping-out, of the last vestiges of 'organic' communities (families, universities, local self-management traditions) at the level of the actual 'micro-practices' of the power exercise. In Fascism, the aestheticized organicist corporate ideology is thus the very form of an unprecedented technological mobilization of society which disrupts 'organic' links.[15] This paradox enables us to avoid the liberal-multiculturalist trap of condemning every call for a return to organic (ethnic, etc.) links as 'proto-Fascist': what defines Fascism is, rather, a specific combination of organicist corporatism and the drive to ruthless modernization. To put it in yet another way: in every actual Fascism, one always encounters elements which make us say: 'This is not yet full-blown Fascism; there are still inconsistent elements of leftist traditions or liberalism in it'; however, this removal from – this distance towards – the phantom of 'pure' Fascism *is* Fascism *tout court*. 'Fascism', in its ideology and practice, is nothing but a certain formal principle of distortion of social antagonism, a certain logic of its displacement by a combination and condensation of inconsistent attitudes.

The same distortion is discernible in the fact that, today, the only class which, in its 'subjective' self-perception, explicitly conceives of and presents itself as a class is the notorious 'middle class' which is precisely the 'non-class': the allegedly hard-working middle strata of society which define themselves not only by their allegiance to firm moral and religious standards, but by a double opposition to both 'extremes' of the social space – non-patriotic 'deracinated' rich corporations on the one side; poor excluded immigrants and ghetto-members on the other. The 'middle class' grounds its identity in the exclusion of both extremes which, when they are directly counterposed, give us 'class antagonism' at its purest. The constitutive lie of the very notion of the 'middle class' is thus the same as that of the true Party line between the two extremes of 'right-wing deviation' and 'left-wing deviation' in Stalinism: the 'middle class' is, in its very 'real' existence, the *embodied lie*, the denial of antagonism – in psychoanalytic terms, the 'middle class' is a *fetish*, the impossible intersection of Left and Right which, by expelling both poles of the antagonism into the position of antisocial 'extremes' which corrode the healthy social body (multinational corporations and intruding immigrants), presents itself as the neutral common ground of Society. In other words, the 'middle class' is the very form of the disavowal of the fact that 'Society doesn't exist' (Laclau) – in it, Society *does* exist. Leftists usually bemoan the fact that the line of division in the class struggle is as a rule blurred, displaced, falsified – most blatantly in the case of rightist populism, which presents itself as speaking on behalf of the people, while in fact advocating the interests of those who rule. However, this constant displacement and 'falsification' of the line of (class) division *is* the 'class struggle': a class society in which the ideological perception of the class division was pure and direct would be a harmonious structure with no struggle – or, to put it in Laclau's terms, class antagonism would thereby be fully symbolized; it would no longer be impossible/real, but a simple differential structural feature.

The Political and Its Disavowals

If, then, the notion of hegemony expresses the elementary structure of ideological domination, are we condemned to shifts within the space of hegemony, or is it possible to suspend – temporarily, at least – its very mechanism? Jacques Rancière's claim is that such a subversion does occur, and that it even constitutes the very core of politics, of a proper political event.

What, for Rancière, is politics proper?[16] A phenomenon which, for the first time, appeared in Ancient Greece when the members of *demos* (those with no firmly determined place in the hierarchical social edifice) not only demanded that their voice be heard against those in power, those who exerted social control – that is, they not only protested the wrong [*le tort*] they suffered, and wanted their voice to be heard, to be recognized as included in the public sphere, on an equal footing with the ruling oligarchy and aristocracy – even more, they, the excluded, those with no fixed place within the social edifice, presented themselves as the representatives, the stand-ins, for the Whole of Society, for the true Universality ('we – the "nothing", not counted in the order – are the people, we are All against others who stand only for their particular privileged interest'). In short, political conflict designates the tension between the structured social body in which each part has its place, and 'the part of no part' which unsettles this order on account of the empty principle of universality – of what Balibar calls *égaliberté*, the principled equality of all men *qua* speaking beings. Politics proper thus always involves a kind of short circuit between the Universal and the Particular: the paradox of a *singulier universel*, a singular which appears as the stand-in for the Universal, destabilizing the 'natural' functional order of relations in the social body. This identification of the non-part with the Whole, of the part of society with no properly defined place within it (or resisting the allocated subordinated place within it) with the Universal, is the elementary gesture of politicization, discernible in all great democratic events from the French Revolution (in which *le troisième état* proclaimed itself identical to the Nation as such, against the aristocracy and the clergy) to the demise of ex-European Socialism (in which dissident 'forums' proclaimed themselves representative of the entire society against the Party *nomenklatura*).

In this precise sense, politics and democracy are synonymous: the basic aim of antidemocratic politics always and by definition is and was depoliticization – that is, the unconditional demand that 'things should go back to normal', with each individual doing his or her particular job. . . . And, as Rancière proves against Habermas, the political struggle proper is therefore not a rational debate between multiple interests, but the struggle for one's voice to be heard and recognized as the voice of a legitimate partner: when the 'excluded', from the Greek *demos* to Polish workers, protested against the ruling elite (aristocracy or *nomenklatura*), the true stakes were not only their explicit demands (for higher wages, better working conditions, etc.), but their very right to be heard and recognized as an equal partner in the debate – in Poland, the *nomenklatura* lost the moment it had to accept Solidarity as an equal partner.

These sudden intrusions of politics proper undermine Rancière's order of *police*, the established social order in which each part is properly accounted for. Rancière, of course, emphasizes how the line of separation between police and politics is always blurred and contested: in the Marxist tradition, say, 'proletariat' can be read as the subjectivization of the 'part of no part' elevating its injustice into the ultimate test of universality and, simultaneously, as the operator which will bring about the establishment of a post-political rational society.[17] Sometimes the shift from politics proper to police can be only a matter of a change from the definite to the indefinite article, like the East German crowds demonstrating against the Communist regime in the last days of the GDR: first they shouted 'We are *the* people!' ['Wir sind *das* Volk!'], thereby performing the gesture of politicization at its purest – they, the excluded counter-revolutionary 'scum' of the official Whole of the People, with no proper place in the official space (or, more precisely, with only titles like 'counter-revolutionaries', 'hooligans', or – at best – 'victims of bourgeois propaganda' reserved for them), claimed to stand for *the* people, for 'all'; a couple of days later, however, the slogan changed into 'We are *a/one* people!' ['Wir sind *ein* Volk!'], clearly signalling the closure of the momentary authentic political opening, the reappropriation of the democratic impetus by the thrust towards the reunification of Germany, which meant rejoining Western Germany's liberal-capitalist police/political order.

In Japan, the caste of untouchables is called the *burakumin*: those who are involved in contact with dead flesh (butchers, leatherworkers, gravediggers) and are sometimes even referred to as *eta* ('much filth'). Even now, in the 'enlightened' present, when they are no longer openly despised, they are silently ignored – not only do companies still avoid hiring them, or parents allowing their children to marry them, but, under the 'politically correct' pretence not of offending them, one prefers to ignore the issue. However, the crucial point, and the proof of the pre-political (or, rather, non-political) 'corporate' functioning of Japanese society, is the fact that although voices are heard on their behalf (we could simply mention the great and recently dead Sue Sumii who, in her impressive series of novels *The River with No Bridge*, used the reference to *burakumin* to expose the meaninglessness of the entire Japanese caste hierarchy – significantly, her primordial traumatic experience was the shock when, as a child, she witnessed how, in order to honour the Emperor, a relative of hers scratched the toilet used by the visiting Emperor to preserve a piece of his shit as a sacred relic), the *burakumin* did not actively *politicize* their destiny, did not constitute their position as that of *singulier universel*, claiming that, precisely as the 'part of no part', they stand for the true universality of Japanese society. . . .[18]

There is a series of disavowals of this political moment, of the proper logic of political conflict:

- *arche-politics*: 'communitarian' attempts to define a traditional close, organically structured homogeneous social space that allows for no void in which the political moment–event can emerge;

- *para-politics*: the attempt to depoliticize politics (to translate it into police logic): one accepts political conflict, but reformulates it into a competition, within the representational space, between acknowledged parties/agents, for the (temporary) occupation of the place of executive power;[19]

- Marxist (or Utopian Socialist) *meta-politics*: political conflict is fully asserted, *but* as a shadow-theatre in which events whose proper place is on Another Scene (of economic processes) are played out; the ultimate goal of 'true' politics is thus its self-cancellation, the transformation of the 'administration of people' into the 'administration of things' within a fully self-transparent rational order of collective Will;[20]

- the fourth form, the most cunning and radical version of the disavowal (not mentioned by Rancière), is what I am tempted to call *ultra-politics*: the attempt to depoliticize the conflict by bringing it to an extreme via the direct militarization of politics – by reformulating it as the *war* between 'Us' and 'Them', our Enemy, where there is no common ground for symbolic conflict – it is deeply symptomatic that, rather than class *struggle*, the radical Right speaks of class (or sexual) *warfare*.[21]

What we have in all these four cases is thus an attempt to gentrify the properly traumatic dimension of the political: something emerged in Ancient Greece under the name of *demos* demanding its rights, and, from the very beginning (i.e. from Plato's *Republic*) to the recent revival of liberal 'political philosophy', 'political philosophy' was an attempt to suspend the destabilizing potential of the political, to disavow and/or regulate it in one way or another: bringing about a return to a pre-political social body, fixing the rules of political competition, and so forth.[22]

'Political philosophy' is thus, in all its different forms, a kind of 'defence-formation', and perhaps its typology could be established via reference to the different modalities of defence against some traumatic experience in psychoanalysis. It may seem, however, that psychoanalysis, the psychoanalytic approach to politics, also involves the reduction of the proper political dimension. That is to say, when one approaches politics through the psychoanalytic network, one usually focuses on Freud's elaboration of the notion of the 'crowd' apropos of the Army and the

Church. This approach, however, seems to provoke justified criticism: are not the Army and the Church precisely examples of the *disavowal* of the proper political dimension, that is, the two forms of social organization in which the logic of collective deliberation and decision on public affairs which defines the political space is replaced by a clear hierarchical chain of command? Is this not a proof by negation that psychoanalysis is unable to define the properly *political* space: the only form of 'sociability' it can articulate is the 'totalitarian' distortion/obfuscation of the political?

Hannah Arendt seemed to point in this direction when she emphasized the distinction between political power and the mere exercise of (social) violence: organizations run by direct non-political authority – by an order of command that is not politically grounded authority (Army, Church, school) – represent examples of violence [*Gewalt*], not of political Power in the strict sense of the term. Here, however, it would be productive to introduce the distinction between the public symbolic Law and its obscene supplement:[23] the notion of the obscene superego double-supplement of Power implies that *there is no Power without violence*. Power always has to rely on an obscene stain of violence; political space is never 'pure', but always involves some kind of reliance on 'pre-political' violence. Of course, the relationship between political power and pre-political violence is one of mutual implication: not only is violence the necessary supplement of power, (political) power itself is always-already at the root of every apparently 'non-political' relationship of violence. The accepted violence and direct relationship of subordination in the Army, the Church, the family, and other 'non-political' social forms is in itself the 'reification' of a certain ethico-*political* struggle and decision – a critical analysis should discern the hidden *political* process that sustains all these 'non-' or 'pre-political' relationships. In human society, the political is the englobing structuring principle, so that every neutralization of some partial content as 'non-political' is a political gesture *par excellence*.

The (Mis)Uses of Appearance

Within these four disavowals of the political moment proper, the most interesting and politically pertinent is the case of meta-politics, in which – to put it in the terms of Lacan's matrix of the four discourses – the place of the 'agent' is occupied by *knowledge*. Marx presented his position as that of '*scientific* materialism'; that is, meta-politics is a politics which legitimizes itself by a direct reference to the scientific status of its knowledge (it is this knowledge which enables meta-politics to draw a line of distinction between those immersed in politico-ideological illusions and the Party basing its historical intervention on knowledge of actual socioeconomic processes). This knowledge (of class society and the relations of production in Marxism) suspends the classic opposition of *Sein* and *Sollen*, of Being and the Ought, of what Is and the ethical Ideal: the ethical Ideal towards which the revolutionary subject strives is directly grounded in (or coincides with) the 'objective', 'disinterested' scientific knowledge of social processes – this coincidence opens up a space for 'totalitarian' violence, since in this way acts which run against the most elementary norms of ethical decency can be legitimized as grounded in the (insight into) historical Necessity (the mass killing of members of the 'bourgeois class' is justified by the scientific insight that this class is already in itself 'condemned to disappear', past its 'progressive role', etc.).

That is the difference between the standard destructive – even murderous – dimension of strictly adhering to the ethical Ideal, and modern totalitarianism: the terrorism of the Jacobins in the French Revolution was grounded in their strict adherence to the ideal of *égaliberté* – in their attempt to realize this ideal directly, to impose it on to reality; this coincidence of the purest idealism with the most destructive violence, analysed already by Hegel in the famous chapter of his *Phenomenology*, cannot explain twentieth-century totalitarianism. What the Jacobins lacked was the reference to objective/neutral 'scientific' knowledge of history legitimizing their exercise of unconditional power. It is only the Leninist revolutionary, not the Jacobin, who thus occupies the properly perverted position of the pure instrument of historical Necessity made accessible by means of scientific knowledge.[24]

Here Rancière follows Claude Lefort's insight into how the space for (Communist) totalitarianism was opened by 'democratic invention' itself: totalitarianism is an inherent perversion of democratic logic.[25] First, we have the logic of the traditional Master who grounds his authority in some transcendent reason (Divine Right, etc.); what then becomes visible with 'democratic invention' is the gap that separates the positive person of the Master from the place he occupies in the symbolic network – with 'democratic invention', the place of Power is posited as originally *empty*, occupied only temporarily and in a contingent way by different subjects. In other words, it now becomes evident that (to quote Marx) people do not treat somebody as a king because he is a king in himself; he is a king *because* and *as long as* people treat him as one. Totalitarianism takes into account this rupture accomplished by the 'democratic invention': the totalitarian Master fully accepts the logic of 'I am a Master only in so far as you treat me as one' – that is to say, his position involves no reference to some transcendent ground; on the contrary, he emphatically tells his followers: 'In myself, I am nothing; all my strength derives from you; I am only the embodiment of your deepest strivings; the moment I lose my roots in you, I am lost . . .'. His entire legitimacy derives from this position of pure servant of the People: the more he 'modestly' diminishes and instrumentalizes his role, the more he emphasizes that he merely expresses and realizes the strivings of the People themselves, who are the true Master, the more all-powerful and untouchable he becomes, since any attack on him is effectively an attack on the People themselves, on their innermost longings. . . . 'The People' is thus split into actual individuals (prone to treason and all kinds of human weaknesses) and *the* People embodied in the Master. These three logics (that of the traditional Master, of the democratic regulated fight for the empty place of Power, of the totalitarian Master) fit the three modes of the disavowal of politics conceptualized by Rancière: the traditional Master functions within the space of arche-politics; democracy involves para-politics, that is, the gentrification of politics proper in regulated agonism (the rules of elections and representative democracy, etc.); the totalitarian Master is possible only within the space of meta-politics.

Perhaps the distinction between the Communist and Fascist Master resides in the fact that – despite all the talk about racial science, and so on – the innermost logic of Fascism is not meta-political but ultra-political: the Fascist Master is a warrior in politics. Stalinism at its 'purest' (the period of great purges in the late 1930s) is a much more paradoxical phenomenon than the Trotskyite narratives of the alleged betrayal of the authentic revolution by the new *nomenklatura* would like to have us believe: Stalinism, rather, is the point of radical (self-relating) negativity that functions as a kind of 'vanishing mediator' between the 'authentic' revolutionary phase of the late 1910s/early 1920s and the stabilization of the *nomenklatura* into a New Class after Stalin's death. That is to say: what characterizes this Stalinist moment, this effective 'point of (revolutionary) madness', is the inherent tension between the new *nomenklatura* and the Leader who is driven to repeated 'irrational' purges, so that the *nomenklatura* is unable to stabilize itself into a New Class: the self-enhancing ('bootstrap') cycle of Terror potentially involves everyone, not only the entire 'ordinary' population but also the highest *nomenklatura* – everyone (with the exception of the One, Stalin himself) was under permanent threat of liquidation.

One is thus led to believe that Stalin in fact lost his fight against the *nomenklatura* (and thereby the bulk of his 'real' power) in the late 1930s, with the end of the Great Purges (ironically, this moment coincided with the ridiculous increase in public adulation of the figure of Stalin, his celebration as the greatest genius of mankind, and so on, as if the loss of 'real' power was somehow compensated by the gain in symbolic power. What the *nomenklatura* offered Stalin was a role comparable to that of the constitutional monarch who dots the i's, but is deprived of actual executive power (or, at least, has to share it with his equals, members of the senior inner circle); Stalin, of course, could not resign himself to such a symbolic role, and his post-World-War-II activity (the Jewish Doctors' Plot, the planned anti-Semitic purge, etc.) betrays his effort to regain real power, an effort which ultimately remained unsuccessful. So, in the last years of his life, with the resistance of the *nomenklatura* growing, Stalin was more and more isolated as a paranoiac madman whose words no longer possessed direct performative efficiency – his words (say, his accusations of treason against the senior members of the *nomenklatura*) were no longer 'acted upon'. In the last Communist Party congress attended by Stalin (in 1952), Stalin, in his speech, accused Molotov and Kaganovich of being traitors and English spies; after Stalin's speech, Molotov simply stood up and claimed that Comrade Stalin was wrong, since he and Kaganovich always had been and remained good Bolsheviks – and, to the amazement of the party delegates present, *nothing happened*: the two accused men retained their senior posts – something that would have been unthinkable a couple of years before.

Also with regard to actual social change, or 'cut in the substance of the social body', the true revolution was not the October Revolution, but the collectivization of the late 1920s. The October Revolution left the substance of the social body (the intricate network of family and other relations) intact; in this respect it was similar to the Fascist revolution, which also merely imposed a new form of executive power on to the existing network of social relations – or rather, precisely in order to maintain this network of social relations. For that reason, the Fascist revolution was a fake event, a revolution – the semblance of a radical change – which took place so that 'nothing would really change', so that things (i.e. the fundamental capitalist relations of production) would basically remain the same. It was only the forced collectivization of the late 1920s which thoroughly subverted and dismembered the 'social substance' (the inherited network of relations), perturbing and cutting deeply into the most fundamental social fabric.[26]

Let us return, however, to Rancière's basic emphasis on the radical ambiguity of the Marxist notion of the 'gap' between formal democracy (human rights, political freedom, etc.) and the economic reality of exploitation and domination. One can read this gap between the 'appearance' of equality–freedom and the social reality of economic, cultural, and other differences either in the standard 'symptomatic' way (the form of universal rights, equality, freedom and democracy is simply a necessary but illusory form of expression of its concrete social content, the universe of exploitation and class domination), or in the much more subversive sense of a tension in which the 'appearance' of *égaliberté*, precisely, is *not* a 'mere appearance' but evinces an effectivity of its own, which allows it to set in motion the process of the rearticulation of actual socio-economic relations by way of their progressive 'politicization'. (Why shouldn't women vote too? Why shouldn't working conditions be of public political concern?, etc.) One is tempted here to use the old Lévi-Straussian term 'symbolic efficiency': the appearance of *égaliberté* is a symbolic fiction which, as such, possesses an actual efficiency of its own – one should resist the properly cynical temptation of reducing it to a mere illusion that conceals a different actuality.

The distinction between *appearance* and the postmodern notion of *simulacrum* as no longer clearly distinguishable from the Real is crucial here.[27] The political as the domain of appearance (opposed to the social reality of class and other distinctions, that is, of society as the articulated social body) has nothing in common with the postmodern notion that we are entering the era of universalized simulacra in which reality itself becomes indistinguishable from its simulated double. The nostalgic longing for the authentic experience of being lost in the deluge of simulacra (detectable in Virilio), as well as the postmodern assertion of the Brave New World of universalized simulacra as the sign that we are finally getting rid of the metaphysical obsession with authentic Being (detectable in Vattimo), both miss the distinction between simulacrum and appearance: what gets lost in today's 'plague of simulations' is not the firm, true, non-simulated Real, but *appearance itself*. To put it in Lacanian terms: simulacrum is imaginary (illusion), while appearance is symbolic (fiction); when the specific dimension of symbolic appearance starts to disintegrate, the Imaginary and the Real become more and more indistinguishable.

The key to today's universe of simulacra, in which the Real is less and less distinguishable from its imaginary simulation, lies in the retreat of 'symbolic efficiency'. In sociopolitical terms, this domain of appearance (of symbolic fiction) is none other than that of politics as distinct from the social body subdivided into parts. There is 'appearance' in so far as a part not included in the Whole of the Social Body (or included/excluded in a way against which it protests) symbolizes its position as that of a Wrong, claiming, against other parts, that it stands for the universality of *égaliberté*: here we are dealing with appearance in contrast to the 'reality' of the structured social body. The old conservative motto of 'keeping up appearances' thus takes a new twist today: it no longer stands for the 'wisdom' according to which it is better not to disturb the rules of social etiquette too much, since social chaos might ensue. Today, the effort to 'keep up appearances' stands, rather, for the effort to maintain the properly political space against the onslaught of the postmodern all-embracing social body, with its multitude of particular identities.[28]

This is also how one has to read Hegel's famous dictum from his *Phenomenology*: 'the Suprasensible is appearance *qua* appearance'. In a sentimental answer to a child asking him what God's face is like, a priest answers that whenever the child encounters a human face irradiating benevolence and goodness, whoever this face belongs to, he catches a glimpse of His face. . . . The truth of this sentimental platitude is that the Suprasensible (God's face) is discernible as a momentary, fleeting appearance, the 'grimace' of an earthly face. It is *this* dimension of 'appearance' transubstantiating a piece of reality into something which, for a brief moment, irradiates the suprasensible Eternity that is missing in the logic of the simulacrum: in the simulacrum, which becomes indistinguishable from the Real, everything is here, and no other, transcendent dimension effectively 'appears' in/through it. Here we are back at the Kantian problematic of the sublime: in Kant's famous reading of the enthusiasm evoked by the French Revolution in the enlightened public around Europe, the revolutionary events functioned as a sign through which the dimension of trans-phenomenal Freedom, of a free society, *appeared*. 'Appearance' is thus not simply the domain of phenomena, but those 'magic moments' in which another, noumenal dimension momentarily 'appears' in ('shines through') some empirical/contingent phenomenon.

So – back to Hegel: 'the Suprasensible is appearance *qua* appearance' does not simply mean that the Suprasensible is not a positive entity *beyond* phenomena, but the inherent power of negativity which makes appearance 'merely an appearance', that is, something that is not in itself fully actual, but condemned to perish in the process of self-sublation. It also means that the Suprasensible is effective only as redoubled, self-reflected, self-related appearance: the Suprasensible comes into existence in the guise of an appearance of Another Dimension which interrupts the standard normal order of appearances *qua* phenomena.

That is also the problem with cyberspace and virtual reality (VR): what VR threatens is *not* 'reality', which is dissolved in the multiplicity of its simulacra, but, on the contrary, *appearance*. So in order to counter the standard fear that cyberspace VR undermines reality, it is not enough to insist on the distinction between reality and the Real (claiming that VR can generate a 'sense of reality', but not the impossible Real); one should also introduce a distinction, correlative to the one between reality and the Real, within the order of appearance itself – the distinction between phenomenal reality and the 'magic' appearances (of Another Dimension) within it. In short, one should distinguish here between two couples of opposites which are absolutely not to be confused in the single opposition of appearance versus reality: the couple of reality and its simulacrum, and the couple of the Real and appearance. The Real is a grimace of reality: say, a disgustingly contorted face in which the Real of a deadly rage transpires/appears. In this sense, the Real itself is an appearance, an elusive semblance whose fleeting presence/absence is discernible in the gaps and discontinuities of the phenomenal order of reality. The true opposition is thus between reality/simulacrum (the two coincide in VR) and Real/appearance. In more detail, one should distinguish four levels of appearance:

- appearance in the simple sense of 'illusion', the false/distorted representation/image of reality ('things are not what they seem' platitudes) – although, of course, a further distinction needs to be introduced here between appearance *qua* mere subjective illusion (distorting the transcendentally constituted order of reality) and appearance *qua* the transcendentally constituted order of phenomenal reality itself, which is opposed to the Thing-in-itself;

- appearance in the sense of symbolic fiction, that is, in Hegelese, appearance as essential: say, the order of symbolic customs and titles ('the honourable judge', etc.) which is 'merely an appearance' – if we disturb it, however, social reality itself disintegrates;

- appearance in the sense of signs indicating that there is something beyond (directly accessible phenomenal reality), that is, the appearance of the Suprasensible: the Suprasensible exists only in so far as it *appears as such* (as the indeterminate presentiment that 'there is something beneath phenomenal reality');

- finally (and it is only here that we encounter what psychoanalysis calls the 'fundamental fantasy', as well as the most radical phenomenological notion of 'phenomena'), the appearance which fills the *void* in the midst of reality, that is, the appearance which conceals the fact that, beneath the phenomena, there is nothing to conceal.

The problem with Kant is that he tends to confuse the last two levels. That is to say, the paradox to be accepted is that the realm of noumenal Freedom, of the Supreme Good, appears as such (as noumenal) only from the phenomenal perspective of the finite subject: in itself, if we get too close to it, it changes into the monstrous Real. . . . Here Heidegger was on the right track with his insistence on temporality as the ultimate unsurpassable horizon, that is, of eternity itself as a category which has meaning only within the temporal experience of a finite subject: in exactly the same way, what Kant was not fully aware of is how the distinction between (our experience of) noumenal freedom and temporal immersion in phenomena is a distinction internal to our finite temporal experience.

Post-Politics

Today, however, we are dealing with another form of the denegation of the political, postmodern *post-politics*, which no longer merely 'represses' the political, trying to contain it and pacify the 'returns of the repressed', but much more effectively 'forecloses' it, so that the postmodern forms of ethnic violence, with their 'irrational' excessive character, are no longer simple 'returns of the repressed' but, rather, represent a case of the foreclosed (from the Symbolic) which, as we know from Lacan, returns in the Real. In post-politics, the conflict of global ideological visions embodied in different parties which compete for power is replaced by the collaboration of enlightened technocrats (economists, public opinion specialists . . .) and liberal multiculturalists; via the process of negotiation of interests, a compromise is reached in the guise of a more or less universal consensus. Post-politics thus emphasizes the need to leave old ideological divisions behind and confront new issues, armed with the necessary expert knowledge and free deliberation that takes people's concrete needs and demands into account.

The best formula that expresses the paradox of post-politics is perhaps Tony Blair's characterization of New Labour as the 'Radical Centre': in the old days of 'ideological' political division, the qualification 'radical' was reserved either for the extreme Left or for the extreme Right. The Centre was, by definition, moderate: measured by the old standards, the term 'Radical Centre' is the same nonsense as 'radical moderation'. What makes New Labour (or Bill Clinton's politics in the USA) 'radical' is its radical abandonment of the 'old ideological divides', usually formulated in the guise of a paraphrase of Deng Xiaoping's motto from the 1960s: 'It doesn't matter if a cat is red or white; what matters is that it actually catches mice': in the same vein, advocates of New Labour like to empha-size that one should take good ideas without any prejudice and apply them, whatever their (ideological) origins. And what are these 'good ideas'? The answer is, of course, *ideas that work*. It is here that we encounter the gap that separates a political act proper from the 'administration of social matters' which remains within the framework of existing sociopoli-tical relations: the political act (intervention) proper is not simply some-thing that works well within the framework of the existing relations, but something that *changes the very framework that determines how things work*. To say that good ideas are 'ideas that work' means that one accepts in advance the (global capitalist) constellation that determines what works (if, for example, one spends too much money on education or healthcare, that 'doesn't work', since it infringes too much on the conditions of capitalist profitability). One can also put it in terms of the well-known definition of politics as the 'art of the possible': authentic politics is, rather, the exact opposite, that is, the art of the *impossible* – it changes the very parameters of what is considered 'possible' in the existing constellation.[29]

When this dimension of the impossible is effectively precluded, the political (the space of litigation in which the excluded can protest the wrong/injustice done to them) foreclosed from the symbolic returns in the Real, in the guise of new forms of *racism*; this 'postmodern racism' emerges as the ultimate consequence of the post-political suspension of the political, the reduction of the State to a mere police-agent servicing the (consensually established) needs of market forces and multicultur-alist tolerant humanitarianism: the 'foreigner' whose status is never prop-erly 'regulated' is the *indivisible remainder* of the transformation of the democratic political struggle into the post-political procedure of nego-tiation and multiculturalist policing. Instead of the *political* subject 'work-ing class' demanding its universal rights, we get, on the one hand, the multiplicity of particular social strata or groups, each with its problems (the dwindling need for manual workers, etc.) and, on the other, the immigrant, ever more prevented from *politicizing* his predicament of exclusion.[30]

The obvious counter-argument here is that today it is the (political) Right that is accomplishing the acts, boldly changing the very rules of what is considered acceptable-admissible in the sphere of public discourse: from the way Reaganism and Thatcherism legitimized the debate about curtailing workers' rights and social benefits, up to the gradual legitimization of the 'open debate' about Nazism in revisionist historiography *à la* Nolte (was it really so bad? Was not Communism worse, that is, cannot Nazism be understood as a reaction to Leninism–Stalinism?). Here, however, it is crucial to introduce a further distinction: for Lacan, a true act does not only retroactively change the rules of the symbolic space; it also disturbs the underlying fantasy – and here, concerning *this* crucial dimension, Fascism emphatically does *not* pass the criterion of the act. Fascist 'Revolution' is, on the contrary, the paradigmatic case of a pseudo-Event, of a spectacular turmoil destined to conceal the fact that, on the most fundamental level (that of the relations of production), *nothing really changes*. The Fascist Revolution is thus the answer to the question: what do we have to change so that, ultimately, nothing will really change? Or – to put it in terms of the libidinal economy of the ideological space – far from disturbing/'traversing' the fantasy that underlies and sustains the capitalist social edifice, Fascist ideological revolution merely brings to the light the phantasmic 'inherent transgression' of the 'normal' bourgeois ideological situation (the set of implicit racist, sexist, etc., 'prejudices' that effectively determine the activity of individuals in it, although they are not publicly recognized).

One of today's common wisdoms is that we are entering a new medieval society in the guise of the New World Order – the grain of truth in this comparison is that the New World Order, as in medieval times, is global, but not universal, since it strives for a new global *order* with each part in its allocated place. A typical advocate of liberalism today throws together workers' protests against reducing their rights and right-wing insistence on fidelity to the Western cultural heritage: he perceives both as pitiful remainders of the 'age of ideology' which have no relevance in today's post-ideological universe. However, the two resistances to globalization follow totally incompatible logics: the Right insists on a *particular* communal identity (*ethnos* or *habitat*) threatened by the onslaught of globalization; while for the Left, the dimension under threat is that of politicization, of articulating 'impossible' *universal* demands ('impossible' from within the existing space of World Order).

Here one should oppose *globalization* and *universalization*: globalization (not only in the sense of global capitalism, the establishment of a global world market, but also in the sense of the assertion of 'humanity' as the global point of reference for human rights, legitimizing the violation of State sovereignty, from trade restrictions to direct military interventions, in parts of the world where global human rights are violated) is precisely the name for the emerging post-political logic which progressively precludes the dimension of universality that appears in politicization proper. The paradox is that there is no *Universal* proper without the process of political litigation, of the 'part of no part', of an out-of-joint entity presenting/manifesting itself as the stand-in for the Universal.

One should link Rancière's notion of post-politics to the notion of excessive, non-functional cruelty as a feature of contemporary life, proposed by Balibar:[31] a cruelty whose manifestations range from 'fundamentalist' racist and/or religious slaughter to the 'senseless' outbursts of violence by adolescents and the homeless in our megalopolises, a violence one is tempted to call *Id*-Evil, a violence grounded in no utilitarian or ideological reason. All the talk about foreigners stealing work from us, or the threat they represent to our Western values, should not deceive us: under closer examination, it soon becomes clear that this talk provides a rather superficial secondary rationalization. The answer we ultimately obtain from a skinhead is that it makes him feel good to beat up foreigners, that their presence disturbs him. . . . What we encounter here is indeed *Id*-Evil, that is, Evil structured and motivated by the most elementary imbalance in the relationship between the Ego and *jouissance*, by the tension between pleasure and the foreign body of *jouissance* at the very heart of it. Id-Evil thus stages the most elementary 'short circuit' in the subject's relationship to the primordially missing object-cause of his desire: what 'bothers' us in the 'other' (Jew, Japanese, African, Turk . . .) is that he appears to enjoy a privileged relationship to the object – the other either possesses the object-treasure, having snatched it away from us (which is why we don't have it), or he poses a threat to our possession of the object.[32]

What one should suggest here, again, is the Hegelian 'infinite judgement' asserting the speculative identity of these 'useless' and 'excessive' outbursts of violence, which display nothing but a pure and naked ('non-sublimated') hatred of Otherness, and the post-political multiculturalist universe of tolerance of difference, in which nobody is excluded. Of course, I have just used the term 'non-sublimated' in its usual sense which, in this case, stands for the exact opposite of its strict psychoanalytic meaning – in short, what takes place in the focusing of our hatred on some representative of the (officially tolerated) Other is the very mechanism of *sublimation* at its most elementary: the all-encompassing nature of the post-political Concrete Universality which accounts for everybody at the level of symbolic inclusion, this multiculturalist vision-and-practice of 'unity in difference' ('all equal, all different'), leaves open, as the only way to mark the Difference, the proto-sublimatory gesture of elevating a contingent Other (of race, sex, religion . . .) into the 'absolute Otherness' of the impossible Thing, the ultimate threat to our identity – this Thing which must be annihilated if we are to survive. Therein lies the properly Hegelian paradox: the final arrival of the truly rational 'concrete universality' – the abolition of antagonisms, the 'mature' universe of the negotiated coexistence of different groups – coincides with its radical opposite, with thoroughly contingent outbursts of violence.

Hegel's fundamental rule is that 'objective' excess (the direct reign of abstract universality which imposes its law 'mechanically', with complete disregard for the concerned subject caught in its web) is always supplemented by the 'subjective' excess (the irregular, arbitrary exercise of whims). An excellent illustration of this interdependence is provided by Balibar,[33] who distinguishes two opposite but complementary modes of excessive violence: the 'ultra-objective' ('structural') violence that is inherent in the social conditions of global capitalism (the 'automatic' creation of excluded and dispensable individuals, from the homeless to the unemployed), and the 'ultra-subjective' violence of newly emerging ethnic and/ or religious (in short: racist) 'fundamentalisms'. This 'excessive' and 'groundless' violence involves its own mode of knowledge, that of impotent cynical reflection – back to our example of *Id*-Evil, of a skinhead beating up foreigners: when he is really pressed for the reasons for his violence, and if he is capable of minimal theoretical reflection, he will suddenly start to talk like social workers, sociologists and social psychologists, quoting diminished social mobility, rising insecurity, the disintegration of paternal authority, the lack of maternal love in his early childhood . . . in short, he will provide the more or less precise psychosociological account of his acts so dear to enlightened liberals eager to 'understand' violent youth as tragic victims of their social and familial conditions.

Here the standard enlightened formula of the efficiency of the 'critique of ideology' from Plato onwards ('They're doing it because they don't know what they're doing' – that is, knowledge in itself is liberating; when the erring subject reflects upon what he is doing, he will no longer be doing it) is turned around: the violent skinhead 'knows very well what he's doing, but he's nevertheless doing it'.[34] The symbolically efficient knowledge embedded in the subject's actual social *praxis* disintegrates into, on the one hand, excessive 'irrational' violence with no ideologico-political foundation and, on the other, impotent external reflection that leaves the subject's acts intact. In the guise of this cynically impotent reflecting skinhead who, with an ironic smile, explains the roots of his senselessly violent behaviour to the perplexed journalist, the enlightened tolerant multiculturalist bent on 'understanding' forms of excessive violence gets his own message in its inverted, true form – in short, as Lacan would have put it, at this point the communication between him and the 'object' of his study, the intolerant skinhead, is thoroughly successful.

The distinction between this excessive 'dysfunctional' violence and the obscene violence that serves as the implicit support of a standard ideological universal notion is crucial here (when 'the rights of man' are 'not really universal' but 'in fact the right of white property-owning males', any attempt to disregard this implicit underlying set of unwritten rules that effectively constrain the universality of rights is met by outbursts of violence). Nowhere is this contrast stronger than in the case of the African-Americans: although they were formally entitled to participate in political life by the mere fact of being American citizens, the old parapolitical democratic racism prevented their actual participation by silently enforcing their exclusion (via verbal and physical threats, etc.). The appropriate answer to this standard exclusion-from-the-Universal was the great Civil Rights movement associated with the name of Martin Luther King: it suspended the implicit obscene supplement that enacted the actual exclusion of Blacks from formal universal equality – of course, it was easy for such a gesture to gain the support of the large majority of the white liberal upper-class establishment, dismissing opponents as dumb low-class Southern rednecks. Today, however, the very terrain of the struggle has changed: the post-political liberal establishment not only fully acknowledges the gap between mere formal equality and its actualization/ implementation, it not only acknowledges the exclusionary logic of 'false' ideological universality; it even actively fights it by applying to it a vast legal-psychological-sociological network of measures, from identifying the specific problems of every group and subgroup (not only homosexuals but African-American lesbians, African-American lesbian mothers, African-American unemployed lesbian mothers . . .) up to proposing a set of measures ('affirmative action', etc.) to rectify the wrong.

What such a tolerant procedure precludes is the gesture of *politicization* proper: although the difficulties of being an African-American unemployed lesbian mother are adequately catalogued right down to its most specific features, the concerned subject none the less somehow 'feels' that there is something 'wrong' and 'frustrating' in this very effort to mete out justice to her specific predicament – what she is deprived of is the possibility of 'metaphoric' elevation of her specific 'wrong' into a stand-in for the universal 'wrong'. The only way to articulate this universality – the fact that I, precisely, am *not* merely that specific individual exposed to a set of specific injustices – consists, then, in its apparent opposite, in the thoroughly 'irrational' excessive outburst of violence. The old Hegelian rule is again confirmed here: the only way for a universality to come into existence, to 'posit' itself 'as such', is in the guise of its very opposite, of what cannot but appear as an excessive 'irrational' whim. These violent *passages à l'acte* bear witness to some underlying *antagonism* that can no longer be formulated-symbolized in properly political terms. The only way to counteract these excessive 'irrational' outbursts is to approach the question of what none the less remains foreclosed in the very all-inclusionary/tolerant post-political logic, and to actualize this foreclosed dimension in some new mode of political subjectivization.

Let us recall the standard example of a popular protest (mass demonstration, strike, boycott) directed at a specific point, that is, focusing on a particular demand ('Abolish that new tax! Justice for the imprisoned! Stop exploiting that natural resource!' . . .) – the situation becomes politicized when this particular demand starts to function as a metaphoric condensation of the global opposition against Them, those in power, so that the protest is no longer actually just about that demand, but about the universal dimension that resonates in that particular demand (for this reason, protesters often feel somehow deceived when those in power against whom their protest was addressed simply accept their demand – as if, in this way, they have somehow frustrated them, depriving them of the true aim of their protest in the very guise of accepting their demand). What post-politics tends to prevent is precisely this metaphoric universalization of particular demands: post-politics mobilizes the vast apparatus of experts, social workers, and so on, to reduce the overall demand (complaint) of a particular group to just this demand, with its particular content – no wonder this suffocating closure gives birth to 'irrational' outbursts of violence as the only way to give expression to the dimension beyond particularity.

This argumentation is not to be confused with the point, made by many a conservative critic, according to which violent outbursts signify the return of the repressed of our anaemic liberal Western civilization.

Exemplary here is Mario Vargas Llosa's argumentation that 'the hooligan is no barbarian: he is an exquisite and terrible product of civilization'.[35] Llosa takes as his starting point the observation that the typical violent soccer fan is not an unemployed *lumpenproletarian* but a comfortably off middle-class worker, that is, the very epitome of gentle good manners and civilized compassion – his violent outbursts are 'returns of the repressed', the reassertion of the violent orgy increasingly prohibited by our civilized liberal societies. Through a misleading reference to Freud, Llosa mystifies and naturalizes current violent outbursts: as if there is a fixed, irreducible propensity towards violent outbursts in human nature, and when sacred orgies are no longer permitted as its legitimate expression, this propensity has to find another way to express itself. . . . In clear contrast to this line of argumentation, my point is much stronger: the neo-Nazi skinhead's ethnic violence is not the 'return of the repressed' of the liberal multiculturalist tolerance, but *directly generated by it*, its own concealed true face.

Is There a Progressive Eurocentrism?

This conceptual frame enables us to approach Eastern European Socialism in a new way. The passage from actually existing Socialism to actually existing capitalism in Eastern Europe brought about a series of comic reversals of sublime democratic enthusiasm into the ridiculous. The dignified East German crowds gathering around Protestant churches and heroically defying *Stasi* terror suddenly turned into vulgar consumers of bananas and cheap pornography; the civilized Czechs mobilized by the appeal of Havel and other cultural icons suddenly turned into cheap swindlers of Western tourists. . . . The disappointment was mutual: the West, which began by idolizing the Eastern dissident movement as the re-invention of its own tired democracy, disappointedly dismisses the present post-Socialist regimes as a mixture of the corrupt ex-Communist oligarchy and/or ethnic and religious fundamentalists (even the dwindling liberals are mistrusted as insufficiently 'politically correct': where is their feminist awareness? etc.); the East, which began by idolizing the West as the example of affluent democracy to be followed, finds itself in the whirlpool of ruthless commercialization and economic colonization. So was all this worth the effort?

The hero of Dashiell Hammett's *Maltese Falcon*, the private detective Sam Spade, narrates the story of his being hired to find a man who had suddenly left his settled job and family, and vanished. Spade is unable to track him down, but a few years later he accidentally encounters the man in a bar in another city. Under an assumed name, the man is leading a life remarkably similar to the one he fled from (a regular boring job, a new wife and children) – despite this similarity, however, he is convinced that his new beginning was not in vain, that it was well worth the trouble to cut his ties and start a new life.... Perhaps the same goes for the passage from actually existing Socialism to acutally existing capitalism in ex-Communist East European countries: despite betrayed enthusiastic expectations, something *did* take place in between, in the passage itself, and it is in this Event which took place in between, this 'vanishing mediator', in this moment of democratic enthusiasm, that we should locate the crucial dimension obfuscated by later renormalization.

It is clear that the protesting crowds in the DDR, Poland and the Czech Republic 'wanted something else', a utopian object of impossible Fullness designated by a multiplicity of names ('solidarity', 'human rights', etc.), *not* what they actually got. There are two possible reactions to this gap between expectations and reality; the best way to capture them is by reference to the well-known opposition between *fool* and *knave*. The fool is a simpleton, a court jester who is allowed to tell the truth precisely because the 'performative power' (the sociopolitical efficacy) of his speech is suspended; the knave is the cynic who openly states the truth, a crook who tries to sell the open admission of his crookedness as honesty, a scoundrel who admits the need for illegitimate repression in order to maintain social stability. Following the fall of Socialism, the knave is a neo-conservative advocate of the free market, who cruelly rejects all forms of social solidarity as counterproductive sentimentalism; while the fool is a multiculturalist 'radical' social critic who, by means of his ludic procedures destined to 'subvert' the existing order, actually serves as its supplement. With regard to Eastern Europe, a knave dismisses the 'third way' project of *Neues Forum* in the ex-DDR as hopelessly outdated utopianism, and exhorts us to accept cruel market reality; while a fool insists that the collapse of Socialism has actually opened up a Third Way, a possibility left unexploited by the Western recolonization of the East.

This cruel reversal of the sublime into the ridiculous was, of course, grounded in the fact that there was a double misunderstanding at work in the public (self-)perception of social protest movements (from Solidarity to *Neues Forum*) in the last years of Eastern European Socialism. On the one hand, there were the attempts of the ruling *nomenklatura* to reinscribe these events in their police/political framework, by distinguishing between 'honest critics' with whom one could discuss matters in a calm, rational, depoliticized atmosphere, and a bunch of extremist provocateurs who served foreign interests.[36] The battle was thus not only for higher wages and better conditions, but also – and above all – for the workers to be acknowledged as legitimate partners in negotiating with representatives of the regime – the moment the powers that be were forced to accept this, the battle was in a way already won.[37] When these movements exploded in a broad mass phenomenon, their demands for freedom and democracy (and solidarity and . . .) were also misperceived by Western commentators who saw in them confirmation that the people of the East also want what the people in the West already have: they automatically translated these demands into the Western liberal-democratic notion of freedom (multiparty representational political game *cum* global market economy).

Emblematic to the point of caricature here was the figure of Dan Rather, the American news reporter, on Tiananmen Square in 1989, standing in front of a copy of the Statue of Liberty and claiming that this statue says everything about what the protesting students were demanding (in short, if you scratch the yellow skin of a Chinese, you find an American). What this statue actually stood for was a utopian longing that had nothing to do with the real USA (incidentally, it was the same with the original immigrants to America, for whom the view of the statue stood for a utopian longing that was soon crushed). The perception of the American media thus offered another example of the reinscription of the explosion of what, as we have seen, Étienne Balibar calls *égaliberté* (the unconditional demand for freedom–equality which explodes any positive order) within the confines of a given order.

Are we, then, condemned to the debilitating alternative of choosing between a knave and a fool, or is there a *tertium datur*? Perhaps the contours of this *tertium datur* can be discerned via reference to the fundamental European legacy. When one says 'European legacy', every self-respecting leftist intellectual has the same reaction as Joseph Goebbels had to culture as such: he reaches for his gun and starts to fire accusations of proto-Fascist Eurocentrist cultural imperialism. . . . Is it possible, however, to imagine a leftist appropriation of the European political tradition? Yes, if we follow Rancière and identify as the core of this tradition the unique gesture of democratic political subjectivization: it was this politicization proper which re-emerged violently in the disintegration of Eastern European Socialism. From my own political past, I remember how, after four journalists were arrested and brought to trial by the Yugoslav Army in Slovenia in 1988, I participated in the 'Committee for the protection of the human rights of the four accused'. Officially, the goal of the Committee was simply to guarantee fair treatment for the four accused; however, the Committee turned into the major oppositional political force, practically the Slovene version of the Czech Civic Forum or East German *Neues Forum*, the body which co-ordinated democratic opposition, a *de facto* representative of civil society.

The Committee's programme consisted of four items; the first three directly concerned the accused, while the 'devil in the detail', of course, was the fourth item, which said that the Committee wanted to clarify the entire background of the arrest of the four accused, and thus contribute to creating circumstances in which such arrests would no longer be possible – a coded way of saying that we wanted the abolition of the existing Socialist regime. Our demand 'Justice for the four accused!' started to function as the metaphoric condensation of the demand for the global overthrow of the Socialist regime. For that reason, in almost daily negotiations with the Committee, Communist Party officials were always accusing us of a 'hidden agenda', claiming that the liberation of the four accused was not our true goal – that we were 'exploiting and manipulating the arrest and trial for other, darker political goals'. In short, the Communists wanted to play the 'rational' depoliticized game: they wanted to deprive the slogan 'Justice for the four accused!' of its explosive general connotation, and reduce it to its literal meaning, which concerned just a minor legal matter; they cynically claimed that it was we, the Committee, who were behaving 'non-democratically' and manipulating the fate of the accused, using global pressure and black-mailing strategies instead of focusing on the particular problem of their plight.

This is politics proper: the moment in which a particular demand is not simply part of the negotiation of interests but aims at something more, and starts to function as the metaphoric condensation of the global restructuring of the entire social space. There is a clear contrast between this subjectivization and today's proliferation of postmodern 'identity politics' whose goal is the exact opposite, that is, precisely the assertion of one's particular identity, of one's proper place within the social structure. The postmodern identity politics of particular (ethnic, sexual, etc.) life-styles perfectly fits the depoliticized notion of society, in which every particular group is 'accounted for', has its specific status (of victim) acknowledged through affirmative action or other measures destined to guarantee social justice. The fact that this kind of justice meted out to victimized minorities requires an intricate police apparatus (for identifying the group in question, for punishing offenders against its rights – how legally to define sexual harassment or racial injury?, and so on – for providing the preferential treatment which should compensate for the wrong this group has suffered) is deeply significant: what is usually praised as 'postmodern politics' (the pursuit of particular issues whose resolution must be negotiated within the 'rational' global order allocating its particular component its proper place) is thus effectively the end of politics proper.

So while everyone seems to agree that today's post-political liberal-democratic global capitalist regime is the regime of the non-event (in Nietzsche's terms, of the Last Man), the question of where we are to look for the Event remains open. The obvious solution is: in so far as we experience contemporary postmodern social life as 'non-substantial' the proper answer is the multitude of passionate, often violent returns to 'roots', to different forms of ethnic and/or religious 'substance'. What is 'substance' in social experience? It is the violent emotional moment of 'recognition', when one becomes aware of one's 'roots', of one's 'true belonging', the moment in the face of which liberal reflexive distance is utterly impotent – all of a sudden, adrift in the world, one finds oneself in the grip of a kind of absolute longing for 'home', and everything else, everyday common concerns, becomes unimportant. . . .[38]

Here, however, one must fully endorse Badiou's point that these 'returns to the Substance' are themselves impotent in the face of the global march of Capital: they are its inherent supplement, the limit/condition of its functioning, since – as Deleuze emphasized years ago – capitalist 'deterritorialization' is always accompanied by re-emerging 'reterritorializations'. More precisely, there is an inherent split in the field of particular identities themselves caused by the onslaught of capitalist globalization: on the one hand, the so-called 'fundamentalisms', whose basic formula is that of the Identity of one's own group, implying the practice of excluding the threatening Other(s): France for the French (against Algerian immigrants), America for Americans (against the Hispanic invasion), Slovenia for Slovenians (against the excessive presence of 'Southerners', immigrants from the ex-Yugoslav republics);[39] on the other hand, there is postmodern multiculturalist 'identity politics', aiming at the tolerant coexistence of ever-shifting, 'hybrid' lifestyle groups, divided into endless subgroups (Hispanic women, black gays, white male AIDS patients, lesbian mothers . . .).

This ever-growing flowering of groups and subgroups in their hybrid and fluid, shifting identities, each insisting on the right to assert its specific way of life and/or culture, this incessant diversification, is possible and thinkable only against the background of capitalist globalization; it is the very way capitalist globalization affects our sense of ethnic and other forms of community belonging: the only link connecting these multiple groups is the link of Capital itself, always ready to satisfy the specific demands of each group and subgroup (gay tourism, Hispanic music . . .). Furthermore, the opposition between fundamentalism and postmodern pluralist identity politics is ultimately a fake, concealing a deeper solidarity (or, to put it in Hegelese, speculative identity): a multiculturalist can easily find even the most 'fundamentalist' ethnic identity attractive, but only in so far as it is the identity of the supposedly authentic Other (say, in the USA, Native American tribal identity); a fundamentalist group can easily adopt, in its social functioning, the postmodern strategies of identity politics, presenting itself as one of the threatened minorities, simply striving to maintain its specific way of life and cultural identity. The line of separation between multiculturalist identity politics and fundamental-ism is thus purely formal; it often depends merely on the different perspective from which the observer views a movement for maintaining a group identity.

Under these conditions, the Event in the guise of the 'return to roots' can be only a semblance that fits the capitalist circular movenent perfectly or – in the worst case – leads to a catastrophe like Nazism. The sign of today's ideologico-political constellation is the fact that these kinds of pseudo-Events constitute the only appearances of Events which seem to pop up (it is only right-wing populism which today displays the authentic *political* passion of accepting the *struggle*, of openly admitting that, pre-cisely in so far as one claims to speak from a universal standpoint, one does not aim to please everybody, but is ready to introduce a *division* of 'Us' versus 'Them'). It has often been remarked that, despite hating the guts of Buchanan in the USA, Le Pen in France or Haider in Austria, even Leftists feel a kind of relief at their appearance – finally, in the midst of the reign of the aseptic post-political administration of public affairs, there is someone who revives a proper political passion of division and confrontation, a committed belief in political issues, albeit in a deplorably repulsive form. . . . We are thus more and more deeply locked into a claustrophobic space within which we can only oscillate between the non-event of the smooth running of the liberal-democratic capitalist global New World Order and fundamentalist Events (the rise of local proto-Fascisms, etc.), which temporarily disturb the calm surface of the capitalist ocean – no wonder that, in these circumstances, Heidegger mistook the pseudo-Event of the Nazi revolution for the Event itself. Today, more than ever, one has to insist that the only way open to the emergence of an Event is that of breaking the vicious cycle of globalization-with-particularization by (re)asserting the dimension of Universality *against* capitalist globalization. Badiou draws an interesting parallel here between our time of American global domination and the late Roman Empire, also a 'multiculturalist' global State in which multiple ethnic groups were thriving, united (not by capital, but) by the non-substantial link of the Roman legal order – so what we need today is the gesture that would undermine capitalist globalization from the standpoint of universal Truth, just as Pauline Christianity did to the Roman global Empire.

For this reason, a renewed Left should aim at fully endorsing Kierkegaard's paradoxical claim that, with regard to the tension between tradition and modernity, *Christianity is on the side of modernity*. In his assertion that authentic Faith can emerge only when one leaves pagan 'organicist' humanism behind, Kierkegaard promulgates a thoroughgoing reversal in the relationship between Inside and Outside (inner faith and religious institution). In his passionate and violent polemics against 'Christendom', he does not simply reject obedience to external institutionalized religion on behalf of a true inner faith: Kierkegaard is well aware that these two aspects (rituals of the external institution and a true inner conviction) are strictly codependent, that they form the two sides of the 'modern age' in which lifeless external ritual is supplemented by the empty sentimentalism of the liberal religion of inner conviction ('dogmas don't matter, what matters is the authentic inner religious sentiment'). Kierkegaard's point is that true religion is simultaneously more 'inner' (it involves an act of absolute faith that cannot even be externalized into the universal medium of language) and more external (when I truly believe, I accept that the source of my faith is not in myself; that, in some inexplicable way, it comes from outside, from God Himself – in His grace, God addressed me, it was not I who raised myself to Him).

In other words, we no longer dwell in the Aristotelian universe in which (ontologically) lower elements spontaneously move and tend towards their Goal, the immovable Good: in Christianity, it is God Himself who 'moves', who embodies Himself in a temporal/mortal man. When Kierkegaard determines faith as the pure internality which the believer is unable to symbolize/socialize, to share with others (Abraham is absolutely alone in the face of God's horrible command to slaughter his son Isaac; he is unable even to share his pain with others); this means that what, in his faith, is absolutely inner, what resists intersubjective symbolic mediation, is the very radical *externality* of the religious Call: Abraham is unable to share God's horrible injunction with others precisely in so far as this injunction in no way expresses his 'inner nature', but is experienced as a radically traumatic intrusion which attacks the subject from outside and which the subject can never internalize, assume as 'his own', discern any meaning in it to be shared with others. The point is thus that the subject cannot externalize God's injunction *precisely because he cannot internalize it.* We can see now how Kierkegaard 'surmounts' the 'modern age' opposition between external lifeless ritual and pure inner sentimental conviction: not through a pseudo-Hegelian synthesis, so that we re-establish an authentic social life in which 'external' social rituals are again permeated with authentic inner conviction – that is, in which subjects fully participate in organic social life (the young Hegel's vision of the Greek community prior to the split into 'subjective' and 'objective'), but by endorsing the paradox of authentic faith in which radical externality coincides with pure internality.

Perhaps one should return here to the well-known Kierkegaardian opposition between Socratic *reminiscence* and Christian *repetition*. The Socratic philosophical principle is the one of reminiscence: the Truth already dwells deep inside me, and in order to discover it I have only to look deep into my soul, to get to 'know myself'. The Christian Truth, in contrast, is the one of Revelation, which is the exact opposite of reminiscence: Truth is not inherent, it is not the (re)discovery of what is already in myself, but an Event, something violently *imposed* on me from the Outside through a traumatic encounter that shatters the very foundations of my being. (For that reason, the New Age Gnostic redefinition of Christianity in terms of the Soul's journey of inner self-discovery and purification is profoundly heretical, and should be ruthlessly rejected.) And Lacan, like Badiou, opts for the Christian–Kierkegaardian view: in contrast to misleading first impressions, psychoanalytic treatment is, at its most fundamental, *not* the path of remembrance, of the return to the inner repressed truth, its bringing to light; its crucial moment, that of 'traversing the fantasy', rather, designates the subject's (symbolic) *rebirth*, his (re-)creation *ex nihilo*, a jump through the 'zero-point' of death drive to the thoroughly new symbolic configuration of his being.

The Three Universals

These impasses demonstrate how the structure of the Universal is much more complex than it appears. It was Balibar[40] who elaborated the three levels of universality which vaguely follow the Lacanian triad of Real, Imaginary and Symbolic: the 'real' universality of globalization, with the supplementary process of 'internal exclusions' (the extent to which, today, the fate of each of us hinges on the intricate web of global market relations); the universality of the fiction that regulates ideological hegemony (Church or State as the universal 'imagined communities', which allow the subject to acquire a distance towards immersion in his immediate social group – class, profession, sex, religion ... – and posit himself as a free subject); the universality of an Ideal, as exemplified by the revolutionary demand for *égaliberté*, which remains an unconditional excess, setting in motion permanent insurrection against the existing order, and can thus never be 'gentrified', included in the existing order.

The point, of course, is that the boundary between these three universals is never stable and fixed: the notion of freedom and equality can serve as the hegemonic idea which enables us to identify with our particular social role (I am a poor artisan, but precisely as such I participate in the life of my nation-state as an equal and free citizen ...), or as the irreducible excess which destabilizes the fixed social order. What, in the Jacobin universe, was the destabilizing universality of the Ideal setting in motion the incessant process of social transformation later became the ideological fiction allowing each individual to identify with his specific place in the social space. The alternative here is: is the universal 'abstract' (potentially opposed to concrete content) or 'concrete' (in the sense that I experience my very particular mode of social life as my specific way of participating in the universal social order)? Balibar's point is, of course, that the tension between the two is irreducible: the excess of abstract-negative-ideal universality, its unsettling-destabilizing force, can never be fully integrated into the harmonious whole of a 'concrete universality'.[41]

However, there is another tension, the tension between the two modes of 'concrete universality' itself, which seems more crucial today. That is to say, the 'real' universality of today's globalization through the market involves its own hegemonic fiction (or even ideal) of multiculturalist tolerance, respect for and protection of human rights and democracy, and so on; it involves its own pseudo-Hegelian 'concrete universality' of a

world order whose universal features of market, human rights and democracy allow each specific 'lifestyle' to flourish in its particularity. So a
tension inevitably emerges between this postmodern, post-nation-state,
'concrete universality', and the earlier 'concrete universality' of the
nation-state.

The story of the emergence of the nation-state is the story of the (often
extremely violent) 'transubstantiation' of local communities and their
traditions into the modern nation *qua* 'imagined community'; this process
involved the repression of authentic local ways of life and/or their
reinscription into the new encompassing 'invented tradition'. In other
words, 'national tradition' is a screen that conceals *not* the process of
modernization but *the true ethnic tradition itself in its unbearable factuality.*[42]
What comes after is the (apparently) opposite 'postmodern' process of
returning to more local, subnational modes of identification; however,
these new modes of identification are no longer experienced as directly
substantial – they are already a matter of the free choice of one's 'lifestyle'. None the less, it is not enough to oppose the previous authentic
ethnic identification to the postmodern arbitrary choice of 'lifestyles': this
opposition fails to acknowledge the extent to which that very previous
'authentic' national identification was an 'artificial', violently imposed
phenomenon, based on the repression of previous local traditions.

Far from being a 'natural' unity of social life, a balanced frame, a kind
of Aristotelian *entelechia* towards which all previous development advanced,
the universal form of nation-state is, rather, a precarious, temporary
balance between the relationship to a particular ethnic Thing (patriotism,
pro patria mori, etc.) and the (potentially) universal function of the market.
On the one hand, the nation-state 'sublates' organic local forms of
identification into universal 'patriotic' identification; on the other, it
posits itself as a kind of pseudo-natural boundary of the market economy,
delimiting 'internal' from 'external' commerce – economic activity is thus
'sublimated', raised to the level of the ethnic Thing, legitimated as a
patriotic contribution to the nation's greatness. This balance is constantly
threatened from both sides: from the side of previous 'organic' forms of
particular identification which do not simply disappear but continue their
subterranean life outside the universal public sphere; and from the side
of the immanent logic of Capital, whose 'transnational' nature is inherently indifferent to nation-state boundaries. And today's new 'fundamentalist' ethnic identifications involve a kind of 'desublimation', a process of
disintegration of this precarious unity of the 'national economy' into its

two constituent parts, the transnational market function and the relationship to the ethnic Thing.[43]

It is therefore only today, in contemporary 'fundamentalist' ethnic, religious, lifestyle, and so on, communities, that the split between the abstract form of commerce and the relationship to the particular ethnic Thing, inaugurated by the Enlightenment project, is fully realized: today's postmodern ethnic or religious 'fundamentalism' and xenophobia are not only not 'regressive' but, on the contrary, offer the supreme proof of the final emancipation of the economic logic of the market from the attachment to the ethnic Thing. That is the highest speculative effort of the dialectic of social life: not in describing the mediation process of the primordial immediacy (say, the disintegration of organic community in 'alienated' individualist society), but in explaining how this very mediation process characteristic of modernity can give birth to new forms of 'organic' immediacy, like the contemporary 'chosen' or 'invented' communities ('lifestyle communities': gays, etc.).[44]

Multiculturalism

How, then, does the universe of Capital relate to the form of nation-state in our era of global capitalism? Perhaps this relationship is best designated as 'autocolonization': with the direct multinational functioning of Capital, we are no longer dealing with the standard opposition between metropolis and colonized countries; a global company, as it were, cuts its umbilical cord with its mother-nation and treats its country of origin as simply another territory to be colonized. This is what is so disturbing to patriotically orientated right-wing populists, from Le Pen to Buchanan: the fact that the new multinationals have exactly the same attitude towards the French or American local population as towards the population of Mexico, Brazil or Taiwan. Is there not a kind of poetic justice in this self-referential turn of today's global capitalism, which functions as a kind of 'negation of negation', after national capitalism and its internationalist/colonialist phase? At the beginning (ideally, of course), there is capitalism within the confines of a nation-state, and with the accompanying international trade (exchange between sovereign nation-states); what follows is the relationship of colonization, in which the colonizing country subordinates and exploits (economically, politically, culturally) the colonized country; the final moment of this process is the paradox of colonization, in which there are only colonies, no colonizing countries – the colonizing power is no longer a nation-state but the global company itself. In the long term, we shall all not only wear Banana Republic shirts but also live in banana republics.

And, of course, the ideal form of ideology of this global capitalism is multiculturalism, the attitude which, from a kind of empty global position, treats *each* local culture as the colonizer treats colonized people – as 'natives' whose *mores* are to be carefully studied and 'respected'. That is to say: the relationship between traditional imperialist colonialism and global capitalist self-colonization is exactly the same as the relationship between Western cultural imperialism and multiculturalism – just as global capitalism involves the paradox of colonization without the colonizing nation-state metropolis, multiculturalism involves a patronizing Eurocentrist distance and/or respect for local cultures without roots in one's own particular culture. In other words, multiculturalism is a disavowed, inverted, self-referential form of racism, a 'racism with a distance' – it 'respects' the Other's identity, conceiving the Other as a self-enclosed 'authentic' community towards which the multiculturalist maintains a distance made possible by his/her privileged universal position. Multiculturalism is a racism which empties its own position of all positive content (the multiculturalist is not a direct racist; he or she does not oppose to the Other the *particular* values of his or her own culture); none the less he or she retains this position as the privileged *empty point of universality* from which one is able to appreciate (and depreciate) other particular cultures properly – multiculturalist respect for the Other's specificity is the very form of asserting one's own superiority.

From the standpoint of the post-Marxist anti-essentialist notion of politics as the field of hegemonic struggle with no pre-established rules that would define its parameters in advance, it is easy to reject the very notion of the 'logic of Capital' as precisely the remainder of the old essentialist stance: far from being reducible to an ideologico-cultural effect of the economic process, the passage from standard cultural imperialism to the more tolerant multiculturalism with its openness towards the wealth of hybrid ethnic, sexual, and so on, identities is the result of a long and difficult politico-cultural *struggle* whose final outcome was in no way guaranteed by the a priori co-ordinates of the 'logic of Capital'. . . . The crucial point, however, is that this struggle for the politicization and assertion of multiple ethnic, sexual, and other identities always took place against the background of an invisible yet all the more forbidding barrier: the global capitalist system was able to incorporate the gains of the postmodern politics of identities to the extent that they did not disturb the smooth circulation of Capital – the moment some political intervention poses a serious threat to that, an elaborate set of exclusionary measures quashes it.

What about the rather obvious counter-argument that the multiculturalist's neutrality is false, since his or her position silently privileges Eurocentrist content? This line of reasoning is right, but for the wrong reason. The particular cultural background or roots which always support the universal multiculturalist position are not its 'truth', hidden beneath the mask of universality ('multiculturalist universalism is really Eurocentrist...') but, rather, the opposite: the stain of particular roots is the phantasmic screen which conceals the fact that the subject is already thoroughly 'rootless', that his true position is the void of universality. Let me recall Darian Leader's example of the man in a restaurant with his female companion, who, when asking the waiter for a table, says: 'Bedroom for two, please!' instead of 'Table for two, please!'. One should reverse the standard Freudian explanation ('Of course, his mind was already on the night of sex he planned after the meal!'): this intervention of the subterranean sexual fantasy is, rather, the screen which serves as the defence against the oral drive which actually matters to him more than sex.[45]

In his analysis of the French Revolution of 1848 (in *The Class Struggles in France*), Marx provides a similar example of such a double deception: the Party of Order which took over after the Revolution publicly supported the Republic, yet secretly it believed in Restoration – members used every opportunity to mock Republican rituals and to signal in every possible way where 'their heart was'. The paradox, however, was that the truth of their activity lay in the external form they privately mocked and despised: this Republican form was not a mere semblance beneath which the Royalist desire lurked – rather, it was the secret clinging to Royalism which enabled them to fulfil their actual historical function: to implement bourgeois Republican law and order. Marx himself mentions how members of the Party of Order derived immense pleasure from their occasional Royalist 'slips of the tongue' against the Republic (referring to France as a Kingdom in their parliamentary debates, etc.): these slips of the tongue articulated their phantasmic illusions which served as the screen enabling them to blind themselves to the social reality of what was going on *on the surface*.

And, *mutatis mutandis*, the same goes for today's capitalist, who still clings to some particular cultural heritage, identifying it as the secret source of his success (Japanese executives following tea ceremonies or

Bushido code, etc.), or for the reverse case of the Western journalist in search of the particular secret of Japanese success: this very reference to a particular cultural formula is a screen for the universal anonymity of Capital. The true horror lies not in the particular content hidden beneath the universality of global Capital but, rather, in the fact that Capital is effectively an anonymous global machine blindly running its course; that there is in fact no particular Secret Agent animating it. The horror is not the (particular living) ghost in the (dead universal) machine, but the (dead universal) machine in the very heart of each (particular living) ghost. The conclusion to be drawn is thus that the problematic of multiculturalism (the hybrid coexistence of diverse cultural life-worlds) which imposes itself today is the form of appearance of its opposite, of the massive presence of capitalism as *global* world system: it bears witness to the unprecedented homogenization of today's world.

It is in fact as if, since the horizon of social imagination no longer allows us to entertain the idea of an eventual demise of capitalism – since, as we might put it, everybody tacitly accepts that *capitalism is here to stay* – critical energy has found a substitute outlet in fighting for cultural differences which leave the basic homogeneity of the capitalist world-system intact. So we are fighting our PC battles for the rights of ethnic minorities, of gays and lesbians, of different lifestyles, and so forth, while capitalism pursues its triumphant march – and today's critical theory, in the guise of 'cultural studies', is performing the ultimate service for the unrestrained development of capitalism by actively participating in the ideological effort to render its massive presence invisible: in the predominant form of postmodern 'cultural criticism', the very mention of capitalism as a world system tends to give rise to accusations of 'essentialism', 'fundamentalism', and so on. The price of this depoliticization of the economy is that the domain of politics itself is in a way depoliticized: political struggle proper is transformed into the cultural struggle for the recognition of marginal identities and the tolerance of differences.[46]

The falsity of elitist multiculturalist liberalism lies in the tension between content and form which already characterized the first great ideological project of tolerant universalism, that of Freemasonry: the doctrine of Freemasonry (the universal brotherhood of all men based on the light of Reason) clearly clashes with its form of expression and organization (a secret society with its initiation rituals); that is, it is the very form of expression and articulation of Freemasonry which belies its positive doctrine. In a strictly homologous way, the contemporary 'politically correct' liberal attitude which perceives itself as surpassing the limitations of its ethnic identity ('citizen of the world' without anchors in any particular ethnic community) functions, *within its own society*, as a narrow elitist upper-middle-class circle clearly opposing itself to the majority of common people, despised for being caught in their narrow ethnic or community confines. No wonder liberal multiculturalist tolerance is caught in the vicious cycle of simultaneously conceding *too much* and *not enough* to the particularity of the Other's culture:

• On the one hand, it tolerates the Other in so far as it is not the *real* Other, but the aseptic Other of premodern ecological wisdom, fascinating rites, and so on – the moment one is dealing with the *real* Other (say, of clitoridectomy, of women compelled to wear the veil, of torturing enemies to death . . .), with the way the Other regulates the specificity of its *jouissance*, tolerance stops. Significantly, the same multiculturalists who oppose Eurocentrism also, as a rule, oppose the death penalty, dismissing it as a remainder of primitive barbaric customs of vengeance – here, their hidden true Eurocentrism becomes visible (their entire argumentation against the death penalty is strictly 'Eurocentrist', involving the liberal notions of human dignity and penalty, and relying on an evolutionary schema from primitive violent societies to modern tolerant societies able to overcome the principle of vengeance).

• On the other hand, the tolerant multiculturalist liberal sometimes tolerates even the most brutal violations of human rights, or is at least reluctant to condemn them, afraid of being accused of imposing one's own values on to the Other. From my own youth, I recall Maoist students preaching and practising the 'sexual revolution'; when they were reminded that the China of the Maoist Cultural Revolution involved an extremely 'repressive' attitude towards sexuality, they were quick to answer that sexuality plays a totally different role in their life-world, so we should not impose on them our standards of what is 'repressive' – their attitude towards sexuality appears 'repressive' only by our Western standards. . . . Do we not encounter the same stance today when multiculturalists warn us not to impose our Eurocentrist notion of universal human rights on to the Other? Furthermore, is not this kind of false 'tolerance' often evoked by spokesmen for multinational Capital itself, in order to legitimize the fact that 'business comes first'?

The key point is to assert the complementarity of these two excesses, of *too much* and *not enough*: if the first attitude is unable to perceive the specific cultural *jouissance* which even a 'victim' can find in a practice of

another culture that appears cruel and barbaric to us (victims of clitoridectomy often perceive it as the way to regain the properly feminine
dignity), the second attitude fails to perceive the fact that the Other is
split in itself – that members of another culture, far from simply identifying with their customs, can acquire a distance towards them and revolt
against them – in such cases, reference to the 'Western' notion of
universal human rights can well serve as the catalyst which sets in motion
an authentic protest against the constraints of one's own culture. In other
words, there is no happy medium between 'too much' and 'not enough';
so when a multiculturalist replies to our criticism with a desperate plea:
'Whatever I do is wrong – either I am too tolerant towards the injustice
the Other suffers, or I am imposing my own values on to the Other – so
what do you want me to do?', our answer should be: 'Nothing! As long as
you remain stuck in your false presuppositions, you can do nothing!'
What the liberal multiculturalist fails to notice is that each of the two
cultures engaged in 'communication' is caught in its own antagonism
which has prevented it from fully 'becoming itself' – and the only
authentic communication is that of 'solidarity in a common struggle',
when I discover that the deadlock which hampers me is also the deadlock
which hampers the Other.

Does this mean that the solution lies in acknowledging the 'hybrid'
character of each identity? It is easy to praise the hybridity of the
postmodern migrant subject, no longer attached to specific ethnic roots,
floating freely between different cultural circles. Unfortunately, two totally
different sociopolitical levels are condensed here: on the one hand the
cosmopolitan upper- and upper-middle-class academic, always with the
proper visas enabling him to cross borders without any problem in order
to carry out his (financial, academic . . .) business, and thus able to 'enjoy
the difference'; on the other hand the poor (im)migrant worker driven
from his home by poverty or (ethnic, religious) violence, for whom the
celebrated 'hybridity' designates a very tangible traumatic experience of
never being able to settle down properly and legalize his status, the subject
for whom such simple tasks as crossing a border or reuniting with his
family can be an experience full of anxiety, and demanding great effort.
For this second subject, being uprooted from his traditional way of life is
a traumatic shock which destabilizes his entire existence – to tell him that
he should enjoy the hybridity and the lack of fixed identity of his daily
life, the fact that his existence is migrant, never identical-to-itself, and so
on, involves the same cynicism as that at work in the (popularized version
of) Deleuze and Guattari's celebration of the schizo-subject whose rhizo-

matic pulverized existence explodes the paranoiac 'proto-Fascist' protective shield of fixed identity: what is, for the concerned subject, an experience of the utmost suffering and despair, the stigma of exclusion, of being unable to participate in the affairs of his community, is – from the point of view of the external and well, 'normal', and fully adapted postmodern theoretician – celebrated as the ultimate assertion of the subversive desiring machine. . . .

For a Leftist Suspension of the Law

How, then, do Leftists who are aware of this falsity of multiculturalist postmodernism react to it? Their reaction assumes the form of the Hegelian *infinite judgement*, which posits the speculative identity of two thoroughly incompatible terms: 'Adorno (the most sophisticated "elitist" critical theorist) is Buchanan (the lowest point of American rightist populism).'[47] That is to say: these critics of postmodern multiculturalist elitism (from Christopher Lasch to Paul Piccone) take the risk of endorsing neo-conservative populism, with its notions of the reassertion of community, local democracy and active citizenship, as the only politically relevant answer to the all-pervasive predominance of 'instrumental Reason', of the bureaucratization and instrumentalization of our life-world.[48] Of course, it is easy to dismiss today's populism as a nostalgic reactive formation against the process of modernization, and as such inherently *paranoiac*, in search of an external cause of malignancy, of a secret agent who pulls the strings and is thus responsible for the woes of modernization (Jews, international Capital, non-patriotic multiculturalist managers, state bureaucracy . . .); the problem is, rather, to conceive of this new populism as a new form of 'false transparency' which, far from presenting a serious obstacle to capitalist modernization, paves the way for it. What these leftist advocates of populism fail to perceive is thus the fact that today's populism, far from presenting a threat to global capitalism, remains its inherent product.

Paradoxically, today's true conservatives are, rather, leftist 'critical theorists' who reject both liberal multiculturalism and fundamentalist populism – who clearly perceive the complicity between global capitalism and ethnic fundamentalism. They point towards a third domain, which belongs neither to the global market society nor to the new forms of ethnic fundamentalism: the domain of the *political*, the public space of civil society, of active responsible citizenship (the fight for human rights, ecology, etc.). However, the problem is that this very form of the political space is increasingly threatened by the onslaught of globalization; consequently, one cannot simply return to it or revitalize it: the post-nation-state logic of Capital remains the Real which lurks in the background, while all three main leftist reactions to the process of globalization (liberal multiculturalism; the attempt to embrace populism by discerning, beneath its fundamentalist appearance, resistance to 'instrumental reason'; the attempt to keep open the space of the political) seem inappropriate. Although the last approach is based on an accurate insight into the complicity between multiculturalism and fundamentalism, it avoids the crucial question: *how are we to reinvent the political space in today's conditions of globalization?* The politicization of the series of particular struggles which leaves the global process of Capital intact is clearly not sufficient. This means that one should reject the opposition which, within the frame of late capitalist liberal democracy, imposes itself as the main axis of ideological struggle: the tension between 'open' post-ideological universalist liberal tolerance and the particularist 'new fundamentalisms'. Against the liberal Centre which presents itself as neutral, post-ideological, relying on the rule of Law, one should reassert the old leftist motif of the necessity to suspend the neutral space of Law.

Of course, both Left and Right involve their own mode of suspension of the Law on behalf of some higher or more fundamental interest. The rightist suspension, from anti-Dreyfussards to Oliver North, acknowledges its violation of the letter of the Law, but justifies it by reference to some higher national interest: it presents its violation as a painful self-sacrifice for the good of the Nation.[49] As for the leftist suspension, it is enough to mention two films, *Under Fire* and *Watch on the Rhine.* The first takes place during the Nicaraguan revolution, when an American photo-journalist faces a troublesome dilemma: just before the victory of the revolution, Somozistas kill a charismatic Sandinista leader, so the Sandinistas ask the journalist to fake a photo of their dead leader, presenting him as still alive and thus belying the Somozistas' claims about his death – in this way, he would contribute to a swift victory for the revolution and shorten the agony of prolonged bloodshed. Professional ethics, of course, strictly prohibit such an act, since it violates the unbiased objectivity of reporting and makes the journalist an instrument of the political fight; the journalist nevertheless chooses the 'leftist' option and fakes the photo. . . . In *Watch on the Rhine,* based on a play by Lillian Hellman, this dilemma is even more acute: in the late 1930s, a fugitive family of German political emigrants involved in the anti-Nazi struggle comes to stay with their distant relatives, an idyllic all-American small-town middle-class family; soon, however, the Germans face an unexpected threat in the form of an acquaintance of the American family, a Rightist who blackmails the emigrants and, through his contacts with the German Embassy, endangers members of the Underground in Germany itself. The father of the emigrant family decides to kill him, and thereby puts the American family in a difficult moral dilemma: their empty moralizing solidarity with the victims of Nazism is over; now they actually have to take sides and dirty their hands with covering up the killing. . . . Here also, the family decides on the 'leftist' option. 'Left' is defined by this readiness to suspend the abstract moral frame – or, to paraphrase Kierkegaard, to accomplish a kind of *political suspension of the Ethical*.[50]

The lesson of all this, which gained actuality apropos of the Western reaction to the Bosnian war, is thus that there is no way to avoid being partial, since the neutral stance itself involves taking sides (in the case of the Bosnian war, the 'balanced' talk about Balkan ethnic 'tribal warfare' already endorses the Serbian standpoint): humanitarian liberal equidistance can easily slip into or coincide with its opposite and in effect tolerate the most violent 'ethnic cleansing'. In short, the Leftist does not simply violate the Liberal's impartial neutrality; what he claims is that *there is no such neutrality*: that the Liberal's impartiality is always-already biased. The cliché of the liberal Centre, of course, is that both suspensions, the rightist and the leftist, ultimately amount to the same: to a totalitarian threat to the rule of law. The entire consistency of the Left hinges on proving that, on the contrary, each of the two suspensions follows a different logic. While the Right legitimizes its suspension of the Ethical by its anti-universalist stance – that is, by a reference to its particular (religious, patriotic) identity which overrules any universal moral or legal standards – the Left legitimizes its suspension of the Ethical precisely by means of a reference to the true Universality to come. Or – to put it another way – the Left simultaneously accepts the antagonistic character of society (there is no neutral position, struggle is constitutive) *and* remains universalist (speaking on behalf of universal emancipation): in the leftist perspective, accepting the radically antagonistic – that is, *political* – character of social life, accepting the necessity of 'taking sides', is the only way to be effectively *universal*.

How are we to comprehend this paradox? It can be conceived only if *the antagonism is inherent to universality itself*, that is, if universality itself is split into the 'false' concrete universality that legitimizes the existing division of the Whole into functional parts, and the impossible/real demand of 'abstract' universality (Balibar's *égaliberté* again). The leftist political gesture *par excellence* (in contrast to the rightist slogan 'to each his or her own place') is thus to question the concrete existing universal order on behalf of its symptom, of the part which, although inherent to the existing universal order, has no 'proper place' within it (say, illegal immigrants or the homeless in our societies). This procedure of *identifying with the symptom* is the exact and necessary obverse of the standard critico-ideological move of recognizing a particular content behind some abstract universal notion, that is, of denouncing neutral universality as false ('the "man" of human rights is actually the white male property-owner . . .'): one pathetically asserts (and identifies with) *the point of inherent exception/exclusion, the 'abject', of the concrete positive order, as the only point of true universality*.

It is easy to show that, say, the subdivision of the people who live in a country into 'full' citizens and temporary immigrant workers privileges 'full' citizens and excludes immigrants from the public space proper (just as man and woman are not two species of a neutral universal genus of humanity, since the content of the genus as such involves some mode of 'repression' of the feminine); much more productive, theoretically as well as politically (since it opens up the way for the 'progressive' subverting of hegemony), is the opposite operation of *identifying universality with the point of exclusion* – in our case, of saying 'we are all immigrant workers'. In a hierarchically structured society, the measure of true universality lies in the way parts relate to those 'at the bottom', excluded by and from all others (in ex-Yugoslavia, for example, universality was represented by Albanian and Bosnian Muslims, looked down on by all other nations). The recent pathetic statement of solidarity 'Sarajevo is the capital of Europe' was also an exemplary case of such a notion of exception as embodying universality: the way enlightened liberal Europe related to Sarajevo bore witness to the way it related to itself, to its universal notion.

The examples we have evoked make it clear that leftist universalism proper does not involve any kind of return to some neutral universal content (a common notion of humanity, etc.); rather, it refers to a universal which comes to exist (which becomes 'for itself', to put it in Hegelese) only in a particular element which is structurally displaced, 'out of joint': within a given social Whole, it is precisely the element which is prevented from actualizing its full particular identity that stands for its universal dimension. The Greek *demos* stood for universality not because it covered the majority of the population, nor because it occupied the lowest place within the social hierarchy, but because *it had no proper place*

within this hierarchy, but was a site of conflicting, self-cancelling determinations – or, to put it in contemporary terms, a site of performative
contradictions (they were addressed as equals – participating in the
community of *logos* – in order to be informed that they were excluded
from this community . . .). To take Marx's classic example, 'proletariat'
stands for universal humanity not because it is the lowest, most exploited
class, but because its very existence is a 'living contradiction' – that is, it
gives body to the fundamental imbalance and inconsistency of the capitalist social Whole. We can see, now, in what precise way the dimension of
the Universal is opposed to globalism: the universal dimension 'shines
through' the symptomatic displaced element which belongs to the Whole
without being properly its part. For this reason, criticism of the possible
ideological functioning of the notion of hybridity should in no way
advocate the return to substantial identities – the point is precisely to
assert *hybridity as the site of the Universal.*[51]

In so far as normative heterosexuality stands for the global Order within
which each sex is assigned its proper place, queer demands are not simply
demands that their sexual practice and lifestyle be recognized in their
specificity, alongside other practices, but something that unsettles the very
global order and its exclusionary hierarchical logic; precisely as such, as
'out of joint' with regard to the existing order, queers stand for the
dimension of Universality (or, rather, *can* stand for it, since politicization
is never directly inscribed into one's objective social position, but involves
the gesture of subjectivization). Judith Butler[52] develops a powerful argument against the abstract and politically regressive opposition between
economic struggle and the 'merely cultural' queer struggle for recognition: far from being 'merely cultural', the social form of sexual reproduction inhabits the very core of the social relations of production; that
is, the nuclear heterosexual family is a key component and condition of
the capitalist relations of ownership, exchange, and so on; for that reason,
the way queer political practice questions and undermines normative
heterosexuality poses a potential threat to the capitalist mode of production itself. . . . My reaction to this thesis is twofold: I fully endorse queer
politics in so far as it 'metaphoricizes' its specific struggle as something
that – if its objectives were to be realized – undermines the very potentials
of capitalism. However, I tend to think that, in the course of the ongoing
transformation into the 'post-political' tolerant multiculturalist regime,
today's capitalist system is able to neutralize queer demands, to absorb
them as a specific 'way of life'. Is not the history of capitalism a long
history of how the predominant ideologico-political framework was able

to accommodate (and soften the subversive edge of) the movements and demands that seemed to threaten its very survival? For a long time, sexual libertarians thought that monogamous sexual repression was necessary for the survival of capitalism – now we know that capitalism can not only tolerate, but even actively incite and exploit, forms of 'perverse' sexuality, not to mention promiscuous indulgence in sexual pleasures. What if the same destiny awaits queer demands?[53] The recent proliferation of different sexual practices and identities (from sadomasochism to bisexuality and drag performances), far from posing a threat to the present regime of biopower (to use the Foucauldian terms), is precisely the form of sexuality that is generated by the present conditions of global capitalism, which clearly favour the mode of subjectivity characterized by multiple shifting identifications.

The key component of the 'leftist' position is thus the equation of the assertion of *Universalism* with a militant, *divisive* position of one engaged in a struggle: true universalists are not those who preach global tolerance of differences and all-encompassing unity, but those who engage in a passionate fight for the assertion of the Truth that enthuses them. Theoretical, religious and political examples abound here: from St Paul, whose unconditional Christian universalism (everyone can be redeemed, since, in the eyes of Christ, there are no Jews and Greeks, no men and women . . .) made him into a proto-Leninist militant fighting different 'deviations', through Marx (whose notion of class struggle is the necessary obverse of the universalism of his theory which aims at the 'redemption' of the whole of humanity) and Freud, up to great political figures – say, when De Gaulle, almost alone in England in 1940, launched his call for resistance to German occupation, he was at the same time presuming to speak on behalf of the universality of France, and, *for this very reason*, introducing a radical split, a fissure, between those who followed him and those who preferred the collaborationist 'Egyptian fleshpots'.

To put it in Badiou's words, it is crucial here not to translate the terms of this struggle (set in motion by the violent and contingent assertion of the new universal Truth) into the terms of the order of Being, with its groups and subgroups, conceiving it as the struggle between two social entities defined by a series of positive characteristics; that was the 'mistake' of Stalinism, which reduced the class struggle to a struggle between 'classes' defined as social groups with a set of positive features (place in the mode of production, etc.). From a truly radical Marxist perspective, although there is a link between 'working class' as a social group and 'proletariat' as the position of the militant fighting for universal Truth, this link is not a determining causal connection, and the two levels must be strictly distinguished: to be a 'proletarian' involves assuming a certain *subjective stance* (of class struggle destined to achieve the Redemption through Revolution) which, in principle, can be adopted by *any* individual – to put it in religious terms, irrespective of his (good) works, any individual can be 'touched by Grace' and interpellated as a proletarian subject. The line that separates the two opposing sides in the class struggle is therefore not 'objective', it is not the line separating two positive social groups, but ultimately *radically subjective* – it involves the position individuals assume towards the Truth-Event. Subjectivity and universalism are thus not only not exclusive, but two sides of the same coin: it is precisely because 'class struggle' interpellates individuals to adopt the subjective stance of a 'proletarian' that its appeal is universal, aiming at everyone without exception. The division it mobilizes is not the division between two well-defined social groups, but the division, which runs 'diagonally' to the social division in the Order of Being, between those who recognize themselves in the call of the Truth-Event, becoming its followers, and those who deny or ignore it. In Hegelese, the existence of the true Universal (as opposed to the false 'concrete' Universality of the all-encompassing global Order of Being) is that of an endless and incessantly divisive struggle; it is ultimately the division between the two notions (and material practices) of Universality: those who advocate the positivity of the Order of Being as the ultimate horizon of knowledge and action, and those who accept the efficiency of the dimension of Truth-Event irreducible to (and unaccountable in the terms of) the Order of Being.

That is the ultimate gap that separates Nazism from Communism: in Nazism, a Jew is ultimately guilty simply because he is a Jew, because of his direct natural properties, because of what he is; while even in the darkest days of Stalinism a member of the bourgeoisie or aristocracy is not guilty *per se*, that is, directly because of his social status – there is always a minimum of subjectivization involved; participation in the class struggle relies on the subjective act of decision. In a perverted way, the very function of confession in the Stalinist show trial attests to this difference: for the guilt of the traitor to be effective, the accused must confess, that is, subjectively assume his guilt, in clear contrast to Nazism, where an analogous confession by a Jew that he was participating in a plot against Germany would be meaningless. It is at this point that the revisionist historians' argumentation according to which the Nazi Holocaust was already foreshadowed by the Leninist liquidation of the ex-ruling classes (in both cases people were killed simply because of what they were, not because of their deeds) misses the point.

For that reason, the anti-Communist revisionist historian's thesis according to which the Nazi Holocaust did not only follow in time the Communist purges of the enemies of the revolution in the Soviet Union, but was also causally conditioned by them (conceived as a reaction or, rather, a preventive strike against them) misses the point. The revisionists are quite right to stress that the Nazi struggle against the Jewish plot was a repetition/copy of the Communist class struggle – however, far from exculpating the Nazis, this fact brings home all the more the difference between Nazism and Communism: what for the Communists was the antagonism that dwells in the very kernel of the social edifice was, in Nazi ideology, 'naturalized' into the biological property of a specific race (the Jews). So instead of the notion of society as divided/traversed by the class struggle, in which everybody is compelled to take sides, we get the notion of society as a corporate body threatened by an external enemy: the Jew as the foreign intruder. Consequently, it is totally misguided to conceive the Communist revolutionary terror and the Nazi Holocaust as the two modes of the same totalitarian violence (in the first case the gap between Us and Them, the enemy, and the enemy's annihilation, were justified in terms of class difference – it is legitimate to destroy members of the opposing class – and in the second, in terms of racial difference – it is legitimate to kill Jews): the true horror of Nazism lies in the very way it displaced/naturalized social antagonism into racial difference, making the Jews guilty because of the simple fact that they were Jews, independently of what they did, of how they subjectivized their condition.

The Ambiguity of Excremental Identification

For Rancière, subjectivization involves the assertion of a *singulier universel*, the singular/excessive part of the social edifice that directly gives body to the dimension of universality. Perhaps this logic of *singulier universel* is, like Badiou's thought, profoundly Christological: is not the ultimate 'universal singular', the singular individual standing for humanity, Christ himself? Does not the revolution of Christianity lie in the fact that, in accordance with the logic of 'identification with the symptom', it offers as this singular point, which stands for the true Universal, not what is 'the highest of Man' but the lowest excremental remainder – only by identifying with this remainder, by *imitatio Christi*, can a person 'reach eternity' and become effectively universal. And perhaps this Christological reference also makes palpable a possible limitation of the political efficiency of the gesture of 'identification with the symptom'.

Christianity's entire theological edifice relies on such an excremental identification – on the identification with the poor figure of the suffering Christ dying in pain between the two thieves. The artifice by means of which Christianity became the ruling ideology was to combine this radical excremental identification with full endorsement of the existing hierarchical social order: 'rich and poor, honest men and sinners, masters and slaves, men and women, neighbours and foreigners, we are all united in Christ'. Although this excremental identification imposed compassion and merciful care for the poor (the 'do not forget that they are also God's children' motif) by reminding the rich and powerful that their position is precarious and contingent, it none the less confirmed them in this position, and even proclaimed every open rebellion against the existing power relations a mortal sin. The pathetic assertion 'We are all [Jews, Blacks, gays, residents of Sarajevo . . .]' can thus work in an extremely ambiguous way: it can *also* induce a hasty claim that our own predicament is in fact the same as that of the true victims, that is, a false metaphoric universalization of the fate of the excluded.

Soon after the publication of Solzhenitsyn's *Gulag* trilogy in the West, it became fashionable in some 'radical' leftist circles to emphasize how 'our entire consumerist Western society is also one gigantic *Gulag*, in which we are imprisoned by the chains of the ruling ideology – and our position is even worse, since we are unaware of our true predicament'. In a recent discussion about clitoridectomy, a 'radical' feminist pathetically claimed that Western women are in a way also thoroughly circumcised, having to undergo stressful diets, rigorous body training and painful breast- or face-lifting operations in order to remain attractive to men. . . . Although, of course, there is in both cases, an element of truth in the claims made, there is none the less something fundamentally faked in the pathetic statement of a radical upper-middle-class student that 'the Berkeley campus is also a gigantic *Gulag*'. Is it not deeply significant that the best-known example of such a pathetic identification with the outcast/victim is J.F. Kennedy's 'Ich bin ein Berliner' from 1963 – a statement which is definitely not what Rancière had in mind (and, incidentally, a statement which, because of a grammatical error, means, when retranslated into English, 'I am a doughnut')?

The way out of this predicament seems easy enough: the measure of the authenticity of the pathetic identification lies in its sociopolitical efficiency. To what effective measures does it amount? In short, how does this political stance of *singulier universel* affect what Rancière calls the *police* structure? Is there a legitimate distinction between two 'polices (orders of being)': the one which is (or tends to be) self-contained, and the one which is more open to the incorporation of properly political demands? Is there something like a 'police of politics'? Of course, the Kantian answer (shared even by Badiou) would be that any direct identification of police (the Order of Being) with politics (the Truth-Event), any procedure by means of which the Truth posits itself directly as the constitutive structuring principle of the sociopolitical Order of Being, leads to its opposite, to the 'politics of the police', to revolutionary Terror, whose exemplary case is the Stalinist *désastre*. The problem is that the moment we try to provide the pathetic identification with the symptom, the assertion of the *universel singulier*, with a determinate content (What do protesters who pathetically claim 'We are all immigrant workers!' actually *want*? What is their *demand* to the Police Power?), the old contrast between the radical universalism of *égaliberté* and the 'postmodern' assertion of particular identities reappears with a vengeance, as is clear from the deadlock of gay politics, which fears losing its specificity when gays are acknowledged by the public discourse: do you want *equal rights* or *specific rights* to safeguard your particular way of life? The answer, of course, is that the pathetic gesture of *singulier universel* effectively functions as a hysterical gesture made to avoid the decision by *postponing* its satisfaction indefinitely. That is to say: the gesture of *singulier universel* flourishes on bombarding the Police/Power edifice with *impossible* demands, with demands which are 'made to be rejected'; its logic is that of 'In demanding that you do this, I am actually demanding that you do not do it, because *that's not it.*' The situation here is properly undecidable: not only is a radical political project often 'betrayed' by a compromise with the Police Order (the eternal complaint of revolutionary radicals: once the reformists take over, they change only the form and accommodate themselves to the old masters), there can also be the opposite case of pseudo-radicalization, which fits the existing power relations much better than a modest reformist proposal.[54]

The further distinction to be made here is between the two opposed subjects of the enunciation of the statement that asserts the *universel singulier*: is this statement the direct statement of *the excluded victim itself* (of *demos* in old Athens; of the *troisième état* in the French Revolution; of Jews, Palestinians, Blacks, women, gays ... today), which proposes its particular plight as representative of the universality of 'humanity', or is it the statement of solidarity made by *others*, the concerned 'enlightened public'? How do these two modes of functioning relate to one another? The difference in question is the difference between the universal Public claiming: 'We are all *them* (the excluded non-part)!' and the excluded non-part claiming: 'We are the true Universal [the People, Society, Nation . . .!]' – this reversal, although apparently purely symmetrical, never produces direct symmetrical effects. What we encounter here is a key feature of the mechanism that generates (ideological) semblance: the symmetrical reversal that produces an asymmetrical result. In Marx, for example, the simple inversion of the 'developed' to the 'general' form of equivalence (from the state in which commodity A expresses its value in the series of commodities B, C, D, E, F . . ., to the state in which commodity A itself expresses – gives body to – the value of commodities B, C, D, E, F . . .) gives rise to the effect of fetishism; that is, it confers on A the aura of a commodity that has to possess some mysterious ingredient enabling it to function as the equivalent of all the others.

Hegel also often brings about the deepest speculative shift, a change in the whole terrain of thought, by means of a simple symmetrical inversion. The statement 'The Self is the Substance' is in no way equivalent to the statement 'The Substance is the Self': the first asserts the simple subordination of the Self to the Substance ('I recognize myself as belonging to my social Substance'), while the second involves the subjectivization of the Substance itself. Louis XIV did not say: 'I am the State'; what he said was: '*L'État c'est moi*': only in the second version is the finite Self posited as the truth of the Substance itself, so that when Louis XIV issues a decree, it is not only him (this finite individual) who is speaking, it is the Substance itself which speaks through him (in the precise sense of the Lacanian '*moi, la vérité, parle*'). Therein, in the necessity of this reversal, lies one of Hegel's crucial insights: the apparently modest gesture of asserting the subordination (the belonging) of subject to Substance sooner or later reveals itself as standing for its exact opposite, for the subjectivization of the Substance itself. Therein also lies the core of Christianity: not only is man divine, *God Himself has to become man* (with all the latter's finite attributes). For that same reason, 'life is an illusion' is not the same as 'illusion is life': 'life is an illusion' stands for the Baroque attitude of the melancholic awareness of the illusory character of terrestrial life (*à la* Calderón), while 'illusion is life' involves a positive Nietzschean attitude of fully embracing and asserting the game of appearances against the 'nihilist' search for a transcendent 'true' reality – or, if we return to our example, 'We [the nation] are all immigrant workers' is not the same as 'We [immigrant workers] are the true nation.'

Embracing the Act

This is perhaps the moment to return to our starting point: how well are the authors we have been dealing with equipped to accomplish this step of political universalization? Here, the reference to Althusser as their starting point again becomes crucial. As I have already emphasized, their theoretical edifices are to be conceived as four different ways of negating this common starting point, of maintaining (or, rather, gaining) a distance towards Althusser; perhaps it would even be possible to conceptualize their differences by reference to the different ways one can negate/ 'repress' a traumatic kernel in psychoanalysis: denegation, disavowal, repression *stricto sensu* (coinciding with the return of the repressed), foreclosure . . . why?

Although these authors made important progress with regard to their Althusserian starting point (their everlasting merit is that they went forward from Althusser without allowing themselves to be immersed in the postmodern and/or deconstructionist morass), they seem to fall into the trap of 'marginalist' politics, accepting the logic of momentary outbursts of an 'impossible' radical politicization that contains the seeds of its own failure and has to recede in the face of the existing Order (the couples of Truth-Event versus Order of Being; of politics versus police; of *égaliberté* versus imaginary universality). This common feature is closely linked to the reduction of the subject to the process of *subjectivization*. What Rancière aims at is the process by means of which a 'part of no part' becomes involved in litigation for its place within the social visibility; what Badiou aims at is engagement grounded in fidelity to the Truth-Event; what Balibar aims at is a political agent insisting on his 'impossible' demand for *égaliberté* against any positive order of its actualization. In all these cases, subjectivization, of course, is not to be confused with what Althusser had in mind when he elaborated the notion of ideological (mis)recognition and interpellation: here subjectivity is not dismissed as a form of misrecognition; on the contrary, it is asserted as the moment in which the ontological gap/void becomes palpable, as a gesture that undermines the positive order of Being, of the differential structure of Society, of politics as police.

It is crucial to perceive the link between this reduction of the subject to subjectivization and the way the theoretical edifice of these authors relies on the basic opposition of two logics: *la politique/police* and *le politique* in Rancière; Being and Truth-Event in Badiou; even, perhaps, the imaginary universal order versus *égaliberté* in Balibar. In all these cases, the second point is properly political, introduces the gap in the positive order of Being: a situation becomes 'politicized' when a particular demand starts to function as a stand-in for the impossible Universal. Thus we have various forms of the opposition between Substance and Subject, between a positive ontological order (police, Being, structure) and a gap of impossibility which prevents a final closure of this order and/or disturbs its balance. The ultimate reference of these three forms of duality seems to be the Kantian opposition between the constituted order of objective reality and the Idea of Freedom that can function only as a regulative point of reference, since it is never ontologically fully actualized. 'Justice', the rectification of the fundamental and constitutive ontological injustice of the universe, is presented as an unconditional impossible demand, possible only against the background of its own impossibility: the moment a political movement pretends fully to realize Justice, to translate it into an actual state of things, to pass from the spectral *démocratie à venir* to 'actual democracy', we are in totalitarian catastrophe – in Kantian terms, the Sublime changes into the Monstrous. . . . Of course, these two levels are not simply external: the space for the political Truth-Event is opened up by the symptomatic void in the order of Being, by the necessary inconsistency in its structural order, by the constitutive presence of a *surnuméraire*, of an element which is included in the totality of Order, although there is no proper place for it in this totality, and which, for this very reason – since it is an element without further particular specifica- tions – professes to be the immediate embodiment of the Whole. On the other hand, the properly political intervention endeavours to bring about change in the order of police, its restructuring (so that what was hitherto 'invisible' and/or 'nonexistent' in its space becomes visible).

Two Hegelian conclusions should be drawn from this: (1) the very notion of politics involves conflict between the political and apolitical/ police – that is, politics is the antagonism between politics proper and the apolitical attitude ('disorder' and Order); (2) for this reason, 'politics' is a genus which is its own species: which, ultimately, has two species, itself and its 'corporatist'/police negation. Despite this Hegelian twist, however, we are dealing here with a logic which includes its own failure in advance, which considers its full success as its ultimate failure, which sticks to its marginal character as the ultimate sign of its authenticity, and thus entertains an ambiguous attitude towards its politico-ontological opposite, the police Order of Being: it has to refer to it, it *needs* it as the big enemy ('Power') which must be there in order for us to engage in our marginal/ subversive activity – the very idea of accomplishing a total subversion of this Order ('global revolution') is dismissed as proto-totalitarian.

This criticism should not be misread as relying on the traditional Hegelian opposition of abstract and concrete universality: against the assertion of radical negativity as the obverse of universality – of the logic of the Ought that indefinitely postpones its actualization – I am not advocating the necessity of embracing the 'concrete' positive order as the realized Supreme Good. The Hegelian move here is not a resigned-heroic acceptance of the positive Order as the only possible actualization of Reason, but to focus on, to reveal, how the police/political Order itself already relies on a series of disavowed/misrecognized *political* acts, how its founding gesture is political (in the radical sense of the term, as opposed to police) – in Hegelese, how positive Order is nothing but the positivation of the radical negativity.

Let us take Rancière's central notion of *mésentente* ('misapprehension'), which occurs when the excluded/invisible 'part of no part' politicizes its predicament and disturbs the established police/political structure of the social space, its subdivision in parts, by asserting itself as the stand-in for the Whole and demanding the rearticulation of its particular position, that is, a new mode of its visibility (say, a woman 'politicizes' her predicament the moment she presents her limitation to the *private* family space as a case of *political* injustice). Does not the ambiguous relationship between the explicit power/police discourse and its obscene double also involve a kind of *mésentente*? Is not this obscene double (the publicly disavowed message 'between the lines') the 'invisible', non-public condition of possibility of the functioning of the police apparatus? Power is thus not a unique/flat domain of visibility, the self-transparent machine to which the 'people' opposes its demand to reveal, to accept into the public discursive space, its demands – that is, to reject/subvert the (non-)identical status it enjoys within the power/police discourse; the (almost) symmetrical opposite to this is *the refusal of the public power/police discourse to 'hear/understand' its own message between the lines,* the obscene support of its functioning – confronted with it, it rejects it with contempt as unworthy of its dignity. . . .

What Power 'refuses to see' is not so much the (non-)part of the 'people' excluded from the police space but, rather, the invisible support of its own public police apparatus. (In terms of a vulgar class analysis:

there is no rule of aristocracy without the hidden – publicly unacknowledged – support of the *Lumpenproletariat.*) Our point is thus that the marginalist radical refusal to assume responsibility for Power (in Lacanese: its hidden demand for the Master in the guise of his public provocation – see Lacan's diagnosis of the hysterical character of the student rebellion of May '68) is strictly correlative to (or the obverse of) Power's hidden link with its own disavowed obscene supplement – what a truly 'subversive' political intervention has to strive to include in the public space is above all this obscene supplement on which the Power/Police itself relies. The order of police is never simply a positive order: to function at all, it has to cheat, to misname, and so on – *in short, to engage in politics*, to do what its subversive opponents are supposed to do.

In Kant's political thought, the basic principle (the equivalent of the moral categorical imperative) is the 'transcendental principle of publicity': 'All acts which concern the rights of other people and whose maxim does not coincide with their publicly announced aim, are wrong. . . . All guiding principles which need publicity (if they are not to miss their goal) are in accord with justice and with politics.'[55] In the political domain, wrong or evil is an act whose actual aim contradicts its publicly announced goal: as Kant emphasizes again and again, even the worst tyrant publicly pretends to work for the good of the people, while pursuing his own power and wealth. We may put this same maxim in a negative way: a politics is 'wrong (unjust)' when it holds that the public disclosure of its actual motives (or, rather, maxims) would be self-defeating: even a tyrant cannot *publicly* say: 'I am imposing this law in order to crush my enemies and increase my wealth.' – It is against this background that one should locate the thesis on the superego supplement of public ideological discourse: the superego obscene supplement is precisely the support of the public ideological text which, in order to be operative, *has to remain publicly disavowed*: its public avowal is self-defeating. And our point is that such a disavowal is constitutive of what Rancière calls the order of 'police'.

The notion of the Ideal of *égaliberté* as a real/impossible unconditional demand betrayed in its every positivization, a demand which can actualize itself only in those short intermediary moments of Power/Police Vacuum when the 'people' 'spontaneously' organizes itself outside the official representative political machinery (see the fascination of many Leftists for 'spontaneous council democracy' in the early, 'authentic' stages of the revolution), brings radical revolutionary purists uncannily close to those conservatives who endeavour to prove the necessary and unavoidable betrayal or 'regression into terror' of every revolution, as if the only possible actualization of *égaliberté* is the Khmer Rouge or the Sendero Luminoso. One is tempted to claim that Leninist politics is the true counterpoint to this Kantian marginalist leftist attitude which insists on its own inherent impossibility. That is to say: what a true Leninist and a political conservative have in common is the fact that they reject what one could call liberal leftist 'irresponsibility' (advocating grand projects of solidarity, freedom, and so on, yet ducking out when one has to pay the price for them in the guise of concrete and often 'cruel' political measures): like an authentic conservative, a true Leninist is not afraid of the *passage à l'acte*, of accepting all the consequences, unpleasant as they may be, of realizing his political project. Kipling (whom Brecht admired very much) despised British liberals who advocated freedom and justice, while silently counting on the Conservatives to do the necessary dirty work for them; the same can be said for the liberal Leftist's (or 'democratic Socialist's') relationship to Leninist Communists: liberal Leftists reject social-democratic 'compromise', they want a true revolution, yet they shirk the actual price to be paid for it, and thus prefer to adopt the attitude of a Beautiful Soul and keep their hands clean. In contrast to this false liberal leftist position (they want true democracy for the people, but without secret police to fight counter-revolution, without their academic privileges being threatened . . .), a Leninist, like a Conservative, is *authentic* in the sense of *fully assuming the consequences of his choice*, of being fully aware of what it actually means to take power and to exert it.

I am now in a position to specify what seems to me the fatal weakness of the proto-Kantian opposition between the positive order of Being (or of the *service des biens* or of the politics as Police) and the radical, unconditional demand for *égaliberté* which signals the presence of the Truth-Event (or the Political), that is, the opposition between the *global* social order and the dimension of Universality proper, which cuts a line of separation into this global order: what it leaves out of consideration is the 'excess' of the founding gesture of the Master without which the positive order of the *service des biens* cannot maintain itself. What we are aiming at here is the 'non-economical' excess of the Master over the smooth functioning of the positive police order of Being. In a pluralist society, the marginal 'radical' parties or political agents are able to play the game of unconditional demands, of 'we want this [higher salaries for teachers and doctors, better retirement and social security conditions . . .], *pereat mundus*', leaving it to the Master to find a way of meeting their demand – this unconditional demand targets the political Master not simply in his capacity as the administrator of the *service des biens*, but in his capacity as guarantor of the survival of the Order. That is the other crucial aspect of the Master's position: he does not shirk the responsibility of breaking the egg when people demand an omelette – of imposing unpopular but necessary measures. In short, the Master is the one who forever relinquishes the right to claim: 'But I didn't want this!' when things go wrong.

Of course, this position is ultimately that of an impostor: his mastery is an illusion; none the less, the very fact that someone is ready to occupy this untenable place has a pacifying effect on his subjects – we can indulge in our petty narcissistic demands, well aware that the Master is here to guarantee that the whole structure will not collapse. The heroism of an authentic Master consists precisely in his willingness to assume this impossible position of ultimate responsibility, and to take upon himself the implementation of unpopular measures which prevent the system from disintegrating. That was the greatness of Lenin after the Bolsheviks took power: in contrast to hysterical revolutionary fervour caught in the vicious cycle, the fervour of those who prefer to stay in opposition and prefer (publicly or secretly) to avoid the burden of taking over, of accomplishing the shift from subversive activity to responsibility for the smooth running of the social edifice, he heroically embraced the onerous task of actually *running the State* – of making all the necessary compromises, but also taking the necessary harsh measures, to assure that the Bolshevik power would not collapse.

So when Rancière or Badiou dismisses politics as a Police which merely takes care of the smooth *service des biens*, they leave out of consideration the fact that the social Order cannot reproduce itself if it is constrained to the terms of the *service des biens*: there must be One who assumes the ultimate responsibility, inclusive of a ruthless readiness to make the necessary compromises or break the letter of the Law in order to guarantee the system's survival; and it is totally erroneous to interpret this function as that of an unprincipled pragmatic sticking to power, whatever the cost. The advocates of the Political as opposed to Police fail to take into account this inherent excess of the Master which sustains the *service des biens* itself: they are unaware of the fact that what they are fighting, what they are provoking with their unconditional demand, is *not* the 'servicing of goods', but the unconditional responsibility of the Master. In short, what they are unaware of is that their unconditional demand for *égaliberté* remains within the confines of the hysterical provocation aimed at the Master, testing the limits of his ability: 'Can he reject – or meet – our demands, and still maintain the appearance of omnipotence?'.

The test of the true revolutionary, as opposed to this game of hysterical provocation, is the heroic readiness to endure the conversion of the subversive undermining of the existing System into the principle of a new positive Order which gives body to this negativity – or, in Badiou's terms, the conversion of Truth into Being.[56] To put it in more abstract philosophical terms: the fear of the impending 'ontologization' of the proper political act, of its catastrophic transposition into the positive order of Being, is a false fear that results from a kind of perspective illusion: it puts too much trust in the substantial power of the positive order of Being, overlooking the fact that the order of Being is never simply given, but is itself grounded in some preceding Act. *There is no Order of Being as a positive ontologically consistent Whole*: the false semblance of such an Order relies on the self-obliteration of the Act. In other words, the gap of the Act is not introduced into the Order of Being afterwards: it is there all the time as the condition that actually *sustains* every Order of Being.

Perhaps the ultimate philosophical formulation of the political opposition police/politics is Derrida's opposition between ontology and *heauntology*, the impossible logic of spectrality that forever prevents/differs/displaces the closure of the ontological edifice: the proper deconstructionist gesture is to maintain the spectral opening, to resist the temptation of its ontological closure. Again, it is easy to translate this into Lacanese: spectrality is another name for the phantasmic semblance that fills the irreducible ontological gap. The properly Hegelian gesture here would be to turn around this notion of spectrality as the irreducible supplement which is the condition of (im)possibility of any ontology: what if there is a need for *a minimal ontological support of the very dimension of spectrality*, for some inert *peu de réel* which sustains the spectral opening? In a way, Hegel agrees with Kant that the direct attempt to actualize the abstract negativity of *égaliberté* (what Kant would have characterized as the political equivalent of the epistemological mistake of treating regulative ideas as constitutive) necessarily ends in terror. The difference between them is that each draws the opposite conclusion: for Kant, it means that *égaliberté* should remain an inaccessible Ideal to come, *démocratie à venir*, slowly approached but always kept at a distance in order to avoid the Monstrosity of the abstract absolute negativity; while for Hegel, it means that this monstrous moment of absolute abstract negativity, this self-destructive fury which washes away every positive Order, has *always-already happened*, since it is the very foundation of the positive rational order of human society. In short, while, for Kant, absolute negativity designates an impossible moment of the *future*, a future which will never turn into the present, for Hegel it designates an impossible moment of the *past*, a past which was never fully experienced as the present, since its withdrawal opens up the space for the minimal (social) organization of the Present. There are many names for this eruption of abstract negativity, from Adam's Fall, through Socrates and Christ's crucifixion, to the French Revolution – in all these cases, a negative gesture corrosive of the given (social) substantial order grounded a higher, more rational order.

Notes

1. Is this not also the version of the Lacanian ISR (Imaginary–Symbolic–Real): traditionalism is centred on imaginary Good embodied in the community way of life; modernism on universal Duty; postmodernism on the dissemination of the Real?

2. What one encounters in Lyotard is the ambiguity of the Lacanian Real as that which resists symbolization: on the one hand, we have the dispersal of the pure Multiple not yet totalized/homogenized through some form of the symbolic One – each such form of symbolization is already exclusionary, it 'represses' the *différend*; on the other hand, the ineffable has the form of the absolute Injustice/Crime, the *Holocaust*, the unique event which cannot be put into words, where no work of symbolic mourning can provide reconciliation. (In ethical terms, this split is the split between the Real as pre-symbolic, prelapsarian, the innocence of the multiple; and the Real as the singular, unique point of absolute, ineffable Evil.) In the first case, injustice is *the act of symbolization of the pure Multiple itself* which is by nature exclusionary; in the second case, injustice is the traumatic point which, precisely, *cannot* be symbolized. Violence/injustice is thus simultaneously the act of symbolization and that which eludes symbolization.... The solution to this paradox is that between the primordial Real of the pure Multiple and the symbolic universe there is a 'vanishing mediator', the gesture of/in the Real that grounds symbolization itself, the violent opening up of a gap in the Real which is not yet symbolic.

3. In his criticism of Derrida, Laclau emphasized the gap between Derrida's global philosophical stance (*différance*, the unavoidable 'out-of-joint' of every identity, etc.) and his politics of *démocratie à venir*, of openness towards the Event of irreducible Otherness: why shouldn't one draw, from the fact that identity is impossible, the *opposite* 'totalitarian' conclusion that, for that very reason, we need a strong Power to prevent explosion and guarantee a fragile minimum of order? (See Ernesto Laclau, 'The Time is Out of Joint', in *Emancipation(s)*, London: Verso 1996.) However, does not the same hold for Laclau himself? Why shouldn't one, from the notion of a hegemony which involves the irreducible gap between the Universal and the Particular, and thus the structural impossibility of society, opt for a 'strong' totalitarian politics that limits the effects of this gap as much as possible?

4. Laclau, 'The Time is Out of Joint', p. 123.

5. Another name for this short circuit between the Universal and the Particular, by means of which a particular content hegemonizes the Universal, is, of course, *suture*: the operation of hegemony 'sutures' the empty Universal to a particular content. For that reason, F.W.J. Schelling must be considered the originator of the modern notion of critique of ideology: he was the first to elaborate the notion of 'false' unity and/or universality. For him, 'evil' lies not in the split (between the Universal and the Particular) as such but, rather, in

their 'false'/distorted unity, that is, in a Universality that effectively privileges some narrow particular content and is impenetrably 'anchored' in it. Schelling was thus the first to elaborate the elementary procedure of the critique of ideology: the gesture of discerning, beneath the appearance of neutral universality (say, of 'human rights'), the privileged particular content (say, white upper-middle-class males) which 'hegemonizes' it. See Part I of Slavoj Žižek, *The Indivisible Remainder*, London: Verso 1995.

6. Laclau, 'The Time is Out of Joint', pp. 14–15.

7. Ibid., p. 44.

8. Ibid., p. 14.

9. Laclau develops this logic apropos of the notion of national unity – see ibid., pp. 94–5.

10. The problem with Jürgen Habermas is that he abandons this 'symptomal' approach to the Universal. Just recall his notion of modernity as an 'unfinished project': what gets lost in Habermas's endeavour to realize the hitherto blocked potentials of the Enlightenment is the properly dialectical insight into how what look like external empirical obstacles preventing the full realization of the Enlightenment project are actually *inherent to the very notion of this project*. The fundamental Hegelian move is to transpose external into internal limit: the Enlightenment is an 'unfinished project' not because of contingent external circumstances preventing its full implementation, but 'in its very notion' – the fully realized project of Enlightenment would undermine its very notion.

11. See Quentin Skinner, 'Language and Social Change', in *Meaning and Context: Quentin Skinner and His Critics*, Oxford: Polity Press 1988.

12. No wonder the examples which fit the operation of hegemony as described by Laclau most perfectly are those of rightist populism, from Fascism to Perónism: *the* royal example of hegemony is the way a conservative attitude reappropriates and inscribes popular-revolutionary motifs into its field.

13. Lacan tries to do almost the exact opposite: in the last years of his teaching, he desperately endeavoured to formulate the precarious status of an 'acephalous', desubjectivized knowledge which would no longer rely on a previous Truth-Event – Lacan's name for such knowledge is drive.

14. This point is elaborated in detail in Étienne Balibar, *La crainte des masses*, Paris: Galilée 1997.

15. This, perhaps, expresses *per negationem* the formula of true anti-Fascism today: the reversal of the Fascist constellation, that is, technological desacralization at the level of ideology, supplemented by concrete, 'micro-practice', motions to save and strengthen local 'organic' links.

16. Here I draw on Jacques Rancière, *La mésentente*, Paris: Galilée 1995.

17. One can see why tribal, pre-State societies, with all their authentic proto-democratic procedures for deciding common matters (gathering of all the people, common deliberation, discussion and vote, etc.), are not yet *democratic*: not because politics as such involves society's self-alienation – not because politics is the sphere elevated above concrete social antagonisms (as the standard Marxist argument would claim) – but because the litigation in these pre-political tribal gatherings lacks the properly political paradox of *singulier universel*, of the 'part of no part' that presents itself as an immediate stand-in for universality as such.

18. The excremental identification of the *burakumin* is crucial: when Sue Sumii saw her relative cherishing the Emperor's excrement, her conclusion was that, in the same way, following the tradition of the 'king's two bodies' – of the king's body standing for the social body as such – the *burakumin*, as the excrement of the social body, should also be cherished. In other words, Sue Sumii took the structural homology between the two Emperor's bodies more literally and further than usual: even the lowest part (excrement) of the Emperor's body has to be reduplicated in his other, sublime body, which stands for the body of society. Her predicament was similar to that of Plato who, in *Parmenides*, bravely confronts the embarrassing problem of the precise scope of the relationship between eternal forms/ideas

and their material copies: which material objects are 'ontologically covered' by eternal Ideas as their models? Is there also an eternal Idea of 'low' objects like mud, filth or excrement?

19. This para-politics, of course, has a series of different successive versions: the main rupture is the one between its classical and modern Hobbesian formulation, which focuses on the problematic of the social contract, the alienation of individual rights in the emergence of sovereign power. Habermasian or Rawlsian ethics are perhaps the last philosophical vestiges of this attitude: the attempt to de-antagonize politics by formulating clear rules to be obeyed so that the agonic procedure of litigation does not explode into politics proper.

20. More precisely, Marxism is more ambiguous, since the very term 'political economy' also opens up the space for the opposite gesture of introducing politics into the very heart of the economy, that is, of denouncing the very 'apolitical' character of the economic processes as the supreme ideological illusion. Class struggle does not 'express' some objective economic contradiction, it *is* the very *form of existence* of this contradiction. This ambiguity can also be formulated in the terms of Lacan's 'formulas of sexuation': we can read the statement 'everything is political' as the universal statement which involves its point of exception, the objective economic process (so that the ferocious discernment of a hidden political stance in apparently apolitical sublime artistic or ideological products can go hand in hand with the assertion of the economic process as the point of suspension of the political), or according to the logic of 'non-all', that is, in the sense of 'there is nothing which is not political' – here, 'everything is political' means precisely that there is no way of formulating/defining the political itself in a univocal universal way, since every statement about the political is itself already 'politicized'.

Fredric Jameson boldly asserts the paradoxical coincidence between the most extreme version of neo-liberalism – the universal modelling of human behaviour as utility-maximization – and Marxist socialism with its emphasis on the economic organization of society, on the 'administration of things', in that both do away with the need for any political thought proper: there is a Marxist political practice, but there is no Marxist political thought. From this standpoint, the traditional complaint against Marxism (that it lacks an autonomous political reflection) appears more as a strength than as a weakness – or, as Jameson concludes: '[w]e have much in common with the neo-liberals, in fact virtually everything – save the essentials!' (Fredric Jameson, *Postmodernism, or, the Cultural Logic of Late Capitalism*, London: Verso 1992, p. 265 – would it be possible, in this sense, to define the stance towards neo-conservatist communitarianism as the obverse one, in so far as a Marxist has in common with it only the essentials [the need for a harmonious organic society]?) The counter-argument would be that, perhaps, this neglect of the proper political dimension had very precise political consequences for the history of the Communist movement – do not phenomena like Stalinism indicate precisely a violent return of the repressed political dimension?

21. The clearest indication of this Schmittian disavowal of the political is the primacy of external politics (relations between sovereign states) over internal politics (inner social antagonisms) on which he insists: is not the relationship to an external Other as the Enemy a way of disavowing the *internal* struggle that traverses the social body? In contrast to Schmitt, a leftist position should insist on the unconditional primacy of the inherent antagonism as constitutive of the political.

22. The metaphoric frame we use in order to account for the political process is thus never innocent and neutral: it 'schematizes' the concrete meaning of politics. Ultra-politics has recourse to the model of *warfare*: politics is conceived as a form of social warfare, as the relationship to 'Them', to an Enemy. Arche-politics prefers to refer to the *medical* model: society is a corporate body, an organism; social divisions are like illnesses of this organism – that is, what we should fight, our enemy, is a cancerous intruder, a pest, a foreign parasite to be exterminated if the health of the social body is to be re-established. Para-politics uses the model of *agonistic* competition which follows some commonly accepted rules, like a sporting

event. Meta-politics relies on the model of scientific-technological *instrumental* procedure, while post-politics involves the model of business *negotiation* and strategic *compromise*.

23. See Chapter 2 of Slavoj Žižek, *The Plague of Fantasies*, London: Verso 1997.

24. Incidentally, *this* version of 'freedom as conceived necessity', although it may sound 'Hegelian', is the very opposite of the properly Hegelian speculative identification of true Freedom with Necessity: Hegelian freedom is not the act of freely assuming the role of the instrument of a preordained Necessity.

25. See Claude Lefort, *L'invention démocratique*, Paris: Fayard 1981.

26. On the other hand, the difference between capitalism and Communism is that Communism was perceived as an Idea which then failed in its realization, while capitalism functioned 'spontaneously': there is no Capitalist Manifesto. In the case of Communism, we can thus play the game of finding the culprit, blaming the Party, Stalin, Lenin, ultimately Marx himself, for the millions of dead, their 'lustration'; while in capitalism, there is nobody on whom one can pin guilt or responsibility; things just happened that way, although capitalism has been no less destructive in terms of human and environmental costs, destroying aboriginal cultures, and so òn.

27. See Rancière, *La mésentente*, pp. 144–6.

28. This crucial distinction between simulacrum (overlapping with the Real) and appearance is easily discernible in the domain of sexuality, as the distinction between pornography and seduction: pornography 'shows it all', 'real sex', and for that very reason produces the mere simulacrum of sexuality; while the process of seduction consists entirely in the play of appearances, hints and promises, and thereby evokes the elusive domain of the suprasensible sublime Thing.

29. In this sense, even Nixon's visit to China and the ensuing establishment of diplomatic relations between the USA and China was a kind of political act, in so far as it actually changed the parameters of what was considered 'possible' (or 'feasible') in the domain of international relations – yes, one could do the unthinkable, and talk normally with the ultimate enemy.

30. See Rancière, *La mésentente*, p. 162.

31. See Balibar, 'La violence: idéalité et cruauté', in *La crainte des masses*.

32. For a further development of this motif, see Chapter 3 of Slavoj Žižek, *The Metastases of Enjoyment*, London: Verso 1995.

33. See Balibar, *La crainte des masses*, pp. 42–3.

34. For a more detailed account of this reflected cynical attitude, see Chapter 3 of Žižek, *The Indivisible Remainder*.

35. See Mario Vargas Llosa, 'Hooligans, the product of a high civilisation', *The Independent*, 27 June 1998, The Weekend Review, p. 5.

36. This logic was brought to its absurd extreme in ex-Yugoslavia, in which the very notion of a workers' strike was incomprehensible, since, according to the ruling ideology, workers already rule in the self-management of their companies – against whom, then, could they possibly strike?

37. The interesting point here is how, in this struggle within Socialism in decay, the very term 'political' functioned in an inverted way: it was the Communist Party (standing for the police logic) which 'politicized' the situation (speaking of 'counter-revolutionary tendencies', etc.), while the opposition movement insisted on their fundamentally 'apolitical', civic-ethical character: they just stood for 'simple values' of dignity, freedom, etc. – no wonder their main signifier was the 'apolitical' notion of solidarity.

38. To put it in yet another way: substance is a name for the *inert resistance of the falsity*; when, for example, rational subjective insight tells us that some notion is wrong, that it hinges on our misperception, on our 'blind, superstitious prejudices', and this notion nevertheless inexplicably persists, we are dealing with a substance. Far from designating the Truth, substance is the inert persistence of the false appearance. For this reason, Jungian archetypes point towards the dimension of the 'psychic substance': they designate the

dimension of inert psychic formations that return again and again, although we theoretically undermined them long ago.

39. Abraham Lincoln's comment on spiritualism ('For those who like that sort of thing, I should think it is just about the sort of thing they would like') expresses this tautological character of nationalist self-enclosure perfectly, and, for this reason, works even better if one uses it to characterize nationalists, while it does *not* work if one applies it to authentic radical democrats: one *cannot* say of authentic democratic engagement: 'For those who like that sort of thing, it is just about the sort of thing they would like.'

40. See, especially, 'Les universels', in Balibar, *La crainte des masses*, pp. 421–54.

41. Here, the parallel with Laclau's opposition between the logic of difference – society as a differential symbolic structure – and the logic of antagonism – society as 'impossible', thwarted by an antagonistic split – is clear. Today, the tension between the logic of difference and the logic of antagonism takes the form of the tension between the liberal-democratic universe of negotiation and the 'fundamentalist' universe of the fight to the death between Good and Evil, Us and Them.

42. When, at the beginning of this century, Béla Bartók transcribed hundreds of Hungarian folk songs, he provoked the lasting animosity of the partisans of Romantic national revival precisely by literally executing their programme of reviving authentic ethnic roots. ... In Slovenia, the Catholic Church and nationalists paint an idyllic picture of the nineteenth-century countryside – so no wonder that when, a couple of years ago, the ethnological notebooks of a Slovene writer from that time (Janez Trdina) were published, they were largely ignored: they provide a picture of daily life in the countryside full of child fornication and rape, alcoholism, brutal violence....

43. One of the minor yet telltale events that bear witness to this 'withering-away' of the nation-state is the slow spread of the obscene institution of *private prisons* in the USA and other Western countries: the exercise of what should be the monopoly of the State (physical violence and coercion) becomes the object of a contract between the State and a private company which exerts coercion on individuals for the sake of profit – what we have here is simply the end of the monopoly on the legitimate use of violence which (according to Max Weber) defines the modern State.

44. See Scott Lash and John Urry, *Economies of Signs and Space*, London: Sage 1994.

45. See Darian Leader, *Why Do Women Write More Letters Than They Post?*, London: Faber & Faber 1996, pp. 67–8. The reversal at work in this anecdote quoted by Leader is beautifully illustrated in a recent German publicity spot for Magnum, a brand of gigantic ice-cream-on-a-stick. First we see a poor working-class couple passionately embracing; when they agree to make love, the girl sends the boy to the seaside shop nearby to buy a condom, so that they will be able to make love safely. The boy goes into the corridor with the condom vending machine and notices another vending machine close to it selling Magnum; he looks in his pocket and notices that he has only one 5-mark coin, enough for either a condom or an ice cream, not for both. After some moments of desperate hesitation, we see him passionately licking the ice cream, with the inscription on the screen: 'Sometimes you have to get your priorities right!' Of special interest here is the rather obvious phallic connotation of the Magnum ice-cream-on-a-stick, the 'big' penis: when, in the last shot, the boy is licking the ice cream, his quick jerky gestures imitate an intense fellatio; so the message of getting your priorities right can also be read in a direct sexual way: better the quasi-homoerotic experience of oral sex than the straight heterosexual experience....

46. One can argue, of course, that the circular movement of Capital itself is already a symbolic phenomenon, not something externally opposed to culture (did not Lacan emphasize that the first chapter of *Capital I* is a magisterial exercise in the logic of the signifier?); while, on the other hand, cultural phenomena themselves are no less sites of material production, caught in the web of socioeconomic power relations. While fully endorsing both these points, one should none the less insist that the socioeconomic logic of Capital provides the global framework which (over)determines the totality of cultural processes.

47. Another example of infinite judgement in our techno-New-Age is: 'The spirit (transcendental illumination, awareness) is a capsule (the so-called "cognitive enhancer" pill).'

48. See Paul Piccone, 'Postmodern Populism', *Telos* 103 (Spring 1995). We should also note here by Elizabeth Fox-Genovese's attempt to oppose to upper-middle-class feminism interested in the problems of literary and cinema theory, lesbian rights, etc., the 'family feminism' which focuses on the actual concerns of ordinary working women, and articulates concrete questions of how to survive within the family, with children and a career. See Elizabeth Fox-Genovese, *Feminism Is Not the Story of My Life*, New York: Doubleday 1996.

49. The most concise formulation of the rightist suspension of public (legal) norms was provided by Eamon de Valera: 'The people has no right to do wrong.'

50. This acceptance of violence, this 'political suspension of the Ethical', is the limit of that which even the most 'tolerant' liberal stance is unable to trespass – witness the uneasiness of 'radical' post-colonialist Afro-American studies apropos of Frantz Fanon's fundamental insight into the unavoidability of violence in the process of actual decolonization.

51. The universality we are speaking about is thus not a positive universality with a determinate content but an empty universality, a universality without a positive notion that would specify its contours, a universality that exists only in the guise of the experience of the injustice done to the particular subject who politicizes his/her predicament. The Habermasian answer to it would be, of course, that the very fact that subjects experience their predicament as 'unjust' points towards some implicit normative structure that must be operative in their protest; Rancière's point, however, is that this is precisely the philosophical lure to be avoided: every translation of this 'empty universality' into some determinate positive content already betrays its radical character.

52. See Judith Butler, 'Merely Cultural', *New Left Review* 227 (January/February 1998), pp. 33–44.

53. Butler emphasizes that the difference which characterizes a particular social movement is not the external difference from other movements, but its internal self-difference – following Laclau, I am tempted to claim that this difference is the site of the inscription of the Universal – that Universality is, in its actual existence, the violent, splitting self-difference, which prevents a particular moment from achieving its self-identity (say, the self-difference of the queer movement between its particular demands and its universal anti-capitalist thrust). Butler says that Universality is the site of violent erasure and exclusion, and emphasizes how, for that reason, it should be resisted – differing with her, I am tempted to say that, *for the same reason, it should be endorsed.*

54. Therein lies the grain of truth of Richard Rorty's recent polemics against 'radical' cultural studies elitists (see Richard Rorty, *Achieving Our America*, Cambridge, MA: Harvard University Press 1998): under the pretence of radically questioning the mythical spectre of Power, they perfectly fit the reproduction of the *existing power relations*, posing no threat to them whatsoever – or, to paraphrase Walter Benjamin's thesis, their declared attitude of radical opposition *to* the existing social relations coexists with their perfect functioning *within* these relations, rather like the proverbial hysteric who perfectly fits the network of exploitation against which he complains, and effectively endorses its reproduction.

55. Immanuel Kant, 'Perpetual Peace: A Philosophical Sketch', in *Kant's Political Writings*, Cambridge: Cambridge University Press 1991, p. 129.

56. It was one of the merits of Carl Schmitt that he clearly identified this unconditional will to assume responsibility as the kernel of political authority beyond – or, rather, beneath – the typical liberal legitimization of those who exert power by reference to the smooth servicing of goods.

PART III

From Subjection to Subjective Destitution

5

Passionate (Dis)Attachments, or, Judith Butler as a Reader of Freud

Why Perversion Is Not Subversion

One of the key conclusions to be drawn from the theme of 'Kant avec Sade' is that those who, like Michel Foucault, advocate the subversive potential of perversions are sooner or later led to the denial of the Freudian Unconscious. This denial is theoretically grounded in the fact, emphasized by Freud himself, that for psychoanalysis, hysteria and psychosis – *not perversion* – offer a way into the Unconscious: the Unconscious is *not* accessible via perversions. Following Freud, Lacan repeatedly insisted that perversion is always a socially constructive attitude, while hysteria is much more subversive and threatening to the predominant hegemony. It may seem that the situation is the opposite: don't perverts openly realize and practise what hysterics only secretly dream about? Or, with regard to the Master: do hysterics not merely provoke the Master in an ambiguous way which, in effect, amounts to an appeal addressed to the Master to assert his authority again and more strongly, while perverts actually undermine the Master's position? (This is how one usually understands Freud's thesis that perversion is the negative of neurosis.) This very fact, however, confronts us with the paradox of the Freudian Unconscious: the Unconscious does *not* consist of the secret perverse scenarios we daydream about and (in so far as we remain hysterics) shirk from realizing, while perverts heroically 'do it'. When we do this, when we realize ('act out') our secret perverse fantasies, everything is disclosed, yet the Unconscious is somehow missed – why?

Because the Freudian Unconscious is *not* the secret phantasmic content, but something that intervenes *in between*, in the process of the translation/ transposition of the secret phantasmic content into the text of the dream (or the hysterical symptom). The Unconscious is that which, precisely, is *obfuscated* by the phantasmic scenarios the pervert is acting out: the pervert, with his certainty about what brings enjoyment, obfuscates the gap, the 'burning question', the stumbling block, that 'is' the core of the Unconscious. The pervert is thus the 'inherent transgressor' *par excellence*: he brings to light, stages, practises the secret fantasies that sustain the predominant public discourse, while the hysterical position precisely displays doubt about whether those secret perverse fantasies are 'really *it*'. Hysteria is not simply the battleground between secret desires and symbolic prohibitions; it also, and above all, articulates the gnawing doubt whether secret desires really contain what they promise – whether our inability to enjoy really hinges only on symbolic prohibitions. In other words, the pervert precludes the Unconscious because he *knows* the answer (to what brings *jouissance*; to the Other); he has no doubts about it; his position is unshakeable; while the hysteric doubts – that is, her position is that of an eternal and constitutive (self-)questioning: What does the Other want from me? What am I for the Other? . . .

This opposition of perversion and hysteria is especially pertinent today, in our era of the 'decline of Oedipus', when the paradigmatic mode of subjectivity is no longer the subject integrated into the paternal Law through symbolic castration, but the 'polymorphously perverse' subject following the superego injunction to enjoy. The question of how we are to hystericize the subject caught in the closed loop of perversion (how we are to inculcate the dimension of lack and questioning in him) becomes more urgent in view of today's political scene: the subject of late capitalist market relations is perverse, while the 'democratic subject' (the mode of subjectivity implied by the modern democracy) is inherently hysterical (the abstract citizen correlative to the empty place of Power). In other words, the relationship between the *bourgeois* caught up in market mechanisms and the *citoyen* engaged in the universal political sphere is, in its subjective economy, the relationship between perversion and hysteria. So when Rancière calls our age 'post-political', he is aiming precisely at this shift in political discourse (the social link) from hysteria to perversion: 'post-politics' is the perverse mode of administering social affairs, the mode deprived of the 'hystericized' universal/out-of-joint dimension.

One often hears the claim that today hysteria is no longer sexualized but is, rather, to be located in the domain of non-sexualized victimization, of the wound of some traumatic violence that cuts into the very soul of our being. However, we are dealing with hysteria only in so far as the victimized subject entertains an ambiguous attitude of fascination towards the wound, in so far as he secretly takes 'perverse' pleasure in it, in so far as the very source of pain exerts a magnetism – hysteria is precisely the name for this stance of ambivalent fascination in the face of the object that terrifies and repels us. And this excess of pleasure in pain is another name for *sexualization*: the moment it is there, the situation is sexualized, the subject is caught in the perverse loop. In other words, one should none the less stick to the old Freudian thesis on the fundamentally sexual character of hysteria: wasn't Freud's Dora, the paradigmatic case of hysteria, continually complaining about being victimized by the manipulations of her father and Mr K?

What complicates the issue further is that one should definitely *not* directly qualify homosexuality (or any other sexual practice that violates the heterosexual norm) as a 'perversion'. The question to be asked is, rather: how is the fact of homosexuality inscribed into the subject's symbolic universe? What subjective attitude sustains it? There definitely is a perverse homosexuality (the masochist or sadist pretending to possess knowledge about what provides *jouissance* to the Other); but there is also a hysterical homosexuality (opting for it in order to confront the enigma of 'What am I for the Other? What does the Other want (from me)?', and so on. So, for Lacan, there is no direct correlation between forms of sexual practice (gay, lesbian, straight) and the 'pathological' subjective symbolic economy (perverse, hysterical, psychotic). Let us take the extreme case of coprophagy (eating excrement): even such a practice is not necessarily 'perverse', since it can well be inscribed into a hysterical economy – that is to say, it can well function as an element of the hysterical provocation and questioning of the Other's desire: what if I eat shit in order to test how I stand with regard to the Other's desire – will he still love me when he sees me doing it? Will he finally abandon me as his object? It can also function as psychotic if, say, the subject identifies his partner's shit as the miraculous Divine substance, so that by swallowing it he gets in touch with God, receives His energy. Or, of course, it can function as perversion if the subject, while doing it, assumes the position of the object-instrument of the Other's desire (if he does it in order to generate enjoyment in his partner).

On a more general level, it is interesting to note how, when one describes new phenomena, one as a rule overlooks their predominant hysterical functioning and prefers the allegedly more 'radical' perverse or psychotic functioning. Say, in the case of cyberspace, we are bombarded with interpretations which emphasize how cyberspace opens up the possibility of polymorphous perverse playing with and permanent reshaping of one's symbolic identity, or how it involves a regression to the psychotic incestuous immersion into the Screen as the maternal Thing that swallows us, depriving us of the capacity of symbolic distance and reflection. It can, however, be argued that the most common reaction of all of us when we are confronted with cyberspace is still that of hysterical perplexity, of permanent questioning: 'How do I stand with respect to this anonymous Other? What does It want from me? What game is it playing with me?' . . .

With regard to this crucial opposition between hysteria and perversion, it is important to note that Adorno's *Philosophy of the New Music*, that masterpiece of the dialectical analysis of the 'class struggle in music', resorts to the clinical categories of, precisely, hysteria and perversion in order to elaborate the opposition of the two fundamental tendencies in modern music, designated by the names Schoenberg and Stravinsky: Schoenberg's 'progressive' music displays the clear features of an extreme hysterical tension (anxiety-laden reactions to traumatic encounters); while Stravinsky, in his pastiche-like traversing of all possible musical styles, displays no less clear features of perversion, that is, of renouncing the dimension of subjectivity proper, of adopting the stance of exploiting the polymorphous multitude, with no real subjective engagement with any specific element or mode.

And – to give this opposition a philosophical twist – one is tempted to claim that this fidelity to the truth of hysteria against the pervert's false transgression is what led Lacan, in the last years of his teaching, to claim pathetically: 'I rebel against philosophy [*Je m'insurge contre la philosophie*].' Apropos of this general claim, the Leninist question should be asked immediately: which (singular) philosophy did Lacan have in mind; which philosophy was, for him, a stand-in for philosophy 'as such'? Following a suggestion by François Regnault (who draws attention to the fact that Lacan made this statement in 1975, in the wake of the publication of *Anti-Oedipus*[1]), one could argue that the philosophy actually under fire, far from standing for some traditional Hegelian metaphysics, is none other than that of Gilles Deleuze, a philosopher of globalized perversion if ever there was one. That is to say, is not Deleuze's critique of 'Oedipal' psychoanalysis an exemplary case of the perverse rejection of hysteria? Against the hysterical subject who maintains an ambiguous attitude towards symbolic authority (like the psychoanalyst who acknowledges the pathological consequences of 'repression', but none the less claims that 'repression' is the condition of cultural progress, since outside symbolic authority there is only the psychotic void), the pervert bravely goes to the limit in undermining the very foundations of symbolic authority and fully endorsing the multiple productivity of pre-symbolic libidinal flux . . . for

Lacan, of course, this 'anti-Oedipal' radicalization of psychoanalysis is the very model of the trap to be avoided at any cost: the model of false subversive radicalization that fits the existing power constellation perfectly. In other words, for Lacan, the philosopher's 'radicality', his fearless questioning of all presuppositions, is the model of the false transgressive radicality.

For Foucault, a perverse philosopher if ever there was one, the relationship between prohibition and desire is circular, and one of absolute immanence: power and resistance (counter-power) presuppose and generate each other – that is, the very prohibitive measures that categorize and regulate illicit desires effectively generate them. Simply recall the proverbial figure of the early Christian ascetic who, in his detailed description of situations to be avoided, since they provoke sexual temptations, displays an extraordinary knowledge of how seduction works (of how a simple smile, a glance, a defensive gesture of the hands, a demand for help, can carry a sexual innuendo . . .). The problem here is that, after insisting that the disciplinary power mechanisms produce the very object on which they exert their force (the subject is not only that which is oppressed by the power but emerges himself as the product of this oppression) –

> The man described for us, whom we are invited to free, is already in himself the effect of a subjection [*assujettissement*] much more profound than himself. A 'soul' inhabits him and brings him to existence, which is itself a factor in the mastery that power exercises over the body. The soul is the effect and instrument of a political autonomy; the soul is the prison of the body.[2]

– it is as if Foucault himself tacitly acknowledges that this absolute continuity of resistance to power is not enough to ground effective resistance to power, a resistance that would not be 'part of the game' but would allow the subject to assume a position that exempts him from the disciplinary/confessional mode of power practised from early Christianity to psychoanalysis. Foucault thought that he located such an exception in Antiquity: the Antique notions of the 'use of pleasures' and 'care for the Self' do not yet involve reference to a universal Law. However, the image of Antiquity deployed in Foucault's last two books is *stricto sensu* phantasmic, the fantasy of a discipline which, even in its most ascetic version, needs no reference to the symbolic Law/Prohibition of pleasures without sexuality. In his attempt to break out of the vicious cycle of power and resistance, Foucault resorts to the myth of a state 'before the Fall' in which discipline was self-fashioned, not a procedure imposed by the culpabilizing universal moral order. In this phantasmic Beyond, one encounters the same disciplinary mechanisms as later, only in a different modality, a kind of correlate to Malinowski–Mead's mythical description of non-repressed South Pacific sexuality. No wonder Foucault reads pre-Christian texts in a way which totally differs from his usual practice of reading: his last two books are much closer to the standard academic 'history of ideas'. In other words, Foucault's description of the Self in pre-Christian Antiquity is the necessary Romantic-naive supplement to his cynical description of power relations after the Fall, where power and resistance overlap.[3]

So when, in *Discipline and Punish* and Volume I of *The History of Sexuality*, Foucault endlessly varies the theme of power as productive, with respect to political and educational power as well as power over sexuality; when he emphasizes again and again how, in the course of the nineteenth century, 'repressive' attempts to categorize, discipline, etc. sexuality, far from constraining and limiting their object, 'natural' sexuality, in fact produced it and led to its proliferation (sex was affirmed as the ultimate 'secret', the point of reference, of human activity), is he not, in a way, asserting the Hegelian thesis on how reflexive probing into a transcendent In-itself produces the very inaccessible X that seems forever to elude its final grasp? (This point can be made very clearly apropos of the mysterious 'dark continent' of Feminine Sexuality allegedly eluding the grasp of patriarchal discourse: is not this mysterious Beyond the very product of male discourse? Is not Feminine Mystery the ultimate *male* fantasy?)

As for disciplining and controlling, Foucault's point is not only how the object these measures want to control and subdue is already their effect (legal and criminal measures engender their own forms of criminal transgression, etc.): the very subject who resists these disciplinary measures and tries to elude their grasp is, in his heart of hearts, branded by them, formed by them. Foucault's ultimate example would have been the nineteenth-century workers' movement for the 'liberation of work': as early libertarian criticisms like Paul Lafargue's *Right to Laziness* had already pointed out, the Worker who wanted himself liberated was the product of disciplinary ethics, that is, in his very attempt to get rid of the domination of Capital, he wanted to establish himself as the disciplined worker who works for himself, who is fully his own master (and thus loses the right to resist, since he cannot resist himself . . .). On this level, Power and Resistance are effectively caught in a deadly mutual embrace: there is no Power without Resistance (in order to function, Power needs an X which eludes its grasp); there is no Resistance without Power (Power is already formative of that very kernel on behalf of which the oppressed subject resists the hold of Power).

There is thus nothing more misguided than to argue that Foucault, in Volume 1 of his *History of Sexuality*, opens up the way for individuals to rearticulate-resignify-displace the power mechanisms they are caught in: the whole point and strength of his forceful argumentation lies in his claim that resistances to power are generated by the very matrix they seem to oppose. In other words, the point of his notion of 'biopower' is precisely to give an account of how disciplinary power mechanisms can constitute individuals *directly*, by penetrating individual bodies and *bypassing the level of 'subjectivization'* (that is, the whole problematic of how individuals ideologically subjectivize their predicament, how they relate to their conditions of existence). It is therefore meaningless, in a way, to criticize him for not rendering this subjectivization thematic: his whole point is that if one is to account for social discipline and subordination, one *has* to bypass it! Later, however (starting from Volume II of his *History of Sexuality*), he is compelled to return to this very ostracized topic of subjectivization: how individuals subjectivize their condition, how they relate to it – or, to put it in Althusserian terms, how they are not only individuals caught in disciplinary state apparatuses, but also interpellated subjects.

How, then, does Foucault relate to Hegel? According to Judith Butler,[4] the difference between the two is that Hegel does not take the *proliferating* effect of disciplinatory activity into account: in Hegel, formative disciplining simply works on the body that is presupposed as an In-itself, given as part of inert human nature, and gradually 'sublates'/mediates its immediacy; while Foucault emphasizes how disciplining mechanisms themselves set in motion a wild proliferation of what they endeavour to suppress and regulate: the very 'repression' of sexuality gives rise to new forms of sexual pleasure. . . .[5] However, what seems to be missing in Foucault, the anti-dialectician *par excellence*, is precisely the properly Hegelian self-referential turn in the relationship between sexuality and its disciplinatory control: not only does confessional self-probing unearth new forms of sexuality – *the confessional activity itself becomes sexualized, gives rise to a satisfaction of its own*: 'The repressive law is not external to the libido that it represses, but the repressive law represses to the extent that repression becomes a libidinal activity.'[6]

Take politically correct probing into hate speech and sexual harassment: the trap into which this effort falls is not only that it makes us aware of (and thus generates) new forms and layers of humiliation and harassment (we learn that 'fat', 'stupid', 'short-sighted' ... are to be replaced by 'weight-challenged', etc.); the catch is, rather, that this censoring activity itself, by a kind of devilish dialectical reversal, starts to participate in what it purports to censor and fight – is it not immediately evident how, in designating somebody as 'mentally challenged' instead of 'stupid', an ironic distance can always creep in and give rise to an excess of humiliating aggressivity – one adds insult to injury, as it were, by the supplementary polite patronizing dimension (it is well known that aggressivity coated in politeness can be much more painful than directly abusive words, since violence is heightened by the additional contrast between the aggressive content and the polite surface form . . .). In short, what Foucault's account of the discourses that discipline and regulate sexuality leaves out of consideration is the process by means of which the power mechanism itself becomes eroticized, that is, contaminated by what it endeavours to 'repress'. It is not enough to claim that the ascetic Christian subject who, in order to fight temptation, enumerates and categorizes the various forms of temptation, actually proliferates the object he tries to combat; the point is, rather, to conceive of how the ascetic who flagellates in order to resist temptation finds sexual pleasure in this very act of inflicting wounds on himself.

The paradox at work here is that the very fact that there is no pre-existing positive Body in which one could ontologically ground our resistance to disciplinary power mechanisms makes effective resistance possible. That is to say: the standard Habermasian argument against Foucault and 'post-structuralists' in general is that since they deny any normative standard exempt from the contingent historical context, they are unable to ground resistance to the existing power edifice. The Foucauldian counter-argument is that the 'repressive' disciplinary mechanisms themselves open up the space for resistance, in so far as they generate a surplus in their object. Although the reference to some Feminine Essence (from the Eternal Feminine to more contemporary feminine writing) seems to ground women's resistance to the masculine symbolic order, this reference none the less confirms femininity as the pre-given foundation upon which the masculine discursive machine works – here resistance is simply the resistance of the pre-symbolic foundation to its symbolic working-through. If, however, one posits that the patriarchal endeavour to contain and categorize femininity itself generates forms of resistance, one opens up a space for a feminine resistance that is no longer resistance on behalf of the underlying foundation but resistance as the active principle in excess over the oppressive force.

To avoid the standard example of sexuality, however, let us recall the formation of national identity through resistance to colonialist domination: what precedes colonialist domination is self-enclosed ethnic awareness, which lacks the strong will to resist and to assert its identity forcefully against the Other; only as a reaction to colonialist domination is this awareness transformed into active political will to assert one's national identity against the oppressor – anti-colonialist national liberation movements are *stricto sensu* generated by colonialist oppression; that is to say, it is this oppression which brings about the shift from passive ethnic self-awareness grounded in mythical tradition to the eminently modern will to assert one's ethnic identity in the form of a nation-state. One is tempted to say that the will to gain political independence from the colonizer in the guise of a new independent nation-state is the ultimate proof that the colonized ethnic group is thoroughly integrated into the ideological universe of the colonizer. We are dealing here with the contradiction between the enunciated content and the position of enunciation: as for the enunciated content, the anti-colonialist movement, of course, conceives itself as a return to pre-colonial roots, as asserting one's cultural, etc., independence from the colonizer – but the very form of this assertion is already taken over from the colonizer: it is the form of Western nation-state political autonomy – no wonder the Congress Party in India, which led to independence, was instigated by English liberals and organized by Indian intellectuals studying at Oxford. Does not the same hold for the multitude of quests for national sovereignty among the ethnic groups of the ex-Soviet Union? Although Chechens evoke their hundred-year-old struggle against Russian domination, today's form of this struggle is clearly the outcome of the modernizing effect of the Russian colonization of traditional Chechen society.

Against Butler, one is thus tempted to emphasize that Hegel *was* well aware of the retroactive process by means of which oppressive power itself generates the form of resistance – is not this very paradox contained in Hegel's notion of positing the presuppositions, that is, of how the activity of positing-mediating does not merely elaborate the presupposed immediate-natural Ground, but thoroughly transforms the very core of its identity? The very In-itself to which Chechens endeavour to return is already mediated-posited by the process of modernization, which deprived them of their ethnic roots.

This argumentation may appear Eurocentrist, condemning the colonized to repeat the European imperialist pattern by means of the very gesture of resisting it – however, it is also possible to give it precisely the opposite reading. That is to say: if we ground our resistance to imperialist Eurocentrism in the reference to some kernel of previous ethnic identity, we automatically adopt the position of a victim resisting modernization, of a passive object on which imperialist procedures work. If, however, we conceive our resistance as an excess that results from the way brutal imperialist intervention disturbed our previous self-enclosed identity, our position becomes much stronger, since we can claim that our resistance is grounded in the inherent dynamics of the imperialist system – that the imperialist system itself, through its inherent antagonism, activates the forces that will bring about its demise. (The situation here is strictly homologous to that of how to ground feminine resistance: if woman is 'a symptom of man', the locus at which the inherent antagonisms of the patriarchal symbolic order emerge, this in no way constrains the scope of feminist resistance but provides it with an even stronger detonating force.) Or – to put it in yet another way – the premiss according to which resistance to power is inherent and immanent to the power edifice (in the sense that it is generated by the inherent dynamic of the power edifice) in no way obliges us to draw the conclusion that every resistance is co-opted in advance, included in the eternal game Power plays with itself – the key point is that through the effect of proliferation, of producing an excess of resistance, the very inherent antagonism of a system may well set in motion a process which leads to its own ultimate downfall.[7]

It seems that such a notion of antagonism is what Foucault lacks: from the fact that every resistance is generated ('posited') by the Power edifice itself, from this absolute inherence of resistance to Power, he seems to draw the conclusion that resistance is co-opted in advance, that it cannot seriously undermine the system – that is, he precludes the possibility that the system itself, on account of its inherent inconsistency, may give birth to a force whose excess it is no longer able to master and which thus detonates its unity, its capacity to reproduce itself. In short, Foucault does not consider the possibility of an effect escaping, outgrowing its cause, so that although it emerges as a form of resistance to power and is as such absolutely inherent to it, it can outgrow and explode it. (The philosophical point to be made here is that this is the fundamental feature of the dialectical-materialist notion of 'effect': the effect can 'outdo' its cause; it can be ontologically 'higher' than its cause.) One is thus tempted to reverse the Foucauldian notion of an all-encompassing power edifice which always-already contains its transgression, that which allegedly eludes it: what if the price to be paid is that the power mechanism cannot even control *itself*, but has to rely on an obscene protuberance at its very heart? In other words: what effectively eludes the controlling grasp of Power is not so much the external In-itself it tries to dominate but, rather, the obscene supplement which sustains its own operation.[8]

And this is why Foucault lacks the appropriate notion of the subject: the subject is by definition in excess over its cause, and as such it emerges with the reversal of the repression of sexuality into the sexualization of the repressive measures themselves. This insufficiency of Foucault's theoretical edifice can be discerned in the way, in his early *History of Madness*, he is already oscillating between two radically opposed views: the view that madness is not simply a phenomenon that exists in itself and is only secondarily the object of discourses, but is *itself* the product of a multitude of (medical, legal, biological . . .) discourses about itself; and the opposite view, according to which one should 'liberate' madness from the hold exerted over it by these discourses, and 'let madness itself speak'.[9]

Ideological Interpellation

The work of Judith Butler is of special interest here: while she takes as her starting point the Foucauldian account of subjectivization as subjection through performative disciplinatory practices, she none the less perceives the aforementioned flaws in Foucault's edifice, and endeavours to supplement it by reference to a series of other theoretical concepts and edifices, from Hegel via psychoanalysis to Althusser's notion of ideological interpellation as constitutive of subjectivity, combining all these references in a way which is far from the eclectic monstrosity usually referred to as 'creative synthesis'.

In her reading of the Hegelian dialectics of lord and bondsman, Butler focuses on the hidden contract between the two: 'the imperative to the bondsman consists in the following formulation: you be my body for me, but do not let me know that the body that you are is my body'.[10] The disavowal on the part of the lord is thus double: first, the lord disavows his own body, he poses as a disembodied desire and compels the bondsman to act as his body; secondly, the bondsman has to disavow the fact that he acts merely as the lord's body and act as an autonomous agent, as if the bondsman's bodily labouring for the lord is not imposed on him but is his autonomous activity. . . .[11] This structure of double (and thereby self-effacing) disavowal also expresses the patriarchal matrix of the relationship between man and woman: in a first move, woman is posited as a mere projection/reflection of man, his insubstantial shadow, hysterically imitating but never able really to acquire the moral stature of a fully constituted self-identical subjectivity; however, this status of a mere reflection has itself to be disavowed and the woman provided with a false autonomy, as if she acts as she does within the logic of patriarchy on account of her own autonomous logic (women are 'by nature' submissive, compassionate, self-sacrificing . . .). The paradox not to be missed here is that the bondsman (servant) is all the more the servant, the more he (mis)perceives his position as that of an autonomous agent; and the same goes for woman – the ultimate form of her servitude is to (mis)perceive herself, when she acts in a 'feminine' submissive-compassionate way, as an autonomous agent. For that reason, the Weiningerian ontological denigration of woman as a mere 'symptom' of man – as the embodiment of male fantasy, as the hysterical imitation of true male subjectivity – is, when it is openly admitted and fully accepted, far more subversive than the false direct assertion of feminine autonomy – perhaps the ultimate feminist statement is to proclaim openly: 'I do not exist in myself, I am merely the Other's fantasy embodied'.

The same holds for the relationship between the subject and the Institution: the bureaucratic/symbolic Institution not only reduces the subject to its mouthpiece, but also wants the subject to disavow the fact that he is merely its mouthpiece and to (pretend to) act as an autonomous agent – a person with a human touch and personality, not just a faceless bureaucrat. The point, of course, is not only that such an autonomization is doubly false, since it involves a double disavowal, but also that there is no subject prior to the Institution (prior to language as the ultimate institution): subjectivity is produced as the void in the very submission of the life-substance of the Real to the Institution. If, then – as Althusser would have put it – the perception that, prior to interpellation, the subject is always-already there is precisely the effect and proof of successful interpellation, does not the Lacanian assertion of a subject prior to interpellation/subjectivization repeat the very ideological illusion that Althusser endeavours to denounce? Or – to take another aspect of the same critical argument – in so far as ideological identification succeeds precisely inasmuch as I perceive myself as a 'full human person' who 'cannot be reduced to a puppet, to an instrument of some ideological big Other', is not the thesis on interpellation's necessary failure the very sign of its ultimate success? An interpellation succeeds precisely when I perceive myself as 'not only *that*,' but a 'complex person who, among other things, is also *that* – in short, imaginary distance towards symbolic identification is the very sign of its success.

For Lacan, however, the dimension of subjectivity that eludes symbolic identification is *not* the imaginary wealth/texture of experiences which allows me to assume an illusory distance towards my symbolic identity: the Lacanian 'barred subject' (s) is 'empty' not in the sense of some psychologico-existential 'experience of a void' but, rather, in the sense of a dimension of self-relating negativity which a priori eludes the domain of *vécu*, of lived experience. The old story of the prince who disguises himself as a stable boy to seduce the princess, his bride, in order to be sure that she loves him for what he really is, not for his title, is thus not appropriate to mark the distinction we are dealing with here: the Lacanian subject *qua* s is neither the title which constitutes my symbolic identity nor the phantasmic object, that 'something in me' beyond my symbolic identities which makes me worthy of the Other's desire.

A funny thing happened recently in a Slovene theatre: a half-educated *nouveau riche* was late for the performance and tried to reach his seat half an hour into the show; quite accidentally, at that very moment, the actor on the stage had to pronounce, pathetically, the phrase: 'Who is disturbing my silence?' – the poor *nouveau riche*, who did not feel quite at home in the theatre, out of guilt for being late, recognized himself as the addressee of this phrase – that is, he interpreted this phrase as the outburst of the actor's rage because of the sudden commotion in the front row – and answered loudly, for everyone to hear: 'My name is X. Sorry I was late, but my car broke down on the way to the theatre!' The theoretical point of this ridiculous unfortunate event is that a similar 'misunderstanding' defines interpellation *as such*: whenever we recognize ourselves in the call of the Other, there is a minimum of such a misunderstanding at work; our recognition in the call is always a misrecognition, an act of falling into ridicule by boastfully assuming the place of the addressee which is not really ours. . . .

Does not this gap, however, also indicate an excess on the side of the 'big Other' of the symbolic institution? That is to say: is it not a fact that today, more than ever, we, as individuals, are interpellated without even being aware of it: our identity is constituted for the big Other by a series of digitalized informational (medical, police, educational . . .) files we are mostly not even aware of, so that interpellation functions (determines our place and activity in the social space) without any gesture of recognition on the part of the subject concerned. This, however, is not the problem Althusser is addressing with the notion of interpellation; his problem, rather, is that of *subjectivization*: how do individuals themselves subjectivize their condition, how do they experience themselves as subjects? If I am inscribed into a secret state file without being aware of it, this simply doesn't concern my subjectivity. Much more interesting is the opposite case, in which the subject recognizes himself in the call of an Other which 'doesn't exist' – say, in the Call of God: Althusser's point is that my recognition in the interpellative call of the Other is performative in the sense that, in the very gesture of recognition, it *constitutes* (or 'posits') this big Other – God 'exists' in so far as believers recognize themselves as hearing and (dis)obeying His Call; the Stalinist politician exerts his power in so far as he recognizes himself as interpellated by the big Other of History, serving its Progress; a democratic politician who 'serves the people' constitutes the agency (People) the reference to which legitimizes his activity.

If, then, today, in the guise of detailed databases that circulate in the corporate cyberspace and determine what we effectively are for the big Other of the power structure[12] – that is, how our symbolic identity is constructed – and we are in this sense 'interpellated' by institutions even without being aware of it, one should nevertheless insist that this 'objective interpellation' actually affects my subjectivity only by means of the fact that *I myself am well aware of how, outside the grasp of my knowledge, databases circulate which determine my symbolic identity in the eyes of the social 'big Other'*. My very awareness of the fact that 'the truth is out there', that files on me circulate which, even if they are factually 'inaccurate', none the less performatively determine my socio-symbolic status, is what gives rise to the specific proto-paranoiac mode of subjectivization characteristic of today's subject: it constitutes me as a subject inherently related to and hassled by an elusive piece of database in which, beyond my reach, 'my fate is writ large'.

From Resistance to the Act

The political focus of Butler's theoretical endeavour is the old leftist one: how is it possible not only actually to resist, but also to undermine and/ or displace the existing socio-symbolic network (the Lacanian 'big Other') which predetermines the space within which the subject can only exist?[13] She is well aware, of course, that the site of this resistance cannot be simply and directly identified as the Unconscious: the existing order of Power is also supported by unconscious 'passionate attachments' – attachments that must remain publicly non-acknowledged if they are to fulfil their role:

> If the unconscious escapes from a given normative injunction, to what other injunction does it form an attachment? What makes us think that the unconscious is any less structured by the power relations that pervade cultural signifiers than is the language of the subject? If we find an attachment to subjection at the level of the unconscious, what kind of resistance is to be wrought from that?[14]

The outstanding case of such unconscious 'passionate attachments' that sustain Power is precisely the inherent reflexive eroticization of regulatory power mechanisms and procedures themselves: in an obsessional ritual, the very performance of the compulsive ritual destined to keep illicit temptation at bay becomes the source of libidinal satisfaction. It is thus the 'reflexivity' involved in the relationship between regulatory power and sexuality, the way repressive regulatory procedures themselves are libidinally invested and function as a source of libidinal satisfaction, this 'masochistic' reflexive turn, which remains unaccounted for in the standard notion of the 'internalization' of social norms into psychic prohibitions. The second problem with the quick identification of the Unconscious as the site of resistance is that even if we concede that the Unconscious *is* the site of resistance which forever prevents the smooth functioning of power mechanisms, that is, that interpellation – the subject's recognition in his/her allotted symbolic place – is always ultimately incomplete, failed, 'does such resistance do anything to alter or expand the dominant injunctions or interpellations of subject formation?'[15] In short: '[t]his resistance establishes the incomplete character of any effort to produce a subject by disciplinary means, but it remains unable to rearticulate the dominant terms of productive power'.[16]

That is the kernel of Butler's criticism of Lacan: according to her, Lacan reduces resistance to the imaginary misrecognition of the symbolic structure; such a resistance, although it thwarts the full symbolic realization, nevertheless depends on it and asserts it in its very opposition, unable to rearticulate its terms: 'For the Lacanian, then, the imaginary signifies the impossibility of the discursive – that is, symbolic – constitution of identity.'[17] Along these lines, she even qualifies the Lacanian Unconscious itself as imaginary, that is, as 'that which thwarts any effort of the symbolic to constitute sexed identity coherently and fully, an unconscious indicated by the slips and gaps that characterize the workings of the imaginary in language'.[18] Against this background, it is then possible to claim that, in Lacan, 'psychic resistance presumes the continuation of the law in its anterior, symbolic form and, in that sense, contributes to its status quo. In such a view, resistance appears doomed to perpetual defeat.'[19]

The first thing to note here is that Butler seems to conflate two radically opposed uses of the term 'resistance': one is the *socio-critical* use (resistance to power, etc.), the other the *clinical* use operative in psychoanalysis (the patient's resistance to acknowledging the unconscious truth of his symptoms, the meaning of his dreams, etc.). When Lacan effectively determines resistance as 'imaginary', he has in mind the misrecognition of the symbolic network which determines us. On the other hand, for Lacan, radical rearticulation of the predominant symbolic Order is altogether possible – this is what his notion of *point de capiton* (the 'quilting point' or the Master-Signifier) is about: when a new *point de capiton* emerges, the socio-symbolic field is not only displaced, its very structuring principle changes. One is thus tempted to reverse the opposition between Lacan and Foucault as elaborated by Butler (Lacan constrains resistance to imaginary thwarting, while Foucault, who has a more pluralistic notion of discourse as a heterogeneous field of multiple practices, allows for a more thorough symbolic subversion and rearticulation): it is Foucault who insists on the immanence of resistance to Power, while Lacan leaves open the possibility of a radical rearticulation of the entire symbolic field by means of an *act* proper, a passage through 'symbolic death'. In short, it is Lacan who allows us to conceptualize the distinction between imaginary resistance (false transgression that reasserts the symbolic status quo and even serves as a positive condition of its functioning) and actual symbolic rearticulation via the intervention of the Real of an *act*.

Only on this level – if we take into account the Lacanian notions of *point de capiton* and the act as real – does a meaningful dialogue with Butler become possible. Butler's matrix of social existence (as well as Lacan's) is that of a forced choice: in order to exist at all (within the socio-symbolic space) one has to accept the fundamental alienation, the definition of one's existence in the terms of the 'big Other', the predominant structure of the socio-symbolic space. As she is quick to add, however, this should not constrain us to (what she perceives as) the Lacanian view according to which the symbolic Order is a given that can be effectively transgressed only if the subject pays the price of psychotic exclusion; so that on the one hand we have false imaginary resistance to the symbolic Norm and, on the other, psychotic breakdown, with the full acceptance of alienation in the symbolic Order (the goal of psychoanalytic treatment) as the only 'realistic' option.

Butler opposes to this Lacanian fixity of the Symbolic the Hegelian dialectics of presupposing and positing: not only is the symbolic Order always-already presupposed as the sole milieu of the subject's social existence; this Order itself exists, is reproduced, only in so far as subjects recognize themselves in it and, via repeated performative gestures, again and again assume their places in it – this, of course, opens up the possibility of changing the symbolic contours of our socio-symbolic existence by way of its parodically displaced performative enactings. That is the thrust of Butler's anti-Kantianism: she rejects the Lacanian symbolic a priori as a new version of the transcendental framework which fixes the co-ordinates of our existence in advance, leaving no space for the retroactive displacement of these presupposed conditions. So when, in a key passage, Butler asks –

> What would it mean for the subject to desire something other than its continued 'social existence'? If such an existence cannot be undone without falling into some kind of death, can existence nevertheless be risked, death courted or pursued, in order to expose and open to transformation the hold of social power on the conditions of life's persistence? The subject is compelled to repeat the norms by which it is produced, but the repetition establishes a domain of risk, for if one fails to reinstate the norm 'in the right way,' one becomes subject to further sanction, one feels the prevailing conditions of existence threatened. And yet, without a repetition that risks life – in its current organization – how might we begin to imagine the contingency of that organization, and performatively reconfigure the contours of the conditions of life?[20]

– the Lacanian answer is clear: 'to desire something other than its continued "social existence"', and thus to fall 'into some kind of death', to risk a gesture by means of which death is 'courted or pursued', indicates precisely how Lacan reconceptualized the Freudian death drive as the elementary form of the *ethical act*, the act as irreducible to a 'speech act' which relies for its performative power on the pre-established set of symbolic rules and/or norms.

Is this not the whole point of Lacan's reading of *Antigone*: Antigone effectively risks her entire social existence, defying the socio-symbolic power of the City embodied in the ruler (Creon), thereby 'falling into some kind of death' (i.e. sustaining a symbolic death, exclusion from the socio-symbolic space). For Lacan, there is no ethical act proper without taking the risk of such a momentary 'suspension of the big Other', of the socio-symbolic network that guarantees the subject's identity: an authentic *act* occurs only when the subject risks a gesture that is no longer 'covered up' by the big Other. Lacan pursues all possible versions of this entering the domain 'between the two deaths': not only Antigone after her expulsion, but also Oedipus at Colonnus, King Lear, Poe's Mr Valdemar, and so on, up to Sygne from Claudel's Coufontaine trilogy – their common predicament is that they all found themselves in this domain of the undead, 'beyond death and life', in which the causality of symbolic Fate is suspended.

One should criticize Butler for conflating this act in its radical dimension with the performative reconfiguration of one's symbolic condition via its repetitive displacements: the two are not the same – that is to say, one should maintain the crucial distinction between a mere 'performative reconfiguration', a subversive displacement which remains *within* the hegemonic field and, as it were, conducts an internal guerrilla war of turning the terms of the hegemonic field against itself, *and* the much more radical *act* of a thorough reconfiguration of the entire field which redefines the very conditions of socially sustained performativity. It is thus Butler herself who ends up in a position of allowing precisely for marginal 'reconfigurations' of the predominant discourse – who remains constrained to a position of 'inherent transgression', which needs as a point of reference the Other in the guise of a predominant discourse that can be only marginally displaced or transgressed.[21]

From the Lacanian standpoint, Butler is thus simultaneously too optimistic and too pessimistic. On the one hand she overestimates the subversive potential of disturbing the functioning of the big Other through the practices of performative reconfiguration/displacement: such practices ultimately support what they intend to subvert, since the very field of such 'transgressions' is already taken into account, even engendered, by the hegemonic form of the big Other – what Lacan calls 'the big Other' are symbolic norms *and* their codified transgressions. The Oedipal order, this gargantuan symbolic matrix embodied in a vast set of ideological institutions, rituals and practices, is a much too deeply rooted and 'substantial' entity to be effectively undermined by the marginal gestures of performative displacement. On the other hand, Butler does not allow for the radical gesture of the thorough restructuring of the hegemonic symbolic order in its totality.

'Traversing the Fantasy'

Is it possible also to undermine the most fundamental level of subjection, what Butler calls 'passionate attachments'? The Lacanian name for the primordial 'passionate attachments' on which the very consistency of the subject's being hinges is, of course, *fundamental fantasy*. The 'attachment to subjectivization' constitutive of the subject is thus none other than the primordial 'masochist' scene in which the subject 'makes/sees himself suffering', that is, assumes *la douleur d'exister*, and thus provides the minimum of support to his being (like Freud's primordially repressed middle term 'Father is beating me' in the triad of 'A child is being beaten'). This fundamental fantasy is thoroughly *inter-passive*.[22] in it, a scene of passive suffering (subjection) is staged which simultaneously sustains and threatens the subject's being – which sustains this being only in so far as it remains foreclosed (primordially repressed). From this perspective, a new approach opens up to the recent artistic practices of sadomasochistic performance: is it not a fact that, in them, this very foreclosure is ultimately undone? In other words, what if the open assuming/staging of the phantasmic scene of primordial 'passionate attachments' is far more subversive than the dialectic rearticulation and/ or displacement of this scene?

The difference between Butler and Lacan is that for Butler, the primordial repression (foreclosure) equals the foreclosure of the primordial 'passionate attachment', while for Lacan the fundamental fantasy (the stuff 'primordial attachments' are made of) is already a filler, a formation which covers up a certain gap/void. It is here, on this very point at which the difference between Butler and Lacan is almost imperceptible, that we encounter the ultimate gap that separates them. Butler again interprets these 'primordial attachments' as the subject's presuppositions in a proto-Hegelian sense of the term, and therefore counts on the subject's ability dialectically to rearticulate these presuppositions of his/her being, to reconfigure/displace them: the subject's identity 'will remain always and forever rooted in its injury as long as it remains an identity, but it does imply that the possibilities of resignification will rework and unsettle the passionate attachment to subjection without which subject formation – and re-formation – cannot succeed'.[23] When subjects are confronted with a forced choice in which rejecting an injurious interpellation amounts to not existing at all – when, under the threat of nonexistence, they are, as it were, emotionally blackmailed into identifying with the imposed symbolic identity ('nigger', 'bitch', etc.) – it is nevertheless possible for them to displace this identity, to recontextualize it, to make it work for other purposes, to turn it against its hegemonic mode of functioning, since symbolic identity retains its hold only by its incessant repetitive re-enacting.

What Lacan does here is to introduce a distinction between two terms that are identified in Butler: the *fundamental fantasy* that serves as the ultimate support of the subject's being, and the *symbolic identification* that is already a symbolic response to the trauma of the phantasmic 'passionate attachment'. The symbolic identity we assume in a forced choice, when we recognize ourselves in ideological interpellation, relies on the disavowal of the phantasmic 'passionate attachment' that serves as its ultimate support. (In army life, for example, such a 'passionate attachment' is provided by the homosexual link which has to be disavowed if it is to remain operative.[24]) This leads to a further distinction between symbolic rearticulations, or variations on the fundamental fantasy that do not actually undermine its hold (like the variations on 'Father is beating me' in Freud's 'A child is being beaten' fantasy), and the possible 'traversing' of, gaining a distance towards, the very fundamental fantasy – the ultimate aim of psychoanalytic treatment is for the subject to undo the ultimate 'passionate attachment' that guarantees the consistency of his/her being, and thus to undergo what Lacan calls 'subjective destitution'. At its most fundamental, the primordial 'passionate attachment' to the scene of fundamental fantasy is not 'dialecticizable': it can only be traversed.

Clint Eastwood's 'Dirty Harry' series of films provides an exemplary case of the dialectical reconfiguration/variation of the fantasy: in the first film, the masochist fantasy is almost directly acknowledged in all its ambiguity, while in subsequent instalments it looks as if Eastwood self-consciously accepted politically correct criticism and displaced the fantasy to give the story a more acceptable 'progressive' flavour – in all these reconfigurations, however, *the same fundamental fantasy remains operative*. With all due respect for the political efficiency of such reconfigurations, they thus do not really disturb the hard phantasmic core, but even sustain it. And, in contrast to Butler, Lacan's wager is that even and also in politics, it *is* possible to accomplish a more radical gesture of 'traversing' the very fundamental fantasy – only such gestures which disturb this phantasmic core are authentic *acts*.[25]

This compels us to redefine the very fundamental notion of (social) identification: because the passionate attachment is operative only in so far as it is not openly admitted, in so far as we maintain our distance towards it, what holds a community together is not the directly shared mode of identification with the same object but, rather, its exact opposite: the shared mode of *disidentification*, of *delegating* the members' hatred or love to another agent *through whom* they love or hate. The Christian community, for instance, is held together by the shared delegation of their belief to some selected individuals (saints, priests, maybe only Christ alone) who are 'supposed to really believe'. The function of *symbolic* identification is thus the very opposite of direct immersion in (or fusion with) the object of identification: it is to maintain the *proper distance* towards the object (for this reason, the Church as Institution always perceived zealots as its ultimate enemies: because of their direct identification and belief, they threaten the distance through which the religious institution maintains itself). Another example: if, in a love melodrama depicting a couple making love, we were all of a sudden to perceive that the couple is actually having sex (or if, in a snuff movie, we become aware that the victim is actually being tortured to death), this thoroughly *ruins* the proper identification with the narrative reality. From my youth, I remember the Polish spectacle *Pharaoh* (1960), in which there is a scene where a horse is sacrificed: when I, the spectator, noticed that the horse was actually being stabbed to death by lances, this instantly obstructed my identification with the narrative. . . . And the point is that the same goes for 'real life': our sense of reality is always sustained by a minimum of disidentification (for example, when we engage in communication with other people, we 'repress' our awareness of how they sweat, defecate and urinate).

Butler is right to emphasize that subjectivity involves a two-level operation: a primordial 'passionate attachment', a submission/subjection to an Other, *and* its denial – that is, the gaining of a minimal distance towards it which opens up the space of freedom and autonomy. The primordial 'passionate attachment' is thus – to put it in Derridan terms – the condition of (im)possibility of freedom and resistance: there is no subjectivity outside it, that is, subjectivity can assert itself only as the gaining of a distance towards its ground which can never be fully 'sublated'. However, it is none the less theoretically and politically crucial to distinguish between the primordial *phantasmic* 'passionate attachment' that the subject is compelled to repress/disavow in order to gain socio-symbolic existence, and subjection to this very socio-symbolic order, which provides the subject with a determinate symbolic 'mandate' (a place of interpellatory recognition/identification). While the two cannot simply be opposed as 'good' and 'bad' (the very socio-symbolic identification can sustain itself only if it maintains a non-acknowledged phantasmic support), they nevertheless function according to different logics.

This confusion between phantasmic 'passionate attachments' and socio-symbolic identification also accounts for the fact that – surprisingly – Butler uses the couple of superego and ego ideal in a naive pre-Lacanian way, defining superego as the agency that measures the gap between the subject's actual ego and the ego ideal the subject is supposed to emulate, and finds the subject guilty of failure in this endeavour. Would it not be much more productive to follow Lacan and insist on the opposition between the two terms – on the fact that the guilt materialized in the pressure exerted on the subject by the superego is not as straightforward as it may seem: it is not the guilt caused by the failed emulation of the ego ideal, but the more fundamental guilt of accepting the ego ideal (the socially determined symbolic role) as the ideal to be followed in the first place, and thus of betraying one's more fundamental desire (the primordial 'passionate attachment', as Butler would have put it)? If one follows Lacan, one can thus account for the basic paradox of the superego, which lies in the fact that the more I follow the orders of the ego ideal, the more guilty I am – Lacan's point is that, in following the demands of the ego ideal, I am in effect guilty – guilty of betraying my fundamental phantasmic 'passionate attachment'. In other words, far from feeding off some 'irrational' guilt, the superego manipulates the subject's actual betrayal of his fundamental 'passionate attachment' as the price he had to pay for entering the socio-symbolic space, and assuming a pre-determined place within it.

So what is superego in its opposition to the symbolic Law? The parental figure who is simply 'repressive' in the mode of symbolic authority tells a child: 'You must go to Grandma's birthday party and behave nicely, even if you're bored to death – I don't care how you feel, just do it!' The superego figure, in contrast, tells the child: 'Although you know how much Grandma would like to see you, you should visit her only if you really want to – if not, you should stay at home!' The superego trick lies in this false appearance of a free choice, which, as every child knows, is actually a forced choice that involves an even stronger order – not only 'You must visit Grandma, however you feel!', but 'You must visit Grandma, and, furthermore, *you must be glad to do it!*' – the superego orders you to *enjoy* doing what you have to do. The same goes for the strained relationship between lovers or a married couple: when a spouse says to his partner: 'We should visit my sister only if you really want to!', the order between the lines is, of course: 'Not only must you agree to visit my sister, but you must do it gladly, of your own free will, for your own pleasure, not as a favour to me!' The proof of this lies in what happens if the unfortunate partner takes the offer as an actual free choice and says: 'No!' – the predictable spouse's answer then is: 'How could you say that! How can you be so cruel! What has my poor sister done to you that you don't like her?'

The Melancholic Double-Bind

In recent years, Butler has endeavoured to supplement her early 'constructionist' criticism of psychoanalysis by a 'positive' account of the formation of (masculine or feminine) sexual identity, which draws on the Freudian mechanism of mourning and melancholy. She relies here on the old Freudian distinction between foreclosure and repression: repression is an act performed by the subject, an act by means of which a subject (who is already there as an agent) represses part of his psychic content; while foreclosure is a negative gesture of exclusion which grounds the subject, a gesture on which the very consistency of the subject's identity hinges: this gesture cannot be 'assumed' by the subject, since such an assumption would involve the subject's disintegration.

Butler links this primordial and constitutive foreclosure to homosexuality: it is the foreclosure of the passionate attachment to Sameness (to the parent of the same sex) which has to be sacrificed if the subject is to enter the space of the socio-symbolic Order and acquire an identity in it. This leads to the melancholy constitutive of the subject, including the reflexive turn which defines subjectivity: one represses the primordial attachment – that is, one starts to hate to love the same-sex parent; then, in a gesture of reflexive reversal proper, this 'hate to love' turns around into 'love to hate' – one 'loves to hate' those who remind one of the primordially lost objects of love (gays). . . . Butler's logic is impeccable in its very simplicity: Freud insists that the result of the loss of a libidinal object – the way to overcome the melancholy apropos of this loss – is identification with the lost object: does this not also hold for our sexual identities? Is not the 'normal' heterosexual identity the result of successfully overcoming melancholy by identifying with the lost object of the same sex, while the homosexual is the one who refuses fully to come to terms with this loss, and continues to cling to the lost object? Butler's first result is thus that the primordial Foreclosure is not the prohibition of incest: the prohibition of incest already presupposes the predominance of the heterosexual norm (the repressed incestuous wish is for the parent of the opposite sex), and this norm itself came into place through the foreclosure of the homosexual attachment:

> The oedipal conflict presumes that heterosexual desire has already been *accomplished*, that the distinction between heterosexual and homosexual has been enforced . . .; in this sense, the prohibition on incest presupposes the prohibition on homosexuality, for it presumes the heterosexualization of desire.[26]

The primordial 'passionate attachment' to the same sex is thus posited as not only repressed but foreclosed in the radical sense of something which never positively existed, since it was excluded from the very start: 'To the extent that homosexual attachments remain unacknowledged within normative heterosexuality, they are not merely constituted as desires which emerge and subsequently become prohibited; rather, these desires are proscribed from the start.' So, paradoxically, it is the very excessive and compulsive 'straight' identification which – if we take into account the fact that, for Freud, identification relies on the melancholic incorporation of the lost object – demonstrates that the primordial attachment was homosexual:

> In this sense, the 'truest' lesbian melancholic is the strictly straight woman, and the 'truest' gay male melancholic is the strictly straight man. . . . The straight man *becomes* (mimes, cites, appropriates, assumes the status of) the man he 'never' loved and 'never' grieved; the straight woman *becomes* the woman she 'never' loved and 'never' grieved.[27]

Here Butler seems to get involved in a kind of Jungianism *à l'envers*: a man is longing not for his complementary feminine counterpart (*animus* for *anima*, etc.), but for sameness – it is not sameness which 'represses' difference, it is (the desire for) difference which forecloses (the desire for) sameness. . . . However, what about the fact, quoted by Butler herself, that the man, in remaining attached to the compulsive male identification, fears being put in the 'passive' position of femininity as the one who desires (another) man? What we have here is the obverse of the melancholic incorporation: if, in the latter, one *becomes* what one was compelled to give up – *desiring as an object* (a man), then, in the first case, one *desires as an object* what one is afraid to *become* (a woman): a man 'wants the woman he would never be. He wouldn't be caught dead being her: therefore he wants her. . . . Indeed, he will not identify with her, and he will not desire another man. That refusal to desire, that sacrifice of desire under the force of prohibition, will incorporate homosexuality as an identification with masculinity.'[28] Here we encounter the key ambiguity of Butler's argument, an ambiguity which also affects the inconclusive character of her important discussion of transsexual drag dressing: her definition of the foreclosed primordial 'passionate attachment' oscillates between two subjective positions *from which* one desires another man – is it that one desires another man *as a man*, or that one desires to be *a woman* desired by (and desiring) another man? In other words, is my straight masculine identification the melancholic incorporation of my foreclosed attachment to another man, or a defence against assuming the subjective position of a woman (desiring a man)? Butler herself touches upon this ambiguity later in the text, when she asks:

> Does it follow that if one desires a woman, one is desiring from a masculine disposition, or is that disposition retroactively attributed to the desiring position as a way of retaining heterosexuality as the way of understanding the separateness or alterity that conditions desire?[29]

This question, of course, is rhetorical – that is, Butler clearly opts for the second choice. In that case, however, why does she, in the quoted passage, identify desiring another man with assuming a feminine disposition, as if a man 'wouldn't be caught dead being her', since this would mean that he desires another man? Does not all this indicate that the primordial loss constitutive of subjectivity cannot be defined in terms of the foreclosure of a *homosexual* attachment? In other words, *why* does a man fear becoming a woman; why 'wouldn't [he] be caught dead being her'? Is it only because, as such, he would desire (and be desired by) another man? Let us recall Neil Jordan's *The Crying Game*, a film in which we have a passionate love between two men, structured as a heterosexual affair: the black transsexual Dil is a man who desires another man *as a woman*. It thus seems more productive to posit as the central enigma that of sexual difference – *not* as the already established symbolic difference (heterosexual normativity) but, precisely, as that which forever eludes the grasp of normative symbolization.

Butler is right in opposing the Platonic–Jungian notion that the loss involved in sexuation is the loss of the other sex (the notion which opens up the path to various obscurantist androgynous myths of the two halves, feminine and masculine, joined in a complete human being): it is wrong 'to assume from the outset that we only and always lose the other sex, for it is as often the case that we are often in the melancholic bind of *having lost our own sex in order, paradoxically, to become it*'.[30] In short, what the Platonic–Jungian myth fails to take into account is that the obstacle or loss is strictly *inherent*, not external: the loss a woman has to assume in order to become one is not the renunciation of masculinity but, paradoxically, the loss of something which, precisely, forever prevents her from fully becoming a woman – 'femininity' is a masquerade, a mask supplementing a failure to become a woman. Or – to put it in Laclau's terms – sexual difference is the Real of an antagonism, not the Symbolic of a differential opposition: sexual difference is not the opposition allocating to each of the two sexes its positive identity defined in opposition to the other sex (so that woman is what man is not, and vice versa), but a common Loss on account of which woman is never fully a woman and man is never fully a man – 'masculine' and 'feminine' positions are merely two modes of coping with this inherent obstacle/loss.

For that reason, the paradox of 'having lost our own sex in order to become it' holds even more for sexual difference: what one has to lose in order to assume sexual difference *qua* the established set of symbolic oppositions that define the complementary roles of 'man' and 'woman' is sexual difference itself *qua* impossible/real. This dialectical paradox of how an entity can *become* X only in so far as it has to renounce directly *being* X is precisely what Lacan calls 'symbolic castration': the gap between the symbolic place and the element which fills it, the gap on account of which an element can *fill* its place in the structure only in so far as it *is not* directly this place.

Although the title of the recent bestseller *Men are from Mars, Women are from Venus* may appear to provide a version of Lacan's 'there is no sexual relationship' (no complementary relationship between the two sexes, since they are made of different, incompatible stuff), what Lacan has in mind is completely different: men and women are not incompatible simply because they are 'from different planets', each involving a different psychic economy, and so on, but precisely because there is an inextricable antagonistic link between them – that is to say, because they are *from the same planet* which is, as it were, split from within. In other words, the mistake of the *Men are from Mars, Women are from Venus* version of 'there is no sexual relationship' is that it conceives of each of the two sexes as a fully constituted positive entity, which is given independently of the other sex and is, as such, 'out of sync' with it. Lacan, on the contrary, grounds the impossibility of sexual relationship in the fact that the identity of each of the two sexes is hampered from within by the antagonistic relationship to the other sex which prevents its full actualization. 'There is no sexual relationship' not because the other sex is too far away, totally strange to me, but because it is *too close to me*, the foreign intruder at the very heart of my (impossible) identity. Consequently, each of the two sexes functions as the inherent obstacle on account of which the other sex is never 'fully itself': 'man' is that on account of which woman can never fully realize herself as a woman, achieve her feminine self-identity; and, vice versa, 'woman' materializes the obstacle which prevents man's self-fulfilment. So when we claim that, in order to become a man, one must first lose oneself as man, this means that sexual difference is already inscribed into the very notion of 'becoming a man'.

The Real of Sexual Difference

This is the key problem: when Butler rejects sexual difference as 'the primary *guarantor* of loss in our psychic lives' – when she disputes the premiss that 'all separation and loss [can] be traced back to that structuring loss of the other sex by which we emerge as this sexed being in the world',[31] she silently equates sexual difference with the heterosexual symbolic norm determining what it is to be a 'man' or a 'woman', while for Lacan sexual difference is real precisely in the sense that it can never be properly symbolized, transposed/translated into a symbolic norm which fixes the subject's sexual identity – 'there is no such thing as a sexual relationship'. When Lacan claims that sexual difference is 'real', he is therefore far from elevating a historical contingent form of sexuation into a transhistorical norm ('if you do not occupy your proper preor-dained place in the heterosexual order, as either man or woman, you are excluded, exiled into a psychotic abyss outside the symbolic domain'): the claim that sexual difference is 'real' equals the claim that it is 'impossible' – impossible to symbolize, to formulate as a symbolic norm. In other words, it is not that we have homosexuals, fetishists, and other perverts *in spite of* the normative fact of sexual difference – that is, as proofs of the failure of sexual difference to impose its norm; it is not that sexual difference is the ultimate point of reference which anchors the contingent drifting of sexuality; it is, on the contrary, on account of the gap which forever persists between the real of sexual difference and the determinate forms of heterosexual symbolic norms that we have the multitude of 'perverse' forms of sexuality. That is also the problem with the accusation that sexual difference involves 'binary logic': in so far as sexual difference is real/impossible, it is precisely *not* 'binary' but, again, that because of which every 'binary' account of it (every translation of sexual difference into a couple of opposed symbolic features: reason versus emotion, active versus passive . . .) always fails.

So when Butler complains that 'it's a hell of a thing to live in the world being called the impossible real – being called the traumatic, the unthinkable, the psychotic',[32] the Lacanian answer is that, in a sense, *everyone is 'outside'*: those who think they are really 'inside' are, precisely, psychotics. . . . In short, Lacan's well-known dictum according to which a madman is not only a beggar who thinks he is a king but also a king who thinks he is a king (i.e. who perceives his symbolic mandate 'king' as directly grounded in the real of his being) applies also to his assertion of the impossibility of the sexual relationship: a madman is the one who, from the fact that 'there is no sexual relationship', draws the conclusion that the sexual act (the act of copulation) is impossible in reality – he thereby confuses the symbolic void (the absence of the symbolic 'formula' of sexual relationship) with a gap in reality – that is, he confuses the order of 'words' and the order of 'things', which, precisely, is the most elementary and succinct definition of psychosis.[33]

So when Lacan equates the Real with what Freud calls 'psychic reality', this 'psychic reality' is not simply the inner psychic life of dreams, wishes, and so on, as opposed to perceived external reality, but the hard core of primordial 'passionate attachments', which are real in the precise sense of resisting the movement of symbolization and/or dialectical mediation:

> . . . the expression 'psychical reality' itself is not simply synonymous with 'internal world', 'psychological domain', etc. If taken in the most basic sense that it has for Freud, this expression denotes a nucleus within that domain which is heterogeneous and resistant and which is alone in being truly 'real' as compared with the majority of psychical phenomena.[34]

In what sense, then, does the Oedipus complex touch on the Real? Let us answer this via another question: what do Hegel and psychoanalysis have in common when it comes to the notion of subject? For both of them, the 'free' subject, integrated into the symbolic network of mutual recognition, is the result of a process in which traumatic cuts, 'repressions', and the power struggle intervene, not something primordially given. Thus both aim at a kind of 'meta-transcendental' gesture of accounting for the very genesis of the a priori transcendental frame. Every 'historicization', every symbolization, has to 're-enact' the passage from the pre-symbolic X to history. Apropos of Oedipus, for example, it is easy to play the game of historicization, and to demonstrate how the Oedipal constellation is embedded in a specific patriarchal context; it requires a far greater effort of thought to discern, in the very historical contingency of the Oedipus complex, one of the re-enactments of the gap which opens up the horizon of historicity.

In her more recent writings, Butler herself seems to concede this point, when she accepts the key distinction between sexual difference and the 'social construction of gender': the status of sexual difference is not directly that of a contingent socio-symbolic formation; rather, sexual difference indicates the enigmatic domain which lies in between, no longer biology and not yet the space of socio-symbolic construction. Our point here would be to emphasize how this in-between is the very 'cut' which sustains the gap between the Real and the contingent multitude of the modes of its symbolization. In short: yes, of course, the way we symbolize sexuality is not determined by nature, it is the outcome of a complex and contingent socio-symbolic power struggle; however, this very space of contingent symbolization, this very gap between the Real and its symbolization, must be sustained by a cut, and 'symbolic castration' is the Lacanian name for this cut. So 'symbolic castration' is not the ultimate point of symbolic reference which somehow limits the free flow of the multitude of symbolizations: on the contrary, it is the very gesture which sustains, keeps open, the space of contingent symbolizations.[35]

So, to recapitulate: the attraction of Butler's account of sexual difference is that it makes it possible to see the apparently 'natural' state of things (psychic acceptance of the 'natural' sexual difference) as the result of a redoubled 'pathological' process – of repressing the 'passionate attachment' to the same sex. The problem with it, however, is: if we agree that the entry into symbolic Law that regulates human sexuality is paid for by a fundamental renunciation, is this renunciation in fact that of the same-sex attachment? When Butler asks the crucial question 'Is there some part of the body which is not preserved in sublimation, some part of the body which remains unsublimated?' (i.e. not included in the symbolic texture), her answer is: 'This bodily remainder, I would suggest, survives for such a subject in the mode of already, if not always, having been destroyed, in a kind of constitutive loss. The body is not a site on which a construction takes place; it is a destruction on the occasion of which a subject is formed.'[36] Does this not bring her close to the Lacanian notion of *lamella*, of the undead organ-without-body?

This organ must be called 'unreal,' in the sense that the unreal is not the imaginary and precedes the subjective it conditions, being in direct contact with the real. . . . My lamella represents here the part of a living being that is lost when that being is produced through the straits of sex.[37]

This organ-without-body that 'is' the non-symbolized libido is precisely 'asexual' – neither masculine nor feminine but, rather, that which *both* sexes lose when they enter symbolic sexuation. Lacan himself presents his notion of lamella as a myth on a par with Plato's myth (in *Symposium*) on the origins of sexual difference, and one should bear in mind the key difference: for Lacan, what the two sexes lose in order to be One is not the complementary lost half, but an asexual third object. One could say that this object is marked by a Sameness – however, this Sameness is not the sameness of the 'same sex,' but, rather, the mythical asexual Sameness, libido not yet marked by the cut of sexual difference.[38]

In socioeconomic terms, one is tempted to claim that Capital itself is the Real of our age. That is to say, when Marx describes the mad self-enhancing circulation of Capital, whose solipsistic path of self-fecundation reaches its apogee in today's meta-reflexive speculations on futures, it is far too simplistic to claim that the spectre of this self-engendering monster which pursues its path regardless of any human or environmental concern is an ideological abstraction, and one should never forget that behind this abstraction there are real people and natural objects on whose productive capacities and resources Capital's circulation is based, and on which it feeds like a gigantic parasite. The problem is that this 'abstraction' is not only in our (financial speculator's) misperception of social reality – it is 'real' in the precise sense of determining the structure of the material social processes themselves: the fate of whole strata of populations, and sometimes of whole countries, can be decided by the 'solipsistic' speculative dance of Capital, which pursues its goal of profitability in a benign indifference to how its movement will affect social reality. Here we encounter the Lacanian difference between reality and the Real: 'reality' is the social reality of the actual people involved in interaction and in the productive processes, while the Real is the inexorable 'abstract' spectral logic of Capital which determines what goes on in social reality.

This reference to the Real also enables us to answer one of the recurrent criticisms of Lacan according to which he is a formalist who, in a Kantian way, asserts an a priori 'transcendental' void around which the symbolic universe is structured, a void which can then be filled by a contingent positive object.[39] So is Lacan actually a kind of structuralist Kantian, asserting the ontological priority of the symbolic order over the contingent material elements which occupy its places (claiming, say, that the 'real' father is nothing but a contingent bearer of the purely formal structural function of symbolic prohibition)? What blurs this clear distinction between the empty symbolic form and its contingent positive content is precisely the *Real*: a stain which sutures the empty frame on to a part of its content, the 'indivisible remainder' of some 'pathological' contingent materiality which, as it were, 'colours' the allegedly neutral universality of the symbolic frame, and thus functions as a kind of umbilical cord through which the empty framework of the symbolic form is anchored in its content. This short circuit between form and content provides the most succinct rejection or subversion of (what one usually perceives as) 'Kantian formalism': the very transcendental-formal frame which forms the horizon, the condition of possibility, of the content which appears within it is enframed by a part of its content, since it is attached to a particular point within its content. What we are dealing with here is the paradox of a kind of 'pathological a priori': a pathological (in the Kantian sense of innerworldly contingency) element that sustains the consistency of the formal frame within which it occurs.

This is also one of the possible definitions of the Lacanian *sinthome* as real: the pathological contingent formation that sustains the a priori universal frame. In this precise sense, the Lacanian *sinthome* is a 'knot': a particular innerworldly phenomenon whose existence is experienced as contingent – however, the moment one touches it or approaches it too closely, this 'knot' unravels and, with it, our entire universe – that is, the very place from which we speak and perceive reality disintegrates; we literally lose the ground from beneath our feet. . . . Perhaps the best illustration is the patriarchal melodramatic theme of 'going in through the wrong door' (the wife who accidentally reaches into the pocket of her husband's jacket and finds his confidential love letter, thus ruining her entire family life), which is raised to a much higher power in its science-fiction version (you accidentally open the wrong door and witness the secret meeting of the aliens). However, there is no need to get involved in such eccentricities; simply think of the elementary case of the fragile balance of a situation in which one is formally allowed to do something (ask a certain question, perform a certain act), but is none the less expected *not* to do it, as if some unwritten rule prohibited it – if one actually does it, the whole situation explodes.

Apropos of this point, we can elaborate the line of separation between Marx and the standard 'bourgeois' sociologists of modernity who emphasize the universal features of post-traditional life (the modern individual is no longer directly immersed in a particular tradition, but experiences himself as a universal agent caught in a contingent particular context and free to choose his way of life; he thus entertains a reflected relationship towards his life-world, relying even in his most 'spontaneous' activities (sexuality, leisure) on 'how-to-do-it' manuals. Nowhere is this paradox of reflexivity more evident than in desperate attempts to break out of the reflected ways of modernity and return to a more spontaneous 'holistic' life: in a tragicomic way, these very attempts are supported by a host of *specialists* who teach us how to discover our true spontaneous Self. . . . There is also probably nothing more scientific than the growing of 'organic food': it takes high science to be able to *subtract* the harmful effects of industrial agriculture. 'Organic agriculture' is thus a kind of Hegelian 'negation of negation', the third link in the triad whose first two links are pre-industrial 'natural' agriculture and its negation/mediation, industrialized agriculture: it is a return to nature, to an organic way of doing things; but this very return is 'mediated' by science.

Standard sociologists of modernity conceive of this 'reflexivity' as a quasi-transcendental universal feature which expresses itself in a specific way in different domains of social life: in politics as the replacement of the traditional organic authoritarian structure by modern formal democracy (and its inherent counterpoint, the formalist insistence on the principle of authority for its own sake); in economy as the predominance of commodification and 'alienated' market relations over the more organic forms of the communal production process; in the ethical domain as the split of traditional *mores* into formal external legality and an individual's inner morality; in learning as the replacement of traditional initiatory wisdom by the reflected forms of scientific knowledge transmitted by the school system; in art as the artist's freedom to choose from the multitude of available 'styles'; and so on. 'Reflexivity' (or its various incarnations, up to the Frankfurt School's 'instrumental Reason') is thus conceived as a kind of historical a priori, a form which 'constitutes', moulds into the same universal shape, different layers of social life. Marx, however, adds to this a crucial supplementary turn of the screw: for him, all particular 'empirical' domains of social life do not entertain the same relationship towards this universal frame; they are not all cases of a passive positive stuff formed by it – there is one exceptional 'pathological', innerworldly particular content in which the very universal form of reflexivity is grounded, to which it is attached by a kind of umbilical cord, by which the frame of this form itself is enframed; for Marx, of course, this particular content is the social universe of commodity exchange.[40]

And are we not dealing with the same paradox in the case of the

Lacanian notion of fantasy (*objet petit a* qua phantasmic object) as a supplement to the nonexistence of the sexual relationship? Precisely because there is no universal symbolic form(ula) of a complementary relationship between the two sexes, any relationship between them has to be supplemented by a 'pathological' particular scenario, a kind of phantasmic crutch which can sustain only our 'having actual sex with another person' – if the knot of the fantasy is dissolved, the subject loses his/her universal capacity to engage in sexual activity. So the criticism that Lacan is a proto-Kantian formalist should be turned back on its perpetrators – it is the 'social constructionists' who are all too 'formalist': in an impeccably Kantian way, they presuppose the contingent space of symbolization as simply given, and do not ask Hegel's key post-Kantian meta-transcendental question: how does this very space of historicity, of the multitude of contingent modes of symbolization, sustain itself?[41]

Masochistic Deception

Butler's elaboration of the logic of melancholic identification with the lost object in fact provides a theoretical model which allows us to avoid the ill-fated notion of the 'internalization' of externally imposed social norms: what this simplistic notion of 'internalization' misses is the reflexive turn by means of which, in the emergence of the subject, external power (the pressure it exerts on the subject) is not simply internalized but vanishes, is lost; and this loss is internalized in the guise of the 'voice of conscience', the internalization which gives birth to the internal space itself:

> In the absence of explicit regulation, the subject emerges as one for whom power has become voice, and voice, the regulatory instrument of the psyche . . . the subject is produced, paradoxically, through this withdrawal of power, its dissimulation and fabulation of the psyche as a speaking topos.[42]

This reversal is embodied in Kant, *the* philosopher of moral autonomy, who identifies this autonomy with a certain mode of subjection, namely, the subjection to (even the humiliation in the face of) the universal moral Law. The key point here is to bear in mind the tension between the two forms of this Law: far from being a mere extension or internalization of the external law, the inner Law (Call of Conscience) emerges when the external law fails to appear, in order to compensate for its absence. In this perspective, liberation from the external pressure of norms embodied in one's social conditioning (in the Enlightenment vein) is strictly identical to submission to the unconditional inner Call of Conscience. That is to say: the opposition between external social regulations and internal moral Law is that between reality and the Real: social regulations can still be justified (or pretend to be justified) by objective requirements of social coexistence (they belong to the domain of the 'reality principle'); while the demand of the moral Law is unconditional, brooking no excuse – 'You can, because you must!', as Kant put it. For that reason, social regulations make peaceful coexistence possible, while moral Law is a traumatic injunction that disrupts it. One is thus tempted to go a step further and to invert once more the relationship between 'external' social norms and the inner moral Law: what if the subject invents external social norms precisely in order to escape the unbearable pressure of the moral Law? Isn't it much easier to have an external Master who can be duped, towards whom one can maintain a minimal distance and private space, than to have an ex-timate Master, a stranger, a foreign body in the very heart of one's being? Doesn't the minimal definition of Power (the agency experienced by the subject as the force that exerts its pressure on him from the Outside, opposing his inclinations, thwarting his goals) rely precisely on this *externalization* of the ex-timate inherent compulsion of the Law, of that which is 'in you more than yourself'? This tension between external norms and the inner Law, which can also give rise to subversive effects (say, of opposing public authority on behalf of one's inner moral stance), is neglected by Foucault.

Again, the crucial point is that this subjection to the inner Law does not simply 'extend' or 'internalize' external pressure; rather, it is correlative to the suspension of external pressure, to the withdrawal-into-self which creates so-called 'free inner space'. This leads us back to the problematic of *fundamental fantasy*: what the fundamental fantasy stages is precisely the scene of constitutive submission/subjection that sustains the subject's 'inner freedom'. This primordial 'passionate attachment' – that is, the scene of passive submission staged in the fundamental fantasy – must be distinguished from masochism in the strict, narrow clinical sense: as it was elaborated in detail by Deleuze,[43] this masochism *stricto sensu* already involves an intricate attitude of disavowal towards the frame of Oedipal symbolic reality. The masochist's suffering does not attest to some perverse enjoyment of pain as such, but is thoroughly in the service of pleasure – its exquisite spectacle (masquerade) of torture and pain, of humiliation to which the masochist subject submits itself, serves to dupe the attentive guard of the superego. In short, clinical masochism is a way for the subject to attain pleasure by accepting the punishment required for it by the superego in advance – the faked spectacle of punishment serves to demonstrate the underlying Real of pleasure.

Just picture the standard scene of moral masochism: the everyday masochistic subject often finds it deeply satisfying to imagine that a person to whom he is deeply attached will wrongly accuse him of some misdeed or accomplish some similar act of mistaken accusation; the satisfaction is provided by imagining the future scene in which the beloved other, who has unknowingly injured him, will deeply regret his unjust accusation. . . . It is the same in masochistic theatre: the masochist's passivity conceals his activity (he is the director who arranges the scene and tells the domina what to do to him); his moral pain barely conceals his active pleasure in the moral victory that humiliates the other. Such an intricate scene can take place only within a space already organized by the symbolic order: masochistic theatre relies on the *contract* between the masochist and his master (domina).

The crucial question to be raised here concerns the role of deception in the masochism of the fundamental fantasy: whom does *this* scene of suffering and submission serve to deceive? The Lacanian answer is that there is a deception at work on this level too: the fundamental fantasy provides the subject with the minimum of being, it serves as a support for his existence – in short, its deceptive gesture is 'Look, I suffer, therefore I am, I exist, I participate in the positive order of being.' It is thus not guilt and/or pleasure, but existence itself which is at stake in the fundamental fantasy, and it is precisely this deception of the fundamental fantasy that the act of 'traversing the fantasy' serves to dispel: by traversing the fantasy, the subject accepts the void of his nonexistence.

A nice Lacanian example of masochistic deception is that of the citizen of a country in which one's head is cut off if one says publicly that the king is stupid; if this subject dreams that his head is to be cut off, this dream has nothing whatsoever to do with any kind of death wish, etc., it simply means that the subject thinks his king is stupid – that is, the predicament of suffering masks the pleasure of attacking the dignity of the king. . . .[44] Here, pain and suffering are clearly the masquerade in the service of pleasure, destined to dupe superego censorship. Such a strategy of deception, however, in which a scene of pain and suffering is put in the service of the pleasure of deceiving the superego, can function only on the basis of a more fundamental 'sadomasochistic' stance in which the subject engages in fantasizing about being exposed to passive painful experiences and is thus ready to accept, outside any deceptive strategy, *pain itself as the source of libidinal satisfaction.*[45]

Along these lines, one should reread Laplanche's old classic ideas about the primal seduction fantasy in which the reflexive inward turn, 'fantasization', sexualization and masochism all coincide – that is, are all generated in one and the same gesture of 'turning around'.[46] In his detailed commentary on the three phases of the Freudian 'A child is being beaten' fantasy (1: 'My father is beating the child whom I hate'; 2: 'I am being beaten by my father'; 3: 'A child is being beaten'), Laplanche insists on the crucial difference between the first phase and the second: they are both unconscious, that is, they represent the secret genesis of the final, conscious phase of the fantasy ('A child is being beaten'); however, while the first phase is simply the repressed memory of some real event witnessed by the child (the parent beating his brother), and can as such be remembered in the course of psychoanalytic treatment, the second is properly phantasmic and, for that very reason, 'primordially repressed'. This phase was never consciously imagined, but was foreclosed from the very beginning (here we have a perfect case of the foreclosed same-sex primordial 'passionate attachment' Butler focuses on); for this reason, it can never be remembered (i.e. subjectively assumed by the subject), but simply retroactively reconstructed as the Real which has to be presupposed if one is to account for the final, conscious phase of the fantasy: '. . . *what is repressed is not the memory but the fantasy derived from it or subtending it*: in this case, not the actual scene in which the father would have beaten another child, but the fantasy of being beaten by the father'.[47]

So the passage from the initial, outward-directed aggressivity (satisfaction found in beating another child or observing a parent beating him/ her) to the foreclosed phantasmic scene in which the subject imagines *himself* being beaten by the parent is crucial – the role of the first phase is that of the proverbial 'grain of sand', the little piece of reality (a scene witnessed in reality by the child), which triggers the phantasmic formation of a scene that provides the co-ordinates of the primordial 'passionate attachment'. Again, what is primordially repressed and, as such, forever inaccessible to subjectivization (since subjectivization itself relies on this repression) is the second phase. Several things occur simultaneously in the passage from the first phase to the second:

- as Freud himself emphasizes, only in the second phase is the situation properly *sexualized* – that is, the passage from phase 1 to phase 2 is the passage from pre-sexual aggressivity to properly sexualized 'pleasure in pain';

- this sexualization is strictly consubstantial with the reflexive gesture of 'introjection': instead of actually attacking another human being I fantasize about it, I imagine a scene of submission and pain; instead of being an agent in real interaction, I become an impassive observer of an 'inner' scene that fascinates me;

- furthermore, as for its content, this scene stages a situation within which I assume a passive position of being subjected to humiliation and pain, or at least the position of an impassive, impotent observer.

The crucial point is that these three features are strictly consubstantial: at its most radical, sexualization *equals* phantasmization, which *equals* assuming the passive position of impotence, humiliation and pain:

> ... the process of turning-around is not to be thought of only at the level of the content of the fantasy, but *in the very movement of fantasmatization*. The shift to the reflexive is not only or even necessarily to give a reflexive content to the 'sentence' of the fantasy; it is also and above all to reflect the action, internalize it, make it enter into oneself as fantasy. To fantasize aggression is to turn it around upon oneself, to aggress oneself: such is the moment of autoerotism, in which the indissoluble bond between fantasy as such, sexuality, and the unconscious is confirmed.[48]

The point of the reflexive turn is thus not simply a symmetrical reversal of aggressivity (destroying/attacking an external object) into being attacked by an external object; rather, it lies in the act of 'internalizing' passivity, actively imagining the scene of one's impassive submission. Thus in fantasizing, the clear-cut opposition of activity and passivity is subverted: in 'internalizing' a scene of being beaten by another, I immobilize myself in a double sense (instead of being active in reality, I assume the passive stance of a fascinated observer who merely imagines/fantasizes a scene in which he participates; within the very content of this scene, I imagine myself in a passive, immobile position of suffering humiliation and pain) – however, precisely this double passivity presupposes my active engagement – that is to say, the accomplishment of a reflexive turn by means of which, in an autoerotic way, I myself, not an external agent, thwart my external activity, the spontaneous outflow of energy, and 'dominate myself', replacing activity in reality by the outburst of fantasizing. Apropos of his definition of *drive* (as opposed to instinct), Lacan made this point nicely by emphasizing how drive always and by definition involves a position of *'se faire . . .'*, of 'making oneself . . .': scopic drive is neither a voyeuristic tendency to see nor the exhibitionistic tendency to be seen by another, to expose oneself to another's eyes, but the 'middle voice', the attitude of 'making oneself visible', of deriving libidinal satisfaction from actively sustaining the scene of one's own passive submission. Consequently, from the Lacanian standpoint, this primordial gesture of 'fantasmatization' is the very birthplace and the ultimate mystery of what Kant and the entire tradition of German Idealism refers to as 'transcendental imagination', this abyssal capacity of freedom that enables the subject to disengage itself from its immersion in its surrroundings.

Later in his work, Laplanche elaborated this gesture of reflexive 'fantasmatization' into a theory of the original seduction scene as the true 'primordial scene' of psychoanalysis: a child impotently witnessing a scene of sexual interaction, or being himself submitted to gestures (from parents or other adults) which possess some mysterious sexual connotation that is impenetrable to him. It is in this gap that human sexuality and the Unconscious originate: in the fact that a child (every one of us) is at some point the impotent observer, caught in some sexualized situation which remains impenetrable to him, which he cannot symbolize, integrate into the universe of meaning (observing parental coitus, being submitted to excessive maternal caressing, etc.). Where, however, is the Unconscious in all this? The Unconscious encountered here, in this primordial scene of seduction, is *the adult's (parent's)* Unconscious, not the child's: when a child is exposed to excessive maternal caressing, say, he observes that Mother herself does something that goes beyond what she is fully aware of, that she derives from fondling him a satisfaction whose basis is beyond her grasp. Lacan's dictum 'the Unconscious is the discourse of the Other' is therefore to be taken quite literally, beyond the standard platitudes about how I am not the subject/master of my speech, since it is the big Other who speaks through me, and so on: the primordial encounter of the Unconscious is the encounter with the Other's inconsistency, with the fact that the [parental] Other is not actually the master of his acts and words, that he emits signals of whose meaning he is unaware, that he performs acts whose true libidinal tenor is inaccessible to him. One is thus tempted to repeat here Hegel's famous dictum that the secrets of the Egyptians (the meaning of their rituals and monuments, impenetrable to our modern Western gaze) were also secrets for the Egyptians themselves: the whole construction of the scene of primordial seduction as the original site of sexualization holds only if we presuppose that it is not only the observing and/or victimized child for whom the scene is impenetrable and enigmatic – what baffles the observing/victimized child is the fact that he is witnessing a scene which is obviously impenetrable also to the active adult perpetrators themselves – that they, too, 'don't know what they're doing'.

This constellation also enables us to throw new light on Lacan's claim (mentioned above) that 'there is no sexual relationship': if the enigma and confusion were to be only on the side of the child, in his (mis)perception as something mysterious of what, for the parents themselves, is a thoroughly natural and unproblematic activity, then there definitely would be a 'normal' sexual relationship. However, the worn-out phrase 'deep inside every adult, there is a child who is still alive' is not without foundation, if it is properly understood as meaning that even when the proverbial two consenting adults engage in 'normal and healthy' sex in the privacy of their bedroom, they are never quite alone in there: there is always a 'fantasmatized' *child's gaze* observing them, a gaze – usually 'internalized' – on account of which their activity is ultimately impenetrable to themselves. Or – to put it in yet another way – the point of the scene of primordial seduction is not that adults accidentally infringe upon the child, disturbing his fragile balance with a display of their *jouissance* – the point, rather, is that the child's gaze is included, comprehended, from the very beginning in the situation of adult parental sexuality, rather like Kafka's parable of the Door of the Law: just as the man from the country discovers at the end that the scene of the majestic entrance to the palace of the Law was staged only for his gaze, the parental sexual display, far from unintentionally disturbing the child's equilibrium, is in a way 'there only for the child's gaze'. Is not the ultimate paradisiacal fantasy that of parents copulating in front of their child, who observes them and makes comments? We are thus dealing with the structure of a temporal loop: there is sexuality not only because of a gap between adult sexuality and the child's unprepared gaze traumatized by its display, but because this child's perplexity continues to sustain adult sexual activity itself.[49] This paradox also explains the blind spot of the topic of sexual harassment: *there is no sex without an element of 'harassment'* (of the perplexed gaze violently shocked, traumatized, by the uncanny character of what is going on). The protest against sexual harassment, against violently imposed sex, is thus ultimately *the protest against sex as such*: if one subtracts from the sexual interplay its painfully traumatic character, the remainder is simply no longer sexual. 'Mature' sex between the proverbial consenting adults, deprived of the traumatic element of shocking imposition, is by definition *desexualized*, turned into mechanic coupling.

From my youth, I remember obscene rhyming songs five-year-old children used to recite to each other, songs of ridiculous sexual exploits whose hero was a mythical anonymous 'cowboy'. One of these songs (which, of course, rhymes only in Slovene) went as follows: 'The cowboy without a hat / is screwing a woman behind a tree. / However, when she tries to escape him and runs away / he for a brief moment sees [catches a glimpse of] her naked ass.' The charm – if we may put it that way – of this childhood song lies in the fact that, in its perspective, there is nothing especially exciting in the act of copulation; this act speaks for itself – what is truly exciting, rather, is the brief moment of catching sight of a woman's naked ass. . . . [50] And, of course, my point is that this childish song is basically right: contrary to the standard view, which depicts copulation as the most exciting, climactic moment of sexual activity, one should insist that, in order for the subject to be aroused in the first place and be able to perform the act of copulation, some particular 'partial' element must fascinate him (or her) – as, in the case of this song, the brief glance of the naked ass. 'There is no sexual relationship' also means that there is no direct representation of the act of copulation which would immediately 'turn us on', that sexuality must be supported by partial *jouissances* – a glance here, a squeeze or touch there – which in fact sustain it. Again, the answer to the obvious criticism that it is *children* who have no proper representation of the act of copulation itself – that is, their horizon of sexuality is limited to experiences like catching a glance of another person's ass – is that, at a certain phantasmic level, we remain children and never really 'grow up', in so far as, for a truly grown-up and mature person, there would be a sexual relationship – in so far, that is, as he or she was able to copulate 'directly', without the phantasmic support of some scene involving a partial object. [51]

Is not the supreme case of such a particular feature that sustains the impossible sexual relationship the curling blonde hair in Hitchcock's *Vertigo*? When, in the love scene in the barn towards the end of the film, Scottie passionately embraces Judy refashioned into the dead Madeleine, during their famous 360-degree kiss, he stops kissing her just long enough to steal a look at her newly blonde hair, as if to reassure himself that the particular feature which makes her into the object of desire is still there. . . . Here the opposition between the vortex that threatens to swallow Scottie (the 'vertigo' of the title, the deadly Thing) and the curl of the blonde hair that imitates the vertigo of the Thing, but in a miniaturized, gentrified form. This curl is the *objet petit a* which condenses the impossible-deadly Thing, serving as its stand-in and thus enabling us to entertain a livable relationship with it without being swallowed by it.

Orson Welles's film *The Immortal Story*, based on Karen Blixen's novel, is of interest not only because it focuses on the ambiguous relationship between myth and reality: the rich old merchant wants to act out the sailors' mythic narrative of a rich old husband who pays a young sailor to spend the night with his young wife, and thus procure an heir to his wealth – he wants, as it were, to close the gap between myth and reality, that is, to produce a sailor who will finally be able to relate this mythic narrative as something that actually happened to him (the attempt, of course, fails: the sailor announces that no amount of money will induce him to tell anyone what happened to him). More interesting is the phantasmic staging of the scene of lovemaking: behind a half-transparent curtain, on a brightly lit bed, the couple are making love, while the old merchant sits half-concealed in a deep armchair in the darkness nearby, and overhears their act of love – here we have the Third Gaze as the ultimate guarantee of the sexual relationship. That is to say, it is the very presence of the silent witness who listens to the couple making love that transubstantiates what is ultimately an encounter between a paid sailor and an aged prostitute into a mythic event that transcends its material conditions. In other words, the miracle that occurs is not that the two lovers somehow transcend their miserable real-life situation, forget about the ridiculous conditions of their encounter, get immersed in each other and thus produce an authentic love-encounter; they succeed in transubstantiating that miserable situation into the miracle of an authentic love-encounter precisely *because* they are aware that they are doing it for a silent witness, that they are 'realizing a myth' – the two lovers behave as if they are no longer miserable real people, but *actors/agents in another person's dream*. The silent witness, far from intruding in an intimate situation and spoiling it, is its key constituent. It is a standard cliché that, simple and austere as it is, *The Immortal Story* is Welles's ultimate exercise in self-reflection – that the old merchant who stages the scene of love-making (played, of course, by Welles himself) is the obvious stand-in for Welles himself as director – perhaps this cliché should be turned around, and the old merchant observing the scene is the stand-in for the spectator.

The difference between Lacan and Laplanche is nevertheless crucial here: for Laplanche, drive is consubstantial with fantasy – that is to say, it is the very reflexive turn into phantasmic 'internalization' which brings about the transformation of instinct into drive; for Lacan, on the contrary, there is a drive beyond fantasy. What does this drive beyond fantasy mean? Perhaps another difference allows us to throw some light on this key point: while one could claim that, for Lacan also, the 'birthplace' of psychoanalysis is the child's traumatic experience with the impenetrable 'dark spot' of the Other's *jouissance* which disturbs the calm of his psychic homeostasis, Lacan determines fantasy as an *answer* to the enigma of this 'dark spot' (designated, in his 'graph of desire', by the question *Che vuoi?* – 'What does the Other want from me? What [as an object] am I for the Other, for his desire?'[52]). The pre-phantasmic drive would then designate the stance of exposing oneself to the 'dark spot' of the Other's enigma without filling it with a phantasmic answer. . . . Thus for Lacan fantasy is a minimal 'defence-formation', a stratagem to elude – what?

Here, one should return to the Freudian notion of the original *Hilflosigkeit* (helplessness/distress) of the infant. The first feature to be noted is that this 'distress' covers two interconnected but none the less different levels: purely organic helplessness (the small child's inability to survive, to satisfy his/her most elementary needs, without the parents' help), as well as the traumatic perplexity which occurs when the child is thrown into the position of a helpless witness to sexual interplay between his/her parents or other adults, or between adult(s) and himself: the child is helpless, without 'cognitive mapping', when he or she is confronted by the enigma of the Other's *jouissance*, unable to symbolize the mysterious sexual gestures and innuendos he is witnessing. Crucial for 'becoming human' is the overlapping of the two levels – the implicit 'sexualization' of the way a parent satisfies a child's bodily needs (say, when the mother feeds the child while caressing him excessively and the child detects in this excess the mystery of sexual *jouissance*).

So, back to Butler: the crucial question concerns the philosophical status of this original and constitutive *Hilflosigkeit*: is it not another name for the gap of the primordial *dis-attachment* that triggers the need for the phantasmic primordial 'passionate attachment'? In other words, what if we turn the perspective around and conceive of the obstacle which prevents the infant from fully fitting into its environment, of this original 'out-of-joint', also in its positive aspect, as another name for the very abyss of freedom, for that gesture of 'disconnecting' which liberates a subject from its direct immersion in its surroundings? Or – to put it in yet another way – true, the subject is, as it were, 'blackmailed' into passively submitting to some form of primordial 'passionate attachment', since, outside of this, he simply does not exist – however, this nonexistence is not directly the absence of existence, but a certain gap or void in the order of being which 'is' the subject itself. The need for 'passionate attachment' to provide for a minimum of being implies that the subject *qua* 'abstract negativity' – the primordial gesture of dis-attachment from its environment – *is already there.* Fantasy is thus a defence-formation against the primordial abyss of dis-attachment, of the loss of (the support in) being, which 'is' the subject itself. At this precise point, then, Butler should be supplemented: the emergence of the subject is not strictly equivalent to subjection (in the sense of 'passionate attachment', of submission to some figure of the Other), since for 'passionate attachment' to take place the gap that 'is' the subject must already be there. Only if this gap is already there can we explain how it is possible for the subject to escape the hold of the fundamental fantasy.

One could also link this opposition of attachment and dis-attachment to the old Freudian metapsychological opposition of life and death drive: in *The Ego and the Id*, Freud himself defines them as the opposition between the forces of connection/unity and the forces of disconnection/ disunity. Dis-attachment is thus the death drive at its purest, the gesture of ontological 'derailment' which throws the order of Being 'out of joint', the gesture of dis-investment, of 'contraction'/withdrawal from being immersed in the world, and primordial attachment is the counter-move to this negative gesture. In the last resort, this negative tendency to disruption is none other than *libido* itself: what throws a (future) subject 'out of joint' is none other than the traumatic encounter with *jouissance.*[53]

Apropos of this primordial gap, one should avoid the temptation to conceive of it as the effect of the intervention of the paternal Law/ Prohibition that disturbs the incestuous dyad of the child and his/her Mother, compelling the child to enter the dimension of symbolic castration/distance: the gap, the experience of the 'dismembered body', is primordial; it is the effect of the death drive, of the intrusion of some excessive/traumatic *jouissance* that disturbs the smooth balance of the pleasure principle, and the paternal Law – not unlike the imaginary identification with the mirror-image – is an attempt to gentrify/stabilize this gap. One should never forget that, for Lacan, the Oedipal paternal Law is ultimately *in the service of the 'pleasure principle':* it is the agency of pacification–normalization which, far from disturbing the balance of pleasure, 'stabilizes the impossible', bringing about the minimal conditions for the tolerable coexistence of subjects. (Misreadings like this sustain the temptation to write a kind of negative introduction to Lacan, taking as the starting point a false cliché about him, and then describing his actual position through its rectification. Apart from the above-mentioned

cliché on the paternal Law as the agency that introduces the gap, there
are the clichés on the piece of wood in the *Fort–Da* game as signifying
Mother's presence/absence; on 'empty speech' as inauthentic babble; on
jouissance féminine as the mystical abyss outside the symbolic domain; on
gaze as the male subject's look which confines woman to the role of its
object; etc.)

From Desire to Drive . . . and Back

Our critical remarks on Butler are based on a full endorsement of her
basic insight into the profound link between – even the ultimate identity
of – the two aspects or modes of reflexivity: reflexivity in the strict
philosophical sense of negative self-relating, which is constitutive of subjectivity in the tradition of German Idealism from Kant to Hegel (the fact
emphasized especially by, among recent interpreters, Robert Pippin: in its
relating to its Other, the subject always-already relates to itself, that is,
consciousness is always-already self-consciousness), and reflexivity in the
psychoanalytic sense of the reflexive turn that defines the gesture of
'primordial repression' (the reversal of the regulation of desire into the
desire for regulation, etc.).[54] This reflexive turn is already clearly discernible in what is arguably the paradigmatic narrative of the defence against
excessive *jouissance*, that of Ulysses meeting the Sirens; the order he gives
his sailors prior to the meeting is: 'You must tie me hard in hurtful bonds,
to hold me fast in position upright against the mast, with the ropes' ends
fastened around it; but if I supplicate you and implore you to set me free,
then you must tie me fast with even more lashings.'[55] The order to 'tie me
hard in *hurtful* bonds' is clearly excessive in the context of Circe's
instructions: we pass from bonding as a defence against the excessive
jouissance of the Sirens' song to bonding itself as the source of erotic
satisfaction.

This reflexivity none the less assumes different modalities – not only
between philosophy and psychoanalysis, but also within psychoanalysis
itself: the reflexivity of *drive* we have focused on in this chapter is not the
same as the hysterical reflexivity of *desire* we discussed in Chapter 2 (i.e.
the fact that hysteria is defined by the reversal of the impossibility to
satisfy desire into the desire to keep desire itself unsatisfied, etc.). How
are these two reflexivities related? The opposition here is between perversion and hysteria: if desire 'as such' is hysterical, drive 'as such' is perverse.
That is to say, hysteria and perversion are caught in a kind of closed

deadly loop within which each of the two can be conceived of as the reaction to its opposite. Drive defines the masochistic parameters of the primordial 'passionate attachment', of the fundamental fantasy which guarantees the minimum of being to the subject; subjectivity proper then emerges through the hysterical disavowal of this primordial 'passionate attachment' – through the subject's refusal to assume the position of the object–instrument of the Other's *jouissance* – the hysterical subject incessantly questions his/her position (his/her basic question is 'What am I for the Other? Why am I what the Other says I am?'). So not only can hysterical desire be conceived of as the disavowal of the fundamental fantasy endorsed by the pervert; perversion itself (assuming the position of the object–instrument of the Other's *jouissance*) can also be conceived of as the escape into self-objectivization which enables me to avoid the deadlock of the radical uncertainty of what I am as an object – the pervert, by definition, *knows* what, as an object, he is for the Other.

Desire and drive are clearly opposed with respect to the way they relate to *jouissance*. For Lacan, the trouble with *jouissance* is not only that it is unattainable, always-already lost, that it forever eludes our grasp, but, even more, that *one can never get rid of it*, that its stain drags on for ever – that is the point of Lacan's concept of surplus-enjoyment: the very renunciation of *jouissance* brings about a remainder/surplus of *jouissance*. Desire stands for the economy in which whatever object we get hold of is 'never *it*', the 'Real Thing', that which the subject is forever trying to attain but which eludes him again and again, while drive stands for the opposite economy, within which the stain of *jouissance* always accompanies our acts. This also explains the difference in the reflexivity of drive and desire: desire reflexively desires its own unsatisfaction, the postponement of the encounter with *jouissance* – that is, the basic formula of the reflexivity of desire is to turn the impossibility of satisfying desire into the desire for nonsatisfaction; drive, on the contrary, finds satisfaction in (i.e. besmirches with the stain of satisfaction) the very movement destined to 'repress' satisfaction.

What, then, is drive, especially in its most radical form, that of the death drive? A look at Wagnerian heroes can be of some help here: from their first paradigmatic case, the Flying Dutchman, they are possessed by an unconditional passion for dying, for finding ultimate peace and redemption in death. Their predicament is that at some time in the past they have committed some unspeakable evil deed, so that they are condemned to pay for it not by death, but by being condemned to a life of eternal suffering, of helplessly wandering around, unable to fulfil their symbolic function. Where is the death drive here? It precisely does *not* lie in their longing to die, to find peace in death: the death drive, on the contrary, is *the very opposite of dying*, it is a name for the 'undead' eternal life itself, for the horrible fate of being caught in the endless repetitive cycle of wandering around in guilt and pain. The final passing-away of the Wagnerian hero (the death of the Dutchman, Wotan, Tristan, Amfortas) is therefore the moment of their *liberation* from the clutches of the death drive. Tristan in Act III is not desperate because of his fear of dying: what makes him so desperate is the fact that, without Isolde, he *cannot die* and is condemned to eternal longing – he anxiously awaits her arrival so that he can die. The prospect he dreads is not that of dying without Isolde (the standard complaint of a lover) but, rather, that of endless life without her. . . .

This gives us a clue to the paradigmatic Wagnerian song, which, precisely, is the *complaint* [*Klage*] of the hero, expressing his horror at being condemned to a life of eternal suffering, to wandering around or living as the 'undead' monster, longing for peace in death (from its first example, the Dutchman's great introductory monologue, to the lament of the dying Tristan and the two great complaints of the suffering Amfortas). Although there is no great complaint by Wotan, Brünnhilde's final farewell to him – '*Ruhe, ruhe, du Gott!*' – points in the same direction: when the gold is returned to the Rhine, Wotan is finally allowed to die in peace. The standard commentary which emphasizes the alleged 'contradiction' in the plot of the *Ring* (why do the gods still perish, although their debt is paid, that is, the gold is returned to the Rhine? Wasn't this unpaid debt the cause of the gods' downfall?) therefore misses the point: the unpaid debt, the 'original sin' of disturbing the natural equilibrium, is what *prevents* Wotan from dying – he can die and find peace only after he settles his debt. One can also see why *Tannhäuser* and *Lohengrin* are not truly Wagnerian operas:[56] they lack a proper Wagnerian hero. Tannhäuser is 'too common', simply split between pure spiritual love (for Elisabeth) and the excess of earthly erotic enjoyment (provided by Venus), unable to renounce earthly pleasures while longing to get rid of them; Lohengrin, on the contrary, is 'too celestial', a divine creature (artist) longing to live like a common mortal with a faithful woman who will trust him absolutely. Neither of the two is in the position of a proper Wagnerian hero, condemned to the 'undead' existence of eternal suffering.[57]

So Wagnerian heroes do suffer from 'sickness unto death', but in the strict Kierkegaardian sense of the term. In his notion of 'sickness unto death', Kierkegaard inverted the standard despair of the individual who is split between the certainty that death is the end, that there is no Beyond of eternal life, and the unquenchable desire to believe that death is not the last thing: that there is another life, with its promise of redemption and eternal bliss: Kierkegaard's 'sickness unto death' involves the opposite paradox of the subject who knows that death is not the end, that he has an immortal soul, but cannot face the exorbitant demands of this fact (the necessity to abandon vain aesthetic pleasures and work for his salvation), and desperately wants to believe that death *is* the end, that there is no divine unconditional demand exerting its pressure upon him. ... So we have here the individual who desperately wants to die, to disappear for ever, but knows that he cannot do it, since he is condemned to eternal life: immortality, not death, becomes the ultimate horror. In a way this reversal is analogous to the one we just mentioned, to the Lacanian shift from desire to drive: desire desperately strives to achieve *jouissance*, its ultimate object which forever eludes it; while drive, on the contrary, involves the opposite impossibility – not the impossibility of attaining *jouissance*, but the impossibility of getting *rid of it*.

The lesson of drive is that *we are condemned to jouissance*: whatever we do, *jouissance* will stick to it; we shall never get rid of it; even in our most thorough endeavour to renounce it, it will contaminate the very effort to get rid of it (like the ascetic who perversely enjoys flagellating himself). And the prospect of contemporary genetic technology seems to involve a homologous Kierkegaardian horror: it raises the terrifying prospect not of death, but of immortality. That is to say: what makes genetic manipulation so uncanny is not only that it will be possible to objectivize our existence entirely (in the genome, I will be confronted with the formula of what I 'objectively am', that is, a genome will function as the ultimate version of the old Indian mystical formula '*Ta twam atsi*' – 'Thou art that!') but also that, in a way, I will become immortal and indestructible, endlessly reproducible, with my doubles popping up all around me through cloning.[58] Again, this domain is that of drives: of asexual immortality through endless repetitive cloning. That is to say: the crucial point to be made here is to oppose genetic cloning to sexual reproduction: genetic cloning signals the end of sexual difference as the impossible/real which structures our lives, and, as such, also the end of the symbolic universe in which we dwell as finite, mortal beings-of-language. This notion of a spectral undead existence also allows us to account for the fundamental paradox of the Freudian/Lacanian death drive: like the Kierkegaardian sickness unto death, the death drive is not the mark of human finitude, but its very opposite, the name for 'eternal (spectral) life', the index of a dimension in human existence that persists for ever, beyond our physical death, and of which we can never rid ourselves.

We can now see in what precise sense Lacan is to be opposed to Heidegger: for Lacan, the death drive is precisely the ultimate Freudian name for the dimension traditional metaphysics designated as that of *immortality* – for a drive, a 'thrust', which persists beyond the (biological) cycle of generation and corruption, beyond the 'way of all flesh'. In other words, in the death drive, the concept 'dead' functions in exactly the same way as '*heimlich*' in the Freudian *unheimlich*, as coinciding with its negation: the 'death drive' designates the dimension of what horror fiction calls the 'undead', a strange, immortal, indestructible life that persists beyond death. This is the 'infinity' compatible with the Lacanian theoretical edifice: not the 'spurious (bad) infinity' of endlessly striving to achieve the final Goal or Ideal that forever eludes our grasp, but an even *worse* infinity of *jouissance* which persists for ever, since we can never get rid of it. Lacan's answer to 'bad infinity' is thus not the idealist pseudo-Hegelian assertion of a true positive infinity of the Idea, but a gesture of 'from bad to worse': the assertion of an *even worse* infinity of an 'indivisible remainder' of *jouissance* which always sticks to everything we do. . . .

How is sexual difference related to this 'undead' drive? Jacques-Alain Miller[59] endeavours to introduce sexual difference into the conclusion of psychoanalytic treatment: women are not so fully identified with their fantasy, 'not all' of their being is caught in it; this is why, for them, it is easier to acquire a distance towards fantasy, to traverse it; while men, as a rule, come up against a condensed phantasmic kernel, a 'fundamental symptom', the basic formula of *jouissance* that they are unable to renounce, so that all they can do is accept it as an imposed necessity. In short, 'traversing the fantasy' is conceived as feminine, and 'identification with the symptom' as masculine.[60]

Miller tackles the unresolved tension between desire and drive discernible in this solution in another of his conferences, 'Le monologue de l'*apparole*',[61] where he focuses on Lacan's obscure claim '*le pas-de-dialogue a sa limite dans l-interprétation, par où s'assure le réel*'. Miller reads this 'lack-of-dialogue' as *l'apparole*, the speech that functions as the apparatus of *jouissance*, no longer as the means of communicating some meaning; *apparole* does not involve intersubjectivity, not even as the empty big Other that is present when we speak in an 'interior monologue', trying to clarify our thoughts; not even as the *jouis-sense* of hurting the Other in the core of his/her being, as is the case with injurious speech – it involves a radically self-enclosed assertion of *jouissance* of empty (meaningless) speech. (In short, *l'apparole* is to *la parole* what *lalangue* is to *le langage*.)

In so far as, in *l'apparole*, we are thus dealing with an idiotic-happy circuit of the apparatus which produces *jouissance*, is this not the very definition of *drive*? How, then, does interpretation limit this self-enclosed circuit by introducing the dimension of the Real? The Real here is the impossible, the impossibility of sexual relationship: the happy babble of *l'apparole* is asexual; as such, it does not involve any experience of the Real *qua* impossible – that is, of some traumatic inherent Limit. Interpretation must therefore 'sober' the subject down from his blissful immersion in the babble of *l'apparole*, and compel him to confront the impossible Real of the human condition. Interpretation is conceived here not as unlimited/infinite ('there is always a new way to read a text') but, on the contrary, as the very gesture of introducing a *limit* to the unconstrained play of *l'apparole*. . . . The problem with this reading is that it identifies *l'apparole* with the unconstrained reign of the 'pleasure principle' which precludes the dimension of the Real. In this case, however, *l'apparole* could *not* be identified with drive, since drive involves the Real of the compulsion to repeat that is by definition 'beyond the pleasure principle'.

The problem Miller is struggling with is the central one in late Lacan: after penetrating beneath the (Oedipus) complex of Law/desire, of desire grounded in prohibition, to the enigmatic 'dark continent' of drive and its satisfaction in the repeated circuit of *jouissance*, how do we (re)introduce a Limit, and thus *return* to the domain of prohibition/Law, communication of/and meaning? The only consistent solution here is that *l'apparole* (the Lacanian version of 'primary narcissism' prior to the introduction of the symbolic Law) is not 'primordial'; that there is something which (logically, at least) precedes it – this, precisely, is what we have called the violence of pre-synthetic imagination, which is *not* to be identified with the blissful circuit of self-satisfied drive. This circuit of drive is the ultimate matrix of *self-affection*, of self-affective circulation (Lacan himself evokes lips kissing themselves as the perfect figure of drive; his very formula of drive – '*se faire* . . .' – already evokes self-affection); while pre-synthetic imagination is the very opposite of self-affection: it stands for a kind of ontological 'Big Bang', for the primordial 'violence' of breaking out of the immersion and enclosure, exploding the closed circuit, tearing apart any unity of Life into the free-floating multiplicity of spectral and monstrous 'partial objects'.

Even Lacan's own position on this point is not without its ambiguities. His 'official' stance is best exemplified by the short but crucial text at the end of his *Écrits*, 'From the Freudian *Trieb* to the Desire of the Analyst':[62] what is the analysand to do when he reaches the end of the analytic cure, that is, when he 'regresses' from desire (sustained by fantasy) to drive? Is he to abandon himself to the self-enclosed circuit of drive? Different mystical and philosophical traditions, from Christian mysticism to Nietzsche, seem to advocate this way: accept the circuit of the 'eternal return of the same', find satisfaction not in reaching a Goal but in the very path which leads to it, that is, in repeatedly missing the Goal. . . . Lacan, however, insists that 'going through the fantasy' is not strictly equivalent to the shift from drive to desire: there is a desire that remains even after we have traversed our fundamental fantasy, a desire not sustained by a fantasy, and this desire, of course, is *the desire of the analyst* – not the desire to become an analyst, but the desire which fits the subjective position of the analyst, the desire of someone who has undergone 'subjective destitution' and accepted the role of the excremental abject, desire delivered of the phantasmic notion that 'there is something in me more than myself', a secret treasure which makes me worthy of the Other's desire. This unique desire is what, even after I have fully assumed 'the big Other's nonexistence' – that is, the fact that the symbolic order is a mere semblance – prevents me from immersing myself in the self-enclosure of drive's circuit and its debilitating satisfaction. The desire of the analyst is thus supposed to sustain the analytic community in the absence of any phantasmic support; it is supposed to make possible a communal 'big Other' that avoids the transferential effect of the 'subject supposed to . . . [know, believe, enjoy]'. In other words, the desire of the analyst is Lacan's tentative answer to the question: after we have traversed the fantasy, and accepted the 'nonexistence of the big Other', how do we none the less return to some (new) form of the big Other that again makes collective coexistence possible?

What one should also not lose sight of is the fact that, for Lacan, drive is not 'primordial', a foundation out of which, by means of the intervention of the symbolic Law, desire emerges. A close reading of Lacan's 'graph of desire'[63] shows how drive is a montage of elements which emerges as a kind of 'necessary by-product' of the instinctual body getting caught in the web of the symbolic order. The fact that an instinctual need is caught in the signifier's web means that the object that satisfies this need starts to function as the sign of the (M)Other's love; consequently, the only way to break out of the deadlock of the subject's enslavement to the Other's demand is via the intervention of the symbolic Prohibition/Law which makes the full satisfaction of desire forever impossible. All the well-known paradoxes of desire are engendered in this way, from 'I can't love you unless I give you up' to 'Don't give me what I ask you for, because that's not *it*' – desire is defined by this *ce n'est pas ça*: that is, its most elementary and ultimate aim is to sustain itself as desire, in its state of non-satisfaction.[64] Drive, on the other hand, stands for the paradoxical possibility that the subject, forever prevented from achieving his Goal (and thus fully satisfying his desire), can nevertheless find satisfaction in the very circular movement of repeatedly missing its object, of circulating around it: the gap constitutive of desire is thus closed; the self-enclosed loop of a circular repetitive movement replaces infinite striving. In this precise sense, drive equals *jouissance*, since *jouissance* is, at its most elementary, 'pleasure in pain', that is, a perverted pleasure provided by the very painful experience of repeatedly missing one's goal.[65]

The fact that drive is a 'by-product' is also to be taken also in the precise meaning this term has acquired in the contemporary theory of rational action:[66] in contrast to desire, which can be characterized as an intentional attitude, drive is something in which the subject is caught, a kind of acephalous force which persists in its repetitive movement. For that reason, one can propose as the ethical motto of psychoanalysis the famous *ne pas céder sur son désir*, 'don't compromise your desire'; while the complementary motto, 'don't compromise your drive', is meaningless, since it is superfluous: the problem with drive is not how not to betray it but, rather, how to break its loop, the hold of its inert power over us. . . . For the same reason, Lacan speaks of the '*desire* of the analyst', *never* of the '*drive* of the analyst': in so far as the analyst is defined by a certain subjective attitude – that of 'subjective destitution' – the specificity of his position can be determined only at the level of desire. Drive is pre-subjective/acephalous, it is not the name *of* a subjective attitude: one can only assume an attitude *towards* drive.

In religious terms, this problem is the problem of different *heresies*. The Christian Church as a social institution effectively functions as the guarantee of human desire, which can thrive only under the protection of the paternal Law (the Name-of-the-Father): far from prohibiting bodily passions (sexuality), the Church endeavours to regulate them. In its long history, it has also developed a series of strategies for 'domesticating' the excess of *jouissance* which cannot be contained in the paternal Law (say, the option opened up to women to become nuns and thus engage in a *jouissance féminine* of mystical experiences). The achievement of the Cathar heresy (*the* heresy if ever there was one) was precisely to undermine this strategic role of the Church in regulating sexual pleasure (the role emphasized by Foucault) – that is, to take disregard for the body literally, to preach and practise true chastity (since, as the Cathars put it, *every* sexual reunion is incestuous).[67] The paradox, of course, is that this radical renunciation of sexual pleasure not only does not deprive the subject of *jouissance*, but even amplifies it (the ascetic mystic has an access to *jouissance* that is much more intense than the usual standard sexual pleasure). That is the connection between the Cathar heresy and courtly love: when, instead of being allowed sexual pleasure within the confines of the Law, bodily sexuality is totally prohibited, this prohibition of the final sexual unification, this structure of *amor interruptus* prolonged *ad infinitum*, gives birth to courtly love in which desire shifts into drive – in which satisfaction is provided by the very indefinite postponement of the sexual union that would bring about 'actual' satisfaction. Christian crusaders against the Cathars were therefore, in a way, right in their suspicion that the ascetic renunciation of earthly pleasures among the Cathars was deeply ambiguous, since it engendered a much more intense *jouissance* that undermined the very regulating power of the paternal symbolic Law.

Our ultimate result is thus that desire and drive, in a way, *presuppose one another*: one cannot deduce one from the other. Drive is not simply the loop of self-satisfaction that emerges as a by-product of desire, nor is desire the result of shrinking back from the circuit of drive. What if, consequently, desire and drive are the two ways of avoiding the deadlock of negativity that 'is' the subject: by finding satisfaction in the repetitive circular movement of drive or, alternatively, by opening up the unending metonymic search for the lost object of desire? These two ways – that of desire and that of drive – involve two thoroughly different notions of subjectivity. Since enough theoretical eulogies have been written about the notorious 'subject of desire' (the subject divided/thwarted by the symbolic Law/Prohibition, the Void of negativity caught in the eternal search for its lost object-cause – saying 'I am a desiring subject' equals saying 'I am the lack, the gap, in the order of Being' . . .), it is perhaps time to focus on the much more mysterious subjectivity brought about by the circular movement of drive.

Lacan's fundamental *doxa* about drive is clear enough, as we have seen: drive involves a kind of self-reflexive turn, not a simple reversal of the active into the passive mode: say, in the scopic drive, the desire 'to see it all' is not simply turned around into the proclivity to be seen by the Other, but into the more ambiguous middle way of *se faire voir*, of making-oneself-seen.[68] (This reversal of desire into drive can also be specified apropos of choice: at the level of the subject of desire, there is choice –

inclusive of the fundamental forced choice – that is, the subject *chooses*, while we go on to the level of drive when the act of choice is inverted into *se faire choisir*, 'making-oneself-chosen', as in predestination, in which the religious subject does not simply choose God, but 'makes himself chosen' by Him. Or – to put it another way – the only – but crucial and highest – freedom I am granted in drive is the freedom to choose the inevitable, freely to embrace my Destiny, what will happen to me in any case.) However, what kind – if any – of *subjectivity* does this reversal of desire into drive involve?[69] Two series of cinematic and/or literary examples are perhaps best suited to illustrate the paradox of drive:

• That of the time-loop in science fiction (the subject travels into the past – or the future – where he encounters a certain mysterious entity that eludes his gaze again and again, until it occurs to him that this 'impossible' entity is *the subject himself*; or – the opposite case – the subject travels into the past with the express purpose of engendering himself, or into the future to witness his own death . . .). In order to avoid the standard examples like *Back to the Future*, let us recall David Lynch's *Lost Highway*. A crucial ingredient of Lynch's universe is a phrase, a signifying chain, which resonates as a Real that persists and always returns – a kind of basic formula that suspends and cuts across the linear flow of time: in *Dune*, it is 'The sleeper must awake', in *Twin Peaks*, 'The owls are not what they seem', in *Blue Velvet*, 'Daddy wants to fuck'; and, of course, in *Lost Highway*, the phrase which contains the first and the last spoken words in the film, 'Dick Laurent is dead', anouncing the death of the obscene paternal figure (Mr Eddy) – the entire narrative of the film takes place in the suspension of time between these two moments. At the beginning, Fred, the hero, hears these words on the interphone in his house; at the end, just before running away, he himself speaks them into the interphone – so we have a circular situation – first a message which is heard but not understood by the hero, then the hero himself pronouncing this message. In short, the whole film is based on the impossibility of the hero encountering *himself*, as in the famous time-warp scene in science-fiction novels where the hero, travelling back in time, encounters himself in an earlier time. . . .

Do we not have here a situation like the one in psychoanalysis, in which, at the beginning, the patient is troubled by some obscure, indecipherable but persistent message – the symptom – which, as it were, bombards him from outside; then, at the conclusion of the treatment, the patient is able to assume this message as his own, to pronounce it in the first person singular? The temporal loop that structures *Lost Highway* is thus the very loop of psychoanalytic treatment in which, after a long detour, we return to our starting point from another perspective. In his very first *Seminar*, Lacan invokes this temporal-loop structure of the symptom when he emphasizes that the Freudian symptom is like a signal bearing a message that comes *not*, as one would expect, from the 'deeply buried past' of ancient traumas, but from the (Subject's) *future* – from the future in which, through the work of psychoanalytic treatment, the meaning of this symptom will be realized.[70] (In this sense, the above-mentioned 360-degree shot of the passionately embracing couple from Hitchcock's *Vertigo*, in the course of which the background behind them transposes us from the present – Scottie kissing Judy refashioned into Madeleine in her ordinary hotel room – to the past – Scottie kissing Madeleine herself just before her suicidal leap from the old barn at the Juan Bautista Mission – and then back to the present, perfectly illustrates drive's temporal loop, the way its movement is folded into itself. Perhaps, then, the 'vertigo' of the film's title ultimately indicates the way Scottie is caught up in drive's endless loop.)

• That of the narrative in which, in the first moment, we (the subject from whose viewpoint the story is told) confront some horrifying object (Alien Thing, Monster, Murderer . . .), presented as the point with which no identification is possible – all of a sudden, however, we, the spectators, are violently thrown into the perspective of this very Alien Thing. Recall examples like *Frankenstein* (the novel), in which, after the Monster is presented to us as the Alien Horror Thing, we are thrown all of a sudden into *his* perspective – that is, *he* is allowed to tell his side of the story.[71] In Wes Craven's supreme *When a Stranger Calls*, also, we are thrown all of a sudden into the standpoint of the pathological compulsive killer presented in the first part of the film as absolute Otherness – not to mention Hitchcock's *Psycho*, in which, after the Mother is constructed as the horrifying Thing, we are, in some shots (like the killing of the detective Arbogast), viewing the action from *its* perspective.[72]

In all these cases, the inaccessible/traumatic Thing-beyond-representation itself becomes 'subjectivized': this subjectivization does not 'humanize' the Thing, demonstrating that what we thought was a Monster is in fact an ordinary, vulnerable person – the Thing retains its unbearable Otherness, it is *as such* that it subjectivizes itself. Or, to put it in the terms of vision: the Thing is first constructed as the inaccessible X around which my desire circulates, as the blind spot I want to see but simultaneously dread and avoid seeing, too strong for my eyes; then, in the shift towards drive, I (the subject) 'make myself seen' as the Thing – in a reflexive turn, I see *myself* as It, the traumatic object-Thing I didn't want to see.

Again, do we not find the ultimate example of this impossible Thing that 'is' ourselves in the science-fiction theme of the so-called *Id*-Machine, a mechanism that directly materializes our unacknowledged fantasies (from Fred Wilcox's *The Forbidden Planet* to Andrei Tarkovsky's *Solaris*)? The latest variation on this theme is Barry Levinson's *Sphere* (1997), in which, beneath the ocean surface in the midst of the Pacific, a gigantic spacecraft is suddenly discovered, having sat there on the ocean floor for three hundred years. The three scientists who penetrate it gradually discover that the mysterious Sphere in the middle of the spacecraft can reach into your mind: it knows your worst fears and starts to make them come true, to materialize them. . . .[73]

Uninteresting as *Sphere* is, it none the less deserves attention for its title: as Lacan showed in the chapter of his Seminar on Transference dedicated to this very theme ('La dérision de la sphère'[74]), the fascination exerted on us by the untouchable, impenetrable, self-enclosed and self-contained form of a sphere lies in the fact that it expresses perfectly, on the imaginary level, the foreclosure of castration, of a cut that would signal the presence of a lack and/or an excess. And, paradoxically, since our access to reality is conditioned by the cut of castration, the status of this sphere, far from embodying ontological perfection, is *stricto sensu* pre-ontological: the Sphere-Thing appears to us as something which, in cinematic terms, one could designate as a blurred object, an object that is by definition, a priori, out of focus.[75] This is nicely conveyed in Levinson's film, in which the Sphere is perfectly round yet simultaneously somehow alive, undulating and vibrating, as if its surface consists of the infinity of microscopic waves.

The Sphere is thus like the surface of Tarkovsky's Solaris–Ocean in its coincidence of global, overall calm and infinite mobility – although it is perfectly at peace, it is simultaneously extremely agitated, scintillating all the time, so that it is impossible to fix it, to get hold of it in its positive existence. As such, the Sphere is nothing in itself – a pure medium, a perfect mirror that does not mirror/materialize reality but only the Real of the subject's fundamental fantasies. When, in the film, the Dustin Hoffman character angrily rebukes Samuel Jackson (playing the African-American mathematician) because he does not want to divulge what is in the sphere to others, Jackson retorts angrily: 'But you also have been in it! You know very well that *there is nothing in the sphere!*' That is to say: nothing but what the subject himself puts there – or, to quote Hegel's classic formulation about the content of the suprasensible Beyond: 'It is manifest that behind the so-called curtain which is supposed to conceal the inner world, there is nothing to be seen unless *we* go behind it ourselves, as much in order that we may see, as that there may be something behind there which can be seen.'[76]

So it is crucial to bear in mind that precisely as Real, as the impossible Thing, the Sphere is an entity of *pure semblance*, an entity that is 'in itself' anamorphically distorted, an undulating, scintillating, out-of-focus surface concealing (or sustained by) Nothing – *as such*, it is the perfect neutral medium for fundamental fantasies. *Sphere* also makes it clear how the notion of a Zone or Thing in which our desires are directly realized is to be located in the lineage of the old fairy-tale theme of three wishes analysed by Freud (the peasant to whom a fairy grants three wishes wishes for a sausage; his wife wishes that the sausage should be stuck to his nose for the stupidity of such a wish; then they use the only remaining wish to get the sausage back from the nose on to the table . . .). The insight beneath this theme is, of course, that of the incommensurability between the subject's true desire and its formulation in a determinate demand: our desire is never actually in the explicit wish we are able to formulate – that is, we never truly desire what we wish for or will – for that reason, there is nothing more horrible – more undesirable, precisely – than a Thing that inexorably actualizes our true desire. . . . For that reason, the only way to evoke desire is to offer the object *and then immediately retract it*, as in the nice seduction scene from *Brassed Off*, when, in front of her house late in the evening, the girl says to the miner whom she intends to seduce: 'Would you care to come into my place for a cup of coffee?' 'Well, I don't drink coffee. . . .' 'No problem, I haven't got any!'[77]

Thus the coincidence of utter alterity with absolute proximity is crucial for the Thing: the Thing is even more 'ourselves', our own inaccessible kernel, than the Unconscious – it is an Otherness which directly 'is' ourselves, staging the phantasmic core of our being. The communication with the Thing thus fails not because it is too alien, the harbinger of an Intellect infinitely surpassing our limited abilities, playing some perverse games with us whose rationale remains forever outside our grasp, but because it brings us too close to what, in ourselves, must remain at a distance if we are to sustain the consistency of our symbolic universe. In its very Otherness, the Thing generates spectral phenomena that obey our innermost idiosyncratic whims: if there is a puppet-master who pulls the strings, it is ourselves, 'the Thing that thinks' in our heart.

And is not the ultimate example of this coincidence of the very kernel of my being with the ultimate externality of the Alien Thing Oedipus himself, who, in search of the murderer of his father, discovers that he himself is the perpetrator? In this precise sense, one can claim that Freud's term *Triebschicksale*, the 'destinies/vicissitudes of drive', is deeply justified, even tautological: the Freudian 'drive' *is* ultimately another name for 'Destiny', for the reversal through which the circle of Destiny accomplishes/closes itself (when Destiny catches up with Oedipus, he is confronted with the fact that he is the monster he is looking for). And in order to bring home how this dimension of Destiny overlaps with the temporal loop, recall the standard tragic science-fiction theme of a scientist who travels into the past in order to intervene in it and thus retroactively change (undo) the catastrophic present; all of a sudden (when it is already too late), he becomes aware not only that the result (the present catastrophe) is the same, but that *his very attempt to change the present through his retroactive intervention in the past produced the very catastrophe he wanted to undo* – his intervention was included in the course of things from the very outset. In this properly dialectical reversal, the alternative reality the agent wanted to bring about turns out to be the very present catastrophic reality.

To those versed in Hegelian philosophy, these two features of drive – its temporal loop; the pitiless and inexorable identification of the subject with the inaccessible Thing whose lack or withdrawal sustains the space of desire – cannot but evoke two fundamental features of the Hegelian dialectical process: does not Hegel reiterate again and again how the dialectical process displays the circular structure of a loop (the subject of the process, the absolute Idea, is not given in advance, but is generated by the process itself – so, in a paradoxical temporal short circuit, the final Result retroactively *causes itself*, generates its own causes); and, furthermore, how the basic matrix of the dialectical process is that of the subject's self-recognition in the In-itself of its absolute Otherness (recall the standard figure of Hegel according to which I have to recognize my own substance in the very force that seems to resist and thwart my endeavour).

Does this mean that 'drive' is inherently metaphysical, that it provides the elementary matrix of the closed circle of teleology and of self-recognition in Otherness? Yes, but with a twist: it is as if, in drive, this closed loop of teleology is minimally displaced on account of the failure that sets it in motion. It may appear that drive is the paradigmatic case of the closed circle of auto-affection, of the subject's body affecting itself within the domain of Sameness – as we have seen, does not Lacan himself suggest, as the supreme metaphor of drive, lips kissing themselves? One should bear in mind, however, that this reflexive reversal-into-self constitutive of drive relies on a fundamental, constitutive *failure*. The most succinct definition of the reversal constitutive of drive is the moment when, in our engagement in a purposeful activity (activity directed towards some goal), the way towards this goal, the gestures we make to achieve it, start to function as a goal in itself, as its own aim, as something that brings its own satisfaction. This closed loop of circular satisfaction, of the repetitive movement that finds satisfaction in its own circular loop, thus none the less relies on the failure to achieve the goal we were aiming at: drive's self-affection is never fully self-enclosed, it relies on some radically inaccessible X that forever eludes its grasp – the drive's repetition is the repetition of a failure. And – back to German Idealism – is not the same failure clearly discernible in the very fundamental structure of *Selbst-Bewusstsein*, of self-consciousness? Is it not clear already in Kant that there is *transcendental* self-consciousness, that I am aware of 'myself' only in so far as I am ultimately inaccessible to myself in my noumenal (*transcendent*) dimension, as the 'I or He or It (the Thing) that thinks' (Kant)? So the basic lesson of the transcendental self-consciousness is that it is the very opposite of full self-transparence and self-presence: I am aware of myself, I am compelled to turn reflexively on to myself, only in so far as I can never 'encounter myself' in my noumenal dimension, as the Thing I actually am.[78]

We can now pinpoint the opposition between the subject of desire and the subject of drive: while the subject of desire is grounded in the constitutive *lack* (it ex-sists in so far as it is in search of the missing Object-Cause), the subject of drive is grounded in a constitutive *surplus* – that is to say, in the excessive presence of some Thing that is inherently 'impossible' and should not be here, in our present reality – the Thing which, of course, is ultimately *the subject itself*. The standard heterosexual 'fatal attraction' scene is that of male desire captivated and fascinated by a deadly *jouissance féminine*: a woman is desubjectivized, caught in the self-enclosed cycle of acephalous drive, ignorant of the fascination she exerts on man, and it is precisely this self-sufficient ignorance which makes her irresistible; the paradigmatic mythical example of this scene, of course, is that of Ulysses captivated by the Sirens' song, this pure *jouis-sense*. What happens, however, when the Woman-Thing herself becomes subjectivized? This, perhaps, is the most mysterious libidinal inversion of all: the moment at which the 'impossible' Thing subjectivizes itself. In his short essay on the 'Silence of the Sirens', Franz Kafka accomplished such a reversal: his point is that Ulysses was in fact so absorbed in himself, in his own longing, that he did not notice that the Sirens did not sing, but just stared at him, transfixed by his image.[79] And again, the crucial point here is that this reversal is not symmetrical: the subjectivity of the subjectivized Sirens is not the same as the subjectivity of the male desire transfixed by the irresistible look of the Woman-Thing. When desire subjectivizes itself, when it is subjectively assumed, the flow of words is set in motion, since the subject is finally able to acknowledge it, to integrate it into its symbolic universe; when drive subjectivizes itself, when the subject sees itself as the dreadful Thing, this other subjectivization is, on the contrary, signalled by the sudden onset of *silence* – the idiotic babble of *jouissance* is interrupted, the subject *disengages* itself from its flow. The subjectivization of drive is this very withdrawal, this pulling away from the Thing that I myself am, this realization that *the Monster out there is myself.*

The subject of drive is thus related to the subject of desire, as Oedipus at Colonnus is related to the 'standard' Oedipus who unknowingly killed his father and married his mother: he is the subject who got back his own message from the Other and was compelled to assume his act, that is, to identify himself as the Evil Thing he was looking for. Was this recognition reason enough for him to blind himself? It is here that sexual difference is to be taken into account: perhaps a woman is more able to endure this identification of the core of one's being with the Evil Thing. In the Louvre, a couple of yards to the left of the *Mona Lisa*, inconspicuous among much more acclaimed paintings, is Luini's *Salome is brought the head of John the Baptist.* Bernardino Luini (1480–1532), a follower of Leonardo in Milan, sentimentalized Leonardo's style: he is known for his series of portraits of the Virgin Mary, painted as a beautiful, somewhat dreamy figure. The surprise of his 'Salome' is that Salome herself is drawn in the same style as his Virgin Marys: although the moment depicted is abhorrent (Salome is brought John's head on a platter, and the painting is dominated by the two heads, Salome's and John's, against the dark background), the expression on Salome's face is far from ecstatic. She is not on the verge of embracing the head and kissing it wildly – the finally obtained partial object (a strict equivalent to the 'bloody head here' mentioned in the passage quoted from Hegel's *Jenaer Realphilosophie*). Her expression is rather melancholic, constrained, her gaze fixed on some unspecified distant point – now that she has got what she was asking for, the finally obtained object is not 'swallowed' but merely encircled,

rendered indifferent.... Perhaps this painting is the closest one can get
to the depiction of the unique moment of the emergence of the subject
of drive.

Notes

1. François Regnault, *Conférences d'esthétique lacanienne*, Paris: Agalma 1997.
2. Michel Foucault, *Discipline and Punish*, New York: Vintage 1979, p. 30. Here Foucault
enables us to specify Althusser's definition of interpellation as the process which transforms
individuals into subjects: these mysterious individuals whose status remains unspecified in
Althusser are the objects and the product of disciplinary micro-practices; they are the bodily
'stuff' on which these practices work. In other words, interpellation is to the subject what
individuals are to the disciplinary micro-practices.
3. Of course, in the above criticism we have focused on the specific Foucauldian notion
of power and resistance from *Discipline and Punish* and Volume I of *History of Sexuality*: in
these two books, the notion of Power remains confined to the procedure of discipline–
confession–control that took shape in early Christianity. When, in his later interviews,
Foucault speaks about power and counter-power, he imperceptibly changes the terrain and
moves to a kind of Nietzschean general ontology of power: power is everywhere and
everything; it is the very air we breathe, the very stuff of our lives. This general ontology of
power also involves a different notion of subject as the 'fold' of power; this subject is no
longer the Self which, while waiting to be liberated from the repressive power, is effectively
constituted by it.
4. Judith Butler, *The Psychic Life of Power*, Stanford, CA: Stanford University Press 1997,
p. 43.
5. Is not this bodily excess generated by the disciplinatory mechanisms the Lacanian
plus-de-jouir? Is the fact that Hegel does not take this excess into account, then, not correlative
to the fact, emphasized by Lacan, that Hegel misses the surplus-enjoyment which keeps the
servant in the position of servitude?
6. Butler, *The Psychic Life of Power*, p. 49.
7. Marx made the same point about capitalism: it will meet its end not because of
resistance to it from external forces of pre-capitalist tradition, but because of its ultimate
inability to master and restrain its own inherent antagonism – as Marx put it, the limit of
capitalism is Capital itself, not the islands of resistance that still elude its control (sexuality,
nature, old cultural traditions).
8. On this obscene supplement of Power, see Chapters 1 and 2 of Slavoj Žižek, *The
Plague of Fantasies*, London: Verso 1997.
9. Is this oscillation not discernible also in Foucault's shifting from one political extreme
to its opposite: from fascination with the Iranian Revolution to immersion in the radical
lifestyle of the San Francisco gay community?
10. Butler, *The Psychic Life of Power*, p. 47.
11. Do we not encounter here the same double disavowal as in Marxian commodity
fetishism? First, a commodity is deprived of its bodily autonomy and reduced to a medium
which embodies social relations; then this network of social relations is projected into a
commodity as its direct material property, as if a commodity has a certain value in itself, or
as if money is in itself a universal equivalent.
12. This point has already been made by Mark Poster in *The Second Media Age*, Cambridge:
Polity Press 1995.
13. Significantly, Butler identifies 'subject' with the symbolic position occupied within this

space, while she reserves the term 'psyche' for the larger unity also encompassing what, in the individual, resists being included in the symbolic space.

14. Butler, *The Psychic Life of Power*, p. 88.

15. Ibid.

16. Ibid., p. 89.

17. Ibid., pp. 96–7.

18. Ibid., p. 97. Here Butler blatantly contradicts Lacan, for whom the Unconscious is 'the Other's *discourse*', that is, symbolic, *not* imaginary – isn't Lacan's best-known single line 'the Unconscious is structured like a language'? 'Slips and gaps' are thoroughly symbolic for Lacan; they concern the (mis)functioning of the signifying network. The situation is therefore the exact obverse of what Butler claims: it is not the Unconscious which is the imaginary resistance to the symbolic Law; on the contrary, it is *consciousness*, the conscious *ego*, which is the agency of the imaginary misrecognition of and resistance to the unconscious symbolic Law!

19. Ibid., p. 98.

20. Ibid., pp. 28–9.

21. Is this not also the problem of the 'marginal' homosexual position, which functions only as the transgression of the heterosexual predominant norm, and thus *needs*, relies on, this norm as its inherent presupposition? Witness Butler's obviously exaggerated insistence on how homosexuality is an experience which, for most individuals, involves the loss of one's identity, as if to imagine oneself engaged in a homosexual act is still an unheard-of traumatic experience today; witness the uneasiness experienced by queers when they are threatened not by censorship, but by the permissive attitude of being simply and indifferently accepted, no longer experienced as a traumatic subversion – as if they are somehow deprived of their subversive sting....

22. For an explanation of this term, see Chapter 3 of Žižek, *The Plague of Fantasies*.

23. Butler, *The Psychic Life of Power*, p. 105.

24. See Chapter 2 of Žižek, *The Plague of Fantasies*.

25. The standard Lacanian notion of the act focuses on the gesture of retroactively changing its own discursive (pre)conditions, the 'big Other' on which it relies, the background against which it occurs: an act proper 'miraculously' changes the very standard by which we measure and value our activity; that is, it is synonymous with what Nietzsche called 'transvaluation of values'. In this precise sense, an act involves the choice of 'the Worst [*le pire*]': the act occurs when one makes the choice of (what, within the situation, appears as) the Worst changes the very standards of what is good or bad. In politics, for example, the usual form of the pragmatic liberal centrists' complaint is that one should not be too radical and go too far in advocating gay rights or minority rights or ...; that one should take into account what majority opinion is still able to swallow, and so on; in such a context, one accomplishes an act proper when one makes precisely what the pragmatic centrist considers a catastrophic choice of the 'impossible', and when this gesture miraculously affects the frame of what is considered 'acceptable'. However, the later Lacan goes a step further and locates the act at an even more radical level, that of disturbing the very fundamental fantasy as the ultimate framework of our world-experience.

26. Butler, *The Psychic Life of Power*, p. 135.

27. Ibid., pp. 147, 146–7.

28. Ibid., pp. 137–8.

29. Ibid., p. 165.

30. Ibid., p. 166.

31. Ibid., p. 165.

32. See Butler's interview with Peter Osborne in *A Critical Sense*, ed. Peter Osborne, London: Routledge 1966, p. 83.

33. Another way of putting it is that for the psychotic, as for the Cathar heretics, every sexual act is incestuous.

34. J. Laplanche and J.-B. Pontalis, *The Language of Psychoanalysis*, London: Karnac 1988, p. 315.

35. Symbolic castration is thus somehow the exact opposite of the well-known pathological phenomenon of a person who feels a limb he no longer has (like the proverbial soldier who still feels the pain in the leg he lost in battle): *symbolic* castration designates, rather, the state in which one does not feel (or rather, more precisely, one does not manipulate freely and master) the organ (penis) one actually still possesses. . . .

36. Butler, *The Psychic Life of Power*, p. 92.

37. Jacques Lacan, 'Positions of the Unconscious', in *Reading Seminar XI*, ed. Richard Feldstein, Bruce Fink and Maire Jaanus, Albany, NY: SUNY Press 1995, p. 274.

38. Incidentally, in psychoanalysis the status of the body is not merely 'psychosomatic', that is, the body is not treated merely as the medium of the inscription of some symbolic impasse, as in the case of conversion hysteria: although psychoanalysis rejects a direct bodily causality of psychic troubles (such an approach reduces psychoanalysis to the constraints of the medical order), it none the less insists on how a pathological psychic process always refers to the Real of some organic disturbance, which functions as the proverbial grain of sand triggering the process of the crystallization of the symptom. When I have a violent toothache, the tooth itself soon becomes the object of narcissistic libidinal investment: I suck it, encircle it with my tongue, touch and inspect it with my fingers, look at it with the aid of a mirror, and so on – in short, the pain of the toothache itself turns into the source of *jouissance*. Along the same lines, Sandór Ferenczi reported the extreme case of a man whose testicle had to be removed because of a dangerous infection: this removal ('real' castration) triggered the onslaught of paranoia, since it resuscitated – actualized, gave a second life to – long-dormant homosexual fantasies (the same often goes for rectal cancer). In cases like these, the cause of paranoia lies not in the subject's inability to sustain the loss of his virility, of his phallic male posture; what he is in fact unable to sustain is, rather, the confrontation with his fundamental passive fantasy, which forms the 'primordially repressed' (foreclosed) 'other scene' of his subjective identity, and was all of a sudden actualized in his very physical reality. See Paul-Laurent Assoun, *Corps et Symptôme*, vol. 1: *Clinique du Corps*, Paris: Anthropos 1997, pp. 34–43.

39. This criticism of formalism is usually coupled with the opposite criticism: with the critical notion that Lacan is too branded by a specific historical content, the patriarchal Oedipal mode of socialization, elevating it into a transcendental a priori of human history.

40. It was Alfred Sohn-Rethel, a 'fellow-traveller' of the Frankfurt School, who described in detail this idea of the commodity form as the secret generator of the universal form of transcendental subjectivity. See Alfred Sohn-Rethel, *Geistige und körperliche Arbeit*, Frankfurt: Suhrkamp 1970.

41. In his criticism of Lacan, Henry Staten proposes a specific version of this point (see *Eros in Mourning*, Baltimore, MD: Johns Hopkins University Press 1995). According to Staten, Lacan inscribes himself into the Platonic–Christian lineage which devalues all positive-empirical objects subjected to the cycle of generation and corruption: for Lacan, as for Plato, every finite positive object is a mere semblance/lure which betrays the truth of desire. Lacan's merit consists in the fact that he brings this Platonic rejection of all finite material objects as worthy of love to its truth, concealed by Plato: finite empirical objects are not fragile copies of (or stand-ins for) their eternal Models – beneath or beyond them there is nothing, that is, they are place-holders of a primordial Void, of Nothingness. To put it in Nietzsche's terms, Lacan thus reveals the nihilistic essence of the metaphysical longing for eternal Objects beyond the earthly cycle of generation and corruption: the desire for these Objects is the desire for Nothingness, that is, these Objects are metaphors of Death.

Here Staten reduces Lacan to a postmodern advocate of the impossibility of the authentic encounter with a Thing: no positive object ever adequately fills in or fits the structural void which sustains desire; all we ever get are furtive semblances, so we are condemned to the repeated experience of *ce n'est pas ça*. . . . What is missing here is the obverse of this logic of the primordial Void which can never be filled by an adequate object: the correlative notion of an excessive, *surnuméraire* object for which there is no place in the symbolic structure. If, for Lacan, desire is effectively sustained by a Void which can never be filled, libido, on the contrary, is the Real of an excessive *object* which remains forever out of joint, in search of its 'proper place'.

42. Butler, *The Psychic Life of Power*, pp. 197–8.

43. See Gilles Deleuze, *Coldness and Cruelty*, New York: Zone 1991.

44. In an otherwise critical review of my first book, Jean-Jacques Lecercle claimed: 'if he [Žižek] does not know about contemporary philosophy, I [Lecercle] am the bishop of Ulan Bator'. Now let us imagine a follower of mine who, due to an attachment to me, is unable openly to admit to himself that he has noticed some serious faults in my knowledge of contemporary philosophy – if this disciple fantasizes about Lecercle dressed up as the bishop of Ulan Bator, this simply means that he thinks my knowledge of contemporary philosophy is flawed. . . .

45. In a more detailed elaboration, one should also distinguish further between the two modes of clinical masochism: on the one hand the properly perverse 'contractual' masochism, that is, the masochism of a subject who is able to 'externalize' his fantasy, to pass to the act and realize his masochistic scenario in an actual interaction with another subject; on the other hand, the (hysterical) secret masochistic daydreaming which is unable to endure its actualization – when the content of such secret masochistic daydreamings is imposed on the subject in reality, the result can be catastrophic: from utter humiliation and shame to the disintegration of his self-identity.

46. See Jean Laplanche, *Life and Death in Psychoanalysis*, Baltimore, MD: Johns Hopkins University Press 1976.

47. Quoted from Jean Laplanche, 'Aggressiveness and Sadomasochism', in *Essential Papers on Masochism*, ed. Margaret A.F. Hanly, New York: New York University Press 1995, p. 122.

48. Ibid.

49. Does not this constellation also provide the elementary matrix of the problematic of (religious) *predestination*? When the child asks himself 'Why was I born? Why did they want me?', one cannot satisfy him by simply answering: 'Because we loved you and wanted to have you.' How could my parents love me when I did not yet exist? Is it not that they have to love me (or hate me – in short, predestine my fate) and then create me, just as the Protestant God decides the fate of a human being prior to his birth?

50. Incidentally, why is the cowboy *without a hat*? Apart from the fact that, in Slovene, 'without a hat' rhymes with 'is fucking', one could propose as the reason for this enigmatic feature that, in the perspective of male children, fucking a woman is considered a non-manly, subservient activity – by doing it, one humiliates oneself by 'servicing' the woman, and it is this humiliating aspect, this loss of male dignity, that is signalled by losing one's hat. Seeing the woman's ass is thus perceived as a kind of revenge for her humiliation of the man: now it's her turn to pay for enticing him to fuck her. . . .

51. This glimpse at the naked ass, which is to be read in exactly the same way as Freud's famous example of the 'glance on the nose' from his article on fetishism, tells us where the mistake of the fetishist pervert lies: this mistake is correlative to the mistake of the standard heterosexual stance that dismisses partial objects as mere foreplays to the 'real thing' (the sexual act itself). From the correct insight that there is no (direct) sexual relationship – that all we have as supports of our enjoyment are fetishistic partial objects that fill the void of the impossible sexual relationship – the fetishist draws the mistaken conclusion that these partial objects are directly the 'thing itself', that one can get rid of the reference to the impossible sexual act and stick to the partial objects themselves. The solution is thus to maintain the tension between the void of the sexual relationship and the partial objects that support our enjoyment: although all we have are these partial objects/scenes, they none the less rely on the tension with the absent sexual act – they presuppose the reference to the void of the (impossible) act.

52. See Jacques Lacan, 'The Subversion of the Subject and the Dialectics of Desire', in *Écrits: A Selection*, New York: Norton 1977.

53. It would also be very productive to link the Freudian *Hilflosigkeit* to the Kantian notion of the Sublime, especially the dynamic Sublime, which also expresses something like the Kantian scene of primordial seduction: the scene of a man reduced to a particle of dust with whom enormous powers of nature are playing, yet observing this fascinating spectacle from the safety of a minimal distance, and thus enjoying it as a passive observer – isn't this the satisfaction provided by the fact that I observe myself reduced to an impotent particle of dust, that I see myself reduced to a helpless element overwhelmed by gigantic forces beyond my comprehension?

54. This topic of reflexivity is already announced and formulated in Butler's first book, her excellent essay on Hegel *Subjects of Desire* (New York: Columbia University Press 1987).

55. *The Odyssey of Homer*, XII, 160–64, trans. Richmond Lattimore, New York: Harper 1991.

56. See Michael Tanner, *Wagner*, London: Flamingo 1997.

57. A further opposition can be made here between two ultimate Wagnerian laments, that of the dying Tristan and that of Amfortas in *Parsifal* – this opposition concerns their different relation to the Oedipal triangulation. *Tristan* reproduces the standard Oedipal situation (stealing Isolde, a woman who belongs to another man, from the paternal figure of King Mark), while – as Claude Lévi-Strauss pointed out – the underlying structure of *Parsifal* is anti-Oedipal, the reversal of Oedipus. In *Parsifal*, the lament is performed by the *paternal* figure of Amfortas, finally delivered by Parsifal. In *Tristan*, the dignified Mark forgives Tristan at the end for his transgressive passion, while in *Parsifal*, the 'asexual' young Parsifal, this 'pure fool', delivers the paternal Amfortas from the painful consequences of his transgressive sin (allowing himself to be seduced by Kundry). This reversal, this displacement of the stain of transgression from son to father, is what makes *Parsifal* a properly *modern* work of art, leaving behind the traditional Oedipal problematic of the son transgressing the paternal prohibition, rebelling against paternal authority.

58. On a much more modest level of everyday life, the same horror is often encountered by anyone who works with a PC: what remains so uncanny about a PC is not only that, due to a virus or some malfunction, we can lose or inadvertently erase the result of hours and days of work, but also the opposite prospect: once you have written something and it is registered in your PC, it is practically impossible really to erase it: as we all know, even if you do apply the *delete* function to some text, the text remains in the computer; it is just that it is no longer registered – for that reason, computers have the function *undelete*, which gives you a fair chance of recovering the text you stupidly deleted. A simple PC thus contains a kind of 'undead' spectral domain of deleted texts which nevertheless continue to lead a shadowy existence 'between the two deaths', officially deleted but still there, waiting to be recovered. That is the ultimate horror of the digital universe: in it, everything remains forever inscribed; it is practically impossible really to get rid of, to erase, a text. . . .

59. See Jacques-Alain Miller, 'Des semblants dans la relation entre les sexes', *La Cause freudienne* 36, Paris 1997, pp. 7–15.

60. Here Miller seems to renounce the notion of symptom as *sinthome*, the knot of *jouissance beyond* fantasy, which persists even when the subject traverses his/her fundamental fantasy, and to reduce the symptom to a 'condensed' kernel of fantasy that regulates the subject's access to *jouissance*.

61. Jacques-Alain Miller, 'Le monologue de l'*apparole*', *La Cause freudienne* 34, Paris 1996, pp. 7–18.

62. See Jacques Lacan, 'Du "Trieb" de Freud au désir du psychanalyste', in *Écrits*, Paris: Éditions du Seuil 1966, pp. 851–4.

63. See Jacques Lacan, 'The Subversion of the Subject and the Dialectics of Desire', in *Écrits: A Selection*.

64. Jenny Holzer's famous truism 'Protect me from what I want' expresses very precisely

the fundamental ambiguity involved in the fact that desire is always the desire of the Other. It can be read either as 'Protect me from the excessive self-destructive desire in me that I myself am not able to dominate' – that is, as an ironic reference to the standard male chauvinist wisdom that a woman, left to herself, gets caught in self-destructive fury, so that she must be protected from herself by benevolent male domination; or in a more radical way, as indicating the fact that in today's patriarchal society woman's desire is radically alienated, that she desires what men expect her to desire, that she desires to be desired, and so on – in this case, 'Protect me from what I want' means 'What I want is already imposed on me by the patriarchal socio-symbolic order that tells me what to desire, so the first condition of my liberation is that I break up the vicious cycle of my alienated desire and learn to formulate my desire in an autonomous way.' The problem, of course, is that this second reading implies a rather naive opposition between 'heteronomous' alienated desire and truly autonomous desire – what if desire as such is 'desire of the other', so that there is ultimately no way to break out of the hysterical deadlock of 'I demand of you to refuse what I demand of you, because that is not *it*'?

65. Even if drive is thus conceived as a secondary by-product of desire, one can still maintain that desire is a defence against drive: the paradox is that desire functions as a *defence against its own product*, against its own 'pathological' outgrowth, that is, against the suffocating *jouissance* provided by drive's self-enclosed circular movement.

66. See Jon Elster, *Sour Grapes*, Cambridge: Cambridge University Press 1982.

67. According to Cathar teaching, our terrestrial world was created by the Devil, that is, the Creator who, at the beginning of the Bible, forms the world we know (the one who says 'Let there be light!', etc.) is none other than the *Devil himself*.

68. See Chapter XIV of Jacques Lacan, *The Four Fundamental Concepts of Psycho-Analysis*, New York: Norton 1979.

69. Here I draw on Alenka Zupančič's unpublished paper, 'La subjectivation sans sujet'.

70. '. . . what we see in the return of the repressed is the effaced signal of something which only takes on its value in the future, through its symbolic realization, its integration into the history of the subject' (*The Seminar of Jacques Lacan, Book I: Freud's Papers on Technique*, New York: Norton 1988, p. 159).

71. Concerning the ultimate example of the Monstrous Thing in contemporary popular culture, that of the Alien, Ridley Scott mentions in an interview that if he were to be allowed to film the sequel to his *Alien*, he would tell the story from the Alien's perspective.

72. For a closer analysis of this subjectivization of the Thing in *Psycho*, see Slavoj Žižek, 'Hitchcock's Universe', in *Everything You Ever Wanted to Know About Lacan (But Were Afraid to Ask Hitchcock)*, ed. Slavoj Žižek, London: Verso 1993.

73. Although it may appear difficult to imagine a more different film than Levinson's own *Wag the Dog* from the same year, are not the two films none the less connected? Is not the Sphere the Zone in which, once we enter it, the tail itself (our phantasmic shadows) wags the dog (our Selves that are supposed to control our personalities)? *Wag the Dog*, the story of the public relations specialists who concoct the media spectacle of a war with Albania in order to distract public attention from the sexual scandal in which the President got involved just weeks before his re-election, and *Sphere* thus both deal with the power of the pure phantasmic semblance, with the way phantasmic semblance can shape our (experience of) reality itself.

74. Jacques Lacan, *Le Séminaire, livre VIII: Le transfert*, Paris: Seuil 1991, pp. 97–116.

75. We find a rough equivalent to it in Woody Allen's *Deconstructing Harry*, in which Robin Williams plays the character who is, as it were, ontologically a blob, blurred, out of focus: his contours are out of focus not only for the subject who looks at him, not only when he is part of the generally blurred background – they are also blurred when he stands among people whom we can perceive quite clearly. This idea (unfortunately a *hapax*, a notion that can in fact be used only once) of a person who is in himself anamorphic, for whom there is no proper perspective that would make his contours clear (even when he himself looks at his

hands, they appear blurred to him), expresses, in a naive but adequate way, the Lacanian notion of a stain constitutive of reality itself.

76. *Hegel's Phenomenology of Spirit*, Oxford: Oxford University Press 1977, p. 103.

77. Unfortunately, *Sphere* mars the purity of its insight by retranslating it into common New Age wisdom: at the end, the three surviving heroes decide that since even for them, three highly educated civilized humans, contact with the Sphere (i.e. the opportunity to translate into reality, to materialize, their innermost fears and dreams) led to such (self-) destructive results, it is better for them to forget (erase from their memories) their entire experience of the Sphere – humanity is not yet spiritually mature enough for such a device. The ultimate message of the film is thus the resigned conservative thesis that, in our imperfect state, it is better not to penetrate too deep into our innermost secrets – if we did so, we might unleash tremendous destructive forces. . . .

78. See Chapter 1 of Slavoj Žižek, *Tarrying With the Negative*, Durham, NC: Duke University Press 1993.

79. See Franz Kafka, 'The Silence of the Sirens', in *Homer: A Collection of Critical Essays*, ed. George Steiner and Robert Fagles, Englewood Cliffs, NJ: Prentice-Hall 1963. For a Lacanian reading of this Kafka text, see Renata Salecl, 'The Silence of the Feminine *jouissance*', in Slavoj Žižek, ed., *Cogito and the Unconscious*, Durham, NC: Duke University Press 1998.

6

Whither Oedipus?

The Three Fathers

From the early days of his *Complexes familiaux*,[1] Lacan focused on the *historicity* of the Oedipus complex itself, as well as of its discovery by Freud. In the modern bourgeois nuclear family, the two functions of the father which were previously separated, that is, embodied in different people (the pacifying Ego Ideal, the point of ideal identification, and the ferocious superego, the agent of cruel prohibition; the symbolic function of totem and the horror of taboo), are *united in one and the same person.* (The previous separate personification of the two functions accounts for the apparent 'stupidity' of some aborigines who thought that the true father of a child is a stone or an animal or a spirit: the aborigines were well aware that the mother was inseminated by the 'real' father; they merely separated the real father from its symbolic function.) The ambiguous rivalry with the father figure, which emerged with the unification of the two functions in the bourgeois nuclear family, created the psychic conditions for modern Western dynamic creative individualism; at the same time, however, it sowed the seeds of the subsequent 'crisis of Oedipus' (or, more generally, with regard to figures of authority as such, of the 'crisis of investiture' that erupted in the late nineteenth century[2]): symbolic authority was more and more smeared by the mark of obscenity and thus, as it were, undermined from within. Lacan's point, of course, is that this identity is the 'truth' of the Oedipus complex: it can 'function normally' and accomplish its job of the child's integration into the socio-symbolic order only in so far as this identity remains concealed – the moment it is posited as such, the figure of paternal authority potentially turns into an obscene *jouisseur* (the German word is *Luder*) in whom impotence and excessive rage coincide, a 'humiliated father' caught in imaginary rivalry with his son.

Here we have the paradigmatic case of a properly historical dialectic:

precisely because Freud was 'the son of his Victorian times' – as many historicist critics of psychoanalysis are never tired of repeating – he was able to express its universal feature, which remains invisible in its 'normal' functioning. The other great example of the state of crisis as the only historical moment which allows for an insight into universality is, of course, that of Marx, who articulated the universal logic of the historical development of humanity on the basis of his analysis of capitalism as the excessive (imbalanced) system of production. Capitalism is a contingent monstrous formation whose very 'normal' state is permanent dislocation, a kind of 'freak of history', a social system caught in the vicious superego cycle of incessant expansion – yet precisely as such, it is the 'truth' of the entire preceding 'normal' history.[3]

In his early theory of the historicity of the Oedipus complex, Lacan thus already establishes the connection between the psychoanalytic problematic of Oedipus as the elementary form of 'socialization', of the subject's integration into the symbolic order, and the standard sociopsychological *topoi* on how modernity is characterized by individualist competitiveness – on how, in modern societies, subjects are no longer fully immersed in (and identified with) the particular social place into which they were born, but can – in principle, at least – move freely between different 'roles'. The emergence of the modern 'abstract' individual who relates to his particular 'way of life' as to something with which he is not directly identified – which, that is, depends on a set of contingent circumstances; this fundamental experience that the particularities of my birth and social status (sex, religion, wealth, etc.) do not determine me fully, do not concern my innermost identity – relies on mutation in the functioning of the Oedipus complex: on the unification of the two sides of paternal authority (Ego Ideal and the prohibitive superego) in one and the same person of the 'real father' described above.

Another aspect of this duality is the crucial distinction between the 'big Other' *qua* the symbolic order, the anonymous circuitry which mediates any intersubjective communication and induces an irreducible 'alienation' as the price for entering its circuit, and the subject's 'impossible' relationship to an Otherness which is not yet the symbolic big Other but the Other *qua* the Real Thing. The point is that one should not identify this Real Thing too hastily with the incestuous object of desire rendered inaccessible by symbolic prohibition (i.e. the maternal Thing); this Thing is, rather, *Father himself*, namely, the obscene Father-*jouissance* prior to his murder and subsequent elevation into the agency of symbolic authority (Name-of-the-Father). This is why, on the level of mythical narrative,

Freud felt the compulsion to supplement the Oedipal myth with another mythical narrative, that of the 'primordial father' (in *Totem and Taboo* [*T&T*]) – the lesson of this myth is the exact obverse of that of Oedipus; that is to say, here, far from having to deal with the father who intervenes as the Third, the agent who prevents direct contact with the incestuous object (and so sustains the illusion that his annihilation would give us free access to this object), it is the killing of the Father-Thing (the *realization* of the Oedipal wish) which gives rise to symbolic prohibition (the dead father returns as his Name). And what occurs in today's much-decried 'decline of Oedipus' (decline of paternal symbolic authority) is precisely the return of figures which function according to the logic of the 'primordial father', from 'totalitarian' political Leaders to the paternal sexual harasser – why? When the 'pacifying' symbolic authority is suspended, the only way to avoid the debilitating deadlock of desire, its inherent impossibility, is to locate the cause of its inaccessibility in a despotic figure which stands for the primordial *jouisseur*: we cannot enjoy because *he* appropriates all enjoyment. . . .

We can now see, in what, precisely, consists the crucial shift from Oedipus to *T&T*: in the 'Oedipus complex', the parricide (and the incest with the mother) has the status of the unconscious desire – we, ordinary (male) subjects, all dream about it, since the paternal figure prevents our access to the maternal object, disturbs our symbiosis with it; while Oedipus himself is the exceptional figure, the One who actually *did it*. In *T&T*, on the contrary, the parricide is not the object of our dreams, the goal of our unconscious wish – it is, as Freud emphasizes again and again, a prehistoric fact which 'really had to happen': the murder of the father is an event which had to take place in reality in order for the passage from animal state to Culture to take place. Or – to put it in yet another way – in the standard Oedipus myth, Oedipus is *the exception who did* what we all merely dream about (kill his father, etc.); while in *T&T we all did it*, and this universally shared crime grounded human community. . . . In short, the traumatic event is not something we dream about, entertaining its future prospect, but never really happens and thus, via its postponement, sustains the state of Culture (since the realization of this wish, i.e. the consummation of the incestuous link with the mother, would abolish the symbolic distance/prohibition that defines the universe of Culture); the traumatic event is, rather, what *always-already had to happen* the moment we are within the order of Culture.

So how are we to explain that, although we did actually kill the father, the outcome is not the longed-for incestuous union? There, in this paradox, lies the central thesis of *T&T*: the actual bearer of prohibition, what prevents our access to the incestuous object, is not the living but the *dead* father, the father who, after his death, returns as his Name, that is, as the embodiment of the symbolic Law/Prohibition. What the matrix of *T&T* accounts for is thus the structural necessity of the parricide: the passage from direct brutal force to the rule of symbolic authority, of the prohibitory Law, is always grounded in a (disavowed) act of primordial crime. That is the dialectic of 'You can prove that you love me only by betraying me': the father is elevated into the venerated symbol of Law only after his betrayal and murder. This problematic also opens up the vagaries of ignorance – not the subject's, but the big Other's: 'the father is dead, but he is not aware of it', that is, he doesn't know that his loving followers have (always-already) betrayed him. On the other hand, this means that the father 'really thinks that he is a father', that his authority emanates directly from his person, not merely from the empty symbolic place he occupies and/or fills. What the faithful follower should conceal from the paternal figure of the Leader is precisely this gap between the Leader in the immediacy of his personality and the symbolic place he occupies, the gap on account of which father *qua* effective person is utterly impotent and ridiculous (exemplary here, of course, is the figure of King Lear, who was confronted violently with this betrayal and the ensuing unmasking of his impotence – deprived of his symbolic title, he is reduced to a raging old impotent fool). The heretic legend according to which Christ himself ordered Judas to betray him (or at least, let him know his wishes between the lines . . .) is therefore well founded: there, in this necessity of the betrayal of the Great Man which alone can assure his fame, lies the ultimate mystery of Power.

The relationship between Michael Collins and Eamon de Valera in the fight for Irish independence illustrates another aspect of this necessity of betrayal. In 1921, De Valera's problem was that he saw the necessity of concluding a deal with the British government, as well as the catastrophic results of the return to a state of war, yet he did not want to conclude this deal himself, and thus take full public responsibility for it, because this would force him to display his impotence, his limitation, publicly (he was well aware that the British government would never concede two key demands: the separate status of the six Ulster counties and the renunciation of Ireland as a Republic, that is, the recognition of the British King as sovereign over the Commonwealth, and thus also over Ireland). In order to retain his charisma, he had to manipulate another (Collins) into concluding the deal, reserving for himself the freedom to disavow it publicly, while later silently accepting its terms – in this way, the semblance of his charisma would be saved. De Valera himself was heard to say of Collins and other members of the Irish delegation to the London negotiations: 'We must have scapegoats'.[4] Collins's tragedy was that he readily assumed this role of 'vanishing mediator', of the subject whose compromising pragmatic stance enables the Master to retain his messianic charisma: 'You might say the trap is sprung,'[5] he wrote after he had agreed to head the London delegation, while after signing the treaty he said, with dark premonition: 'I may have signed my actual death-warrant.'[6] The cliché of the post-revolutionary pragmatic leader who betrays the revolutionary idealist is thus reversed: it is the passionate nationalist idealist (De Valera) who exploits and then betrays the pragmatic realist, the true founding figure.[7]

How, however, is this reversal possible? In the *T&T* matrix, there is still something missing: it is not enough to have the murdered father returning as the agency of symbolic prohibition – in order for this prohibition to be effectual, actually to exert its power, it must be sustained by a positive act of Willing. This insight paved the way for the further and last Freudian variation on the Oedipal matrix, the one in *Moses and Monotheism* [*M&M*], in which we are also dealing with *two* paternal figures; this duality, however, is not the same as the one in *T&T*: here, the two figures are not the pre-symbolic obscene/non-castrated Father-*Jouissance* and the (dead) father *qua* the bearer of symbolic authority (the Name-of-the-Father), but the old Egyptian Moses, the one who imposed monotheism – who dispensed with old polytheistic superstitions and introduced the notion of a universe determined and ruled by a unique rational Order, and the Semitic Moses, who is actually none other than Jehovah (Yahweh), the jealous God who displays vengeful rage when He feels betrayed by His people. In short, *M&M* reverses the matrix of *T&T* yet again: the father who is 'betrayed' and killed by his followers/sons is *not* the obscene primordial Father-*Jouissance* but the very 'rational' father who embodies symbolic authority, the figure which personifies the unified rational structure of the universe [*logos*]. Instead of the obscene primordial pre-symbolic father returning after his murder in the guise of its Name, of symbolic authority, we now have the symbolic authority [*logos*] betrayed, killed by his followers/sons, and then returning in the guise of the jealous and unforgiving superego figure of God full of murderous rage.[8] It is only here, after this second reversal of the Oedipal matrix, that we reach the well-known Pascalian distinction between the God of Philosophers (God *qua* the universal structure of *logos*, identified with the rational structure of the universe) and the God of Theologists (the God of love and hate, the inscrutable 'dark God' of capricious 'irrational' Predestination).

Again, the crucial point is that this God is *not* the same as the obscene primordial Father-*Jouisseur*: in contrast to the primordial father endowed with a *knowledge* of *jouissance*, the fundamental feature of this uncompromising God is that He says 'No!' to *jouissance* – this is a God possessed by ferocious ignorance ('*la féroce ignorance de Yahvé*'[9]), by an attitude of 'I refuse to know, I do not want to hear, anything about your dirty and secret ways of *jouissance*'; a God who banishes the universe of traditional sexualized wisdom, a universe in which there is still a semblance of the ultimate harmony between the big Other (the symbolic order) and *jouissance*, the notion of macrocosm as regulated by some underlying sexual tension between male and female 'principles' (*Yin* and *Yang*, Light and Darkness, Earth and Heaven). This is the proto-existentialist God whose existence – to apply to Him anachronistically Sartre's definition of man – does not simply coincide with His essence (as with the medieval God of St Thomas Aquinas), but precedes His essence; for that reason, He speaks in tautologies, not only concerning His own *quidditas* ('I am what I am'), but also and above all in what concerns *logos*, the *reasons* for what He is doing – or, more precisely, for His injunctions, for what He is asking us to do or prohibiting us to do: the inexorable insistence of His orders is ultimately grounded in an 'It is so *because I say it is so*!'. In short, this God is the God of pure Will, of the capricious abyss that lies beyond any global rational order of *logos*, a God who does not have to *account* for anything He does.

In the history of philosophy, this crack in the global rational edifice of the macrocosm in which the Divine Will appears was first opened up by Duns Scotus; but it was F.W.J. Schelling to whom we owe the most piercing descriptions of this horrifying abyss of Will. Schelling opposed the Will to the 'principle of sufficient reason': pure Willing is always self-identical, it relies only on its own act – 'I want it because I want it!'. In his descriptions, radiating an awesome poetic beauty, Schelling emphasizes how ordinary people are horrified when they encounter a person whose behaviour displays such an unconditional Will: there is something fascinating, properly hypnotic, about it; one is as if bewitched by it. . . . Schelling's emphasis on the abyss of pure Willing, of course, targets Hegel's alleged 'panlogicism': what Schelling wants to prove is that the Hegelian universal logical system is in itself *impotent* – it is a system of pure *potentialities* and, as such, in need of the supplementary 'irrational' act of pure Will in order to *actualize* itself.

This God is the God who *speaks* to His followers/sons, to His 'people' – the intervention of *voice* is crucial here. As Lacan put it in his unpublished Seminar on *Anxiety* (from 1960–61), the voice (the actual 'speech act') brings about the *passage à l'acte* of the signifying network, its 'symbolic efficiency'. This voice is inherently meaningless – nonsensical, even; it is just a negative gesture which gives expression to God's malicious and vengeful anger (all meaning is already there in the symbolic order which structures our universe), but it is precisely as such that it actualizes the purely structural meaning, transforming it into an experience of Sense.[10] This, of course, is another way of saying that through this uttering of the Voice which manifests His Will, God *subjectivizes* Himself. The old Egyptian Moses betrayed and killed by his people was the all-inclusive One of *logos*, the rational substantial structure of the universe, the 'writing' accessible to those who know how to read the 'Great Book of Nature', not yet the all-exclusive One of subjectivity who imposes His unconditional Will on His creation. And, again, the crucial point not to be missed is that this God, although alogical, 'capricious', vengeful, 'irrational', is *not* the pre-symbolic 'primordial' Father-*Jouissance* but, on the contrary, the agent of prohibition carried by a 'ferocious ignorance' of the ways of *jouissance*.

The paradox one has to bear in mind here is that this God of groundless Willing and ferocious 'irrational' rage is the God who, by means of His Prohibition, accomplishes the destruction of the old sexualized Wisdom, and thus opens up the space for the de-sexualized 'abstract' knowledge of modern science: there is 'objective' scientific knowledge (in the modern, post-Cartesian sense of the term) only if the universe of scientific knowledge itself is supplemented and sustained by this excessive 'irrational' figure of the 'real father'. In short, Descartes's 'voluntarism' (see his infamous statement that $2 + 2$ would be 5 if such were God's Will – there are no eternal truths directly consubstantial with Divine Nature) is the necessary obverse of modern scientific knowledge. Premodern Aristotelian and medieval knowledge was not yet 'objective' rational scientific knowledge precisely because it lacked this excessive element of God *qua* the subjectivity of pure 'irrational' Willing: in Aristotle, 'God' directly equals His own eternal rational Nature; He 'is' nothing but the logical Order of Things. The further paradox is that this 'irrational' God as the prohibitory paternal figure also opens up the space for the entire development of modernity, up to the deconstructionist notion that our sexual identity is a contingent socio-symbolic formation: the moment this prohibitory figure recedes, we are back into the Jungian neo-obscurantist notion of the masculine and feminine eternal archetypes which thrives today.

This paradox is crucial if we are not to misunderstand completely the gap that separates the proper authority of the symbolic Law/Prohibition from mere 'regulation by rules': the domain of symbolic rules, if it is actually to count as such, has to be grounded in some tautological authority *beyond rules*, which says 'It is so because I say it is so!'.[11] In short, beyond divine Reason there is the abyss of God's Will, of His contingent Decision which sustains even the Eternal Truths. Above and beyond opening up the space for modern reflexive freedom, this same gap also opens up the space for modern tragedy. In political terms, the difference between classical tragedy and modern tragedy is the difference between (traditional) *tyranny* and (modern) *terror*.[12] The traditional *hero* sacrifices himself for the Cause; he resists the pressure of the Tyrant and accomplishes his Duty, cost what it may; as such, he is appreciated, his sacrifice confers on him a sublime aura, his act is inscribed in the register of Tradition as an example to be followed. We enter the domain of modern tragedy when the very logic of sacrifice for the Thing compels us to sacrifice this Thing itself; therein lies the predicament of Paul Claudel's Sygne, who is compelled to betray her faith in order to prove her absolute fidelity to God. Sygne does not sacrifice her empirical life for what matters to her more than her life, she sacrifices precisely that which is 'in her more than herself', and thus survives as a mere shell of her former self, deprived of her *agalma* – we thereby enter the domain of the *monstrosity of heroism*, when our fidelity to the Cause compels us to transgress the threshold of our 'humanity'. Is it not proof of the highest, most absolute faith that, for the love of God, I am ready to lose, to expose to eternal damnation, my eternal Soul itself? It is easy to sacrifice one's life with the certainty of thereby redeeming one's eternal Soul – how much worse is it to sacrifice one's very soul for God!

Perhaps the ultimate historical illustration of this predicament – of the gap which separates the hero (his resistance to tyranny) from the victim of terror -- is provided by the Stalinist victim: this victim is not someone who finally learns that Communism was an ideological mirage, and becomes aware of the positivity of a simple ethical life outside the ideological Cause – the Stalinist victim cannot retreat into a simple ethical life, since he has already forsaken it for his Communist Cause. This predicament accounts for the impression that although the fate of the victims of the great Stalinist show trials (from Bukharin to Slansky) was horrible beyond description, the properly tragic dimension is missing –

that is, they were *not* tragic heroes, but something more horrible and simultaneously more comical: they were deprived of the very dignity that would confer on their fate its properly tragic dimension. For that reason, Antigone cannot serve as the model for resistance to Stalinist power: if we use her like this, we reduce the Stalinist terror to just another version of tyranny. Antigone maintains the reference to the big Other's desire (to accomplish the symbolic ritual and bury her deceased brother properly) as opposed to the tyrant's (pseudo-)Law – the reference which, precisely, is *lacking* in the Stalinist show trials. In humiliating the victim, the Stalinist terror deprives him of the very dimension which could confer sublime beauty on him: the victim goes beyond a certain threshold, he 'loses his dignity' and is reduced to a pure subject bereft of *agalma*, 'destitute', unable to recompose the narrative of his life.

Thus terror is not the power of corruption that undermines the ethical attitude from outside; rather, it undermines it from within, by mobilizing and exploiting to its utmost the inherent gap of the ethical project itself, the gap that separates the ethical Cause *qua* real from Cause in its symbolic dimension (values, etc.) or – to put it in politico-legal terms – the gap that separates the God of the pure act of decision from the God of positive Prohibitions and Commandments. Does not the Kierkegaardian suspension of the (symbolic) Ethical also involve a move beyond tragedy? The ethical hero is tragic, whereas the knight of Faith dwells in the horrible domain beyond or between the two deaths, since he (is ready to) sacrifice(s) what is most precious to him, his *objet petit a* (in the case of Abraham, his son). In other words, Kierkegaard's point is not that Abraham is forced to choose between his duty to God and his duty to humanity (such a choice remains simply tragic), but that he has to choose between the two facets of duty to God, and thereby the two facets of God Himself: God as universal (the system of symbolic norms) and God as the point of absolute singularity that suspends the dimension of the Universal.

For this precise reason, Derrida's reading of (Kierkegaard's reading of) Abraham's gesture in *Donner la mort*,[13] where he interprets Abraham's sacrifice not as a hyperbolic exception but as something which all of us perform again and again, every day, in our most common ethical experience, seems to fall short. According to Derrida, every time we choose to obey a duty to some individual, we neglect – forget – our duty to all others (since *tout autre est tout autre*, every other person is wholly other) – if I attend to my own children, I sacrifice the children of other men; if I help to feed and clothe *this* other person, I abandon other others, and so on. What gets lost in this reduction of Abraham's predicament to a kind of

Heideggerian constitutive guilt of *Dasein* which can never use/actualize all its possibilities is the self-referential nature of this predicament: Abraham's deadlock does not lie in the fact that, on behalf of the ultimate *tout autre* (God), he has to sacrifice another *tout autre*, his most beloved earthly companion (his son) but, rather, in the fact that, on behalf of his Love for God, he has to sacrifice what *the very religion grounded in his faith orders him to love*. The split is thus inherent in faith itself; it is the split between the Symbolic and the Real, between the *symbolic* edifice of faith and the pure, unconditional *act* of faith – *the only way to prove your faith is to betray what this very faith orders you to love.*

The Demise of Symbolic Efficiency

One can now see why Lacan calls this prohibiting God the 'real father' as the 'agent of castration': symbolic castration is another name for the gap between the big Other and *jouissance*, for the fact that the two can never be 'synchronized'. One can also see in what precise sense perversion enacts the disavowal of castration: the fundamental illusion of the pervert is that he possesses a (symbolic) knowledge that enables him to regulate his access to *jouissance* – that is, to put it in more contemporary terms, the pervert's dream is to transform sexual activity into an instrumental purpose-orientated activity that can be projected and executed according to a well-defined plan. So when, today, one speaks of the decline of paternal authority, it is *this* father, the father of the uncompromising 'No!', who is effectively in retreat; in the absence of his prohibitory 'No!', new forms of the phantasmic harmony between the symbolic order and *jouissance* can thrive again – this return to the substantial notion of Reason-as-Life at the expense of the prohibitory 'real father' is what the so-called New Age 'holistic' attitude is ultimately about (the Earth or macrocosm itself as a living entity).[14] What these deadlocks indicate is that today, in a sense, 'the big Other no longer exists' – but in *what* sense? One should be very specific about what this nonexistence actually amounts to. In a way, it is the same with the big Other as it is with God according to Lacan (it is not that God is dead today; God was dead from the very beginning, only He didn't know it . . .): *it never existed in the first place*, that is, the nonexistence of the big Other is ultimately equivalent to the fact that the big Other is the *symbolic* order, the order of symbolic fictions which operate on a level different from that of direct material causality. (In this sense, the only subject for whom the big Other *does* exist is the psychotic, the one who attributes direct material efficacy to words.) In short, the 'nonexistence of the big Other' is strictly correlative to the notion of belief, of symbolic trust, of credence, of taking what others say 'at face value'.

In one of the Marx Brothers' films, Groucho Marx, caught in a lie, answers angrily: 'Whom do you believe, your eyes or my words?' This apparently absurd logic expresses perfectly the functioning of the symbolic order, in which the symbolic mask–mandate matters more than the direct reality of the individual who wears this mask and/or assumes this mandate. This functioning involves the structure of fetishistic disavowal: 'I know very well that things are the way I see them [that this person is a corrupt weakling], but none the less I treat him with respect, since he wears the insignia of a judge, so that when he speaks, it is the Law itself which speaks through him.' So, in a way, I actually believe his words, not my eyes – that is to say, I believe in Another Space (the domain of pure symbolic authority) which matters more than the reality of its spokesmen. The cynical reduction to reality therefore falls short: when a judge speaks, there is in a way more truth in his words (the words of the Institution of Law) than in the direct reality of the person of the judge – if one limits oneself to what one sees, one simply misses the point. This paradox is what Lacan is aiming at with his '*les non-dupes errent*': those who do not let themselves be caught in the symbolic deception/fiction and continue to believe their eyes are the ones who err most. What a cynic who 'believes only his eyes' misses is the efficiency of the symbolic fiction, the way this fiction structures our experience of reality.

The same gap is at work in our most intimate relationship with our neighbours: we behave *as if* we do not know that they also smell bad, secrete excrement, and so on – a minimum of idealization, of fetishizing disavowal, is the basis of our coexistence. And does not the same disavowal account for the sublime beauty of the idealizing gesture discernible from Anne Frank to American Communists who believed in the Soviet Union? Although we know that Stalinist Communism was an appalling thing, we nevertheless admire the victims of the McCarthy witch-hunt who heroically persisted in their belief in Communism and support for the Soviet Union. The logic here is the same as that of Anne Frank who, in her diaries, expresses belief in the ultimate goodness of mankind in spite of the horrors perpetrated against Jews in World War II: what makes such an assertion of belief (in the essential goodness of mankind; in the truly human character of the Soviet regime) sublime is the very gap between it and the overwhelming factual evidence against it, that is, the active *will to disavow* the actual state of things. Perhaps therein lies the most elementary *meta-physical* gesture: in this refusal to accept the Real in its idiocy, to disavow it and to search for Another World behind it.[15]

In his reading of Freud's article on fetishism, Paul-Laurent Assoun[16] suggests that sexual difference is responsible for two different approaches to the gap between what my eyes tell me and the symbolic fiction – to the gap that separates the visible from the invisible. When a small boy sees a naked girl, he chooses not to believe his eyes (and accept the fact that girls are different); he continues to believe the 'word', the symbolic fiction, which led him to expect a penis in the girl as well, so he disavows his immediate perception, interprets it as a superficial lure, and starts to search, to form hypotheses that would account for this gap (girls have a smaller, almost invisible penis; their penis will grow later; it was cut off . . .) – in short, the boy's disavowal propels him in the direction of a 'spontaneous metaphysician', a believer in Another World beneath the visible facts. The girl, on the contrary, 'believes her eyes', she accepts the fact that she does not possess 'it', so a different set of options is opened to her, from the notorious 'penis envy' and the search for substitutes (a child, etc.) to the cynical attitude of a fundamental distrust towards the symbolic order (what if male phallic power is a mere semblance?).

In the history of philosophy, there are three great anecdotal examples of 'believe my words, not your eyes': Diogenes the Cynic, who refuted the Eleatic thesis that there is no movement by simply taking a walk, and then, as Hegel emphasizes, beat his pupil who applauded the Master – that is, believed his eyes more than the words of argumentation (Diogenes' point was that such a direct reference to experience, to 'what your eyes tell you', does not count in philosophy – the task of philosophy is to demonstrate, by means of argumentation, the truth or untruth of what we see); the medieval story of scholastic monks who discussed how many teeth a donkey has, and were then shocked at the proposal by a younger member of their group that they should simply go to a stall outside their house and count; finally, the story of Hegel insisting that there are only eight planets around the Sun even after the discovery of the ninth.

Today, with the new digitalized technologies enabling perfectly faked documentary images, not to mention Virtual Reality, the injunction 'Believe my words (argumentation), not the fascination of your eyes!' is more pertinent than ever. That is to say, the logic of 'Whom do you believe, your eyes or my words?' – that is, of 'I know very well, but none the less . . . [I believe]' – can function in two different ways, that of the symbolic *fiction* and that of the imaginary *simulacrum*. In the case of the efficient symbolic fiction of the judge wearing his insignia, 'I know very well that this person is a corrupt weakling, but I none the less treat him as if [I believe that] the symbolic big Other speaks through him': I disavow what my eyes tell me, and choose to believe the symbolic fiction. In the case of the simulacrum of virtual reality, on the contrary, 'I know very well that what I see is an illusion generated by digital machinery, but I none the less agree to immerse myself in it, to behave as if I believe it' – here, I disavow what my (symbolic) knowledge tells me, and choose to believe my eyes only.

In the history of modern philosophy, the logic of 'Whom do you believe, your eyes or my words?' found its strongest expression in Malebranche's occasionalism: not only is there no sensible proof for occasionalism's central tenet (according to which God is the only causal agent), this tenet is even directly contrary to all sensible experience, which leads us to believe that external objects act directly on our senses, causing sensations in our mind. When Malebranche thus endeavours to convince his readers to believe his words, not their eyes, the central enigma he has to explain is: *why* did God create the universe in such a way that we, mortal humans, necessarily fall prey to the illusion that sensible objects act directly on our senses? His explanation is moral: if we were to be able to perceive the true state of things directly, we would love God invincibly, through instinct, not on account of our free will and rational insight gained through liberation from the tyranny of our senses; that is, there would be no place for our moral activity, for our struggle to undo the consequences of the Fall and regain the lost Goodness. Thus Malebranche delineates the contours of the philosophical position which explains man's epistemological limitation (the fact that man's knowledge is limited to phenomena, that the true state of things is out of his reach) by reference to moral grounds: only a being marked by such an epistemological limitation can be a moral being, that is, can acquire Goodness as the result of free decision and inner struggle against temptation. This attitude (later adopted by Kant) runs directly against the standard Platonic equation of Knowledge and Goodness (evil is the consequence of our ignorance, that is to say, one cannot know the truth and continue to be bad, since the more we know, the closer we are to being good): a certain radical ignorance is the positive condition of our being moral.

So what is symbolic efficiency? We all know the old, worn-out joke about the madman who thought he was a grain of corn; after finally being cured and sent home, he returned immediately to the mental institution and explained his panic to the doctor: 'I met a hen on the road, and I was afraid it would eat me!' To the doctor's surprised exclamation 'But what's the problem now? You know you're not a grain of corn but a human being who can't be swallowed by a hen!', the madman answered: 'Yes, *I* know I'm no longer a grain of corn, but *does the hen?*' . . . This story, nonsensical at the level of factual reality, where you are either a grain or not, is absolutely sensible if one replaces 'a grain' with some feature that determines my *symbolic* identity. Do not similar things happen all the time in our dealings with different levels of bureaucracy? Say a high-level office complies with my demand and gives me a higher title; however, it takes some time for the decree to be properly executed and reach the lower-level administration which actually takes care of the benefits from this title (higher salary, etc.) – we all know the frustration caused by a lower bureaucrat who casts a glance at the decree we confront him with and retorts indifferently: 'Sorry, I haven't been properly informed about this new measure yet, so I can't help you . . .'. Isn't this a bit like telling you: 'Sorry, to us you're still a grain of corn, not yet a human being'? In short, there is a certain mysterious moment at which a measure or a decree actually becomes operative, registered by the big Other of the symbolic institution.

The mysterious character of this moment can best be illustrated by a funny thing that happened during the last election campaign in Slovenia, when a member of the ruling political party was approached by an elderly lady from his local constituency, asking him for help. She was convinced that the street number of her house (not the standard 13, but 23) was bringing her bad luck – the moment her house got this new number, due to some administrative reorganization, misfortunes started to afflict her (burglars broke in, a storm tore the roof off, neighbours began to annoy her), so she asked the candidate to be so kind as to arrange with the municipal authorities for the number to be changed. The candidate made a simple suggestion to the lady: why didn't she do it alone? Why didn't she simply repaint or replace the plate with the street number herself by, for example, adding another number or letter (say, 23A or 231 instead of 23)? The old lady answered: 'Oh, I tried that a couple of weeks ago; I myself replaced the old plate with a new one with the number 23A, but *it didn't work* – my bad luck is still with me; you can't cheat it, it has to be done properly, by the relevant state institution.' The 'it' which cannot be duped in this way is the Lacanian big Other, the symbolic institution.

This, then, is what symbolic efficiency is about: it concerns the minimum of 'reification' on account of which it is not enough for us, all concerned individuals, to know some fact in order to be operative – 'it', the symbolic institution, must also know/'register' this fact if the performative consequences of stating it are to ensue. Ultimately this 'it', of course, can be embodied in the gaze of the absolute big Other, God Himself. That is to say: do we not encounter exactly the same problem as that of the unfortunate old lady with those Catholics who do not practise direct contraception but have intercourse only on days with no ovulation? Whom do they cheat in this way? As if God cannot read their thoughts and know that they really want to have sex for the mere pleasure of it, with no offspring in mind? The Church has always been extremely sensitive about this gap between mere existence and its proper inscription/registration: children who died before being christened were not allowed to be buried properly on consecrated ground, since they were not yet properly inscribed into the community of believers. 'Symbolic efficiency' thus concerns the point at which, when the Other of the symbolic institution confronts me with the choice of 'Whom do you believe, my word or your eyes?', I choose the Other's word without hesitation, dismissing the factual testimony of my eyes.[17]

The notion of the blockbuster provides an excellent example of the redoubling of the order of positive being in the order of naming, that is, of the symbolic inscription in the big Other. First, the term functioned as a direct description of a film which earned a lot of money; then it started to be used to describe a film made as a big production, with the prospect of a huge publicity campaign and big box-office receipts – such a film, of course, can later actually fail at the box office. So, with regard to the two *Postmans*, the Italian *Il Postino* and the failure with Kevin Costner, it is quite consistent to designate *The Postman* as *a failed blockbuster*, while *Il Postino* is not a blockbuster, although it earned a lot more money than *The Postman*. This gap can, of course, also generate rather droll consequences. In the Yugoslavia of the 1970s the subtitles, as a rule, *undertranslated* the vulgar expressions that abound in the Hollywood films of the period – say, when a character on screen says 'Fuck you up your ass!', the subtitle in Slovene read: 'Go to the Devil!' or something similarly moderate. In the late 1980s, however, when all censorship barriers came down in Yugoslavia, while Hollywood became slightly more restrained (perhaps under the influence of Reagan-era Moral Majority pressures), the translators, as if to take revenge for the long years of repression, started to *overtranslate* the vulgar expressions – say, when a character on screen uttered a simple 'Go to hell!', the subtitle read: 'Screw your mother down her throat!', or something similar. . . .

To put it in philosophical terms: symbolic inscription means that the very In-itself, the way a thing actually is, is already there for us, the observers. Take the two dead celebrities Princess Diana and Mother Teresa. According to the cliché, Diana, even when she was engaged in her charities, was basking in media attention, carefully manipulating mediatic dissemination of the innermost details of her private life (her secret patronage of the Morton biography); while Mother Teresa, a true saint, was silently doing her charitable job outside the media limelight, in the hellish slums of Calcutta. . . . The problem with this opposition, however, is that *we all knew about Mother Teresa silently doing her work outside the focus of the media* – this, precisely, is what she was famous for; this image of her created by the media is why she was received by heads of state and had a state funeral. . . . So the very opposition between Diana on a shopping spree with her new boyfriend and Mother Teresa taking care of mortally ill beggars in her grey Calcutta hospital is a mediatic opposition *par excellence.*

Here the gap between reality and the order of its symbolic registration is crucial – the gap on account of which symbolic registration is ultimately contingent. Let me mention the recent trend to portray the President of the USA as a brutal murderer (*Absolute Power, Murder at 1600*): this trend flouts a prohibition that was in force until quite recently: even a couple of years ago, a film like this would have been unthinkable. It is like the detective in a TV series who, sometime in the 1960s, was no longer required to be a noble figure: he could be a cripple, a gay, a woman. . . . This sudden apperception that the prohibition doesn't matter is crucial: you can have a President who is a murderer, but the presidency still retains its charisma. . . . This does not mean that it was simply 'like this all the time': it was like this *in* itself, but not *for* itself. If one had made a film like *Absolute Power* in the 1950s, the ideological impact would have been too traumatic; after the shift in the system of symbolic prohibition, the personal honesty of the President no longer matters, the system has accommodated to the change. . . .

With every social shift, one should look for this crucial symbolic change: in the hippie era, businessmen could wear jeans, be bearded, and so on, but nevertheless be ruthless profiteers. This moment of change is the crucial moment at which the system restructures its rules in order to accommodate itself to new conditions by incorporating the originally subversive moment. This, then, is the true underlying story beneath the disintegration of the Hayes Code of self-censorship in Hollywood – within a brief span in the 1960s, all of a sudden, 'everything became possible', the taboos were falling almost day by day (explicit references to drugs, to the sexual act, to homosexuality, to racial tension, up to the sympathetic portrayal of Communists); none the less, 'the system' survived intact: nothing really changed. Here capitalism is much more flexible than Communism, which was unable to afford such radical alleviations: when Gorbachev gradually tried to ease the constraints in order to strengthen the system, the system disintegrated.

The big Other is thus the order of the lie, of lying sincerely. Take Bill Clinton and Monica Lewinsky: we all know (or at least surmise) that they did it; nevertheless we support Clinton as long as this can be concealed from the big Other's gaze. . . . So here we have the paradox of the big Other at its purest. The majority of people believe there was something between the two of them; they believe that Clinton was lying when he denied it; none the less, they support him. Although (they assumed that) Clinton lied when he denied his sexual affair with 'that woman', Monica Lewinsky, he *lied sincerely*, with inner conviction, somehow believing in his very lie, taking it seriously – this paradox itself is to be taken quite seriously, since it designates the key element of the efficiency of an ideological statement. In other words, as long as Clinton's lie is not perceived/registered by the big Other, as long as it is possible for him to keep up appearances (of presidential 'dignity'), the very fact that we all know (or presume) that he is lying serves as a further ground for the public's identification with him – not only does the public's awareness that he is lying, and that there actually was something going on between him and Monica Lewinsky, not hurt his popularity, it even actively boosts it. One should never forget that the Leader's charisma is sustained by the very features (signs of weakness, of common 'humanity') that may seem to undermine it. This tension was deftly manipulated and brought to its extreme by Hitler: in his speeches in front of large crowds, he regularly staged the act of 'losing his cool', of engaging in a hysterical acting out, helplessly shouting and waving his hands, like a spoilt child frustrated by the fact that his demands are not immediately gratified – again, these very features which seemed to contradict the Leader's impassioned dignity sustained the crowd's identification with him.

All these paradoxes have a fundamental bearing on the way cyberspace affects the subject's symbolic identity. The poor madman who met a hen adopted the attitude of 'I know very well that I am a man, but . . . [does the big Other know it?]' – in short, he believed that the change in identity had not yet been registered by the big Other, that for the big Other he was still a grain of corn. Now, let us imagine a rather common case of a shy and inhibited man who, in cyberspace, participates in a virtual community in which he adopts the screen persona of a promiscuous woman; his stance, of course, is that of 'I know very well I am really just a shy, modest guy, so why shouldn't I briefly indulge in posing as a promiscuous woman, doing things I could never do in real life?' – however, are things really so simple and straightforward? What if this man's real-life persona (the Self he adopts, the way he behaves in his actual social interaction) is a kind of secondary 'defence-formation', an identity he adopts as a mask in order to 'repress' or keep at bay his true 'inner Self', the hard core of his phantasmic identity, which lies in being a promiscuous woman, and for which he can find an outlet only in his private daydreaming or in anonymous virtual community sexual games? In *Seminar XI*, Lacan mentions the old Chinese paradox of Tchuang-Tze, who awakens after dreaming that he is a butterfly, and then asks himself: 'How do I know I am not a butterfly who is now dreaming that he is a man?' Does not the same hold for our shy virtual community member: is he not in fact a promiscuous woman dreaming that she is an inhibited man?

The temptation to be avoided here is the easy 'postmodern' conclusion that we do not possess any ultimate fixed socio-symbolic identity, but are drifting, more or less freely, among an inconsistent multitude of Selves, each of them displaying a partial aspect of my personality, without any unifying agent guaranteeing the ultimate consistency of this 'pandemonium'. The Lacanian hypothesis of the big Other involves the claim that all these different partial identifications are not equivalent in their symbolic status: there is one level at which symbolic efficiency sets in, a level which determines my socio-symbolic position. This level is not that of 'reality' as opposed to the play of my imagination – Lacan's point is not that, behind the multiplicity of phantasmic identities, there is a hard core of some 'real Self'; we are dealing with a symbolic fiction, but a fiction which, for contingent reasons that have nothing to do with its inherent nature, possesses performative power – is socially operative, structures the socio-symbolic reality in which I participate. The status of the same person, inclusive of his/her very 'real' features, can appear in an entirely different light the moment the modality of his/her relationship to the big Other changes.

So the problem today is not that subjects are more dispersed than they were before, in the alleged good old days of the self-identical Ego; the fact that 'the big Other no longer exists' implies, rather, that the symbolic fiction which confers a performative status on one level of my identity, determining which of my acts will display 'symbolic efficiency', is no longer fully operative. Perhaps the supreme example of this shift is provided by the recent trends in Christianity. Christianity proper – the belief in Christ's Resurrection – is the highest religious expression of the power of symbolic fiction as the medium of universality: the death of the 'real' Christ is 'sublated' in the Holy Spirit, that is, in the spiritual community of believers. This authentic kernel of Christianity, first articulated by St Paul, is under attack today: the danger comes in the guise of the New Age Gnostic/dualist (mis)reading, which reduces the Resurrection to a metaphor of the 'inner' spiritual growth of the individual soul. What is lost thereby is the very central tenet of Christianity, already emphasized by Hegel: the break with the Old Testament logic of Sin and Punishment, that is, the belief in the *miracle* of Grace which retroactively 'undoes' our past sins. This is the 'good news' of the New Testament: the miracle of the *creatio ex nihilo*, of a New Beginning, of starting a new life 'from nothing', is possible. (*Creatio ex nihilo*, of course, is feasible only within a symbolic universe, as the establishment of a new symbolic fiction which erases the past one.) And the crucial point is that this New Beginning is possible only through Divine Grace – its impetus must come from *outside*; it is not the result of man's inner effort to overcome his/her limitations and elevate his/her soul above egotistic material interests; in this precise sense, the properly Christian New Beginning is absolutely incompatible with the pagan Gnostic problematic of the 'purification of the soul'. So what is actually at stake in recent New Age pop-Gnostic endeavours to reassert a kind of 'Christ's secret teaching' beneath the official Pauline dogma is the effort to undo the 'Event–Christ', reducing it to a continuation of the preceding Gnostic lineage.

Another important aspect of this Gnostic (mis)reading of Christianity is the growing obsession of popular pseudo-science with the mystery of Christ's alleged tomb and/or progeny (from his alleged marriage with Mary Magdalene) – bestsellers like *The Holy Blood and the Holy Grail* or *The Tomb of God*, which focus on the region around Rennes-le-Château in the south of France, weaving into a large coherent narrative the Grail myth, Cathars, Templars, Freemasons . . . : these narratives endeavour to supplant the diminishing power of the *symbolic fiction* of the Holy Spirit (the community of believers) with the *bodily Real* of Christ and/or his descendants. And again, the fact that Christ left his body or bodily descendants behind serves the purpose of undermining the Christian–Pauline narrative of Resurrection: Christ's body was not actually resurrected; 'the true message of Jesus was lost with the Resurrection'.[18] This 'true message' allegedly lies in promoting 'the path of self-determination, as distinct from obedience to the written word':[19] redemption results from the soul's inner journey, not from an act of pardon coming from outside; that is, 'Resurrection' is to be understood as the inner renewal/rebirth of the soul on its journey of self-purification. Although the advocates of this 'return of/in the Real' promote their discovery as the unearthing of the heretic and subversive secret long repressed by the Church as Institution, one could counter this claim with the question: what if this very unearthing of the 'Secret' is in the service of 'undoing', of getting rid of the truly traumatic, subversive core of Christian teaching, the *skandalon* of Resurrection and the retroactive forgiveness of sins – that is, the unique character of the Event of Resurrection?

These reversals signal that today, the big Other's nonexistence has attained a much more radical dimension: what is increasingly undermined is precisely the symbolic *trust* which persists against all sceptical data. Perhaps the most eye-catching facet of this new status of the nonexistence of the big Other is the sprouting of 'committees' destined to decide upon the so-called ethical dilemmas which crop up when technological developments ever-increasingly affect our life-world:[20] not only cyberspace but also domains as diverse as medicine and biogenetics on the one hand, and the rules of sexual conduct and the protection of human rights on the other, confront us with the need to invent the basic rules of proper ethical conduct, since we lack any form of big Other, any symbolic point of reference that would serve as a safe and unproblematic moral anchor.

In all these domains, the *différend* seems to be irreducible – that is to say, sooner or later we find ourselves in a grey zone whose mist cannot be dispelled by the application of some single universal rule. Here we encounter a kind of counterpoint to the 'uncertainty principle' of quantum physics; there is, for example, a structural difficulty in determining whether some comment was actually a case of sexual harassment or one of racist hate speech. Confronted with such a dubious statement, a 'politically correct' radical a priori tends to believe the complaining victim (if the victim experienced it as harassment, then harassment it was . . .), while a diehard orthodox liberal tends to believe the accused (if he sincerely did not mean it as harassment, then he should be acquitted . . .). The point, of course, is that this undecidability is structural and unavoidable, since it is the big Other (the symbolic network in which victim and offender are both embedded) which ultimately 'decides' on meaning, and the order of the big Other is, by definition, open; nobody can dominate and regulate its effects.

That is the problem with replacing aggressive with 'politically correct' expressions: when one replaces 'short-sighted' with 'visually challenged', one can never be sure that this replacement itself will not generate new effects of patronizing and/or ironic offensiveness, all the more humiliating inasmuch as it is masked as benevolence. The mistake of this 'politically correct' strategy is that it underestimates the resistance of the language we actually speak to the conscious regulation of its effects, especially effects that involve power relations. So to resolve the deadlock, one convenes a committee to formulate, in an ultimately arbitrary way, the precise rules of conduct.... It is the same with medicine and biogenetics (at what point does an acceptable and even desirable genetic experiment or intervention turn into unacceptable manipulation?), in the application of universal human rights (at what point does the protection of the victim's rights turn into an imposition of Western values?), in sexual *mores* (what is the proper, non-patriarchal procedure of seduction?), not to mention the obvious case of cyberspace (what is the status of sexual harassment in a virtual community? How does one distinguish here between 'mere words' and 'deeds'?). The work of these committees is caught in a symptomal vicious cycle: on the one hand, they try to legitimate their decisions by reference to the most advanced scientific knowledge (which, in the case of abortion, tells us that a foetus does not yet possess self-awareness and experience pain; which, in the case of a mortally ill person, defines the threshold beyond which euthanasia is the only meaningful solution); on the other hand, they have to evoke some non-scientific ethical criterion in order to direct and posit a limitation to inherent scientific drive.

The key point here is not to confuse this need to invent specific rules with the standard need of *phronesis* – that is, with the insight, formulated by Aristotle, into how direct application of universal norms to concrete situations is not possible – there is always a need to take into account the 'twist' given to the universal norm by the specific situation. In this standard case, we do have at our disposal some universally accepted 'sacred' Text which provides the horizon of our choices (say, the Bible in the Christian tradition), so that the problem of 'interpretation' is to reactualize the Text of tradition in each new situation, to discover how this Text still 'speaks to us' – today, it is precisely this universally accepted point of reference which is missing, so that we are thrown into a process of radically open and unending symbolic (re)negotiation and (re)invention without even the semblance of some preceding set of presupposed norms. Or – to put it in Hegelese – when I speak about the 'rules to be followed', I already presuppose a reflected attitude of strategically adapting myself to a situation by imposing certain rules on myself (and others) – what gets lost in adopting such an attitude is what Hegel called social *Substance*, the 'objective Spirit' as the true Substance of my being which is always-already there as the ground on which individuals thrive, although it is kept alive only through the incessant activity of those individuals. So when the proponents of virtual community enthusiastically describe the challenge that cyberspace poses to our capacity for ethical invention, for testing new rules of participation in all aspects of virtual community life, we should always bear in mind that these (re)invented rules *supplant the lack of a fundamental Law/Prohibition*: they endeavour to provide the viable frame of interaction for narcissistic post-Oedipal subjects. It is as if the lack of the big Other is supplanted by 'ethical committees' as so many substitute 'small big Others' on to which the subject transposes his responsibility and from which he expects to receive a formula that will resolve his deadlock.

It is crucial to distinguish between this decline of the symbolic paternal authority and the standard Oedipal gap that forever separates the real person of the father from its symbolic place/function – the fact that the real father always turns out to be an impostor, unable actually to live up to his symbolic mandate. As is well known, there lies the problem of the hysteric: the central figure of his universe is the 'humiliated father', that is, he is obsessed with the signs of the real father's weakness and failure, and criticizes him incessantly for not living up to his symbolic mandate – beneath the hysteric's rebellion and challenge to paternal authority there is thus a hidden call for a renewed paternal authority, for a father who would really be a 'true father' and adequately embody his symbolic mandate. Today, however, it is the very symbolic function of the father which is increasingly undermined – that is, which is losing its performative efficiency; for that reason, a father is no longer perceived as one's *Ego Ideal*, the (more or less failed, inadequate) bearer of symbolic authority, but as one's *ideal ego*, imaginary competitor – with the result that subjects never really 'grow up', that we are dealing today with individuals in their thirties and forties who remain, in terms of their psychic economy, 'immature' adolescents competing with their fathers.[21]

The Risk Society and Its Enemies

The fundamental deadlock embodied in the existence of different 'ethical committees' is the focus of the recently popular theory of the 'risk society'.[22] The paradigmatic examples of risks to which this theory refers are global warming, the hole in the ozone layer, mad cow disease, the danger of using nuclear power plants as the source of energy, the unforeseen consequences of the application of genetics to agriculture, and so on. All these cases exemplify what are usually referred to as 'low probability – high consequence' risks: no one knows how great the risks are; the probability of the global catastrophe is small – however, if the catastrophe does occur, it will be really terminal. Biologists warn us that the increased use of chemicals in our food and drugs can make the human race extinct not because of a direct ecological catastrophe, but simply by rendering us infertile – this outcome seems improbable, yet it would be catastrophic. The next crucial feature is that these new threats are so-called 'manufactured risks': they result from human economic, technological and scientific interventions into nature, which disrupt natural processes so radically that it is no longer possible to elude the responsibility by letting nature itself find a way to re-establish the lost balance. It is also absurd to resort to a New Age turn against science, since these threats are, for the most part, invisible, undetectable, without the diagnostic tools of science.

All today's notions of ecological threat, from the hole in the ozone layer to how fertilizers and chemical food additives are threatening our fertility, are strictly dependent on scientific insight (usually of the most advanced kind). Although the effects of the 'hole in the ozone layer' are observable, their causal explanation through reference to this 'hole' is a scientific hypothesis: there is no directly observable 'hole' up there in the sky. These risks are thus generated by a kind of self-reflexive loop, that is, they are not external risks (like a gigantic comet falling on Earth) but the unforeseen outcome of individuals' technological and scientific endeavour to control their lives and increase their productivity. Perhaps the supreme example of the dialectical reversal by means of which a new scientific insight, instead of simply magnifying our domination over nature, generates new risks and uncertainties is provided by the prospect that, in a decade or two, genetics will not only be able to identify an individual's complete genetic inheritance, but even manipulate individual genes technologically to effect the desired results and changes (to eradicate a tendency towards cancer, and so on). Far from resulting in total predictability and certainty, however, this very radical self-objectivization (the situation in which, in the guise of the genetic formula, I will be able to confront what I 'objectively am') will generate even more radical uncertainties about what the actual psychosocial effects of such knowledge and its applications will be. (What will become of the notions of freedom and responsibility? What will be the unforeseen consequences of meddling with genes?)

This conjunction of low probability and high consequence makes the standard Aristotelian strategy of avoiding both extremes virtually impossible: it is as if it is impossible today to assume a moderate rational position between scaremongering (ecologists who depict an impending universal catastrophe) and covering up (downplaying the dangers). The downplaying strategy can always emphasize the fact that scaremongering at best takes as certain conclusions which are not fully grounded in scientific observations; while the scaremongering strategy, of course, is fully justified in retorting that once it is possible to predict the catastrophe with full certainty, it will be, by definition, already too late. The problem is that there is no objective scientific or other way to acquire certainty about existence and extent: it is not simply a matter of exploitative corporations or government agencies downplaying the dangers – there is in fact no way to establish the extent of the risk with certainty; scientists and speculators themselves are unable to provide the final answer; we are bombarded daily by new discoveries which reverse previous common views. What if it turns out that fat really prevents cancer? What if global warming is actually the result of a natural cycle, and we should pump even more carbon dioxide into the atmosphere?

There is a priori no proper measure between the 'excess' of scaremongering and the indecisive procrastination of 'Don't let's panic, we don't yet have conclusive results'. For example, apropos of global warming, the logic of 'let us avoid both extremes, the careless further emission of carbon dioxide as well as the quick shutting-down of thousands of factories, and proceed gradually' is clearly meaningless.[23] Again, this impenetrability is not simply a matter of 'complexity', but of reflexivity: the new opaqueness and impenetrability (the radical uncertainty as to the ultimate consequences of our actions) is not due to the fact that we are puppets in the hands of some transcendent global Power (Fate, Historical Necessity, the Market); on the contrary, it is due to the fact that 'nobody is in charge', that *there is no such power*, no 'Other of the Other' pulling the strings – opaqueness is grounded in the very fact that today's society is thoroughly 'reflexive', that there is no Nature or Tradition providing a firm foundation on which one can rely, that even our innermost impetuses (sexual orientation, etc.) are more and more experienced as something to be chosen. How to feed and educate a child, how to proceed in sexual seduction, how and what to eat, how to relax and amuse oneself – all these spheres are increasingly 'colonized' by reflexivity, that is, experienced as something to be learned and decided upon. Is not the ultimate example of reflexivity in today's art the crucial role of the *curator*? His role is not limited to mere selection – through his selection, he (re)defines what art *is* today. That is to say: today's art exhibitions display objects which, at least for the traditional approach, have nothing to do with art, up to human excrement and dead animals – so why is this to be perceived as art? *Because what we see is the curator's choice.* When we visit an exhibition today, we are thus not directly observing works of art – what we are observing is the curator's notion of what art is; in short, the ultimate artist is not the producer but the curator, his activity of selection.

The ultimate deadlock of the risk society lies in the gap between knowledge and decision, between the chain of reasons and the act which resolves the dilemma (in Lacanese: between S_2 and S_1): there is no one who 'really knows' the global outcome – on the level of positive knowledge, the situation is radically 'indecidable'; but we none the less *have to decide*. Of course, this gap was there all the time: when an act of decision grounds itself in a chain of reasons, it always retroactively 'colours' these reasons so that they support this decision – just think of the believer who is well aware that the reasons for his belief are comprehensible only to those who have already decided to believe. . . . What we encounter in the contemporary risk society, however, is something much more radical: the opposite of the standard forced choice about which Lacan speaks, that is, of a situation in which I am free to choose on condition that I make the right choice, so that the only thing left for me to do is to accomplish the empty gesture of pretending to accomplish freely what is in any case imposed on me.[24] In the contemporary risk society, we are dealing with something entirely different: the choice is really 'free' and is, for this very reason, experienced as even more frustrating – we find ourselves constantly in the position of having to decide about matters that will fundamentally affect our lives, but without a proper foundation in knowledge.

What Ulrich Beck calls the 'second Enlightenment' is thus, with regard to this crucial point, the exact reversal of the aim of the 'first Enlightenment': to bring about a society in which fundamental decisions would lose their 'irrational' character and become fully grounded in good reasons (in a correct insight into the state of things): the 'second Enlightenment' imposes on each of us the burden of making crucial decisions which may affect our very survival without any proper foundation in Knowledge – all the expert government panels and ethical committees, and so on, are there to conceal this radical openness and uncertainty. Again, far from being experienced as liberating, this compulsion to decide freely is experienced as an anxiety-provoking obscene gamble, a kind of ironic reversal of predestination: I am held accountable for decisions which I was forced to make without proper knowledge of the situation. The freedom of decision enjoyed by the subject of the 'risk society' is not the freedom of someone who can freely choose his destiny, but the anxiety-provoking freedom of someone who is constantly compelled to make decisions without being aware of their consequences. There is no guarantee that the democratic politicization of crucial decisions, the active involvement of thousands of concerned individuals, will necessarily improve the quality and accuracy of decisions, and thus effectively lessen the risks – here one is tempted to evoke the answer of a devout Catholic to the atheist liberal criticism that they, Catholics, are so stupid as to believe in the infallibility of the Pope: 'We Catholics at least believe in the infallibility of *one* and only one person; does not democracy rely on a much more risky notion that the majority of the people, millions of them, are infallible?'

The subject thus finds himself in a Kafkaesque situation of being guilty of not even knowing what (if anything) he is guilty of: I am forever haunted by the prospect that I have already made decisions which will endanger me and everyone I love, but I will learn the truth only – if ever – when it is already too late. Here let us recall the figure of Forrest Gump, that perfect 'vanishing mediator', the very opposite of the Master (the one who symbolically registers an event by nominating it, by inscribing it into the big Other): Gump is presented as the innocent bystander who, simply by doing what he does, unknowingly sets in motion a shift of historic proportions. When he visits Berlin to play football, and inadvertently throws the ball across the wall, he thereby starts the process which brings down the wall; when he visits Washington and is given a room in the Watergate complex, he notices some strange things going on in the rooms across the yard in the middle of the night, calls the guard, and sets in motion the events which culminated in Nixon's downfall – is this not the ultimate metaphor for the situation at which the proponents of the notion of 'risk society' aim, a situation in which we are forced to make moves whose ultimate effects are beyond our grasp?

In what precise way does the notion of the 'risk society' involve the nonexistence of the big Other? The most obvious point would be the fact – emphasized again and again by Beck and Giddens – that today we live in a society which comes after Nature and Tradition: in our active engagement with the world around us, we can no longer rely either on Nature as the permanent foundation and resource of our activity (there is always the danger that our activity will disrupt and disturb the stable cycle of natural reproduction), or on Tradition as the substantial form of customs that predetermine our lives. However, the break is more radical. Although the dissolution of all traditional links is the standard theme of nineteenth-century capitalist modernization, repeatedly described by Marx (the 'all that is solid melts into air' theme), the whole point of Marx's analysis is that this unheard-of dissolution of all traditional forms, far from bringing about a society in which individuals run their lives collectively and freely, engenders its own form of anonymous Destiny in the guise of market relations. On the one hand, the market does involve a fundamental dimension of risk: it is an impenetrable mechanism which can, in a wholly unpredictable way, ruin the effort of an honest worker and make a sleazy speculator rich – nobody knows what the final outcome of speculation will be. However, although our acts can have unforeseen and unintended consequences, the notion still persists that they are co-ordinated by the infamous 'invisible hand of the market', the basic premiss of free-market ideology: each of us pursues his/her particular interests, and the ultimate result of this clash and interaction of the multiplicity of individual acts and conflicting intentions is global welfare. In this notion of the 'cunning of Reason', the big Other survives as the social Substance in which we all participate by our acts, as the mysterious spectral agency that somehow re-establishes the balance.

The fundamental Marxist idea, of course, is that this figure of the big Other, of the alienated social Substance – that is, the anonymous market as the modern form of Fate – can be superseded, and social life brought under the control of humanity's 'collective intellect'. In this way, Marx remained within the confines of the 'first modernization', which aimed at the establishment of a self-transparent society regulated by the 'collective intellect'; no wonder this project found its perverted realization in actually existing Socialism, which – despite the extreme uncertainty of an individual's fate, at least in the times of paranoiac political purges – was perhaps the most radical attempt to suspend the uncertainty that pertains to capitalist modernization. Real Socialism's (modest) appeal is best exemplified by the election slogan of Slobodan Milosevic's Socialist Party in the first 'free' elections in Serbia: 'With us, there is no uncertainty!' – although life was poor and drab, there was no need to worry about the future; everyone's modest existence was guaranteed; the Party took care of everything – that is, all decisions were made by Them. Despite their contempt for the regime, people none the less half-consciously trusted 'Them', relied on 'Them', believed that there was somebody holding all the reins and taking care of everything. There was actually a perverse kind of liberation in this possibility of shifting the burden of responsibility on to the Other. In her report on a voyage through post-Communist Poland, the country of her youth, Eva Hoffman relates how the infamous desolate greyness of the socialist environs, with depressing concrete buildings on broad streets without posters or neon lights, looked different, even more oppressive, in 1990:

> I know this grayness; I even used to love it, as part of the mood and weather with which one grew up here, and which sank into the bones with a comforting melancholy. Why, then, does it seem so much more desolate than before? I guess I'm looking at it with different antennae, without the protective filters of the system, which was the justification, the explanation for so much: even for the gray. Indeed, the drabness was partly Their doing, a matter not only of economics but of deliberate puritanism . . . now this neighbourhood is just what it is, bareness stripped of significance.[25]

What we have here is the perversely liberating aspect of alienation in actually existing Socialism: reality was not really 'ours' (the ordinary people's), it belonged to Them (the Party *nomenklatura*); its greyness bore witness to Their oppressive rule and, paradoxically, this made it much easier to endure life; jokes could be told about everyday troubles, about the lack of ordinary objects like soap and toilet paper – although we suffered the material consequences of these troubles, the jokes were at Their expense, we told them from an exempt, liberated position. Now, with Them out of power, we are suddenly and violently compelled to assume this drab greyness: it is no longer Theirs, it is ours. . . . What happens today, with the 'postmodern' risk society, is that there is no 'Invisible Hand' whose mechanism, blind as it may be, somehow re-establishes the balance; no Other Scene in which the accounts are properly kept, no fictional Other Place in which, from the perspective of the Last Judgement, our acts will be properly located and accounted for. Not only do we not know what our acts will in fact amount to, there is even no global mechanism regulating our interactions – *this* is what the properly 'postmodern' nonexistence of the big Other means. Foucault spoke of the 'strategies without subject' that Power uses in its reproduction – here we have almost the exact opposite: subjects caught in the unpredictable consequences of their acts, but no global strategy dominating and regulating their interplay. Individuals who are still caught in the traditional modernist paradigm are desperately looking for another agency which one could legitimately elevate into the position of the

Subject Supposed to Know, and which would somehow guarantee our choice: ethical committees, the scientific community itself, government authority, up to the paranoiac big Other, the secret invisible Master of conspiracy theories.

So what is wrong with the theory of the risk society? Does it not fully endorse the nonexistence of the big Other, and draw all ethico-political consequences from this? The problem is that, paradoxically, this theory is simultaneously too specific and too general: with all its emphasis on how the 'second modernization' forces us to transform old notions of human agency, social organization, and so on, up to the most intimate ways of relating to our sexual identity, the theory of the risk society nevertheless underestimates the impact of the emerging new societal logic on the very fundamental status of subjectivity; on the other hand, in conceiving of risk and manufactured uncertainty as a universal feature of contemporary life, this theory obfuscates the concrete socioeconomic roots of these risks. And it is my contention that psychoanalysis and Marxism, as a rule dismissed by theorists of the risk society as outdated expressions of the first-wave modernization (the fight of the rational agency to bring the impenetrable Unconscious to light; the idea of a self-transparent society controlled by the 'common intellect'), can contribute to a critical clarification of these two points.

The *Unbehagen* in the Risk Society

Psychoanalysis is neither a theory which bemoans the disintegration of the old modes of traditional stability and wisdom, locating in them the cause of modern neuroses and compelling us to discover our roots in old archaic wisdom or profound self-knowledge (the Jungian version), nor just another version of reflexive modern knowledge teaching us how to penetrate and master the innermost secrets of our psychic life – what psychoanalysis focuses on, its proper object, consists, rather, in the unexpected consequences of the disintegration of traditional structures that regulated libidinal life. Why does the decline of paternal authority and fixed social and gender roles generate new anxieties, instead of opening up a Brave New World of individuals engaged in the creative 'care of the Self' and enjoying the perpetual process of shifting and reshaping their fluid multiple identities? What psychoanalysis can do is to focus on the *Unbehagen* in the risk society: on the new anxieties generated by the risk society, which cannot be simply dismissed as the result of the tension or gap between the subjects' sticking to the old notions of personal responsibility and identity (like fixed gender roles and the family structure) and the new situation of fluid, shifting identities and choices.

What the advent of the 'risk society' affects is not simply Tradition or some other reliable symbolic frame of reference, but the symbolic Institution itself in the much more fundamental sense of the functioning of the symbolic order: with the advent of the risk society, the performative dimension of symbolic trust and commitment is potentially undermined. The problem with theorists of the risk society is thus that they underestimate the radical character of this change: with all their insistence on how, in today's risk society, reflexivity is universalized, so that Nature and Tradition no longer exist, in all their talk about the 'second Enlightenment' doing away with the naive certainties of the first wave of modernization, they leave intact the subject's fundamental mode of subjectivity: their subject remains the modern subject, able to reason and reflect freely, to decide on and select his/her set of norms, and so on. Here, the error is the same as that of feminists who want to do away with the Oedipus complex, and so on, and nevertheless expect the basic form of subjectivity that was generated by the Oedipus complex (the subject free to reason and decide, etc.) to survive intact. In short, what if it is not the postmodern pessimists who come to their catastrophic conclusion because they measure the new world with old standards; what if, on the contrary, it is theorists of the risk society themselves who unproblematically rely on the fact that, in the conditions of the disintegration of symbolic Trust, the reflexive subject of the Enlightenment somehow, inexplicably, survives intact?

This disintegration of the big Other is the direct result of universalized reflexivity: notions like 'trust' all rely on a minimum of *non-reflected* acceptance of the symbolic Institution – ultimately, trust always involves a leap of faith: when I trust somebody, I trust him because I simply take him at his word, not for rational reasons which tell me to trust him. To say 'I trust you because I have decided, upon rational reflection, to trust you,' involves the same paradox as the statement 'Having weighed up the reasons for and against, I decided to obey my father.' Symptomatic of this disintegration of fundamental Trust is the recent rise of a US Christian revival group that quite adequately calls itself 'the Promise-Keepers': their plea is a desperate appeal to men to assume again their symbolic mandate of responsibility, of the burden of decision, against the weak and hysterical female sex unable to cope with the stresses of contemporary life. The point to be made against this is not only that we are dealing with the conservative patriarchal reinscription of the sexual difference (weak hysterical women versus men whose Word should again become their Bond), but that the way in which this very explicit emphasis on promises to be kept is already part of a hysterical economy – a trust which has to be reasserted in this public ritualized way, as it were, undermines its own credentials.

The inability of risk society theory to take all the consequences of global reflexivization into account is clearly discernible in its treatment of the family. This theory is right to emphasize how the relationship between parents and children in the traditional family was the last bastion of legal slavery in our Western societies: a large stratum of society – minors – were denied full responsibility and autonomy, and retained in a slave status with regard to their parents (who controlled their lives and were responsible for their acts). With reflexive modernization, children themselves are treated as responsible subjects with freedom of choice (in divorce procedures, they are allowed to influence the decision on which of the two parents they will live with; they can start a court procedure against their parents if they feel that their human rights have been violated; etc.) – in short, parenthood is no longer a natural-substantial notion, but becomes in a way politicized; it turns into another domain of reflexive choice. However, is not the obverse of this reflexivization of family relations, in which the family loses its character of immediate-substantial entity whose members are not autonomous subjects, the progressive *'familialization'* of public professional life itself? Institutions which were supposed to function as an antidote to the family start to function as surrogate families, allowing us somehow to prolong our family dependence and immaturity: schools – even universities – increasingly assume therapeutic functions; corporations provide a new family home, and so on. The standard situation in which, after the period of education and dependency, I am allowed to enter the adult universe of maturity and responsibility is thus doubly turned around: as a child I am already recognized as a mature responsible being; and, simultaneously, my childhood is prolonged indefinitely, that is, I am never really compelled to 'grow up', since all the institutions which follow the family function as *ersatz* families, providing caring surroundings for my Narcissistic endeavours. . . .

In order to grasp all the consequences of this shift, one would have to return to Hegel's triad of family, civil society (free interaction of individuals who enjoy their reflexive freedom) and State: Hegel's construction is based on the distinction between the private sphere of family and the public sphere of civil society, a distinction which is vanishing today, in so

far as family life itself becomes politicized, is turning into part of the
public domain; on the other hand, public professional life becomes
'familialized', that is, subjects participate in it as members of a large
family, not as responsible 'mature' individuals. So the problem here is not
patriarchal authority and the emancipatory struggle against it, as most
feminists continue to claim; the problem, rather, is the new forms of
dependency that arise from the very decline of patriarchal symbolic
authority. It was Max Horkheimer, in his study on authority and family in
the 1930s, who drew attention to the ambiguous consequences of the
gradual disintegration of paternal authority in modern capitalist society:
far from being simply the elementary cell and generator of authoritarian
personalities, the modern nuclear family was simultaneously the structure
that generated the 'autonomous' critical subject able to confront the
predominant social order on account of his/her ethical convictions, so
that the immediate result of the disintegration of paternal authority is
also the rise of what sociologists call the conformist 'other-orientated'
personality.[26] Today, with the shift towards the narcissistic personality, this
process is even stronger, and has entered a new phase.

With regard to the 'postmodern' constellation (or to what the theorists
of the risk society call reflexive modernization characteristic of the second
modernity and/or the second Enlightenment – perhaps their overinsistent
emphasis on how they are opposed to postmodernism is to be read as a
disavowal of their unacknowledged proximity to it[27]), in which patriarchy
is fatally undermined, so that the subject experiences himself as freed
from any traditional constraints, lacking any internalized symbolic Prohibition, bent on experimenting with his life and on pursuing his life-
project, and so on, we have therefore to raise the momentous question of
the disavowed 'passionate attachments' which support the new reflexive
freedom of the subject delivered from the constraints of Nature and/or
Tradition: what if the disintegration of the public ('patriarchal') symbolic
authority is paid for (or counterbalanced) by an even stronger disavowed
'passionate attachment' to subjection, as – among other phenomena – the
growth of sado-maso lesbian couples where the relationship between the
two women follows the strict and severely enacted Master/Slave matrix
seems to indicate: the one who gives the orders is the 'top', the one who
obeys is the 'bottom', and in order to become the 'top' one has to go
through an arduous process of apprenticeship. While it is wrong to read
this 'top/bottom' duality as a sign of direct 'identification with the (male)
aggressor', it is no less wrong to perceive it as a parodic imitation of
patriarchal relations of domination; we are dealing, rather, with the

genuine paradox of the freely chosen Master/Slave form of coexistence which provides a deep libidinal satisfaction.

Thus the standard situation is reversed: we no longer have the public Order of hierarchy, repression and severe regulation, subverted by secret acts of liberating transgression (as when we laugh at our pompous Master privately, behind his back); on the contrary, we have public social relations among free and equal individuals, where the 'passionate attachment' to some extreme form of strictly regulated domination and submission becomes the secret transgressive source of libidinal satisfaction, the obscene supplement to the public sphere of freedom and equality. The rigidly codified Master/Slave relationship turns up as the very form of 'inherent transgression' of subjects living in a society in which all forms of life are experienced as a matter of the free choice of a lifestyle. And this paradoxical reversal is the proper topic of psychoanalysis: psychoanalysis deals not with the severe authoritarian father who forbids you to enjoy, but with the obscene father who enjoins you to enjoy, and thus renders you impotent or frigid much more effectively. The Unconscious is not secret resistance against the Law; the Unconscious is the prohibitive Law itself.

So the answer of psychoanalysis to the risk society *topos* of the global reflexivization of our lives is not that there is none the less some pre-reflexive substance called the Unconscious which resists reflexive mediation; the answer is to emphasize another mode of reflexivity that is neglected by theorists of the risk society, the reflexivity at the very core of the Freudian subject. This reflexivity spoils the game of the postmodern subject free to choose and reshape his identity. As we have already seen, there are numerous variations on this reflexivity in psychoanalysis: in hysteria, the impossibility of satisfying desire is reflexively inverted into the desire for nonsatisfaction, the desire to maintain desire itself unsatisfied; in obsessional neurosis, we are dealing with the reversal of the 'repressive' regulation of desire into the desire for regulation – this 'masochistic' reflexive turn, through which the repressive regulatory procedures themselves are libidinally invested and function as a source of libidinal satisfaction, provides the key to how power mechanisms function: regulatory power mechanisms remain operative only in so far as they are secretly sustained by the very element they endeavour to 'repress'.

Perhaps the ultimate example of the universalized reflexivity of our lives (and thereby of the retreat of the big Other, the loss of symbolic efficiency) is a phenomenon known to most psychoanalysts today: the growing inefficiency of psychoanalytic *interpretation*. Traditional psychoanalysis still relied on a substantial notion of the Unconscious as the non-reflected 'dark continent', the impenetrable 'decentred' Substance of the subject's being to be arduously penetrated, reflected, mediated, by interpretation. Today, however, the formations of the Unconscious (from dreams to hysterical symptoms) have definitely lost their innocence: the 'free associations' of a typical educated analysand consist for the most part of attempts to provide a psychoanalytic explanation of their disturbances, so that one is quite justified in saying that we have not only Jungian, Kleinian, Lacanian ... interpretations of the symptoms, but symptoms which are themselves Jungian, Kleinian, Lacanian ... , that is, whose reality involves implicit reference to some psychoanalytic theory. The unfortunate result of this global reflexivization of interpretation (everything becomes interpretation, the Unconscious interprets itself . . .) is, of course, that the analyst's interpretation loses its performative 'symbolic efficiency' and leaves the symptom intact in its idiotic *jouissance*. In other words, what happens in psychoanalytic treatment is similar to the paradox (already noted) of a neo-Nazi skinhead who, when really pressed to give the reasons for his violence, suddenly starts to talk like social workers, sociologists and social psychologists, quoting diminished social mobility, rising insecurity, the disintegration of paternal authority, lack of maternal love in his early childhood – when the big Other *qua* the substance of our social being disintegrates, the unity of practice and its inherent reflection disintegrates into raw violence and its impotent, inefficient interpretation.

This impotence of interpretation is also one of the necessary obverses of the universalized reflexivity hailed by risk society theorists: it is as if our reflexive power can flourish only in so far as it draws its strength from and relies on some minimal 'pre-reflexive' substantial support which eludes its grasp, so that its universalization is paid for by its inefficiency, that is, by the paradoxical re-emergence of the brute Real of 'irrational' violence, impermeable and insensitive to reflexive interpretation. And the tragedy is that, faced with this deadlock of the inefficiency of their interpretative interventions, even some psychoanalysts who otherwise resist the obvious false solution of abandoning the domain of psychoanalysis proper and taking refuge in biochemistry or body training are tempted to take the direct way of the Real: they emphasize that since the Unconscious is already its own interpretation, all the psychoanalyst can do is *act* – so, instead of the patient acting (say, producing *actes manqués*) and the analyst interpreting the patient's acts, we get a patient interpreting and his analyst introducing a cut into this flow of interpretation with an act (say, of closing the session).[28]

So, in terms of the Frankfurt School, the choice we are facing apropos of the second modernity is again that between Adorno/Horkheimer and Habermas. Habermas's crucial break with Adorno and Horkheimer is to reject their fundamental notion of the *dialectic* of Enlightenment: for Habermas, phenomena like totalitarian political regimes or the so-called alienation of modern life are ultimately generated not by the inherent dialectics of the very project of modernity and Enlightenment, but by its nonconsequent realization – they bear witness to the fact that modernity remained an unfinished project. In contrast, Adorno and Horkheimer remain faithful to the old Hegelian and Marxist dialectical procedure of reading the troubling excess that occurs in the realization of some global project as the symptomal point at which the truth of the entire project emerges: the only way to reach the truth of some notion or project is to focus on where this project went wrong.

It's the *Political* Economy, Stupid!

As for the socioeconomic relations of domination that go with the 'postmodern' constellation, the public image of Bill Gates is worthy of some comment;[29] what matters is not factual accuracy (is Gates really like that?) but the very fact that a certain figure started to function as an icon, filling some phantasmic slot – if the features do not correspond to the 'true' Gates, they are all the more indicative of the underlying phantasmic structure. Gates is not only no longer the patriarchal Father–Master, he is also no longer the corporate Big Brother running a rigid bureaucratic empire, dwelling on the inaccessible top floor, guarded by a host of secretaries and deputees. He is, rather, a kind of *little brother*: his very ordinariness functions as the indication of its opposite, of some monstrous dimension so uncanny that it can no longer be rendered public in the guise of some symbolic title. What we encounter here, most violently, is the deadlock of the Double who is simultaneously like ourselves *and* the harbinger of an uncanny, properly monstrous dimension – indicative of this is the way title-pages, drawings or photomontages present Gates: as an ordinary guy, whose devious smile none the less implies a wholly different underlying dimension of monstrosity beyond representation which threatens to shatter his ordinary-guy image.[30] In this respect, it is also a crucial feature of Gates-as-icon that he is (perceived as) the ex-hacker who made it – one should confer on the term 'hacker' all its subversive/marginal/anti-establishment connotations of those who want to disturb the smooth functioning of large bureaucratic corporations. At the phantasmic level, the underlying notion here is that Gates is a subversive marginal hooligan who has taken over and dresses himself up as a respectable chairman.

In Bill Gates, the Little Brother, the average ugly guy, thus coincides with and contains the figure of the Evil Genius who aims for total control of our lives. In old James Bond movies this Evil Genius was still an eccentric figure, dressed up extravagantly or in a proto-Communist Maoist grey uniform – in the case of Gates, this ridiculous charade is no longer needed; the Evil Genius turns out to be the obverse of the ordinary guy next door. In other words, what we encounter in the icon of Bill Gates is a kind of reversal of the theme of the hero endowed with supernatural powers, but in his everyday life a common, confused, clumsy guy (Superman, who in his ordinary existence is a clumsy bespectacled journalist): here it is the bad guy who is characterized by this kind of split.[31] The ordinariness of Bill Gates is thus not of the same order as the emphasis on the so-called ordinary human features of the traditional patriarchal Master. The fact that this traditional Master never lived up to his mandate – that he was always imperfect, marked by some failure or weakness – not only did not impede his symbolic authority, but even served as its support, bringing home the constitutive gap between the purely formal function of symbolic authority and the empirical individual who occupies its post. In contrast to this gap, Bill Gates's ordinariness points to a different notion of authority, that of the obscene superego that operates in the Real.

There is an old European fairy-tale theme of diligent dwarves (usually controlled by an evil magician) who during the night, while people are asleep, emerge from their hiding-place and accomplish their work (put the house in order, cook the meals . . .) so that when people wake up in the morning, they find their work magically done. This theme persists through Richard Wagner's *Rhinegold* (the Nibelungs who work in their underground caves, driven by their cruel master, the dwarf Alberich) to Fritz Lang's *Metropolis*, in which the enslaved industrial workers live and work deep beneath the earth's surface to produce wealth for the ruling capitalists. This matrix of 'underground' slaves dominated by a manipulative evil Master brings us back to the old duality of the two modes of the Master, the public symbolic Master and the secret Evil Magician who actually pulls the strings and does his work during the night: are not the two Bills who now run the USA, Clinton and Gates, the ultimate exemplifications of this duality? When the subject is endowed with symbolic authority, he acts as an appendix to his symbolic title – that is to say, it is the big Other, the symbolic Institution, which acts through him: recall our previous example of a judge, who may be a miserable and corrupt person, but the moment he puts on his robe and other insignia, his words are the words of the Law itself. On the other hand, the 'invisible' Master (whose paradigmatic case is the anti-Semitic figure of the 'Jew' who, invisible to the public eye, pulls the strings of social life) is a kind of uncanny double of public authority: he has to act in shadow, irradiating a phantom-like, spectral omnipotence.[32]

This, then, is the conclusion to be drawn from the Bill Gates icon: how the disintegration of the patriarchal symbolic authority, of the Name-of-the-Father, gives rise to a new figure of the Master who is simultaneously our common peer, our fellow-creature, our imaginary double, and – *for this very reason* – phantasmically endowed with another dimension of the Evil Genius. In Lacanian terms: the suspension of the Ego Ideal, of the feature of symbolic identification – that is, the reduction of the Master to an imaginary ideal – necessarily gives rise to its monstrous obverse, to the superego figure of the omnipotent Evil Genius who controls our lives. In this figure, the imaginary (semblance) and the real (of paranoia) overlap, owing to the suspension of the proper symbolic efficiency.

The point of insisting that we are dealing with Bill Gates as an icon is that it would be mystifying to elevate the 'real' Gates into a kind of Evil Genius who masterminds a plot to achieve global control over us all. Here, more than ever, it is crucial to remember the lesson of the Marxist dialectic of fetishization: the 'reification' of relations between people (the fact that they assume the form of phantasmagorical 'relations between things') is always redoubled by the apparently opposite process – by the false 'personalization' ('psychologization') of what are in fact objective social processes. It was in the 1930s that the first generation of Frankfurt School theoreticians drew attention to how – at the very moment when global market relations started to exert their full domination, making the individual producer's success or failure dependent on market cycles totally out his of control – the notion of a charismatic 'business genius' reasserted itself in 'spontaneous capitalist ideology', attributing the success or failure of a businessman to some mysterious *je ne sais quoi* which he possesses.[33] And does not the same hold even more today, when the abstraction of market relations that run our lives is brought to an extreme? The book market is overflowing with psychological manuals advising us on how to succeed, how to outdo our partner or competitor – in short, making our success dependent on our proper 'attitude'.

So, in a way, one is tempted to reverse Marx's famous formula: in contemporary capitalism, *the objective market 'relations between things' tend to assume the phantasmagorical form of pseudo-personalized 'relations between people'*. No, Bill Gates is no genius, good or bad, he is just an opportunist who knew how to seize the moment and, as such, the result of the capitalist system run amok. The question is not 'How did Gates do it?' but 'How is the capitalist system structured, what is wrong with it, that an individual can achieve such disproportionate power?' A phenomenon like that of Bill Gates thus seems to indicate its own solution: once we are dealing with a gigantic global network formally owned by a single individual or corporation, is it not a fact that ownership becomes, in a way, irrelevant to its functioning (there is no longer any worthwhile competition; profit is guaranteed), so that it becomes possible simply to cut off this head and to socialize the entire network without greatly disturbing its functioning? Does not such an act amount to a purely formal conversion that simply brings together what, *de facto*, already belongs together – the collective of individuals and the global communicational network they are all using – and which thus forms the substance of their social lives?

This already brings us to the second aspect of our critical distance towards risk society theory: the way it approaches the reality of capitalism. Is it not that, on closer examination, its notion of 'risk' indicates a narrow and precisely defined domain in which risks are generated: the domain of the uncontrolled use of science and technology in the conditions of capitalism? The paradigmatic case of 'risk', which is not simply one among many but risk 'as such', is that of a new scientific-technological invention put to use by a private corporation without proper public democratic debate and control, then generating the spectre of unforeseen catastrophic long-term consequences. However, is not this kind of risk rooted in the fact that the logic of market and profitability is driving privately owned corporations to pursue their course and use scientific and technological innovations (or simply expand their production) without actually taking account of the long-term effects of such activity on the environment, as well as the health of humankind itself?

Thus – despite all the talk about a 'second modernity' which compels us to leave the old ideological dilemmas of Left and Right, of capitalism versus socialism, and so on, behind – is not the conclusion to be drawn that in the present global situation, in which private corporations outside public political control are making decisions which can affect us all, even up to our chances of survival, the only solution lies in a kind of direct socialization of the productive process – in moving towards a society in which global decisions about the fundamental orientation of how to develop and use productive capacities at the disposal of society would somehow be made by the entire collective of the people affected by such decisions? Theorists of the risk society often evoke the need to counteract the reign of the 'depoliticized' global market with a move towards radical *repoliticization*, which will take crucial decisions away from state planners and experts and put them into the hands of the individuals and groups concerned themselves (through the revitalization of active citizenship, broad public debate, and so on) – however, they stop short of putting in question the very basics of the anonymous logic of market relations and global capitalism, which imposes itself today more and more as the 'neutral' Real accepted by all parties and, as such, more and more depoliticized.[34]

Two recent English films, both stories about the traumatic disintegration of old-style working-class male identity, express two opposing versions of this deadlock of depoliticization. *Brassed Off* focuses on the relationship between 'real' political struggle (the miners' struggle against threatened pit closures legitimized in terms of technological progress) and the idealized symbolic expression of the miners' community, their brass band. At first, the two aspects seem to be opposed: to the miners caught up in the struggle for economic survival, the 'Only music matters!' attitude of their old bandmaster dying of lung cancer looks like a vain fetishized insistence on the empty symbolic form deprived of its social substance. Once the miners lose their political struggle, however, the 'Music matters' attitude, their insistence on playing and participating in a national competition, turns into a defiant symbolic gesture, a proper act of asserting fidelity to their political struggle – as one of them puts it, when there's no hope, there are only principles to follow. . . . In short, the *act* occurs when we reach this crisscross or, rather, short circuit of levels, so that insistence on the empty form itself (we'll continue playing in our brass band, whatever happens . . .) becomes the sign of fidelity to the content (to the struggle against the closures, for the continuation of the miners' way of life). The miners' community belongs to a tradition condemned to disappear – none the less, it is precisely here that one should avoid the trap of accusing the miners of standing for the old reactionary male-chauvinist working-class way of life: the principle of community discernible here is well worth fighting for, and should by no means be left to the enemy.

The Full Monty, our second example, is – like *Dead Poets Society* or *City Lights* – one of those films whose entire narrative line moves towards its final climactic moment – in this case, the five unemployed men's 'full Monty' appearance in the striptease club. Their final gesture – 'going to the end', revealing their penises to the packed hall – involves an act which – although in a way opposite to that of *Brassed Off* – ultimately amounts to the same thing: to the acceptance of the loss. The heroism of the final gesture in *The Full Monty* is not that of persisting in the symbolic form (playing in the band) when its social substance disintegrates but, on the contrary, of accepting what, from the perspective of the male working-class ethic, cannot but appear as the ultimate humiliation: readily giving away false male dignity. (Recall the famous bit of dialogue near the beginning, when one of the heroes says that after seeing women urinating in a standing position, he finally understands that they are lost; that their – men's – time is over.) The tragicomic dimension of their predicament lies in the fact that the carnivalesque spectacle (of stripping) is performed not by the usual well-endowed striptease dancers but by ordinary decent and shy middle-aged men who are definitely not beautiful – their *heroism* is that they agree to perform the act, although they are aware that their physical appearance is not appropriate to it. This gap between the performance and the obvious inappropriateness of the performers confers on the act its properly sublime dimension – from the vulgar amusement of stripping, their act becomes a kind of spiritual exercise in abandoning false pride. (Although the oldest among them, their ex-foreman, is informed, just prior to their show, that he has got a new job, he nevertheless decides to join his mates in the act out of fidelity: the point of the show is thus not merely to earn the much-needed money, but a matter of principle.)

What one should bear in mind, however, is that both acts, that of *Brassed Off* and that of *The Full Monty*, are the acts of losers – that is to say, two modes of coming to terms with the catastrophic loss: insisting on the empty form as fidelity to the lost content ('When there's no hope, only principles remain'); heroically renouncing the last vestiges of false narcissistic dignity and accomplishing the act for which one is grotesquely inadequate. And the sad thing is that, in a way, this is our situation today: today, after the breakdown of the Marxist notion that capitalism itself generates the force that will destroy it in the guise of the proletariat, none of the critics of capitalism, none of those who describe so convincingly the deadly vortex into which the so-called process of globalization is drawing us, has any well-defined notion of how we can get rid of capitalism. In short, I am not preaching a simple return to the old notions of class struggle and socialist revolution: the question of how it is really possible to undermine the global capitalist system is not a rhetorical one – maybe it is *not* really possible, at least not in the foreseeable future.

So there are two attitudes: either today's Left nostalgically engages in the ritualistic incantation of old formulas, be it those of revolutionary Communism or those of welfare state reformist Social Democracy, dismissing all talk of new postmodern society as empty fashionable prattle that obfuscates the harsh reality of today's capitalism; or it accepts global capitalism as 'the only game in town', and follows the double tactics of promising the employees that the maximum possible welfare state will be maintained, and the employers that the rules of the (global capitalist) game will be fully respected and the employees' 'irrational' demands firmly censored. So, in today's leftist politics, we seem in effect to be reduced to the choice between the 'solid' orthodox attitude of proudly, out of principle, sticking to the old (Communist or Social Democratic) tune, although we know its time has passed, and the New Labour 'radical centre' attitude of going the 'full Monty' in stripping, getting rid of, the last vestiges of proper leftist discourse. . . . Paradoxically, the ultimate victim of the demise of Really Existing Socialism was thus its great historical opponent throughout most of our century, reformist Social Democracy itself.

The big news of today's post-political age of the 'end of ideology' is thus the radical depoliticization of the sphere of the economy: the way the economy functions (the need to cut social welfare, etc.) is accepted as a simple insight into the objective state of things. However, as long as this fundamental depoliticization of the economic sphere is accepted, all the talk about active citizenship, about public discussion leading to responsible collective decisions, and so on, will remain limited to the 'cultural' issues of religious, sexual, ethnic and other way-of-life differences, without actually encroaching upon the level at which long-term decisions that affect us all are made. In short, the only way effectively to bring about a society in which risky long-term decisions would ensue from public debate involving all concerned is some kind of radical limitation of Capital's freedom, the subordination of the process of production to social control – the radical *repoliticization of the economy*. That is to say: if the problem with today's post-politics ('administration of social affairs') is that it increasingly undermines the possibility of a proper political act, this undermining is directly due to the depoliticization of economics, to the common acceptance of Capital and market mechanisms as neutral tools/ procedures to be exploited.

We can now see why today's post-politics cannot attain the properly political dimension of universality: because it silently precludes the sphere of economy from politicization. The domain of global capitalist market relations is the Other Scene of the so-called repoliticization of civil society advocated by the partisans of 'identity politics' and other postmodern forms of politicization: all the talk about new forms of politics bursting out all over, focused on particular issues (gay rights, ecology, ethnic minorities . . .), all this incessant activity of fluid, shifting identities, of building multiple *ad hoc* coalitions, and so on, has something inauthentic about it, and ultimately resembles the obsessional neurotic who talks all the time and is otherwise frantically active precisely in order to ensure that something – what *really matters* – will *not* be disturbed, that it will remain immobilized.[35] So, instead of celebrating the new freedoms and responsibilities brought about by the 'second modernity', it is much more crucial to focus on what *remains the same* in this global fluidity and reflexivity, on what serves as the very motor of this fluidity: the inexorable logic of Capital. The spectral presence of Capital is the figure of the big Other which not only remains operative when all the traditional embodiments of the symbolic big Other disintegrate, but even directly causes this disintegration: far from being confronted with the abyss of their freedom – that is, laden with the burden of responsibility that cannot be alleviated by the helping hand of Tradition or Nature – today's subject is perhaps more than ever caught in an inexorable compulsion that effectively runs his life.

The irony of history is that, in the Eastern European ex-Communist countries, the 'reformed' Communists were the first to learn this lesson. Why did many of them return to power via free elections in the mid 1990s? This very return offers the ultimate proof that these states have in fact entered capitalism. That is to say: what do ex-Communists stand for today? Due to their privileged links with the newly emerging capitalists (mostly members of the old *nomenklatura* 'privatizing' the companies they once ran), they are first and foremost the party of big Capital; furthermore, to erase the traces of their brief but none the less rather traumatic experience with politically active civil society, they as a rule ferociously advocate a quick deideologization, a retreat from active civil society engagement into passive, apolitical consumerism – the very two features which characterize contemporary capitalism. So dissidents are astonished to discover that they played the role of 'vanishing mediators' on the way from socialism to capitalism, in which the same class as before rules under a new guise. It is therefore wrong to claim that the ex-Communists' return to power shows how people are disappointed by capitalism and long for the old socialist security – in a kind of Hegelian 'negation of negation', it is only with the ex-Communists' return to power that socialism was effectively negated – that is to say, what the political analysts (mis)perceive as 'disappointment with capitalism' is in fact disappointment with the ethico-political enthusiasm for which there is no place in 'normal' capitalism.[36] We should thus reassert the old Marxist critique of 'reification': today, emphasizing the depoliticized 'objective' economic logic against allegedly 'outdated' forms of ideological passions is *the* predominant ideological form, since ideology is always self-referential, that is, it always defines itself through a distance towards an Other dismissed and denounced as 'ideological'.[37] For that precise reason – because *the depoliticized economy is the disavowed 'fundamental fantasy' of postmodern politics* – a properly political *act* would necessarily entail the repoliticization of the economy: within a given situation, a gesture counts as an *act* only in so far as it disturbs ('traverses') its fundamental fantasy.

In so far as today's moderate Left, from Blair to Clinton, fully accepts this depoliticization, we are witnessing a strange reversal of roles: the only serious political force which continues to question the unrestrained rule of the market is the populist extreme Right (Buchanan in the USA; Le Pen in France). When Wall Street reacted negatively to a fall in the unemployment rate, the only one to make the obvious point that what is good for Capital is obviously not what is good for the majority of the population was Buchanan. In contrast to the old wisdom according to which the extreme Right openly says what the moderate Right secretly thinks, but doesn't dare say in public (the open assertion of racism, of the need for strong authority and the cultural hegemony of 'Western values', etc.), we are therefore approaching a situation in which the extreme Right openly says what the moderate *Left* secretly thinks, but doesn't dare say in public (the necessity to curb the freedom of Capital).

One should also not forget that today's rightist survivalist militias often look like a caricaturized version of the extreme militant leftist splinter groups of the 1960s: in both cases we are dealing with radical anti-institutional logic – that is, the ultimate enemy is the repressive State apparatus (the FBI, the Army, the judicial system) which threatens the group's very survival, and the group is organized as a tight disciplined body in order to be able to withstand this pressure. The exact counterpoint to this is a Leftist like Pierre Bourdieu, who defends the idea of a unified Europe as a strong 'social state', guaranteeing the minimum of social rights and welfare against the onslaught of globalization: it is difficult to abstain from irony when one sees a radical Leftist raising barriers against the corrosive global power of Capital, so fervently celebrated by Marx. So, again, it is as if the roles are reversed today: Leftists support a strong State as the last guarantee of social and civil liberties against Capital; while Rightists demonize the State and its apparatuses as the ultimate terrorist machine.

Of course, one should fully acknowledge the tremendous liberating impact of the postmodern politicization of domains which were hitherto considered apolitical (feminism, gay and lesbian politics, ecology, ethnic and other so-called minority issues): the fact that these issues not only became perceived as inherently political but also gave birth to new forms of political subjectivization thoroughly reshaped our entire political and cultural landscape. So the point is not to play down this tremendous advance in favour of the return to some new version of so-called economic essentialism; the point is, rather, that the depoliticization of the economy generates the populist New Right with its Moral Majority ideology, which today is the main obstacle to the realization of the very (feminist, ecological . . .) demands on which postmodern forms of political subjectivization focus. In short, I am pleading for a 'return to the primacy of the economy' not to the detriment of the issues raised by postmodern forms of politicization, but precisely in order to create the conditions for the more effective realization of feminist, ecological, and so on, demands.

A further indicator of the necessity for some kind of politicization of the economy is the overtly 'irrational' prospect of concentrating quasi-monopolistic power in the hands of a single individual or corporation, like Rupert Murdoch or Bill Gates. If the next decade brings the unification of the multitude of communicative media in a single apparatus reuniting the features of interactive computer, TV, video- and audiophone, video and CD player, and if Microsoft actually succeeds in becoming the quasi-monopolistic owner of this new universal medium, controlling not only the language used in it but also the conditions of its application, then we obviously approach the absurd situation in which a single agent, exempt from public control, will in effect dominate the basic communicational structure of our lives and will thus, in a way, be stronger than any government. This opens up the prospect of paranoiac scenarios: since the digital language we shall all use will none the less be man-made, constructed by programmers, is it not possible to imagine the corporation that owns it installing in it some special secret program ingredient which will enable it to control us, or a virus which the corporation can trigger, and thus bring our communication to a halt? When biogenetic corporations assert their ownership of our genes through patenting them, they also give rise to a similar paradox of owning the innermost parts of our body, so that we are already owned by a corporation without even being aware of it.

The prospect we are confronting is thus that both the communicational network we use and the genetic language we are made of will be owned and controlled by corporations (or even a corporation) out of public control. Again, does not the very absurdity of this prospect – the private control of the very public base of our communication and reproduction, the very network of our social being – impose a kind of socialization as the only solution? In other words, is not the impact of the so-called information revolution on capitalism the ultimate exemplification of the old Marxian thesis that 'at a certain stage of their development, the material productive forces of society come into conflict with the existing relations of production, or – what is but a legal expression of the same thing – with the property relations within which they have been at work hitherto'?[38] Do not the two phenomena we have mentioned (the unpredictable global consequences of decisions made by private companies; the patent absurdity of 'owning' a person's genome or the media individuals use for communication), to which one should add at least the antagonism contained in the notion of owning (scientific) *knowledge* (since knowledge is by nature neutral to its propagation, that is, it is not worn out by its spread and universal use), explain why today's capitalism has to resort to more and more absurd strategies to *sustain the economy of scarcity in the sphere of information*, and thus to contain within the frame of private property and market relations the demon it has unleashed (say, by inventing ever new modes of *preventing* the free copying of digitalized information)? In short, does not the prospect of the informational 'global village' signal the *end* of market relations (which are by definition, based on the logic of scarcity), at least in the sphere of digitalized information?

After the demise of Socialism, the ultimate fear of Western capitalism is that another nation or ethnic group will beat the West on its own capitalist terms, combining the productivity of capitalism with a form of social *mores* foreign to us in the West: in the 1970s, the object of fear and fascination was Japan; while now, after a short interlude of fascination with South-East Asia, attention is focusing more and more on China as the next superpower, combining capitalism with the Communist political structure. Such fears ultimately give rise to purely phantasmic formations, like the image of China surpassing the West in productivity while retaining its authoritarian sociopolitical structure – one is tempted to designate this phantasmic combination the 'Asiatic mode of *capitalist* production'.

Against these fears, one should emphasize that China will, sooner or later, pay the price for the unbridled development of capitalism in new forms of social unrest and instability: the 'winning formula' of combining capitalism with the Asiatic 'closed' ethical community life-world is doomed to explode. Now, more than ever, one should reassert Marx's old formula that the limit of capitalism is Capital itself: the danger to Western capitalism comes not from outside, from the Chinese or some other monster beating us at our own game while depriving us of Western liberal individualism, but from the inherent limit of its own process of colonizing ever new (not only geographic but also cultural, psychic, etc.) domains, of eroding the last resistant spheres of non-reflected substantial being, which has to end in some kind of implosion, when Capital will no longer have any substantial content outside itself to feed on.[39] One should take Marx's metaphor of Capital as a vampire-like entity literally: it needs some kind of pre-reflexive 'natural productivity' (talents in different domains of art, inventors in science, etc.) in order to feed on its own blood, and thus to reproduce itself – when the circle closes itself, when reflexivity becomes thoroughly universal, the whole system is threatened.

Another sign which points in this direction is how, in the sphere of what Adorno and Horkheimer called *Kulturindustrie*, the desubstantialization and/or reflexivity of the production process has reached a level that threatens the whole system with global implosion. Even in high art, the recent fashion for exhibitions in which 'everything is permitted' and can pass as an art object, up to mutilated animal bodies, betrays this desperate need of cultural Capital to colonize and include in its circuit even the most extreme and pathological strata of human subjectivity. Paradoxically – and not without irony – the first musical trend which was in a way 'fabricated', exploited for a short time and very soon forgotten, since it lacked the musical substance to survive and attain the status of 'classics' like the early rock of the Beatles and Rolling Stones, was none other than *punk*, which simultaneously marked the strongest intrusion of violent working-class protest into mainstream pop culture – in a kind of mocking version of the Hegelian infinite judgement, in which opposites directly coincide, the raw energy of social protest coincided with the new level of commercial prefabrication which, as it were, creates the object it sells out of itself, with no need for some 'natural talent' to emerge and be subsequently exploited, like Baron Münchhausen saving himself from the swamp by pulling himself up by his own hairs. . . .

Do we not encounter the same logic in politics, where the point is less and less to follow a coherent global programme but, rather, to try to guess, by means of opinion polls, 'what the people want', and offer them that? Even in theory, doesn't the same hold for cultural studies in the Anglo-Saxon domain, or for the very theory of the risk society?[40] Theorists are less and less involved in substantial theoretical work, restraining themselves to writing short 'interventions' which mostly display their anxiety to follow the latest theoretical trends (in feminism, for example, perspicacious theorists soon realized that radical social constructionism – gender as performatively enacted, and so on – is out; that people are getting tired of it; so they start to rediscover psychoanalysis, the Unconscious; in postcolonial studies, the latest trend is to oppose multiculturalism as a false solution . . .). The point is thus not simply that cultural studies or risk society theory is insufficient on account of its content: an inherent commodification is discernible in the very form of the social mode of functioning of what are supposed to be the latest forms of the American or European academic Left. *This* reflexivity, which is also a crucial part of the 'second modernity,' is what the theorists of the reflexive risk society tend to leave out of consideration.[41]

Returns in the Real

The fundamental lesson of *Dialectic of Enlightenment* is therefore still relevant today: it bears directly on what theorists of the risk society and reflexive modernization praise as the advent of the 'second Enlightenment'. Apropos of this second Enlightenment, with subjects delivered from the weight of Nature and/or Tradition, the question of their unconscious 'passionate attachments' must be raised again – the so-called 'dark phenomena' (burgeoning fundamentalisms, neo-racisms, etc.) which accompany this 'second modernity' can in no way be dismissed as simple regressive phenomena, as remainders of the past that will simply vanish when individuals assume the full freedom and responsibility imposed on them by the second modernity.[42]

Proponents of the 'second Enlightenment' praise Kant – so the question of 'Kant avec Sade' arises again. Sade's achievement was to extend the utilitarian logic of instrumentalization to the very intimate relations of sex: sex is no longer a phenomenon confined to the private sphere, exempt from the utilitarian cruelty of public professional life; it must also be made part of the utilitarian rules of equivalent exchange that structure what Hegel called civil society. With the so-called second modernity, the attitude that was hitherto reserved for public as opposed to private life (reflexivity, the right to choose one's way of life instead of accepting it as imposed by tradition, etc.) has also penetrated the most intimate private sphere of sexuality – no wonder the price of this step is the increase in 'sadistic' practices that stage sexuality as the domain of contract and mutual exploitation. And it is precisely at this point that we can see how our two criticisms of risk society theory – that it is simultaneously *too general* (avoiding locating the key risk-generating factor in the specificity of the capitalist market economy) and *too particular* (not taking into account the way the nonexistence of the big Other affects the status of subjectivity) – converge: it is the very 'specific' logic of reflexive commodification of intimate spheres which, in the way it affects subjectivity, undermines the standard figure of the modern free autonomous subject.[43]

One should therefore reject the narrative of the process that leads from the patriarchal Oedipal order to postmodern (or second modernity) multiple contingent identities: what this narrative obliterates are the new forms of domination generated by the 'decline of Oedipus' itself; for this reason, those who continue to locate the enemy in Oedipus are obliged to insist on how postmodernity remains an unfinished project, on how Oedipal patriarchy continues to lead its subterranean life and prevents us from realizing the full potential of postmodern self-fashioning individuality. This properly hysterical endeavour to break with the Oedipal past mislocates the danger: it lies not in the remainders of the past, but in the obscene need for domination and subjection engendered by the new 'post-Oedipal' forms of subjectivity themselves. In other words, today we are witnessing a shift no less radical than the shift from the premodern patriarchal order directly legitimized by the sexualized cosmology (Masculine and Feminine as the two cosmic principles) to the modern patriarchal order that introduced the abstract-universal notion of man; as is always the case with such ruptures, one should be very careful to avoid the trap of measuring the new standards against the old – such blindness leads either to catastrophic visions of total disintegration (the vision of the emerging society as that of proto-psychotic narcissists lacking any notion of trust and obligation) or to a no less false celebration of the new post-Oedipal subjectivity that fails to account for the new forms of domination emerging from postmodern subjectivity itself.

What psychoanalysis enables us to do is to focus on this obscene, disavowed 'supplement' of the reflexive subject freed from the constraints of Nature and Tradition: as Lacan put it, the subject of psychoanalysis is none other than the subject of modern science. Let us begin with the so-called 'culture of complaint',[44] with its underlying logic of *ressentiment*: far from cheerfully assuming the nonexistence of the big Other, the subject blames the Other for its failure and/or impotence, as if *the Other is guilty of the fact that it doesn't exist*, that is, as if impotence is no excuse – the big Other is responsible for the very fact that it wasn't able to do anything: the more the subject's structure is 'narcissistic', the more he puts the blame on the big Other, and thus asserts his dependence on it. The basic feature of the 'culture of complaint' is a call, addressed to the big Other, to intervene and put things right (to compensate the damaged sexual or ethnic minority, etc.) – how, exactly, this is to be done is again a matter for various ethico-legal 'committees'.

The specific feature of the 'culture of complaint' is its legalistic twist, the endeavour to translate the complaint into the legal obligation of the Other (usually the State) to indemnify me – for what? For the very unfathomable *surplus-enjoyment* I am deprived of, whose lack makes me feel underprivileged. Is not the 'culture of complaint' therefore today's version of hysteria, of the hysterical impossible demand addressed to the Other, a demand that actually *wants to be rejected*, since the subject grounds his/her existence in his/her complaint: 'I am in so far as I make the Other responsible for and/or guilty of my misery'? Instead of undermining the position of the Other, the complaining underprivileged address themselves to it: by translating their demand into the terms of legalistic complaint, they *confirm the Other in its position in the very gesture of attacking it*. There is an insurmountable gap between this logic of complaint and the true 'radical' ('revolutionary') act which, instead of complaining to the Other and expecting it to act – that is, displacing the need to act on to it – suspends the existing legal frame and *accomplishes the act itself*.[45] Consequently, this 'culture of complaint' is correlative to sado-maso practices of self-mutilation: they form the two opposed but complementary aspects of the disturbed relationship towards the Law, relating to each other as do hysteria and perversion. The sado-maso practice *acts out the phantasmic scenarios* (of humiliation, rape, victimization . . .) *which traumatize the hysterical subject*. What makes this passage from hysteria to perversion possible is the change in the relationship between Law and *jouissance*: for the hysterical subject, the Law is still the agency which prohibits access to *jouissance* (so he can only fantasize about the obscene *jouissance* hidden beneath the figure of the Law); while for the pervert, the Law emanates from the very figure that embodies *jouissance* (so he can directly assume the role of this obscene Other as the instrument of *jouissance*).[46]

The paradoxical result of the mutation in the nonexistence of the big Other – of the growing collapse of symbolic efficiency – is thus the proliferation of different versions of *a big Other that actually exists, in the Real*, not merely as a symbolic fiction. The belief in the big Other which exists in the Real is, of course, the most succinct definition of paranoia; for this reason, two features which characterize today's ideological stance – cynical distance and full reliance on paranoiac fantasy – are strictly co-dependent: the typical subject today is the one who, while displaying cynical distrust of any public ideology, indulges without restraint in paranoiac fantasies about conspiracies, threats, and excessive forms of enjoyment of the Other. The distrust of the big Other (the order of symbolic fictions), the subject's refusal to 'take it seriously', relies on the belief that there is an 'Other of the Other', that a secret, invisible and all-powerful agent actually 'pulls the strings' and runs the show: behind the visible, public Power there is another obscene, invisible power structure. This other, hidden agent acts the part of the 'Other of the Other' in the Lacanian sense, the part of the meta-guarantee of the consistency of the big Other (the symbolic order that regulates social life).

It is here that we should look for the roots of the recent impasse of narrativization, that is, of the theme of the 'end of great narratives': in our era, when – in politics and ideology as well as in literature and cinema – global, all-encompassing narratives ('the struggle of liberal democracy with totalitarianism', etc.) no longer seem possible, the only way to achieve a kind of global 'cognitive mapping' is through the paranoiac narrative of a 'conspiracy theory'. It is all too simplistic to dismiss conspiracy narratives as the paranoiac proto-Fascist reaction of the infamous 'middle classes' which feel threatened by the process of modernization: they function, rather, as a kind of floating signifier which can be appropriated by different political options, enabling them to obtain a minimal cognitive mapping – not only by right-wing populism and fundamentalism, but also by the liberal centre (the 'mystery' of Kennedy's assassination[47]) and left-wing orientations (recall the old obsession of the American Left with the notion that some mysterious government agency is experimenting with nerve gases which would give them the power to regulate the behaviour of the population).[48]

Another version of the Other's return in the Real is discernible in the guise of the New Age Jungian resexualization of the universe ('men are from Mars, women are from Venus'): according to this, there is an underlying, deeply anchored archetypal identity which provides a kind of safe haven in the flurry of contemporary confusion of roles and identities;

from this perspective, the ultimate origin of today's crisis is not the difficulty in overcoming the tradition of fixed sexual roles, but the disturbed balance in modern man, who puts excessive emphasis on the male-rational-conscious aspect, neglecting the female-compassionate aspect. Although this tendency shares its anti-Cartesian and anti-patriarchal bias with feminism, it rewrites the feminist agenda into a reassertion of archetypal feminine roots repressed in our competitive male mechanistic universe. A further version of the *real* Other is the figure of the father as sexual harasser of his young daughters, the focal point of so-called False Memory Syndrome: here, also, the suspended father as the agent of symbolic authority – that is, the embodiment of a symbolic fiction – 'returns in the Real' (what causes such controversy is the contention of those who advocate rememoration of childhood sexual abuses that sexual harassment by the father is not merely fantasized or, at least, an indissoluble mixture of fact and fantasy, but a plain fact, something which, in the majority of families, 'really happened' in the daughter's childhood – an obstinacy comparable to Freud's no less obstinate insistence on the murder of the 'primordial father' as a real event in humanity's prehistory).

It is easy to discern here the link between False Memory Syndrome and anxiety: False Memory Syndrome is a symptomatic formation that enables the subject to escape anxiety by taking refuge in the antagonistic relationship with the parental Other-harasser. That is to say: one should bear in mind that for Lacan, and in contrast to the Freudian *doxa*, anxiety does not emerge when the object-cause of desire is lost (as when we speak of 'castration-anxiety', usually expressing the fear that the male subject will be deprived of his virile member, or even of birth anxiety expressing the fear of being separated from the mother) – on the contrary, anxiety emerges when (and signals that) the object-cause of desire is too close, when and if we come too near it. We can appreciate Lacan's finesse here: in contrast to the standard notion according to which fear has a determinate object (of which we are afraid), while anxiety is a disposition that lacks any positive/determinate object serving as its cause, for Lacan it is fear which, contrary to misleading appearances, is actually without a determinate object-cause (when I have a dog phobia, say, I do not fear the dog as such, but the irrepresentable 'abstract' void behind him); while anxiety *does* have a determinate object-cause – it is the very overproximity of this object that triggered it. . . .[49]

To get this point clear, we have to bear in mind once more that in the Lacanian perspective desire is ultimately the Other's desire: the question–enigma of desire is ultimately not 'What do I really want?', but 'What does the Other really want from me? What, as an object, am I myself for the Other?' – I myself (the subject), as the object-cause of the Other's desire, am the object whose overproximity triggers anxiety: that is, anxiety emerges when I am reduced to the position of the object exchanged/used by the Other. Along the same lines, in the case of False Memory Syndrome, the antagonistic relationship with the parental harasser enables me to avoid anxiety generated by the fact that I *am* the direct (incestuous) object of parental desire; that I *desire* myself as such.

One last example: in his unpublished paper 'Ideology and its Paradoxes', Glyn Daly draws attention to the topic of 'cracking the code' in today's popular ideology, from New Age pseudo-scientific attempts to use computer technology to crack some sort of fundamental code which gives access to the future destiny of humanity (the Bible code, the code contained in the Egyptian pyramids . . .) up to the paradigmatic scene of cyberspace thrillers in which the hero (or, more often, the heroine, like Sandra Bullock in *The Net*), hunched over a computer, frantically works against time to overcome the obstacle of 'Access Denied' and gain access to the ultra-secret information (say, about the workings of a secret government agency involved in a plot against freedom and democracy, or some equally severe crime). Does this topic not represent a desperate attempt to reassert the big Other's existence, that is, to posit some secret Code or Order that bears witness to the presence of some Agent which actually pulls the strings of our chaotic social life?

The Empty Law

Yet another, much more uncanny assertion of the big Other is discernible, however, in the allegedly 'liberating' notion of the subjects compelled to (re)invent the rules of their coexistence without any guarantee in some meta-norm; Kant's ethical philosophy can already serve as its paradigmatic case. In *Coldness and Cruelty*, Deleuze provides an unsurpassable formulation of Kant's radically new conception of the moral Law:

> . . . the law is no longer regarded as dependent on the Good, but on the contrary, the Good itself is made to depend on the law. This means that the law no longer has its foundation in some higher principle from which it would derive its authority, but that it is self-grounded and valid solely by virtue of its own form. . . . Kant, by establishing THE LAW as an ultimate ground or principle, added an essential dimension to modern thought: the object of the

law is by definition unknowable and elusive.... Clearly THE LAW, as defined by its pure form, without substance or object of any determination whatsoever, is such that no one knows nor can know what it is. It operates without making itself known. It defines a realm of transgression where one is already guilty, and where one oversteps the bounds without knowing what they are, as in the case of Oedipus. Even guilt and punishment do not tell us what the law is, but leave it in a state of indeterminacy equalled only by the extreme specificity of the punishment.[50]

The Kantian Law is thus not merely an empty form applied to a random empirical content in order to ascertain if this content meets the criteria of ethical adequacy – the empty form of the Law, rather, functions as the promise of an absent content (never) to come. This form is not the neutral-universal mould of the plurality of different empirical contents; it bears witness to the persisting uncertainty about the content of our acts – we never know if the determinate content that accounts for the specificity of our acts is the right one, that is, if we have actually acted in accordance with the Law and have not been guided by some hidden pathological motives. Kant thus announces the notion of Law which culminates in Kafka and the experience of modern political 'totalitarianism': since, in the case of the Law, its *Dass-Sein* (the fact of the Law) precedes its *Was-Sein* (what this Law is), the subject finds himself in a situation in which, although he knows there *is* a Law, he never knows (and a priori *cannot* know) *what* this Law is – a gap forever separates *the* Law from its positive incarnations. The subject is thus a priori, in his very existence, guilty: guilty without knowing what he is guilty of (and guilty for that very reason), infringing the law without knowing its exact regulations....[51] What we have here, for the first time in the history of philosophy, is the assertion of the Law as *unconscious*: the experience of Form without content is always the index of a repressed content – the more intensely the subject sticks to the empty form, the more traumatic the repressed content becomes.

The gap that separates this Kantian version of the subject reinventing the rules of his ethical conduct from the postmodern Foucauldian version is easily discernible: although they both assert that ethical judgement ultimately displays the structure of aesthetic judgement (in which, instead of simply applying a universal rule to a particular situation, one has to (re)invent the universal rule in each unique concrete situation), for Foucault this simply means that the subject is thrown into a situation in which he has to shape his ethical project with no support in any transcendent(al) Law; while for Kant this very absence of Law – in the specific sense of a determinate set of positive universal norms – renders all the more sensible the unbearable pressure of the moral Law *qua* the pure empty injunction to do one's Duty. So, from the Lacanian perspective, it is here that we encounter the crucial distinction between rules to be invented and their underlying Law/Prohibition: only when the Law *qua* set of positive universal symbolic norms fails to appear – do we encounter the Law at its most radical, the Law in its aspect of the Real of an unconditional injunction. The paradox to be emphasized here lies in the precise nature of the Prohibition entailed by the moral Law: at its most fundamental, this Prohibition is not the prohibition to accomplish some positive act that would violate the Law, but the self-referential prohibition to confuse the 'impossible' Law with any positive symbolic prescription and/or prohibition, that is, to claim for any positive set of norms the status of *the* law – ultimately, the Prohibition means that *the place of the Law itself must remain empty*.

To put it in classic Freudian terms: in Foucault, we get a set of rules regulating the 'care of the Self' in his 'use of pleasures' (in short, a reasonable application of the 'pleasure principle'); while in Kant, the (re)invention of rules follows an injunction which comes from the 'beyond of the pleasure principle'. Of course, the Foucauldian/Deleuzian answer to this would be that Kant is ultimately the victim of a perspective illusion which leads him to (mis)perceive the radical immanence of ethical norms (the fact that the subject has to invent the norms regulating his conduct autonomously, at his own expense and on his own responsibility, with no big Other to take the blame for it) as its exact opposite: as a radical transcendence, presupposing the existence of an inscrutable transcendent Other which terrorizes us with its unconditional injunction, simultaneously prohibiting us access to it – we are under a compulsion to do our Duty, but forever prevented from clearly knowing what this Duty is. . . . The Freudian answer is that such a solution (the translation of the big Other's inscrutable Call of Duty into immanence) relies on the *disavowal of the Unconscious*: the fact which usually goes unnoticed is that Foucault's rejection of the psychoanalytic account of sexuality also involves a thorough rejection of the Freudian Unconscious. If we read Kant in psychoanalytic terms, the gap between self-invented rules and their underlying Law is none other than the gap between (consciously preconscious) rules we follow and the Law *qua* unconscious: the basic lesson of psychoanalysis is that the Unconscious is, at its most radical, not the wealth of illicit 'repressed' desires but *the fundamental Law itself*.

So even in the case of a narcissistic subject dedicated to the 'care of the

Self', his 'use of pleasures' is sustained by the unconscious unconditional superego injunction to enjoy – is not the ultimate proof the feeling of guilt which haunts him when he *fails* in his pursuit of pleasure? Does not the fact that – according to most opinion polls – people find less and less attraction in sexual activity point in this direction? This uncanny indifference towards intense sexual pleasure contrasts starkly with the official ideology of our postmodern society as bent on instant gratification and pleasure-seeking: today's subject dedicates his life to pleasure and gets so deeply involved in the preparatory activities (jogging, massaging, tanning, applying cream and lotions . . .) that the attraction of the official Goal of his efforts fades away. In the course of a brief stroll along Christopher Street or in Chelsea, one encounters hundreds of gays putting extraordinary energy into body-building, obsessed with the dreadful prospect of getting old, dedicated to pleasure, yet obviously living in permanent anxiety and under the shadow of their ultimate failure.

What is undermined today, in our post-Oedipal 'permissive' societies, is sexual *jouissance* as the foundational 'passionate attachment', as the desired/prohibited focal point around which our life revolves. (From this perspective, even the figure of the paternal 'sexual harasser' looks like a nostalgic image of someone who is still fully able to enjoy 'it'.) Once again the superego has accomplished its task successfully: the direct injunction 'Enjoy!' is a much more effective way to hinder the subject's access to enjoyment than the explicit Prohibition which sustains the space for its transgression. The lesson is that narcissistic 'care of the Self', not the 'repressive' network of social prohibitions, is the ultimate enemy of intense sexual experiences. The utopia of a new post-psychoanalytic subjectivity engaged in the pursuit of new idiosyncratic bodily pleasures beyond sexuality has reverted to its opposite: what we are getting instead is disinterested boredom – and it seems that the direct intervention of pain (sado-masochistic sexual practices) is the only remaining path to the intense experience of pleasure.

In the very last page of *Seminar XI*, Lacan claims that 'any shelter in which may be established a viable, temperate relation of one sex to the other necessitates the intervention – this is what psychoanalysis teaches us – of that medium known as the paternal metaphor':[52] far from hindering its realization, the paternal Law guarantees its conditions. No wonder, then, that the retreat of the big Other, of the symbolic Law, entails the malfunctioning of 'normal' sexuality and the rise of sexual indifference. As Darian Leader has pointed out,[53] the fact that, in *X Files, so many things happen 'out there'* (where the truth dwells: aliens threatening us, etc.) is strictly correlative to the fact that *nothing happens 'down here'*, between the two heroes (Gillian Anderson and David Duchovny) – that there is no sex between them. The suspended paternal Law (which would make sex between the two heroes possible) 'returns in the Real', in the guise of the multitude of 'undead' spectral apparitions which intervene in our ordinary lives.

This disintegration of paternal authority has two facets. On the one hand, *symbolic* prohibitive norms are increasingly replaced by *imaginary* ideals (of social success, of bodily fitness . . .); on the other, the lack of symbolic prohibition is supplemented by the re-emergence of ferocious superego figures. So we have a subject who is extremely narcissistic – who perceives everything as a potential threat to his precarious imaginary balance (take the universalization of the logic of victim; every contact with another human being is experienced as a potential threat: if the other person smokes, if he casts a covetous glance at me, he is already hurting me); far from allowing him to float freely in his undisturbed balance, however, this narcissistic self-enclosure leaves the subject to the (not so) tender mercies of the superego injunction to enjoy.

So-called 'postmodern' subjectivity thus involves a kind of *direct 'superegoization' of the imaginary Ideal,* caused by the lack of the proper symbolic Prohibition; paradigmatic here are the 'postmodern' hackers–programmers, these extravagant eccentrics hired by large corporations to pursue their programming hobbies in an informal environment. They are under the injunction to be what they are, to follow their innermost idiosyncrasies, allowed to ignore social norms of dress and behaviour (they obey only some elementary rules of polite tolerance of each other's idiosyncrasies); they thus seem to realize a kind of proto-Socialist utopia of overcoming the opposition between alienated business, where you earn money, and the private hobby–activity that you pursue for pleasure at weekends. In a way, their job is their hobby, which is why they spend long hours at weekends in their workplace behind the computer screen: when one is paid for indulging in one's hobby, the result is that one is exposed to a superego pressure incomparably stronger than that of the good old 'Protestant work ethic'. Therein lies the unbearable paradox of this postmodern 'disalienation': the tension is no longer between my innermost idiosyncratic creative impulses and the Institution that does not appreciate them or wants to crush them in order to 'normalize' me: what the superego injunction of a postmodern corporation like Microsoft targets is precisely this core of my idiosyncratic creativity – I became useless for them the moment I start losing this 'imp of perversity', the moment I lose my 'countercultural' subversive edge and start to behave like a 'normal' mature subject. What we are dealing with here is thus a strange alliance between the rebellious subversive core of my personality, my 'imp of perversity', and the external corporation.

From Phallus to the Act

The retreat of the big Other thus has two interconnected, albeit opposed, consequences: on the one hand, this failure of the symbolic fiction induces the subject to cling increasingly to imaginary *simulacra*, to the sensual spectacles which bombard us today from all sides; on the other, it triggers the need for violence in the Real of the body itself (piercing the flesh, inserting prosthetic supplements into the body). How does this bodily violence relate to the structure of castration as the condition of symbolic empowerment? In our popular narratives and myths, from Robocop to Stephen Hawking, a person becomes a supernaturally powerful hero only after being the victim of some traumatic accident or illness which literally shatters his body: Robocop becomes the perfect machine-cop when his body is artificially recomposed and supplemented after an almost deadly accident; Hawking's insight into 'the mind of God' is clearly correlated to his crippling illness. . . . The standard analyses of Robocop endeavour to oppose 'progressive' elements – a cyborg which suspends the distinction between human and a machine – and 'regressive' elements – the obvious 'phallic', aggressive-penetrating nature of his metal equipment, which serves as a prosthesis to his mutilated body; these analyses, however, *miss the point*: what is 'phallic' in the strict Lacanian sense is the very structure of the artificial-mechanical prosthesis that supplements the wound to our body, since the phallus itself *qua* signifier is such a prosthesis, empowering its bearer at the price of some traumatic mutilation.

Here it is crucial to maintain the distinction between the phallus as *signified* (the 'meaning of the phallus') and the phallic *signifier*: the phallic signified is the part of *jouissance* integrated into the paternal symbolic order (phallus as the symbol of virility, penetrating power, the force of fertility and insemination, etc.); while the phallus as signifier stands for the price the male subject has to pay if he is to assume the 'meaning of the phallus', its signified. Lacan specifies this 'meaning of the phallus' as the 'imaginary' number (the square root of -1), an 'impossible' number whose value can never be positivized, but which none the less 'functions':

we encounter 'the meaning of the phallus' when, apropos of some notion, we enthusiastically feel that 'this is *it*, the real thing, the true meaning', although we are never able to explain *what*, precisely, this meaning is. Say, in a political discourse, the Master-Signifier (Our Nation) is this kind of empty signifier which stands for the impossible fullness of meaning, that is, its meaning is 'imaginary' in the sense that its content is impossible to positivize – when you ask a member of the Nation to define in what the identity of his Nation consists, his ultimate answer will always be: 'I can't say, you must feel it, it's *it*, what our lives are really about'. . . .

So why is it necessary, in our postmodern age, for the 'wound of castration' to inscribe itself again into the body, as a wound in its very flesh? In the good old times of modern subjectivity, an individual had no need to sacrifice part of his flesh (circumcision, a ritualized initiatory ordeal of risking one's life, tattooing . . .) in order to gain symbolic status: the sacrifice was purely symbolic, that is, a symbolic act of renunciation of all positive substantial content.[54] This renunciation displays the precise structure of the 'loss of a loss' that defines the modern tragedy. *Yanez*, a recent Serb film, deals with the fate of an officer in the Yugoslav Army of Slovene ethnic origin, married to a Macedonian woman, caught in the turmoils of the disintegration of Yugoslavia: when the conflict erupts between Slovenia proclaiming independence and the Yugoslav Army, which endeavoured to keep Slovenia within Yugoslavia, the officer sacrifices his particular (Slovene) ethnic roots, that is, the very substance of his being, for fidelity to the universal Cause (Yugoslav unity), only to discover later that the sad reality of this universal Cause, for which he sacrificed everything that mattered to him most, is the corrupt and deprived Serbia of the nationalist regime of Slobodan Milosevic – so, at the end, we see the hero alone and drunk, totally at a loss. . . .

A similar double movement of renunciation – of first sacrificing everything, the very substance of our being, for some universal Cause, and then being compelled to confront the vacuousness of this Cause itself – is constitutive of modern subjectivity.[55] Today, however, this double movement of renunciation seems no longer to be operative, since subjects increasingly stick to their particular substantial identity, unwilling to sacrifice it for some universal Cause (this is what so-called 'identity politics', as well as the search for ethnic 'roots', are about) – so is this why the cut of symbolic castration had again to be inscribed on to the body, in the guise of some horrifying mutilation as the price of the subject's symbolic empowerment?

Crucial here is the difference between the traditional (premodern) cut in the body (circumcision, etc.) and the postmodern cut:[56] although the two may be superficially alike – that is, although the postmodern cut may look like the 'return to premodern procedures of marking the body' – their inherent libidinal economies are opposed – as with postmodernism, which may look like the return of the premodern archaic forms, but in reality these forms are already 'mediated', colonized by modernity, so that postmodernism signals the moment when modernity no longer has to fight traditional forms, but can use them directly – today's astrologist or fundamentalist preacher, in his very mode of activity, is already marked by modernity. One of the definitions of modernity is the appearance of the 'natural' *naked body* within the symbolic space: nudism and other forms of the celebration of nakedness – not as part of secret initiatory transgressive rituals (as in premodern pagan societies), but as finding pleasure in asserting the 'innocent' beauty of one's natural body – are distinctly modern phenomena.[57]

Here one has to repeat the gesture accomplished by Hegel apropos of the sudden rise of nature as the topos in seventeenth-century art: precisely because the Spirit has returned to itself, that is, is able to grasp itself directly and no longer needs nature as the medium of its symbolic expression, nature becomes perceptible in its innocence, as it is in itself, as a beautiful object of contemplation, not as a symbol of spiritual struggle; along the same lines, when the modern subject 'internalizes' symbolic castration into the 'loss of a loss', the body no longer has to bear the burden of castration and is thus redeemed, free to be celebrated as an object of pleasure and beauty. This appearance of the unmutilated naked body is strictly correlative to the imposition of the disciplinary procedures described in detail by Michel Foucault: with the advent of modernity, when the body is no longer marked, inscribed upon, it becomes the object of strict disciplinary regulations destined to make it fit.

We can thus distinguish four stages in the logic of the 'cut in the body'. First, in pre-Judaean pagan tribal societies, 'I am marked, therefore I am', that is, the cut in my body (tattoo, etc.) stands for my inscription into the socio-symbolic space – outside it I am nothing, more like an animal than a member of a human society. Then comes the Jewish logic of circumcision, 'a cut to end all cuts', that is, the exceptional/negative cut strictly correlative to the prohibition of the pagan multitude of cuts: 'You shall not make any gashes in your flesh for the dead or tattoo any marks upon you: I am the LORD'(Leviticus 19: 28).[58] Finally, with Christianity, this exceptional cut is itself 'internalized', there are no cuts. Where, then, lies the difference between the premodern plethora of ways to shape one's body (tattooing, piercing, mutilation of organs . . .) and the fourth stage, the postmodern 'neo-tribal' cut in the body?

To put it in somewhat simplified terms: the traditional cut ran in the direction *from the Real to the Symbolic*, while the postmodern cut runs in the opposite direction, *from the Symbolic to the Real*. The aim of the traditional cut was to inscribe the symbolic form on to raw flesh, to 'gentrify' raw flesh, to mark its inclusion into the big Other, its subjection to it; the aim of postmodern sado-maso practices of bodily mutilation is, rather, the opposite one – to guarantee, to give access to, the 'pain of existence', the minimum of the bodily Real in the universe of symbolic simulacra. In other words, the function of today's 'postmodern' cut in the body is to serve not as the mark of symbolic castration but, rather, as its exact opposite: to designate the body's resistance against submission to the socio-symbolic Law. When a girl has her ears, cheeks and vaginal lips pierced with rings, the message is not one of submission but one of the 'defiance of the flesh': she changes what, in a traditional society, was the mode of submission to the symbolic big Other of Tradition into its opposite, into the idiosyncratic display of her individuality.

Only in this way is reflexivization thoroughly global: when – to put it in Hegelese – it 'remains by itself in its otherness', that is, when (what was previously) its very opposite starts to function as its expression – as in postmodern architecture, in which a faked return to traditional styles displays the fancies of reflexive individuality. The old motto *plus ça change, plus c'est la même chose* should be supplemented by its opposite, *plus c'est la même chose, plus ça change*: the sign of this radical historical change is the fact that the very features that once defined patriarchal sexual economy are allowed to stay, since they now function in a new way. Simply recall the phenomenon of 'Rule Girls':[59] we are apparently dealing with an attempt to re-establish the old rules of seduction (women are chased and have to make themselves inaccessible, that is, to retain the status of the elusive object and never display an active interest in the man they are attracted to, etc.); however, although the *content* of these 'rules' is, for all practical purposes, the same as that of the old rules regulating the 'patriarchal' process of seduction, the subjective *position of enunciation* differs radically: we are dealing with thoroughly 'postmodern' emancipated subjects who, in order to enhance their pleasure, reflexively adopt a set of rules. So here again the adoption of a past procedure is 'transubstantiated' and serves as the means of expression of its very opposite, of 'postmodern' reflexive freedom.[60]

This brings us to what one is tempted to call the antinomy of postmodern individuality: the injunction to 'be yourself', to disregard the pressure of your surroundings and achieve self-realization by fully asserting your unique creative potential, stumbles sooner or later upon the paradox that if you are completely isolated from your surroundings, you are left with nothing whatsoever, with a void of idiocy pure and simple. The inherent obverse of 'Be your true Self!' is therefore the injunction to cultivate permanent refashioning, in accordance with the postmodern postulate of the subject's indefinite plasticity . . . in short, extreme individualization reverts to its opposite, leading to the ultimate identity crisis: subjects experience themselves as radically unsure, with no 'proper face', changing from one imposed mask to another, since what is behind the mask is ultimately *nothing*, a horrifying void they are frantically trying to fill in with their compulsive activity or by shifting between more and more idiosyncratic hobbies or ways of dressing, meant to accentuate their individual identity. Here we can see how extreme individualization (the endeavour to be true to one's Self outside imposed fixed socio-symbolic roles) tends to overlap with its opposite, with the uncanny, anxiety-provoking feeling of the loss of one's identity – is this not the ultimate confirmation of Lacan's insight into how one can achieve a minimum of identity and 'be oneself' only by accepting the fundamental alienation in the symbolic network?

The paradoxical result of out-and-out narcissistic hedonism is thus that enjoyment itself is increasingly externalized: in the thorough reflexivity of our lives, any direct appeal to our experience is invalidated – that is to say, I no longer trust my own direct experience, but expect the Other to tell me how I really feel, as in the anecdote about the conversation between two behaviourists: 'Tell me how I feel today.' 'Good – what about me?' More precisely, this direct externalization of my innermost experience is much more uncanny than the usual behaviourist reduction: the point is not simply that what counts is the way I behave in observable external reality, not my inner feelings; in contrast to the behaviourist reduction of inner self-experience, I do retain my feelings, but *these feelings themselves are externalized*. The ultimate paradox of individuation, however, is that this complete dependence on others – I am what I am only through my relations with others (see the postmodern obsession with quality 'relationships') – generates the opposite effect of drug dependence, in which I am dependent not on another subject but on a drug that directly provides excessive *jouissance*. Is not the dust of heroin or crack the ultimate figure of surplus-enjoyment: an object on which I am hooked, which threatens to swallow me up in the excessive *jouissance* that suspends the big Other, that is, all symbolic links? Is not the drug user's relationship to the drug therefore the ultimate exemplification of Lacan's formula s−a?

This antinomy can also be formulated as the antinomy between the *simulacrum* (of the masks I wear, of the roles I play in the game of intersubjective relationships) and the *Real* (of traumatic bodily violence and cuts). The key point here is again to assert the Hegelian 'speculative identity' between these two opposites: the price of the global reign of simulacra *is* extreme violence to the bodily Real. (Long ago, Lacan provided the formula for this paradoxical coincidence of opposites: when symbolic efficiency is suspended, the Imaginary falls into the Real.) So how are we to break out of this vicious cycle? Any attempt to return to Oedipal symbolic authority is clearly self-defeating, and can lead only to ridiculous spectacles like those of the Promise-Keepers. What is needed is the assertion of a Real which, instead of being caught in the vicious cycle with its imaginary counterpart, (re)introduces the dimension of the impossibility that shatters the Imaginary; in short, what is needed is an *act* as opposed to mere activity − the authentic act that involves disturbing ('traversing') the fantasy.

Whenever a subject is 'active' (especially when he is driven into frenetic hyperactivity), the question to be asked is: what is the underlying fantasy sustaining this activity? The act − as opposed to activity − occurs only when this phantasmic background itself is disturbed. In this precise sense, act for Lacan is on the side of the object *qua* real as opposed to signifier (to 'speech act'): we can perform speech acts only in so far as we have accepted the fundamental alienation in the symbolic order and the phantasmic support necessary for the functioning of this order, while the act as real is an event which occurs *ex nihilo*, without any phantasmic support. As such, the act as object is also to be opposed to the subject, at least in the standard Lacanian sense of the 'alienated' divided subject: the correlate to the act is a divided subject, but not in the sense that, because of this division, the act is always failed, displaced, and so on − on the contrary, the act in its traumatic *tuche* is that which divides the subject who can never subjectivize it, assume it as 'his own', posit himself as its author−agent − the authentic act that I accomplish is always by definition a foreign body, an intruder which simultaneously attracts/fascinates and repels me, so that if and when I come too close to it, this leads to my *aphanisis*, self-erasure. If there is a subject to the act, it is not the subject of subjectivization, of integrating the act into the universe of symbolic integration and recognition, of assuming the act as 'my own', but, rather, an uncanny 'acephalous' subject through which the act takes place as that which is 'in him more than himself'. The act thus designates the level at which the fundamental divisions and displacements usually associated with the 'Lacanian subject' (the split between the subject of the enunciation and the subject of the enunciated/statement; the subject's 'decentrement' with regard to the symbolic big Other; etc.) are momentarily suspended – in the act, the subject, as Lacan puts it, *posits himself as his own cause*, and is no longer determined by the decentred object-cause.

For that reason, Kant's description of how a direct insight into the Thing in itself (the noumenal God) would deprive us of our freedom and turn us into lifeless puppets if we subtract from it the scenic imagery (fascination with the Divine Majesty) and reduce it to the essential (an entity performing what it does 'automatically', without any inner turmoil and struggle), paradoxically fits the description of the (ethical) act perfectly – this act is precisely something which unexpectedly 'just occurs', it is an occurrence which also (and even most) surprises its agent itself (after an authentic act, my reaction is always 'Even I don't know how I was able to do that, it just happened!'). The paradox is thus that, in an authentic act, the highest freedom coincides with the utmost passivity, with a reduction to a lifeless automaton who blindly performs its gestures. The problematic of the act thus compels us to accept the radical shift of perspective involved in the modern notion of finitude: what is so difficult to accept is not the fact that the true act in which noumenal and phenomenal dimensions coincide is forever out of our reach; the true trauma lies in the opposite awareness that *there are acts*, that they *do occur*, and that we have to come to terms with them.

In the criticism of Kant implicit in this notion of the act, Lacan is thus close to Hegel, who also claimed that the unity of the noumenal and the phenomenal adjourned *ad infinitum* in Kant is precisely what takes place every time an authentic act is accomplished. Kant's mistake was to presuppose that there is an act only in so far as it is adequately 'subjectivized', that is, accomplished with a pure Will (a Will free of any 'pathological' motivations); and, since one can never be sure that what I did was in fact prompted by the moral Law as its sole motive (i.e. since there is always a lurking suspicion that I accomplished a moral act in order to find pleasure in the esteem of my peers, etc.), the moral act turns into something which in fact never happens (there are no saints on this earth), but can only be posited as the final point of an infinite asymptotic approach of the purification of the soul – for that reason, that is, in order none the less to guarantee the ultimate possibility of the act, Kant had to propose his postulate of the immortality of the soul (which, as can be shown, effectively amounts to its very opposite, to the Sadeian fantasy of the immortality of the *body*[61]) – only in such a way can one hope that after endless approximation, one will reach the point of being able to accomplish a true moral act.

The point of Lacan's criticism is thus that an authentic act does *not* – as Kant assumes on misleading self-evidence – presuppose its agent 'on the level of the act' (with his will purified of all pathological motivations, etc.) – it is not only possible, even inevitable, that the agent is *not* 'on the level of its act', that he himself is unpleasantly surprised by the 'crazy thing he has just done', and unable fully to come to terms with it. This, incidentally, is the usual structure of heroic acts: somebody who, for a long time, has led an opportunistic life of manoeuvring and compromises, all of a sudden, inexplicably even to himself, resolves to stand firm, cost what it may – this, precisely, was how Giordano Bruno, after a long history of rather cowardly attacks and retreats, unexpectedly decided to stick to his views. The paradox of the act thus lies in the fact that although it is not 'intentional' in the usual sense of the term of consciously willing it, it is nevertheless accepted as something for which its agent is fully responsible – 'I cannot do otherwise, yet I am none the less fully free in doing it.'

Consequently, this Lacanian notion of act also enables us to break with the deconstructionist ethics of the irreducible finitude, of how our situation is always that of a displaced being caught in a constitutive lack, so that all we can do is heroically assume this lack, the fact that our situation is that of being thrown into an impenetrable finite context;[62] the corollary of this ethics, of course, is that the ultimate source of totalitarian and other catastrophes is man's presumption that he can overcome this condition of finitude, lack and displacement, and 'act like God', in a total transparency, overcoming his constitutive division. Lacan's answer to this is that absolute/unconditional acts do occur, but not in the (idealist) guise of a self-transparent gesture performed by a subject with a pure Will who fully intends them – they occur, on the contrary, as a totally unpredictable *tuche*, a miraculous event which shatters our lives. To put it in somewhat pathetic terms, this is how the 'divine' dimension is present in our lives, and the different modalities of ethical betrayal relate precisely to the different ways of betraying the act–event: the true source of Evil is not a finite mortal man who acts like God, but a man who denies that divine miracles occur and reduces himself to just another finite mortal being.

One should reread Lacan's matrix of the four discourses as the three modes of coming to terms with the trauma of the (analyst's) act;[63] to these three strategies of disavowal of the act, one should add the fourth, properly psychotic one: since an authentic act involves the choice of the Worse, since it is by definition catastrophic (for the existing discursive universe), let us then directly provoke a catastrophe and the act will somehow occur . . . (therein lies the desperate 'terrorist' act of trying to 'sober' the masses lulled into ideological sleep, from the RAF in the Germany of the early 1970s to the Unabomber). While this temptation must, of course, be resisted, one should no less firmly resist the opposite temptation of the different modalities of dissociating the act from its inherent 'catastrophic' consequences.

In so far as the political act *par excellence* is a revolution, two opposing strategies arise here: one can endeavour to separate the noble Idea of the Revolution from its abominable reality (recall Kant's celebration of the sublime feeling the French Revolution evoked in the enlightened public all over Europe, which goes hand in hand with utter disdain for the reality of the revolutionary events themselves), or one can idealize the authentic revolutionary act itself, and bemoan its regrettable but unavoidable later betrayal (recall the nostalgia of Trotskyite and other radical Leftists for the early days of the Revolution, with workers' councils popping up 'spontaneously' everywhere, against the Thermidor, that is, the later ossification of the Revolution into a new hierarchical state structure). Against all these temptations, one should insist on the unconditional need to endorse the act fully in all its consequences. Fidelity is not fidelity to the principles betrayed by the contingent facticity of their actualization, but fidelity to the *consequences* entailed by the full actualization of the (revolutionary) principles. Within the horizon of what precedes the act, the act always and by definition appears as a change 'from Bad to Worse' (the usual criticism of conservatives against revolutionaries: yes, the situation is bad, but your solution is even worse . . .). The proper heroism of the act is fully to assume this Worse.

Beyond the Good

This means that there is none the less something inherently 'terroristic' in every authentic act, in its gesture of thoroughly redefining the 'rules of the game', inclusive of the very basic self-identity of its perpetrator – a proper political act unleashes the force of negativity that shatters the very foundations of our being. So, when a Leftist is accused of laying the ground for the Stalinist or Maoist terror through his otherwise sincere and benevolent proposals, he should learn to avoid the liberal trap of accepting this accusation at face value and then trying to defend himself by pleading not guilty ('Our Socialism will be democratic, respecting human rights, dignity, happiness; there will be no universal obligatory Party Line...'): no, Liberal Democracy is not our ultimate horizon; uneasy as it may sound, the horrible experience of the Stalinist political terror should *not* lead us into abandoning the principle of terror itself – one should search even more stringently for the 'good terror'. Is the structure of a true political act of liberation not, by definition, that of a forced choice and, as such, 'terroristic'? When, in 1940, the French Resistance called on individuals to join its ranks and actively oppose the German occupation of France, the implicit structure of its appeal was not 'You are free to choose between us and the Germans', but 'You *must* choose us! If you choose collaboration, you renounce your very freedom!' In an authentic choice of freedom, I choose what I know I *have* to do.

It was Bertolt Brecht who, in his 'learning' play *The Measure Taken* (1930), fully deployed this 'terroristic' potential of the act, defining the act as the readiness to accept one's thorough self-obliteration ('second death'): the youth who joins the revolutionaries, then endangers them through his humanist compassion for the suffering workers, agrees to be thrown into a pit where his body will disintegrate, with no trace of him left behind.[64] Here, the revolution is endangered by the remainder of naive humanity – that is, by perceiving other people not only as figures in the class struggle but also, and primarily, as suffering human beings. Against this reliance on one's direct sentiments of compassion, Brecht offers the 'excremental' identification of the revolutionary subject with the terror needed to erase the last traces of terror itself, thus accepting the need for its own ultimate self-obliteration: 'Who are you? Stinking, be gone from the room that has been cleaned! Would that you were the last of the filth which you had to remove!'[65]

In his famous short play *Mauser* (1970[66]), Heiner Müller endeavoured to write a dialectical rebuttal of Brecht, confronting this figure of the betrayal of the revolution on account of humanist compassion ('I cannot kill the enemies of revolution, because I also see in them ignorant suffering human beings, helpless victims caught in the historical process') with the opposing figure of the revolutionary executioner who identifies excessively with his brutal work (instead of executing enemies with the necessary impassivity, aware that his murderous work is the painful but necessary measure destined to bring about a state in which killing will no longer be necessary, he elevates the destruction of the enemies of the revolution into an end-in-itself, finding fulfilment in the destructive orgy as such). At the end of the play, it is thus the revolutionary executioner turned into a killing machine, not the compassionate humanist, who is proclaimed the enemy of the revolution and condemned to execution by the Party Chorus. Far from simply undermining *The Measure Taken* with its dialectical counter-example, however, the execution of the revolutionary executioner himself in *Mauser* offers a perfect example of the 'last of the filth which had to be removed'. A revolution is achieved (*not* betrayed) when it 'eats its own children', the excess that was necessary to set it in motion. In other words, the ultimate revolutionary ethical stance is not that of simple devotion and fidelity to the Revolution but, rather, that of willingly accepting the role of 'vanishing mediator', of the excessive executioner to be executed (as the 'traitor') so that the Revolution can achieve its ultimate goal.

More precisely, in *Mauser* the executioner himself is not executed simply for enjoying his killing on behalf of the Revolution as an end-in-itself; he is not caught in some kind of pseudo-Bataillean orgy of (self-) destruction; the point is, rather, that he wants to 'kill the dead themselves again', to obliterate the dead totally from historical memory, to disperse their very bodies, to make them disappear completely, so that the new age will start from the zero-point, with a clean slate – in short, to bring about what Lacan, following Sade, called the 'second death'. Paradoxically, however, it is precisely this that the three revolutionaries in Brecht's *The Measure Taken* aim at: their young comrade must not only be killed, his very disappearance must disappear, no trace of it must be left, his annihilation must be *total* – the young comrade 'must disappear, and totally'.[67] So when the three revolutionaries ask their young comrade to say 'Yes!' to his fate, they want him freely to endorse this total self-obliteration, that is, his second death itself. This is the aspect of *The Measure Taken* that is not covered in Müller's *Mauser*: the problem Brecht is struggling with is not the total annihilation, the 'second death', of the *enemies* of the revolution, but the horrible task of the revolutionary *himself* to accept and endorse *his own 'second death'*, to 'erase himself totally from the picture'. For that reason, also, one can no longer oppose (as Müller does) the destructive total obliteration of the victim to the respectful taking care of the dead, to fully assuming the burden of the killing, once the victim is killed on behalf of the revolution: when, at the end of *The Measure Taken*, in a scene reminiscent of a *pietà*, the three comrades gently take their young friend in their arms, they are carrying him towards the precipice they will throw him into – that is, they are precisely effecting his total obliteration, the disappearance of his disappearance itself. . . .

So is there a third way between humanist hysterical shirking the act and the perverse overidentification with the act, or are we caught in the vicious cycle of violence in which the very revolutionary attempt to break radically with the past reproduces its worst features? Therein lies Müller's displacement with regard to Brecht: the revolutionary act of self-obliteration preached by Brecht doesn't work; the revolutionary negation of the past gets caught in the loop of repeating what it negates, so that history appears to be dominated by a deadly compulsion to repeat. The third way advocated by the Party Chorus in *Mauser* involves a nice paradox: you can maintain a distance towards your act of revolutionary violence (killing the enemies of the revolution) in so far as you conceive of yourself as the instrument of the big Other, that is, in so far as you identify yourself as the one through whom the big Other itself – History – directly acts. This opposition between direct overidentification (in which the violent act turns into the (self-)destructive orgy as an end-in-itself) and identifying oneself as the instrument of the big Other of History (in which the violent act looks like the means of creating conditions in which such acts will no longer be necessary), far from being exhaustive, designates precisely the two ways of eschewing the proper dimension of the ethical act. While the act should not be confused with the (self-)destructive orgy as an end-in-itself, it *is* an 'end-in-itself' in the sense that it is deprived of any guarantee in the big Other (an act is, by definition, 'authorized only by itself', it precludes any self-instrumentalization, any justification through reference to some figure of the big Other). Furthermore, if there is a lesson to be learned from psychoanalysis, it is that direct overidentification and self-instrumentalization ultimately coincide: perverse self-instrumentalization (positing oneself as the instrument of the big Other) necessarily becomes violence as an end-in-itself – to put it in Hegelian terms, the 'truth' of the pervert's claim that he is accomplishing his acts as the instrument of the big Other is its exact opposite: he is staging the fiction of the big Other in order to conceal the *jouissance* he derives from the destructive orgy of his acts.

So where is Evil today? The predominant ideological space provides two opposed answers, the fundamentalist one and the liberal one. According to the first answer, Clinton is Satan (as someone recently claimed at a CNN round table) – not overtly evil, but subtly corroding our moral standards as irrelevant: what does it matter if one lies, commits perjury, obstructs justice, as long as the economy is booming . . .? From this perspective, the true moral catastrophe is not a direct outburst of cruel violence but the subtle loss of moral anchors in an affluent consumerist society where things just run smoothly – the horror of Evil is that it does not look horrible at all, that it lulls us into a meaningless life of pleasures. In short, for a conservative fundamentalist, Clinton is in a way worse than Hitler, because Hitler (Nazism) was an Evil directly experienced as such and provoking moral outrage, while with Clinton's sleaze we are drawn into moral lassitude without even being aware of it. . . .

Although this attitude may appear utterly foreign to a leftist liberal stance, is it not true that, as I have already noted, even today's leftist liberals experience a strange relief at figures like Buchanan in the USA or Le Pen in France: here, at least, we have someone who openly breaks the liberal consensus stalemate and, by passionately advocating a repulsive stance, enables us to engage in an authentic political struggle (it is easy to discern in this stance the repetition of the old leftist stance apropos of Hitler's takeover: for the German Communist Party, Nazis were better than the bourgeois parliamentary regime or even the Social Democrats, because with them, at least we knew where we stood, that is, they forced the working class to get rid of the last parliamentary liberal illusion and accept class struggle as the ultimate reality). In contrast to this position, the liberal version locates the figure of Evil in the Good itself in its fundamentalist, fanatical aspect: Evil is the attitude of a fundamentalist who endeavours to extirpate, prohibit, censor, and so on, all attitudes and practices that do not fit his frame of Goodness and Truth.

These two opposed versions can sometimes also be used to condemn the same event as 'evil' – recall the case of Mary Kay Letourneau, the thirty-six-year-old schoolteacher imprisoned for a passionate love affair with her fourteen-year-old pupil, one of the great recent love stories in which sex is still linked to authentic social transgression: this affair was condemned by Moral Majority fundamentalists (as an obscene illegitimate affair) as well as by politically correct liberals (as a case of child sexual molestation).

The old and often-quoted Hegelian motto that Evil is in the eye of the beholder, that it lies in the point of view which observes Evil all around, has thus found a double confirmation today: each of the two opposed stances, liberal and conservative, ultimately defines Evil as a reflected category, as the gaze that wrongly projects/perceives Evil in its opponent. Is not Evil for today's multiculturalist tolerant liberals the very righteous conservative gaze that perceives moral corruption all around? Is not Evil for Moral Majority conservatives this very multiculturalist tolerance which, a priori, condemns every passionate taking sides and engaged struggle as exclusive and potentially totalitarian? Again, it is the *act* that enables us to cut the Gordian knot of this mutual interweaving of Good and Evil, of Evil reflectively residing in the very eye of the beholder who perceives it. As long as we define ethics in terms of the Good, this Gordian knot is our fate, and, if we want to be 'radical', we end up sooner or later in some delusive, falsely Romantic fascination with radical or diabolical Evil – the only way out is to enforce a *disjunction between the Good and the domain of the ethical act.*[68] As Lacan put it, an ethical act proper by definition involves a move 'beyond the Good' – not 'beyond Good and Evil', but simply beyond the Good.

The fact that acts are still possible today is demonstrated by the case of Mary Kay Letourneau. In order to discern the true contours of Mary Kay's act, one should locate it within the global co-ordinates that determine the fate of sexual love. Today, the opposition between reflexivization and new immediacy is that between sexuality under the regime of science and New Age spontaneity. Both terms ultimately lead to the end of sexuality proper, of sexual passion. The first option – direct scientific-medical intervention into sexuality – is best exemplified by the notorious Viagra, the potency pill that promises to restore the capacity of male erection in a purely biochemical way, bypassing all problems with psychological inhibitions. What will be the psychic effects of Viagra if it actually fulfils its promise?

To those who claim that feminism unleashed a threat to masculinity (men's self-confidence was seriously undermined by being under attack all the time from emancipated women who wanted to be liberated from patriarchal domination, and retain the initiative in sexual contact, and simultaneously demanded full sexual satisfaction from their male partners) Viagra opens up an easy way out of this stressful predicament: men no longer have to worry; they know they will be able to perform properly. On the other hand, feminists can claim that Viagra finally deprives male potency of its mystique, and thus in effect makes men equal to women . . . however, the least one can say against this second argument is that it simplifies the way male potency actually functions: what actually confers a mythical status on it is the threat of impotence. In the male sexual psychic economy, the ever-present shadow of impotence, the threat that, in the next sexual encounter, my penis will refuse to erect is crucial to the very definition of what male potency is.

Let me recall here my own description of the paradox of erection: erection depends entirely on me, on my mind (as the joke goes: 'What is the lightest object in the world? The penis, because it is the only one that can be raised by a mere thought!'), yet it is simultaneously that over which I ultimately have no control (if I am not in the right mood, no amount of willpower will achieve it – that is why, for St Augustine, the fact that erection escapes the control of my will is the Divine punishment for man's arrogance and presumption, for his desire to become master of the universe . . .). To put it in the terms of the Adornian critique of commodification and rationalization: erection is one of the last remainders of authentic spontaneity, something that cannot be thoroughly mastered through rational-instrumental procedures. This minimal gap – the fact that it is never directly 'me', my Self, who can freely decide on erection – is crucial: a sexually potent man elicits a certain attraction and envy not because he can do it at will, but because that unfathomable X which – although beyond conscious control – decides on erection presents no problem for him.

The crucial point here is to distinguish between penis (the erectile organ itself) and phallus (the signifier of potency, of symbolic authority, of the – symbolic, not biological – dimension that confers authority and/ or potency) on me. Just as (as we have noted) a judge, who may be a worthless individual in himself, exerts authority the moment he puts on the insignia that confer his legal authority on him, the moment he no longer simply speaks only for himself, since it is the Law itself that speaks through him, the individual male's potency functions as a sign that another symbolic dimension is active through him: the 'phallus' designates the symbolic support which confers on my penis the dimension of proper potency. Because of this distinction, for Lacan, 'castration anxiety' has nothing to do with the fear of losing one's penis: what makes us anxious, rather, is the threat that the authority of the phallic signifier will be revealed as a fraud. For this reason, Viagra is the ultimate agent of castration: if a man swallows the pill, his penis functions, but he is deprived of the phallic dimension of symbolic potency – the man who is able to copulate thanks to Viagra is a man with a penis but without a phallus.

So can we really imagine how changing erection into something that can be achieved through a direct medical-mechanical intervention (by taking a pill) will affect sexual economy? To put it in somewhat male-chauvinist terms: what will remain of a woman's notion of being properly attractive to a man, of effectively arousing him? Furthermore, is not erection or its absence a kind of signal which lets us know what our true psychic attitude is: turning erection into a mechanically achievable state is somehow similar to being deprived of the capacity to feel pain – how will a male subject get to know what his true attitude is? In what forms will his dissatisfaction or resistance find an outlet, when it is deprived of the simple sign of impotence? The standard designation of a sexually vora-cious man is that when lust takes over he thinks not with his head but with his penis – what happens, however, when his head takes over completely? Will not access to the dimension usually referred to as that of 'emotional intelligence' be further, and perhaps decisively, hindered? It is easy to celebrate the fact that we will no longer have to battle with our psychological traumas, that hidden fears and inhibitions will no longer be able to impede our sexual capacity; however, these hidden fears and inhibitions will, for that very reason, not disappear – they will persist on what Freud called the 'Other Scene', being deprived merely of their main outlet, waiting to explode in what will probably be a much more violent and (self-)destructive way. Ultimately, this turning of erection into a mechanical procedure will simply *desexualize* the act of copulation.

At the opposite end of the spectrum, New Age wisdom seems to offer a way out of this predicament – however, what does it actually offer us? Let me turn to its ultimate popular version, James Redfield's mega-bestseller *The Celestine Prophecy*. According to *The Celestine Prophecy*, the first 'new insight' that will open the path to humanity's 'spiritual awakening' is the awareness that there are no contingent encounters: since our psychic energy participates in the Energy of the universe, which secretly deter-mines the course of things, contingent external encounters always carry a message addressed to us, to our concrete situation; they occur as an answer to our needs and questions (for example, if I am bothered by a certain problem and then something unexpected happens – a long-forgotten friend visits me; something goes wrong at work – this accident certainly contains a message relevant to my problem). We thus find ourselves in a universe in which everything has a meaning, in a proto-psychotic universe in which this meaning is discernible in the very contingency of the Real, and what is of special interest are the conse-quences of all this for intersubjectivity. According to *The Celestine Prophecy*, we are caught today in a false competition with our fellow human beings, seeking in them what we lack, projecting into them our fantasies of this lack, depending on them; and since ultimate harmony is impossible, since the other never provides what we are looking for, tension is irreducible. After spiritual renewal, however, we shall learn to *find in ourselves* what we were seeking in vain in others (one's male or female complement): each human being will become a Platonic complete being, delivered of exclu-sive dependence on another (leader or love partner), delivered of the need to draw energy from him/her. When a truly free subject enters a partnership with another human being, he is thus beyond a passionate attachment to the other: his partner is for him only a vehicle for some message; he endeavours to discern in the other messages that are relevant to his own inner evolution and growth. . . . Here we encounter the necessary obverse of New Age spiritualist elevation: the end of the passionate attachment to the Other, the emergence of a self-sufficient ego to whom his Other–partner is no longer a subject, merely the bearer of a message concerning himself.

In psychoanalysis, we also encounter the position of the bearer of a message: the subject is unaware that he embodies some message, as in some detective novels where someone's life is threatened all of a sudden, a mysterious agent tries to kill him – obviously the subject knows something he shouldn't have known, partakes in some prohibited knowledge (say, the secret which could put a top Mafia figure in prison); the key point here is that *the subject is completely unaware what this knowledge is*, he knows only that he knows something he shouldn't know. . . . This position, however, is the very opposite of the New Age ideology perception of the Other as the bearer of some message which is relevant to me: in psychoanalysis, the subject is not the (potential) reader but the bearer of a message addressed to the Other and therefore, in principle, inaccessible to the subject himself.

Back to Redfield: my point is that the allegedly highest insight of spiritual wisdom overlaps with our most common everyday experience. If we take Redfield's description of the ideal state of spiritual maturity literally, it already holds for late capitalist commercialized everyday interpersonal experience, in which passions proper disappear, in which the Other is no longer an unfathomable abyss concealing and announcing that which is 'in me more than myself', but the bearer of messages for the self-sufficient consumerist subject. New Agers are not giving us even an ideal spiritual supplement to commercialized everyday life; they are giving us the spiritualized/mystified version of this commercialized everyday life itself. . . .

What, then, is the way out of this predicament? Are we condemned to the rather depressing oscillation between scientific objectivization and New Age wisdom, between Viagra and *The Celestine Prophecy*? That there still is a way out is demonstrated by the case of Mary Kay. The ridicule of defining this unique passionate love affair as the case of a woman *raping* an underage boy cannot fail to strike the eye; none the less, practically no one dared to defend the ethical dignity of her act in public; two patterns of reaction emerged: one either simply condemned her as evil, fully responsible for forgetting the elementary sense of duty and decency in letting herself go and engaging in an affair with a sixth-grade schoolboy; or – like her defence lawyer – one took refuge in psychiatric mumbo jumbo, medicalizing her case, treating her as an ill person, describing her as suffering from a 'bipolar disorder' (a new term for manic-depressive states). When she is in one of her manic fits, she is simply not aware of the danger she is getting into – or – as her lawyer put it, repeating the worst anti-feminist cliché – 'The only person to whom Mary Kay poses any threat is herself – she is the greatest danger to herself' (one is tempted to add here: with defence lawyers like that, who needs a prosecution?). Along these lines, Dr Julie Moore, the psychiatrist who 'evaluated' Mary Kay, insisted emphatically that Mary Kay's problem 'is not psychological, but medical', to be treated by drugs that will stabilize her behaviour: 'For Mary Kay, morality begins with a pill.' It was rather uncomfortable to listen to this doctor who brutally medicalized Mary Kay's passion, depriving her of the dignity of an authentic subjective stance: she claimed that when Mary Kay talks about her love for the boy she simply should not be taken seriously – she is transported into some heaven, disconnected from the demands and obligations of her social surroundings. . . .

The notion of 'bipolar disorder' popularized by two Oprah Winfrey shows is interesting: its basic claim is that a person suffering from this disorder still knows the difference between right and wrong, still knows what is right and good for her (patients are, as a rule, women), but when she is in a manic state she goes ahead and makes impulsive decisions, suspending her capacity of rational judgement which tells her what is right and good for her. Is not such a suspension, however, one of the constituents of the notion of the authentic *act* of being truly in love? Crucial here was Mary Kay's unconditional compulsion to accomplish something she knew very well was against her own Good: her passion was simply too strong; she was fully aware that, beyond all social obligations, the very core of her being was at stake in it. . . . This predicament allows us to specify the relationship between act and knowledge. Oedipus didn't know what he was doing (killing his own father), yet he did it; Hamlet knew what he had to do, which is why he procrastinated and was unable to accomplish the act.

There is, however, a third position, that of – among others – Paul Claudel's Sygne de Coufontaine from his drama *The Hostage*,[69] a version of *je sais bien, mais quand même* – Sygne fully knew, was fully aware of, the horrible reality of what she was about to do (bringing ruin to her eternal soul), yet she did it. (Does not the same hold also for the *noir* hero, who is not simply duped by the *femme fatale*, but fully aware that his liaison with her will end in total catastrophe, that she will betray him – nevertheless he goes ahead and commits himself to her?) The fact that this formula of Sygne coincides with the formula of cynicism should not deceive us: Sygne's act stands for the radical opposite of cynicism. We are thus dealing here with the structure of Hegelian speculative judgement: with the statement which can be read in two opposite ways, as the lowest cynicism ('I know that what I am about to do is the lowest depravity, but what the hell, who cares, I'll just do it . . .') and the highest tragic split ('I am fully aware of the catastrophic consequences of what I am about to do, but I can't help it, it's my unconditional duty to do it, so I'll go on with it . . .').

A recent German poster for Davidoff cigarettes deftly manipulates this gap between knowledge and act – this suspension of knowledge in the act, this 'I'll do it, although I'm well aware of the catastrophic consequences of my act' – in order to counteract the effect of the obligatory warning at the bottom of every cigarette advertisement (a variation on the theme 'Smoking may be dangerous for your health'): the image of an experienced man smoking is accompanied by the words 'The More You Know', suggesting the conclusion: if you are truly daring, then the more you know about the dangers of smoking, the more you should demonstrate your defiance by taking the risk and continuing to smoke – that is, by refusing to give up smoking for reasons concerning care for your own survival. . . . This advertisement is the logical counterpart to the obsession with health and longevity that characterizes today's narcissistic individual. And does not this formula of the tragic split also perfectly express Mary Kay's predicament?

This, then, is the sad reality of our late capitalist tolerant liberal society: the very capacity to *act* is brutally medicalized, treated as a manic outburst within the pattern of 'bipolar disorder', and as such to be submitted to biochemical treatment – do we not encounter here our own, Western, liberal-democratic counterpart to the old Soviet attempts to diagnose dissidence as a mental disorder (the practice centred on the infamous Scherbsky Institute in Moscow)? No wonder, then, that part of the sentence was that Mary Kay has to undergo therapy (the lawyer even explained her second transgression – being found with her lover in a car in the middle of the night after her release, which led to her outrageous sentence of over six years in prison – as resulting from the fact that in the days immediately preceding this encounter she was not given her pre-scribed medication regularly).

Oprah Winfrey herself, who dedicated one of her shows to Mary Kay, was at her worst here: she was right to reject the talk of 'bipolar personality' as legal prattle, yet she rejected it for the wrong reason – as a simple excuse allowing Mary Kay to avoid her fundamental *guilt* of behaving irresponsibly. Although Oprah pretended to be neutral and not to take sides, she referred to Mary Kay's love all the time in a mockingly distantiated way ('what she *thought* was love', etc.), and finally passionately voiced the surprised question of her peers, of her husband, of the so-called decent common people: 'How could she have done it, not thinking about the catastrophic consequences of her act? How could she not only put at risk, but effectively abandon and renounce, everything that formed the very substance of her life – her family, with three children, her professional career?' Is not such a suspension of the 'principle of sufficient reason(s)', however, the very definition of the *act*? Undoubtedly the most depressive moment was when, at the trial, under the pressure of her surroundings, Mary Kay conceded, in tears, that she knew she was doing something that was legally and morally wrong – a moment of *ethical betrayal* in the precise sense of 'compromising one's desire' if ever there was one. In other words, her *guilt* at that point lay precisely in renouncing her passion. When she later reasserted her unconditional *fidelity* to her love (stating with dignity that she had learned to remain true and faithful to herself), we have a clear case of someone who, after almost succumbing to the pressure of her surroundings, overcomes her guilt and regains her ethical composure by deciding *not to compromise her desire*.

The ultimate false argument against Mary Kay evoked by a psychologist on the Oprah show was that of gender symmetry: let us imagine the opposite 'Lolita' case of a thirty-four-year-old male teacher who gets involved with a thirteen-year-old girl, his pupil – is it not true that in this case we would insist much more unambiguously on his guilt and responsi-bility? This argument is misleading and wrong – not only for the same reason that the argumentation of those who oppose affirmative action (helping underprivileged minorities) on the grounds that it is a case of inverted racism is wrong (the fact is that men rape women, not vice versa . . .).[70] On a more radical level, one should insist on the uniqueness, the absolute idiosyncrasy, of the ethical act proper – such an act involves its own inherent normativity which 'makes it right'; there is no neutral external standard that would enable us to decide in advance, by a simple application to a single case, on its ethical status.

So our ultimate lesson is that we should supplement the Lacanian notion of 'between two deaths' with 'between the two death drives': the ultimate choice is directly the one between two death drives. The first aspect of the death drive is the indestructible stupidity of superego enjoyment. A supreme example of this idiotic superego compulsion is provided by Charles Russell's film *The Mask*, with Jim Carey (1994), the story of a weak ordinary bank teller, humiliated again and again by his peers and by women, who acquires extraordinary powers when he puts on a mysterious old mask found on a city beach. A series of details are essential to the story's background. When the mask is thrown on to the seashore, it sticks to the slimy decaying remains of a corpse, bearing witness to what remains of the 'person behind the mask' after he totally identifies with the mask: a formless slime like that of Mr Valdemar from Poe's story when he is resuscitated from death, this 'indivisible remainder' of the Real. Another crucial feature is that the hero, before acquiring the mask, is presented as a compulsive TV cartoon-watcher: when he puts on the green wooden mask, and it takes possession of him, he is able to behave, in 'real life', as a cartoon hero (dodging the bullets, dancing and laughing madly, sticking his eyes and tongue far out of his head when he is excited) – in short, he becomes 'undead', entering the spectral phantasmic domain of unconstrained perversion, of 'eternal life' in which there is no death (or sex), in which the plasticity of the bodily surface is no longer constrained by any physical laws (faces can be stretched indefinitely; I can spit out from my body bullets which were shot into me; after I fall from a high building, spread-eagled on the pavement, I simply reassemble myself and walk away . . .).

This universe is inherently *compulsive*: even those who observe it cannot resist its spell. Suffice it to recall perhaps the supreme scene of the film in which the hero, wearing his green mask, is cornered by a large police force (dozens of cars, helicopters): to get out of this impasse he treats the light focused on him as spotlights on a stage, and starts to sing and dance a crazy Hollywood musical version of a seductive Latino song – the policemen are unable to resist its spell; they also start to move and sing as if they are part of a musical-number choreography (a young policewoman is shedding tears, visibly fighting back the power of the mask, but she none the less succumbs to its spell and joins the hero in a popular song-and-dance number . . .). Crucial here is the inherent stupidity of this compulsion: it stands for the way each of us is caught in the inexplicable spell of idiotic *jouissance*, as when we are unable to resist whistling some vulgar popular song whose melody is haunting us. This compulsion is properly ex-timate: imposed from the outside, yet doing nothing but realizing our innermost whims – as the hero himself puts it in a desperate moment: 'When I put the mask on, I lose control – I can do anything I want.' 'Having control over oneself' thus in no way simply relies on the absence of obstacles to the realization of our intentions: I am able to exert control over myself only in so far as some fundamental obstacle makes it impossible for me to 'do anything I want' – the moment this obstacle falls away, I am caught in a demoniac compulsion, at the whim of 'something in me more than myself'. When the mask – the dead object – comes alive by taking possession of us, its hold on us is effectively that of a 'living dead', of a monstrous *automaton* imposing itself on us – is not the lesson to be drawn from this that our fundamental fantasy, the kernel of our being, is itself such a monstrous Thing, a machine of *jouissance*?[71]

On the other hand, against this stupid superego injunction to enjoy which increasingly dominates and regulates the perverse universe of our late capitalist experience, the death drive designates the very opposite gesture, the desperate endeavour to escape the clutches of the 'undead' eternal life, the horrible fate of being caught in the endless repetitive cycle of *jouissance*. The death drive does not relate to the finitude of our contingent temporal existence, but designates the endeavour to escape the dimension that traditional metaphysics described as that of *immortality*, the indestructible life that persists beyond death. It is often a thin, almost imperceptible line which separates these two modalities of the death drive: which separates our yielding to the blind compulsion to repeat more and more intense pleasures, as exemplified by the adolescent transfixed by the video game on the screen, from the thoroughly different experience of traversing the fantasy.

So we not only dwell between the two deaths, as Lacan put it, but our ultimate choice is directly the one between the two death drives: the only way to get rid of the stupid superego death drive of enjoyment is to embrace the death drive in its disruptive dimension of traversing the fantasy. One can beat the death drive only by the death drive itself – so, again, the ultimate choice is between bad and worse. And the same goes for the properly Freudian ethical stance. The superego injunction 'Enjoy!' is ultimately supported by some figure of the 'totalitarian' Master. '*Du darfst!* / You may!', the logo on a brand of fat-free meat products in Germany, provides the most succinct formula of how the 'totalitarian' Master operates. That is to say: one should reject the standard explanation of today's new fundamentalisms as a reaction against the anxiety of excessive freedom in our late capitalist 'permissive' liberal society, offering us a firm anchor by providing strong prohibitions – this cliché about individuals 'escaping from freedom' into the totalitarian haven of closed order is profoundly misleading.

One should also reject the standard Freudo–Marxist thesis according to which the libidinal foundation of the totalitarian (Fascist) subject is the so-called 'authoritarian personality' structure: the individual who finds satisfaction in compulsively obeying authority, repressing spontaneous sexual urges, fearing insecurity and irresponsibility, and so on. The shift from the traditional authoritarian to the totalitarian Master is crucial here: although, on the surface, the totalitarian Master also imposes severe orders, compelling us to renounce our pleasures and to sacrifice ourselves for some higher Duty, his actual injunction, discernible between the lines of his explicit words, is exactly the opposite – the call to unconstrained and unrestrained *transgression*. Far from imposing on us a firm set of standards to be obeyed unconditionally, the totalitarian Master is the agency that suspends (moral) punishment – that is to say, his secret injunction is: *You may!*: the prohibitions that seem to regulate social life and guarantee a minimum of decency are ultimately worthless, just a device to keep the common people at bay, while you are allowed to kill, rape and plunder the Enemy, let yourself go and excessively enjoy, violate ordinary moral prohibitions ... *in so far as* you follow Me. Obedience to the Master is thus the operator that allows you to reject or transgress everyday moral rules: all the obscene dirty things you were dreaming of, all that you had to renounce when you subordinated yourself to the traditional patriarchal symbolic Law – you are now allowed to indulge in them without punishment, exactly like the fat-free German meat which you may eat without any risk to your health. . . .

It is here, however, that we encounter the last, fatal trap to be avoided. What psychoanalytic ethics opposes to this totalitarian *You may!* is not some basic *You mustn't!*, some fundamental prohibition or limitation to be unconditionally respected (Respect the autonomy and dignity of your neighbour! Do not encroach violently upon his/her intimate fantasy space!). The ethical stance of (self-)limitation, of 'No trespassing!' in all its versions, inclusive of its recent ecologico-humanist twist (Do not engage in biogenetic engineering and cloning! Do not tamper too much with natural processes! Do not try to violate the sacred democratic rules and risk a violent social upheaval! Respect the customs and *mores* of other ethnic communities!) is ultimately incompatible with psychoanalysis. One should reject the usual liberal–conservative game of fighting 'totalitarianism' with a reference to some firm set of ethnical standards whose abandonment is supposed to lead to catastrophe: no, the Holocaust and the Gulag did not occur because people forgot about the basic rules of human decency and 'set free the beast in themselves', letting themselves give rein to the unconstrained realization of their murderous impulses. So – once more, and for the last time – the choice is between bad and worse; what Freudian ethics opposes to the 'bad' superego version of *You may!* is another, even more radical *You may!*, a *Scilicet* ('You are allowed to . . .' – the title of the yearbook edited by Lacan in the early 1970s) no longer vouched for by any figure of the Master. Lacan's maxim 'Do not compromise your desire!' fully endorses the pragmatic paradox of ordering you to be free: it exhorts you to dare.

Notes

1. Jacques Lacan, *Les complexes familiaux dans la formation de l'individu* (1938), Paris: Navarin 1984.

2. See Eric Santner, *My Own Private Germany*, Princeton, NJ: Princeton University Press 1996.

3. Is it not, however, that after this description of the crisis of the empirical-social form of the Oedipus complex, Lacan later (in the 1950s) reformulated Oedipus as a kind of formal-transcendental frame independent of concrete historical circumstances and inscribed into the very structure of language (the Oedipal paternal prohibition merely exemplifies the loss, the prohibition of *jouissance*, inherent to the symbolic order as such . . .)? In a strictly homologous gesture, Louis Althusser resolves the 'empirical' crisis of Marxism as the tool for concrete social analysis by transforming it into a formal-structural theoretical edifice with no direct link to determinate historical content. What this criticism (of resolving an 'empirical' crisis by recourse to the a priori symbolic formal order) fails to take into account is that, in the late Lacan of the 1970s, historicity returns with a vengeance.

4. Tim Pat Coogan, *De Valera*, London: Arrow Books 1995, p. 249.

5. Ibid.

6. Ibid., p. 278.

7. The usual comparison of the couple De Valera–Collins with the couple Robespierre–Danton (Robespierre leaving Danton to win the battles, then having him sacrificed) is therefore deeply misleading: it was, rather, Collins himself who was a kind of combined Danton/Robespierre, while De Valera was closer to a Napoleonic figure. Two quotes throw a clear light on their relationship in the crucial phase of negotiating with the British government and then signing the Treaty in 1921. The first, from De Valera's official biography, approved by himself, describes his reasons for not going to London himself to conclude the negotiations, but insisting on a team headed by Collins: De Valera

> believed it was vital at this stage that the symbol of the Republic [i.e. De Valera himself!] should be kept untouched and that it should not be compromised in any sense by any arrangements which it might be necessary for our plenipotentiaries to make . . . it was necessary to keep the Head of State and the symbol untouched and that was why he asked to be left out. (quoted from Coogan, *De Valera*, p. 247)

Collins's main argument for not going to London to negotiate was completely different from this self-appointed position of the 'living symbol of the Republic' – his point was:

in England as in Ireland, the Michael Collins legend existed. It pictured me as a mysterious, active menace, elusive, unknown, unaccountable. . . . Bring me into the spotlight of a London conference and quickly will be discovered the common clay of which I am made. The glamour of the legendary figure will be gone. (quoted from ibid., p. 248)

De Valera and Collins are referring not to any factual reasons concerning their respective abilities, or the dangers and intricacies of the negotiating process, but, rather, to the damage the fact of participating in the negotiations might do to their properly mythical symbolic status: De Valera fears the loss of his status as the symbol of the Republic, which must not be tarnished by any mundane business of dirty negotiations involving necessary compromises; while Collins fears the loss of his status as the invisible Agent, whose spectral omnipotence dwindles once he is brought into daylight and shown to be just another ordinary guy. What we encounter here, of course, is – in Lacanese – the opposition between S_1 and *objet petit a*, between the symbolic Master sustained by the charisma of his public insignia and its spectral double, the mysterious object which, on the contrary, exerts its power only as half-seen, never fully present in daylight.

8. For a concise description of these shifts, see Michel Lapeyre, *Au-delà du complexe d'Œdipe*, Paris: Anthropos–Economica 1997.

9. The title of Chapter 9 of Jacques Lacan, *Le Séminaire, livre XVII: L'envers de la psychanalyse*, Paris: Éditions du Seuil 1991.

10. For a more detailed account of this distinction, see Chapter 2 of Slavoj Žižek, *The Indivisible Remainder*, London: Verso 1996.

11. For this reason, the way the obsessional hysteric and the pervert relate to rules is exactly opposed: the obsessional follows his rules in order to pacify the traumatic impact of the symbolic Law/Prohibition, its unbearable unconditional injunction – that is, for him, rules are there to *normalize* the traumatic excess of the Law (if you follow the clear and explicit rules, you do not have to worry about the ambiguous pressure of your conscience – the Catholic Church has always been skilful in manipulating rules in this way: if you are bothered by the sense of sin, the priest prescribes you a set of procedures – so many prayers, so many good deeds, and so on – which, once you have accomplished them, deliver you of the guilt feeling); while the pervert establishes (and follows) rules in order to conceal the fact that there is no underlying Law in his psychic universe, that is, his rules serve as a kind of *ersatz*-law.

12. See Jacques Lacan, *Le Séminaire, livre VIII: Le transfert*, Paris: Éditions du Seuil 1991.

13. See Jacques Derrida, *Donner la mort*, Paris: Galilée 1995.

14. A sign of how even the Church is not resistant to this shift in the fundamental attitude are the recent grass-roots pressures on the Pope to elevate Mary to the status of co-redemptrix: one expects the Pope to make the Catholic Church viable for the post-paternal third millennium by proclaiming a dogma which asserts that the only way for us, sinful mortals, to gain divine mercy is via our plea to Mary – Mary serves as our mediator; if we convince her, she will speak in our favour to Christ, her son.

15. Hegel, of course, brought this meta-physical search to the point of self-reference: for him, 'the suprasensible is *appearance as appearance*', that is, the Other World beneath appearance is precisely something which *appears*, it is the *appearance* that there is Another World beyond the phenomenal sensible world.

16. See Paul-Laurent Assoun, *La Voix et le Regard*, vol. I, Paris: Anthropos–Economica 1995, pp. 64 ff.

17. That is also the measure of true love: even when I catch my partner red-handed, in bed with another man (or woman), I give preference to his (or her) words – the verbal protestations of innocence – over the hard, stupid fact perceived by my eyes. . . .

18. Richard Andrews and Paul Schellenberger, *The Tomb of God*, London: Warner Books 1997, p. 433.

19. Ibid., p. 428.

20. See Jacques-Alain Miller and Eric Laurent, 'L'Autre qui n'existe pas et ses comités d'éthique', in *La Cause freudienne* 35 (1997), Paris, pp. 7–20.

21. Paul Verhaeghe (see his unpublished paper 'The Collapse of the Father Function and its Effects on Gender Roles') drew attention to another interesting feature of this suspension of paternal symbolic authority: in so far as paternal authority is the 'relay' that enables the subject's entry into the symbolic universe, is not today's 'regression' from language to modes of communication that combine language with other types of signs (say, the replacement of writing with iconic signs: when we deal with a computer, instead of writing orders, we increasingly operate by merely clicking the mouse on to the appropriate iconic sign) also an index of the suspension of paternal authority?

22. See Ulrich Beck's classic *Risk Society: Towards a New Modernity*, London: Sage 1992; and Anthony Giddens's, *The Consequences of Modernity*, Cambridge: Polity Press 1990. For a popular overview of this theory, see *The Politics of the Risk Society*, ed. Jane Franklin, Oxford: Polity Press 1998.

23. For this very reason, the anxiety generated by the risk society is that of a superego: what characterizes the superego is precisely the absence of 'proper measure' – one obeys its commands not enough and/or too much; whatever one does, the result is wrong and one is guilty. The problem with the superego is that its command can never be translated into a positive rule to be followed: the Other issuing the injunction demands something from us, but we are never in a position to guess what, exactly, this demand is. . . .

24. What is an empty gesture? There is tension in Slovenia between the Prime Minister and the President of the republic: the latter, although the constitution reduces his role to protocol functions, wants to play a larger role with effective power. So when, recently, it was clear that the Slovene representative at the meeting of European leaders organized by Jacques Chirac would be the Prime Minister, journalists were told that the President wrote Chirac a letter explaining that since, unfortunately, he was unable to be at the summit, the Prime Minister would take his place. . . . This is the empty gesture at its purest: although it was clear that the Prime Minister should go to France to represent Slovenia, the President acted as if the fact that the Prime Minister went was not 'natural', but resulted from his – the President's – decision not to go and, instead, let the Prime Minister take his place. This is the way to turn defeat into victory – to transform into the result of one's free decision (to withdraw) the fact that one cannot go in any case.

25. Eva Hoffman, *Exit Into History*, London: Minerva 1993.

26. See Max Horkheimer, 'Authority and the Family', in *Critical Theory*, New York: Continuum 1995.

27. This, of course, in no way entails that the difference between the theory of postmodernism and the theory of the second modernity is merely nominal, another name for the same phenomenon; what we are dealing with here, rather, is the inherent split between two fundamentally incompatible notions of postmodernity that are operative today: on the one hand, the idea that postmodernity brings to an end the logic of modernity, deploying all its potential (Fredric Jameson's version – no wonder many of his determinations of postmodernity coincide with those of the second modernity); on the other, the idea that postmodernity negates the basic feature of modernization (rational reflexivity) in favour of some new form of immediacy (the New Age holistic attitude or some other version of the 'post-Cartesian paradigm'). Within this context, it is interesting how recent discussions on globalization again brought into focus the topic of modernization in its different aspects (globalized reflexivity, the dissolution of the last traditional social links . . .): we are becoming increasingly aware that *'postmodernism' was just an endeavour to come to terms with accelerated modernization*. Do not the turbulent events in all spheres of life, from economic and cultural 'globalization' to the reflexivization of the most intimate domains, demonstrate how we still have to learn to cope with the real shock of modernization?

28. In *La fin de l'interprétation* (available on the Internet), Jacques-Alain Miller tried to

resolve this deadlock by situating the analyst at the level of pre-symbolic *jouis-sense*, meaningless gibber, something like the rhizomatic flow of Joyce's *Finnegans Wake*. This reference to Joyce is significant in so far as Joyce is the paradigmatic case of the *reflexive* artist: his works, specifically *Finnegans Wake*, are not simply external to their interpretation but take their possible interpretations into account in advance, and enter into dialogue with them. Since the interpretation or theoretical explanation of a work of art endeavours to 'frame' its object, one can say that this Joyceian dialectics provides another example of how the frame is always included in – is a part of – the framed content: the theory about the work is comprised in the work; the work is a kind of pre-emptive strike at possible theories about itself. So, instead of the S_2 of interpretation (the chain of Knowledge) adding itself to the S_1 of the interpreted signifier, elucidating its meaning, we have in *Finnegans Wake* a gigantic, polymorphous S_1 which not only resists being subordinated to the interpretive S_2, but in a way swallows it (its interpretations) in advance into its own mad dance of *jouis-sense*. . . . Is this really, however, the only way out? Does not this solution merely go from bad to worse, replacing the delirium of interpretation with the immersion in the nightmare of the pre-symbolic/pre-discursive Thing?

29. Here I draw on extensive discussions with Renata Salecl, to whom I also owe a lot of the ideas expressed in this chapter; see Renata Salecl, *(Per)Versions of Love and Hate*, London: Verso 1998.

30. In the 1960s and 1970s, it was possible to buy soft-porn postcards with a girl clad in a bikini or wearing a proper dress; when one moved the postcard a little bit or looked at it from a slightly different perspective, however, the dress magically disappeared, and one was able to see the girl's naked body – is there not something similar about the image of Bill Gates, whose benevolent features, viewed from a slightly different perspective, magically acquire a sinister and threatening dimension?

31. This tendency was already discernible in Bryan Singer's excellent film *The Usual Suspects* (1995), in which the invisible-omnipotent Master-Criminal turns out to be none other than the clumsy, frightened Kevin Spacey character.

32. See Slavoj Žižek, ' "I Hear You with My Eyes"; or, The Invisible Master', in *Gaze and Voice as Love Objects*, Durham, NC: Duke University Press 1996.

33. Adorno pointed out how the very emergence of psychology as 'science', with the individual's psyche as its 'object', is strictly correlative to the predominance of impersonal relations in economic and political life.

34. Among the advocates of risk society politics, it is popular to point out, as a sign that we are moving into a new era 'beyond Left and Right', how none other than George Soros, the very embodiment of financial speculation, came to the insight that the unrestrained rule of the market presents a danger greater than Communist totalitarianism, and thus has to be constrained through some sociopolitical measures – however, is this insight really enough? Should we not rather, instead of celebrating this fact, ask ourselves if this does not prove the contrary: namely, that the new politics 'beyond Left and Right' does not really pose a threat to the reign of Capital?

35. The answer to the question 'Why do we privilege the economic level of the logic of Capital over other spheres of socio-symbolic life (political processes, cultural production, ethnic tensions . . .)? Is this privileging not essentialist in that it neglects the radical plurality of social life, the fact that its multiple levels cannot be conceived as depending on the crucial role of one of the agencies?' is therefore clear: of course we are dealing today with the proliferation of multiple forms of politicization (not only the standard fight for democracy and social justice, but also all the new forms of feminist, homosexual, ecological, ethnic minority, etc., political agents); however, the very space for this proliferation of multiplicity is sustained by the recent stage in the development of capitalism, that is, by its post-nation-state globalization and reflexive colonization of the last vestiges of 'privacy' and substantial immediacy. Contemporary feminism, for example, is strictly correlative to the fact that, in

recent decades, family and sexual life itself has become 'colonized' by market logic, and is thus experienced as something that belongs to the sphere of free choices.

36. Retroactively, one thus becomes aware of how deeply the phenomenon of so-called 'dissidence' was embedded in the socialist ideological framework; of the extent to which 'dissidence', in its very utopian 'moralism' (preaching social solidarity, ethical responsibility, etc.), provided the disavowed ethical core of socialism: perhaps one day historians will note that – in the same sense in which Hegel claimed that the true spiritual result of the Peloponnesian War, its spiritual End, is Thucydides' book about it – 'dissidence' was the true spiritual result of actually existing Socialism. . . .

37. See Slavoj Žižek, 'Introduction', in *Mapping Ideology*, London: Verso 1995.

38. Karl Marx, 'Preface to A *Critique of Political Economy*', in *Selected Writings*, Oxford: Oxford University Press 1977, p. 389.

39. Among today's Marxists, it is Fredric Jameson who has most consistently emphasized this aspect.

40. At least concerning cultural studies, I speak here not from a condescending position of a critic assuming the safe position of an external observer, but as someone who has participated in cultural studies – I, as it were, 'include myself out'. . . .

41. According to Jean-Claude Milner (see *Le salaire de l'idéal*, Paris: Seuil 1997), the same reflexivity determines the status of today's new ruling class, the 'salaried bourgeoisie': the criterion of the ruling class is no longer primarily property, but more and more the fact of belonging to the circle of those who are acknowledged as 'experts' (managers, state administrators, lawyers, academics, journalists, doctors, artists . . .) and are for this reason paid more than average wage-earners. Milner's point is that, contrary to misleading appearances (sustained by the vast network of university diplomas, etc.), this belonging to the circle of experts is ultimately not grounded in any 'actual' qualifications, but is the result of the sociopolitical struggle in the course of which some professional strata gain entry into the privileged 'salaried bourgeoisie': we are dealing here with the closed circle of self-reference, that is, you are paid more if you generate the impression that you should be paid more (a TV news presenter is paid much more than a top scientist whose inventions can change the whole industrial landscape). In short, what Marx evoked as a paradoxical exception (the strange case in which price itself determines value instead of merely expressing it, like the opera singer who is not paid so highly because his singing has such a great value, but is perceived as more valuable because he is so highly paid) is the rule today.

42. It is interesting to note how here theorists of the second modernity follow Habermas, who also tends to dismiss phenomena like Fascism or economic alienation not as results of the inherent trends of Enlightenment, but as proofs that Enlightenment is still an 'unfinished project' – a strategy somewhat similar to that of defunct Socialist regimes, which put all the blame for the present woes on the 'remainders of the (bourgeois or feudal) past'. . . .

43. To put it another way: the theory of second modernity obliterates the double impossibility and/or antagonistic split: on the one hand, the antagonistic complicity between progressive reflexivization and violent returns of substantial identity that characterizes the body politic; on the other, the antagonistic complicity between reflexive freedom and the 'irrational' need for subjection that characterizes the 'postmodern' subject.

44. See Robert Hughes, *Culture of Complaint*, Oxford: Oxford University Press 1993.

45. The shift from traditional Left to 'postmodern' Left is as a rule described by the motto 'from redistribution to recognition': the traditional Social-Democratic Left aimed at the redistribution of wealth and social power on behalf of the exploited-powerless-underprivileged; while today's 'postmodern' Left puts in the foreground the multiculturalist fight for the recognition of a particular (ethnic, lifestyle, sexual orientation, religious . . .) group identity. What, however, if they both participate in the same logic of *ressentiment*, indicated/concealed by the common prefix 're-'? What if they both victimize the underprivileged/excluded, endeavouring to culpabilize the ruling/wealthy and demanding restitution from them? Consequently, what if a certain dose of old-fashioned Marxist criticism is

appropriate here: what if our focus should change from redistribution to the very mode of production which causes 'inequitable' distribution and recognition?

46. The masochistic self-inflicted wound thus serves a different purpose in hysteria and in perversion: in hysteria the aim is to disavow castration (I wound myself in order to conceal the fact that the wound of castration *is already there*); while in perversion I wound myself in order to disavow *the failure/lack of castration* (i.e. I do it to impose the semblance of a Law).

47. Exemplary here is Oliver Stone's *JFK*. Stone is the foremost *meta-nationalist* in Hollywood today; I use the term 'meta-nationalism' in parallel with Balibar's 'meta-racism' (the contemporary paradox of racism formulated in terms of its very opposite, of the fear of racist outbursts: 'one should keep ethnic groups apart in order to prevent racist violence . . .'): Stone seems to undermine great American ideologico-political myths, but he does it in a 'patriotic' way, so that on a deeper level his very subversion reasserts American patriotism as an ideological attitude.

48. The outstanding example of a left-liberal conspiracy movie is *Barracuda* (1978), with its ingenious additional 'turn of the screw' on the standard natural disaster formula: why do sharks and other fish suddenly start to attack swimmers in an idyllic American town resort? It turns out that the whole city was an illegal experimental site for a mysterious government agency injecting the water supply with an untested drug that raises the aggression level (the goal of the experiment is to develop means of raising the combativeness of the American population after the demoralizing influence of the flower-power 1960s), and the fishes' aggressivity was caused by the water dumped in the sea.

X Files goes even a step further in this direction by inverting the standard ideological operation of exchanging all our social and psychic fears (of foreigners, of big business, of other races, of the force of raw nature . . .) for the attacking animal (shark, ants, birds . . .) or for the supernatural monster who comes to embody all of them: in *X Files*, it is the State Conspiracy – the dark Other Power behind the public power – which is presented as a kind of general equivalent hidden behind the multitude of 'supernatural' threats (werewolves, extraterrestrials . . .), that is, the series of supernatural horrors is exchanged for the alienated Social Thing.

49. For that reason, anxiety is clinically not a symptom, but a reaction that occurs when the subject's symptom – the formation that allowed him or her to maintain a proper distance towards the traumatic object-Thing – dissolves, ceases to function: at that moment, when the subject is deprived of the buffer-role of his symptom and is thus directly exposed to the Thing, anxiety emerges to signal this overproximity of the Thing.

50. Gilles Deleuze, *Coldness and Cruelty*, New York: Zone 1991, pp. 82–3.

51. According to the standard narrative of modernity, what distinguishes it from even the most universal versions of premodern Law (Christianity, Judaism, etc.) is that the individual is supposed to entertain a reflected relationship towards ethical norms. Norms are not there simply to be accepted; the subject has to measure not only his acts against them, but also the adequacy of these norms themselves, that is, how they fit the higher meta-rule that legitimizes their use: are the norms themselves truly universal? Do they treat all men – and women – equally and with dignity? Do they allow free expression of their innermost aspirations?, and so forth. This standard narrative gives us a subject who is able to entertain a free reflexive relationship towards every norm he decides to follow – every norm has to pass the judgement of his autonomous reason. What Habermas passes over in silence, however, is the obverse of this reflexive distance towards ethical norms expressed by the above quote from Deleuze: since, apropos of any norm I follow, I can never be sure that it is actually the right norm to follow, the subject is caught in a difficult situation of knowing *that* there are norms to follow, without any external guarantee as to *what* these norms are. . . . There is no modern reflexive freedom from the immediate submission to universal norms without this situation of a priori guilt.

52. Jacques Lacan, *The Four Fundamental Concepts of Psycho-Analysis*, New York: Norton 1977, p. 276.

53. See Darian Leader, *Promises Lovers Make When It Gets Late*, London: Faber & Faber 1997.

54. Was it not St Paul who emphasized this difference in Romans 2: 26–9?

... if those who are uncircumcised keep the requirements of the law, will not their uncircumcision be regarded as circumcision? ... For a person is not a Jew who is one outwardly, nor is true circumcision something external and physical. Rather, a person is a Jew who is one inwardly, and real circumcision is a matter of the heart – it is spiritual and not literal.

55. For a more detailed description of this double movement of the 'sacrifice of a sacrifice', see Chapter 2 of Slavoj Žižek, *The Indivisible Remainder*.

56. Here I draw again on Renata Salecl; see Salecl, *(Per)Versions of Love and Hate*.

57. Here one should emphasize the difference between the sado-maso practices of self-mutilation and the practices of tattooing and other versions of inscription on the bodily surface: tattooing involves the relationship between the naked skin and its covering up by clothes – that is to say, the problem of tattooing is how to transform the naked skin itself into clothing, how to close the gap between the two; so that even while we are naked we are in a way already dressed; on the other hand, the sado-maso practice of self-mutilation cuts into the surface of the skin, revealing the raw flesh beneath. What is threatened in both cases is the notion of the naked body, of the bare surface of the skin: either by direct symbolic inscriptions which cover it up, or by opening up access to the 'raw flesh' beneath; in short, what we get if we put the two practices together is a body which, when it is actually undressed, is no longer a naked body but a mass of raw flesh.

58. Against this background, one can well understand why, in his (unpublished) Seminar on *Anxiety* (1962/63), Lacan emphasizes that the Jewish practice of circumcision is definitely *not* a version of castration (as a vulgar and naive line of association seems to imply) but, rather, its exact opposite: the effect of circumcision is not that of a traumatic cut, but that of pacification, that is, circumcision enables the subject to find its allocated place in the symbolic order.

59. Analysed by Renata Salecl in *(Per)Versions of Love and Hate*.

60. The triad of premodern cut, the modern absence of cut, and the postmodern return to the cut thus effectively forms a kind of Hegelian triad of the 'negation of negation' – not in the sense that in postmodernity we return to the cut at an allegedly higher level, but in a much more precise sense: in premodern society the cut in the body performs the subject's inscription into the symbolic order (the big Other); in modern society we have *the big Other that is operative without the cut* – that is, the subject inscribes itself into the big Other without the mediation of the bodily cut (as was already the case in Christianity, the cut is internalized-spiritualized into an inner gesture of renunciation); in postmodern society, on the contrary, we have *the cut, but without the big Other*. It is thus only in postmodern society that the loss of the big Other (the substantial symbolic order) is fully consummated: in it, we return to the feature that characterizes the first phase (there is again a cut in the body), but this cut now stands for the exact opposite of the first phase – that is to say, it signals not the inscription into the big Other, but its radical nonexistence.

61. See Alenka Zupančič, 'The Subject of the Law', in *SIC 2*, ed. Slavoj Žižek, Durham, NC: Duke University Press 1998.

62. For this reason, Lacan is to be strictly opposed to the recently fashionable 'post-secular' trend of giving theology a deconstructionist spin, reasserting the Divine as the dimension of the unfathomable Otherness, as the 'undeconstructible condition of deconstruction'.

63. See the end of Chapter 3 above.

64. For a detailed reading of Brecht's *The Measure Taken*, see Chapter 5 of Slavoj Žižek, *Enjoy Your Symptom!*, New York: Routledge 1993.

65. Bertolt Brecht, 'The Measure Taken', in *The Jewish Wife and Other Short Plays*, New York: Grove Press 1965, p. 97.

66. See Heiner Müller, 'Mauser', in *Revolutionsstücke*, Stuttgart: Reclam 1995.

67. Brecht, 'The Measure Taken', p. 106.

68. This disjunction between Good and the ethical act also allows us to resolve the following impasse: if we accept the notion of 'diabolical Evil' (Evil elevated to the status of the Kantian ethical duty, that is, accomplished for the sake of principle, not for any pathological profit), to what extent, then, does this parallel with the Good hold? Can there also be a 'voice of Evil Consciousness' rendering us guilty when we did not do our duty to radical Evil? Can we also feel guilty for *not* accomplishing a horrible crime? The problem disappears the moment we cut the link between the ethical domain proper and the problematic of Good (and Evil as its shadow-supplement).

69. For a close reading of Claudel's *The Hostage*, see Chapter 2 of Žižek, *The Indivisible Remainder*.

70. A detailed comparative analysis of the case of Mary Kay with Nabokov's Lolita (if I may be excused for comparing a 'real-life' case with a fictional one) immediately helps us to pinpoint this difference: in *Lolita* (a story which is also, even more than it was when the novel was first published, unacceptable in our politically correct times – remember the problems with the American distribution of the latest cinema version), Humbert Humbert discerns in Lolita a 'nymphet', a girl between nine and fourteen who is *potentially* a woman: the appeal of a nymphet resides in the very indefiniteness of her form – she resembles a young boy much more than a mature woman. So while Mary Kay, the woman, treated her young lover as a grown-up partner, in the Lolita case she is for Humbert Humbert a masturbatory fantasy, the product of *his* solipsistic imagination – as Humbert puts it in the novel: 'What I had madly possessed was not she, but my own creation, another, fanciful Lolita. . . .' As a result, their relationship is teasing-exploitative, cruel on both sides (she is a cruel child towards him; he reduces her to the abused object of his masturbatory solipsistic imagination), in contrast to the sincere passion between Mary Kay and her young lover.

71. Another nice feature of the film is that, in its dénouement, it avoids the standard cliché about 'the real person behind the mask': although, at the end, the hero throws the mask back into the sea, he is able to do so precisely in so far as he incorporates into his actual behaviour elements of what he was doing when he was under its spell. Therein lies our 'growing mature': not in simply discarding masks, but in accepting their symbolic efficiency 'on trust' – in a court of law, when a judge puts on *his* mask (his official insignia), we in effect treat him as if he is under the spell of the symbolic Institution of Law which now speaks through him. . . . However, it would be wrong to conclude from this that the mask is just a more 'primitive' version of symbolic efficiency, of the hold exerted upon us by symbolic authority: it is crucial to maintain a distinction between the proper symbolic authority which operates on a strictly 'metaphoric' level and the obscene 'totemic' literality of the mask. No wonder the hero, when he is wearing the mask, often assumes an animal's face: in the phantasmic space of cartoons, animals (Tom, Jerry, etc.) are perceived precisely as humans wearing animal masks and/or clothing (take the standard scene in which an animal's skin is scratched, and what appears beneath it is ordinary *human skin*).

To paraphrase Lévi-Strauss, what *The Mask* presents us with is thus in effect a case of 'totemism today', of the phantasmic efficiency of the totemic animal mask which is inoperative in today's public social space: when the hero confronts the psychologist who wrote a bestseller on masks, the psychologist calmly answers the hero's questions to the effect that we all wear masks only in the metaphoric meaning of the term; in one of the crucial scenes of the film, which then follows, the hero tries to convince him that in his case the mask really *is* a magical object – when he puts the mask on, however, it remains a dead piece of carved wood; the magical effect fails to occur, so that the hero is reduced to imitating, in a ridiculous way, the wild gestures he is able to perform gracefully when he is under the mask's spell. . . .

Index